In Memory of

Chuck Trapkus

Illustrator of
Living Justice and Peace

21 October 1959 to 21 December 2000

True artisan, loving father, and
compassionate minister to God's poor,
whose strength and dedication are
woven throughout the pages of this
book.

*". . . to comfort the afflicted
and afflict the comfortable."*

Genuine recycled paper with 10% post-consumer waste.
Printed with soy-based ink.

Nihil Obstat: Rev. Andrew Beerman
                Censor Librorum
                10 October 2000
Imprimatur: †Most Rev. Bernard J. Harrington, DD
                Bishop of Winona
                10 October 2000

The publishing team included Jerry Windley-Daoust, development editor; Lorraine Kilmartin, Christine Schmertz Navarro, Kathleen Crawford Hodapp, and Michael Wilt, contributing writers; Barbara Allaire, Shirley Kelter, and Stephan Nagel, consulting editors; Robert Smith, FSC, theological consultant; Katie Thompson, editorial assistant; Laurie Berg-Shaner, copy editor; Barbara Bartelson, production editor and typesetter; Laurie Geisler, art director; Cindi Ramm, design director; Alan S. Hanson, pre-press specialist; Genevieve Nagel, image researcher; Chuck Trapkus, illustrator; and Patricia Deminna, indexer. Special thanks to Susan Windley-Daoust for her contribution of theological consulting and editorial work, and for her support and patience.

The acknowledgments continue on page 330.

Printed in the United States of America

Printing: 9 8 7 6 5 4 3 2 1

Year: 2009 08 07 06 05 04 03 02 01

ISBN 0-88489-632-3

Saint Mary's Press
Christian Brothers Publications
Winona, Minnesota

Library of Congress Cataloging-in-Publication Data

Windley-Daoust, Jerry.
    Living justice and peace : Catholic social teaching in practice /Jerry Windley-Daoust with contributors, Lorraine Kilmartin . . . [et al.].
    p. cm.
ISBN 0-88489-632-3
    1. Christianity and justice—Catholic Church. 2. Peace—Religious aspects—Catholic Church. 3. Sociology, Christian (Catholic). 4. Christian education—Textbooks for teenagers—Catholic. 5. Catholic Church—Doctrines. I. Kilmartin, Lorraine. II. Title.
BX1795.J87 W56 2001
261.8'071'2—dc21

                                                            00-010921

LIVING JUSTICE AND PEACE

Catholic social teaching in practice

Jerry Windley-Daoust

with contributors
Lorraine Kilmartin
Christine Schmertz Navarro
Kathleen Crawford Hodapp
Michael Wilt

1 THE SCRIPTURES AND JUSTICE

~~Individualism~~ Hope
Compassion

Calling Us
to a world of goodness

A WORLD
FULL OF LIGHT
AND SHADOWS

It's been **fifteen or more years** since you were set down in this **world**. What have you found it to be like? **A**

Many people find the world to be full of goodness and joy: a first kiss, music with a dancing spirit, the jeweled beauty of new snow, basketball played so hard your body aches, friends who make you laugh, extra-cheese pizza, a loving family . . . the list could go on and on.

But for many people, this world is not only one of goodness and light but also of shadows and suffering. Perhaps you have already encountered the shadow side of the world, as the following young people did:

Twelve-year-old Craig Kielburger was looking for the comics in the *Toronto Star* one morning when he saw this front-page headline: BATTLED CHILD LABOUR, BOY, 12, MURDERED. The story told of Iqbal Masih, a 12-year-old Pakistani boy who had been sold to a carpet factory owner when he was four and forced to weave carpets, chained to a loom, along with other boys. When human rights activists bought his freedom, he traveled the world speaking out against the widespread practice of child labor—until he was shot dead, presumably by the carpet manufacturers.

The story deeply troubled Craig. But what could he do for kids halfway around the world?

✳ ✳ ✳

"This test is positive," the physician's assistant said. "Are you going to terminate the pregnancy?"

"No," Kelly Jefferson responded. That was an easy question to answer; she opposed all forms of killing, including abortion.

But the next question would prove to be more difficult for the college sophomore. Her boyfriend bailed out of the relationship halfway through the pregnancy, and she soon found that her college offered little support to women in her situation. The school apparently assumed that pregnant students would just have an abortion. Why, she wondered, should she have to sacrifice a decent education in order to choose life for her child?

✳ ✳ ✳

For fourteen years, Ferdinand Marcos had ruled the Philippines under martial law, denying ordinary citizens basic civil rights. When elections were finally held, many people thought that there was a chance of restoring democracy—if Marcos didn't "steal" the election by cheating.

Fifteen-year-old Paulo Mercado and his younger brother worked to ensure free and fair elections by volunteering as newsboys at Radio Veritas, a Catholic radio station that was broadcasting reports of election fraud to the nation. Their efforts weren't enough: Marcos declared himself the winner, and Radio Veritas was kicked off the air.

Soon after, two top-ranking military officers broke ranks with the Marcos regime, along with a contingent of soldiers. A bloody, violent conflict seemed inevitable. Is this what it would take, Paulo wondered, to restore democracy to the country?

Exploitation of children, discrimination, poverty, violence—the world is far from perfect, as these young people found out. Confronted with the harsh reality of such suffering and darkness, each of them had to decide how to respond. **B**

In different ways, we each face the same decision. We will return to the true stories of these young people later in the course. First, let's look at some possible responses to the suffering we encounter in the world. **©**

—the world is far from perfect, as these young people found out.

A What is the world you know like? What is good about it? What is bad about it? Imagine you have the power to change the world. What does this new world look like? You may use writing, song, or art in your response.

B For each example, write down several ways someone could respond to the situation, giving reasons for each response.

How Do We Respond to Suffering?

When we are confronted with suffering in the world around us, we have two basic choices: we can do something about the situation, or we can do nothing. People choose one option or the other for many different reasons. For the sake of simplicity, however, we will consider only four reasons: hopelessness, individualism, enlightened self-interest, and compassion. **C**

Hopelessness

Sometimes it feels as if we hear too much about suffering in the world. Many people deal with the overwhelming nature of all the suffering in the world by choosing to ignore it. Others see or hear news of people suffering, but choose not to act. They might offer several reasons for not responding, such as the following:

- "There are so many problems, and I'm just one person. Even if I make a small contribution, *what difference will it make* in the big picture?"

- "The problems in our community are beyond my control. . . . *I have no power* to change the situation."
- "I'm *afraid* that if I speak up, people might get mad at me. My personal safety might even be at risk. I'd rather stay silent than rock the boat."

These responses to the world's suffering, while understandable, reflect a lack of hope on the part of the people who offer them. To **hope** is to believe in the possibility that what one wants can actually happen. If people do not believe in the possibility that they can make a difference—if they have no hope—they are not likely to act to change things.

Individualism

The independence of individuals to pursue their own destiny is an important value that has led to such good things as democracy, the promotion of equal opportunities for all people, and the notion that people can achieve almost anything if they try hard enough.

Too much emphasis on individual independence, however, can break the ties that connect people with God and one another as community. Have you ever heard comments similar to those that follow?

- "That problem *doesn't affect me* personally, so why should I care?"
- "If homeless people want shelter, they should get a job and work for it like everyone else. *They should help themselves* instead of expecting everyone else to help them."
- "The trouble she has now is the result of her own decisions—she's just *getting what she deserves.*"
- "The pollution our paper mill puts into the water is a *necessary trade-off.* Cleaning it up would cost so much, we would probably lose our jobs."

Such responses to suffering might be called individualistic. Someone who is motivated by **individualism** believes that each person should take responsibility for his or

---

C Read your local newspaper or watch a local television news program. Clip, copy, or write down examples you find that illustrate hopelessness, individualism, enlightened self-interest, and compassion.

her own life, and that when people fail to take responsibility for themselves, others should not be expected to help them. An overemphasis on individualism can lead to a me-first attitude in which individuals seek good things only for themselves—even if others must suffer as a result.

Enlightened self-interest

Hopelessness and individualism lead many people to respond to suffering by doing nothing. However, many other people respond to suffering in the world by attempting to relieve it.

In some cases, such responses are primarily motivated by **enlightened self-interest**—the realization that by helping others we are really helping ourselves in the end. People who act out of enlightened self-interest understand that every person needs other people in order to live a satisfying life. People acting out of enlightened self-interest might make the following comments:

- "The government should spend more money educating people about how to avoid health problems, because it costs less to prevent health problems than to treat them later. *It may take more resources now, but the benefits will be greater in the long run.*"
- "If we continue to let toxins pollute our drinking water, people in our community will face an increased risk of cancer. *We have to act now or we'll face the consequences later.*"
- "I help my elderly neighbor to keep his yard and sidewalk neat because someday I may be in his shoes, unable to do yard work. *If I don't help others, I can't expect them to help me.*"

As these examples illustrate, one reason people choose to help others is that they might receive benefits in return. Sometimes helping others does not result in direct benefits, though. The woman in the third example might never receive help in return from her neighbor. But she knows that in a society in which people value helping one another, she is more likely to get help for herself if she needs it someday. By helping her neighbor, she is contributing to the importance her community places on that value.

Compassion

The realization that everyone in a society benefits when people help one another is one reason people respond to suffering with action. But what about people who help others well beyond any benefit they might receive in return? What about people who help others even when it means that they too will suffer?

When **compassion** is accompanied by **hope**, it moves people to **love**.

✳ *Student art:* Acrylic; Lindsey Warren, Notre Dame High School, Sherman Oaks, California

Consider Jean Donovan, a young single woman who left her job as an accountant to spend some time as a Maryknoll lay missionary in El Salvador. A civil war raged in that country at the time, causing much suffering for the people she served—and putting the lives of the missionaries in danger.

As the violence around her grew worse, Jean considered leaving. It would have been reasonable to protect herself from suffering, but that is not what she chose to do. She explained why in a letter to a friend:

> Several times I have decided to leave El Salvador. I almost could except for the children, the poor, bruised victims of this insanity. Who would care for them? Whose heart could be so staunch as to favor the reasonable thing in a sea of their tears and loneliness? Not mine, dear friend, not mine. (Carrigan, *Salvador Witness,* page 218)

Two weeks later Jean and three nuns were raped and killed by soldiers. Many believe the soldiers wanted to "send a message" to missionaries who work on behalf of the poor.

Jean knew that the reasonable thing to do would have been to leave. Instead she stayed. Why? Certainly not out of enlightened self-interest alone; painful suffering and dying are not typically considered to be in anyone's self-interest.

No, Jean said she stayed because her heart was moved by a "sea of . . .

Jean Donovan chose to care for others, even at great risk to herself.

tears and loneliness" among the people she had come to know. She could give no logical reason for her response beyond her own experience of the people's suffering, which she longed to ease.

Jean Donovan's response was motivated by **compassion,** a word that in Hebrew is the plural of the word *womb*. The biblical sense of compassion, then, is similar to the feeling a mother has for the child in her womb—a feeling of life-giving closeness and protective care. People who have compassion understand, both in their mind and heart, others' experience of suffering. When compassion is accompanied by hope, it moves people to commit themselves to easing suffering. In other words, it moves them to love.

The following are all acts of love, though not quite as dramatic as Jean Donovan's:

- Kyla not only performs the duties she is paid to do as a nurse but also takes extra time to listen to her patient's needs and worries.
- Marc stands up for the kid everyone else picks on, even though he might lose some popularity as a result.
- Josie takes time out of her busy day to e-mail her state representatives about legislation to protect migrant farmworkers from pesticides in the fields. ◗

Called to Respond with Compassion

Although we cannot avoid the shadows of suffering in this world, we can choose how we respond to that suffering. Those who follow Jesus are called to respond to the world's

---

◗ Which of the four responses to encounters with suffering in the world most closely matches your own? Why? Write several paragraphs explaining your position.

suffering as he did, with compassion—even to the point of giving one's self for the good of the world.

For many people, such a response might seem unreasonable and even extreme. Are people like Jean Donovan naive fools? If not, what would bring them to risk their life to help alleviate the suffering of others?

Perhaps the best way to begin to answer that question is to consider the Christian answer to another more basic question: Why is there suffering in the world in the first place?

1. When confronted with suffering in the world, what are two basic ways we can choose to respond?
2. Name four reasons for our responses to suffering, and provide a definition for each.
3. When accompanied by hope, what does compassion lead to?

4. Provide your own example of each of the four types of responses to suffering.

Why Is There Suffering?

Why is there suffering? It is an important and a challenging question, especially for anyone who believes in a good and all-powerful God. Why doesn't God just stop the suffering of the world with a snap of the fingers? To answer that question, Catholics turn to the Tradition of the church and to the Scriptures, which they believe contain the truth that God has revealed to humanity. Two main themes found in God's revelation provide some insight into the question of suffering:

- **God is love.** Love has many meanings in our culture, but in the way Christian faith means it, to **love** is to will the good for another. God is love because God is the source of all goodness, bringing everything into being, and bringing everything into harmony with itself and the rest of creation.

- **When humans fail to love as God does, the result is disorder, destruction, and suffering.** The opposite of love is **selfishness**—seeking things for oneself in a way that ignores the good of others and causes suffering.

According to the Scriptures, God did not create a world of suffering. The original state of the world was one of harmony and abundant goodness. You have probably heard the Creation story many times by now. Still, it contains religious truths that so significantly influence the Christian response to suffering that it is worth examining the story again on a deeper level.

As we revisit the Creation story (you can begin by reading Genesis, chapters 1 to 3), it is important to know that Catholics focus on the religious, rather than the scientific, truth of the story. After all, Genesis was not written for the purpose of recording a scientifically accurate account of Creation. Rather, the purpose of the Genesis Creation stories is to reveal the more important truths about the nature of God, humanity, and creation.

©Fritz Eichenberg Trust/Licensed by VAGA, New York, NY

God created the world to be a place of goodness.
(*The First Seven Days,* by Fritz Eichenberg)

E Can you think of three other examples in which people sacrifice something for a good cause?

Creation: "And God Saw It Was Good"

The Genesis Creation story begins by describing the universe as a deep darkness that would be completely empty except for the spirit of God, which moves through it like a wind (1:1–2). God could have let the universe remain that way, full of nothing but God. Instead, out of love, God creates something else. And so the darkness is dispelled with the words, "Let there be light" (1:3).

God continues to speak new things into being: water, land, plants, stars, animals, and so on. God is depicted working much as an artist does, stepping back occasionally to judge what is being made. God judges it to be *good*. As if to emphasize the point, the phrase "And God saw it was good" is repeated seven times in the Creation account. Creation is good because it unfolds from God's own goodness.

Humans are capable of imitating God's creative giving. Childbirth is perhaps the most obvious example: a pregnant woman gives up part of her physical self for the sake of bringing a new person into being. And both parents inevitably give up part of their lives in order to help their child grow into the best person he or she can be.

Humans: Made in the Image of God

Genesis tells us that the similarity of human love to God's love is no accident. In fact, God intentionally made humans in the **image of God:**

God created man in his image;
in the divine image of God he created him;
male and female he created them.

(1:27, NAB)

What does it mean to be made "in the image of God"? Think of your reflection in a pool of still water: your reflection, or image, is not you, but it resembles you. Similarly, as images of God, humans are reflections of God. Because God is a mystery, what it means to be an image of God is also something of a mystery. But we can be certain of at least three truths: we were made good, we were made to be in relationship with others, and we were made free.

Human dignity

The first attribute of human beings is that they are made essentially good—God says "*very* good," in fact (1:31). The only reason anything or anyone in creation exists is because God wills it to exist, because God loves it. Even Hitler, who is so often given as an example of evil personified, was loved by God; of course, what Hitler did and stood for are another matter.

Draw a portrait of someone you know, or use a mirror to draw a portrait of yourself. The quality of your drawing is unimportant for this activity. Instead, as you form an image of your subject on the paper, reflect on Genesis 2:7, "Then the LORD God formed man from the dust of the ground, and breathed into his nostrils the breath of life; and the man became a living being." When you are finished, record a few words from your reflections at the bottom of the portrait.

THE ENUMA ELISH: A BABYLONIAN CREATION STORY

The Genesis story is not the only ancient creation story. In fact, almost every ancient culture had its own story of how the world came to exist. Each story reflected much about how the people of its culture viewed their world. For that reason, it is interesting to note that the view of the world reflected in the Genesis Creation story was much different from the worldview reflected by the creation stories of other cultures in the ancient world.

For instance, the Babylonians, powerful neighbors of the Israelites who at one time conquered them, had a creation story called the **Enuma Elish.** That story described a world born out of the violence of the gods:

The image is a medieval depiction of Babylon. Although the Babylonians believed that violence was necessary to bring order to a chaotic world, the Genesis Creation stories suggest love, not violence, is the way to a world of goodness.

In the beginning, the gods Apsu and Tiamat give birth to younger gods, who make so much noise that the older gods cannot sleep. Apsu and Tiamat decide to quiet their children by killing them—but one of the young gods, Ea, finds out about the plan and kills Apsu first.

That makes Tiamat very angry, and she vows to avenge her dead mate. Terrified, the children beg the youngest among them, Marduk, to fight Tiamat. He agrees, but only after the other gods say they will make him their ruler if he succeeds.

Marduk catches Tiamat in a net and drives an evil wind down her throat, making her belly blow up like a balloon. Then he shoots an arrow that bursts her belly and pierces her heart. He smashes her skull and stretches out her corpse.

Marduk creates the world out of Tiamat's dead body. The gods who had sided with Tiamat are imprisoned. Marduk and Ea kill one of the captive gods and make human beings out of the god's blood. Human beings, according to the Babylonian story, are made to be servants of the gods. (Adapted from Wink, *Engaging the Powers,* pages 14–15)

The Enuma Elish reflects a basic belief held by Babylonian culture: only violence can bring order out of chaos. By contrast, the Genesis story reflects the belief that love, not violence, is what brings goodness out of chaos.

Although no one believes the Enuma Elish literally anymore, many people believe in its basic assumption—that violence, division, and dominance are necessary to keep order in the world. Christians, by contrast, believe that the way to a world of goodness is love and compassion. ●

Christians, by contrast, believe that **the way to a world of goodness is love and compassion.**

Name three specific examples of how society reflects the belief that violence, division, and domination are necessary to keep order, and three examples of how society reflects the belief that love and compassion are the way to goodness.

The basic goodness of human beings that comes from always being loved by God is called **human dignity.** People may do things that do not reflect their God-given goodness by abusing themselves or someone else. But nothing can take away the love of God, and so nothing a person does can take away his or her inherent dignity.

Made to love and to be loved

God made creation in order to love it by sharing God's own goodness with it. Like any lover, God desires to be loved in return. Because they are made in God's image, people also desire to love and to be loved. In other words, human beings are made not to be alone but to be in relationship:

With other people. In the Genesis story, God makes humans to be "partners" or "helpers" to one another because "it is not good that the man should be alone" (2:18). God brought Adam and Eve together to form a family—the most basic unit of society.

The very nature of God is three persons (Father, Son, and Holy Spirit) united as one through their shared love. As images of God, each of us is also made to be united with all other people through love.

With creation. Human beings are meant to have a loving relationship with creation too. Genesis depicts God giving humans "dominion" over everything on the earth (1:28).

THE WAY
GOD CREATED
THE WORLD
TO BE

God, like sunshine and rain, gives life to humanity and creation . . .

. . . and **each person** is most true to him or her self by living in loving relationship with God, creation, and others.

. . . and for **one another.** In doing so, people love God, . . .

. . . and **creation** is humanity's home. People care for creation . . .

Some people have interpreted this to mean that humans "own" creation and can do whatever they want to with it, but Genesis makes it clear that creation is a gift from God.

Humans are placed in the Garden of Eden, which represents all creation, "to cultivate and care for it" (2:15, NAB). Like God, then, humans are creative. God calls them to share in God's work of creation—work that is carried on today whenever people help to make the world the good place God intended it to be.

With God. Finally, humans are made to have an intimate friendship with God—that is the very reason God made us. In Genesis, Adam and Eve seem to have direct conversations with God; they even hear God "walking" in the garden.

Humans have a deep longing to complete themselves by connecting with the loving power of God. It has been said that all people have a "God-shaped hole" inside themselves. We may try to fill that inner sense of emptiness with many things, but nothing really makes us feel complete until we find God. In the words of Saint Augustine's prayer, "You have made us for yourself, and our heart is restless until it rests in you."

When people open themselves to receiving God's love, that love makes them more completely the people God meant them to be—people who reflect the goodness of God in their own unique way.

Free will

Another attribute that humans have because they are created in God's image is **free will,** the ability to choose what to do. Without free will, people would not be able to love, because love is always a freely given gift—it cannot be forced or taken, bought or sold.

That is why God does not stop people from doing things that cause suffering for themselves or others. If, for instance, you could be forced by God to be nice to others, you would not have free will, and so you would not truly love others. You would be just a puppet in God's hand, not the reflection of God's goodness that you were made to be.

Of course, if humans are free to choose love, it also means they are free not to love. The first humans (represented in Genesis by Adam and Eve) chose to turn away from God's goodness, a choice that disrupted the harmony that existed at the beginning of creation. Ӊ

Original Sin

When most of us hear the story of Adam and Eve eating the forbidden fruit, it reminds us of being disciplined by our parents when we were children. The way the story is told makes it sound as though Adam and Eve got caught with their hands in the cookie jar, and that God sent them to their room without supper as punishment.

It is true that Adam and Eve are a little like children who disobey their parents. But the story told in chapter three of Genesis is about more than stolen fruit.

"You will be like God"

At first, Adam and Eve have a close friendship with God. The love between them is symbolized by the Garden of Eden, a place where Adam and Eve receive God's goodness in abundance.

Then the serpent tells Adam and Eve that if they turn away from God, "your eyes will be opened, and you will be like God, knowing

Ӊ Respond to the following reflection questions with a few sentences for each: In what ways do others see your human dignity? What kind of relationship do you have with other people, with creation, and with God? What is the most important way you have used free will, and why is it important?

good and evil" (3:5). Of course, having been made in the image of God, Adam and Eve already are "like God" in many respects, and God has declared them to be "very good" just as they are.

But the serpent is saying that because Adam and Eve rely on God, they are not good enough. The serpent encourages them to be their own gods, to betray their friendship with God so that they can know good and evil—that is, so that they can decide for themselves what is right and wrong. Adam and Eve go along with the serpent: instead of choosing to live in love, they choose to live selfishly. In the Tradition of the church, this is called the Fall.

As a result, Adam and Eve do indeed come to know evil as well as good. Rather than living in loving relationship with themselves, each other, creation, and God, they become separated:

- **From their own goodness.** Adam and Eve believed the serpent's lie that they were not good enough. So then their nakedness, which was part of their God-given goodness, embarrassed them. By seeking to become something they were not, they failed to respect their own human dignity.

- **From God.** Once Adam and Eve had walked in friendship with God, but now they "[hide] themselves from the presence of the LORD" (3:8). God tells Adam and Eve that their choice will result in suffering and death. This is not a punishment, but a natural consequence of their action. When humans try to live without God, they are like a plant trying to grow without water. Eventually the plant will wither and die.

- **From other people.** When God confronts them about their action, instead of taking responsibility for what they did and repenting, Adam blames Eve and Eve blames the serpent. Selfishness causes division in the human family.

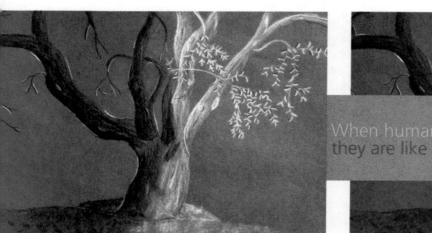

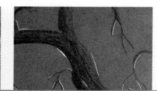

When humans try to live without God, they are like a plant trying to grow without water.

✷ *Student art:* Charcoal pencil; Jason Oglio, Trinity High School, Garfield Heights, Ohio

One way young people experience suffering is through the breakup of romantic relationships. If the Christian understanding of love is to want goodness for another person, is it possible to break up with someone and still have Christian love for them? Explain your answer.

- **From creation.** Rather than living in peace with the animal world, animals and humans will fight each other. Food was plentiful in the garden, but after the Fall, people have to work hard for it: "By the sweat of your face you shall eat bread" (3:19). In the Tradition of the church, even the suffering caused by natural disaster or disease is somehow a result of the Fall.

The sin of our "first parents" had consequences not only for themselves but also for all humankind: all people inherit a broken relationship with God that results in the breakdown of relationships with one's self, other people, and creation. The **original sin** of Adam and Eve—the rejection of their humanity as created in God's image—became a basic tendency of human nature that all people inherit as well. Original sin is a condition people are born into. It is not a personal sin that people commit. Rather, it is a weakened state of human nature that all inherit.

Because of original sin, people have a tendency to sin as their "first parents" did, selfishly betraying the loving relationships they are meant to have with God, with others, and with the earth. These wrongful actions or omissions that humans choose are called **personal sins.**

Cain's murder of Abel vividly illustrates the effects of original sin. When God calls Cain to account, Cain responds, "Am I my brother's keeper?" (4:9). In a world in which people open themselves to love, the answer would be, "Yes!" But with the Fall, that was not the world chosen by the first humans.

Grace: A source of hope

If this were the end of the story of humans' relationship with God, hopelessness would be a realistic response to suffering. But although the first humans chose not to allow God's love to rule their lives, it did not stop God from loving them. When Adam and Eve hid themselves from God's presence, God called out to them, "Where are you?" (3:9).

The call for humanity to return to its friendship with God echoes throughout the rest of the Bible. Ever since the first sin, God's love has worked to restore creation's original goodness. That transforming love of God is known as **grace**, and it is the reason Christians are able to find hope amid suffering. Grace overcomes original sin, restoring our relationship with God and one another; it is what enables us to work with God to make the world all that God meant it to be.

That **transforming love of God** is known as **grace**, and it is the reason Christians are able to find hope amid suffering.

✳ *Student art:* "Darkest Hour." Balsa foam; Annie Bursiek, Boylan Central Catholic High School, Rockford, Illinois

5. What are three truths about human beings that result from their being made in the image of God?
6. What is human dignity? Can anyone lose his or her human dignity? Why or why not?
7. Define the following terms: *original sin, grace.*
8. What is a consequence of original sin?

In Depth

9. What is the difference between wanting what is good for oneself and being selfish? Use examples to explain your answer.

Justice: The Reign of God's Goodness

The story of Creation and the Fall teaches us that God did not bring suffering into the world, people did, because the original sin of Adam and Eve disrupted the order of God's creation. God does not take away the freedom that allows people to bring suffering into the world because that same freedom is what enables us to love.

Although God allows people to bring suffering into the world, God does not will that people suffer. In fact, the whole history of God's relationship with humanity is the story of how God has acted to lead us out of a world of suffering into a world of goodness.

"I Have Heard My People's Cry"

Throughout the Scriptures, God shows compassion for the poor, the oppressed, the weak, and the outcasts from society—not because God loves

Just as God called Moses to lead the Israelites out of Egypt, God calls each of us to lead people out of suffering.

them more than others, but because they are more in need of God's attention by virtue of their suffering.

In the Old Testament, the best-known story of God's concern for oppressed people is the story found in the Book of Exodus about how God frees the Israelites from slavery in Egypt.

As slaves, the Israelites work hard building cities and farming the land—yet all the benefit of their work goes to the Egyptians. To ensure that the Israelites do not become powerful enough to revolt against their oppressors, Pharaoh decrees that all newborn Israelite boys be drowned in the Nile River, which the Egyptians regard as a god.

When the people of Israel cry out to God for help, God responds through a revelation to Moses. The words of God that follow are directed to the Israelites specifically, but they are also an expression of compassion for suffering people everywhere:

Then the LORD said, "I have observed the misery of my people who are in Egypt; I have heard their cry on account of their taskmasters. Indeed, I know their sufferings, and I have come down to deliver them from the Egyptians, and to bring them up out of that land to a good and broad land flowing with milk and honey. . . . So come, I will send you to Pharaoh to bring my people, the Israelites, out of Egypt." (Exodus 3:7–10)

Note that although God promises to take the people from a place of suffering (Egypt) to a place of goodness (the Promised Land), God will not accomplish that transition with a snap of the fingers. Rather, God recruits Moses, who at the time is a shepherd and a fugitive from the Egyptians, to help win freedom for the Israelites.

Moses balks at God's invitation to leadership. As it turns out, he has good reason to be hesitant. The road to freedom is not quick and easy, but takes many years of struggle and hardship. Moses himself never lives to enter the Promised Land. Yet in the end, God and God's people are victorious.

A source of hope for people everywhere

The Exodus story is the central story of the Jewish people. But it also has long been a source of hope for oppressed peoples everywhere, one that has motivated them to take courageous action for the sake of goodness. Slaves in the United States often referred to the Exodus story in their songs, and it inspired the leaders of the twentieth-century civil rights movement as well. Most recently, the Exodus story has influenced liberation theology movements in South America and around the globe. More will be said about liberation theology in chapter two.

"Indeed, I know their sufferings, and I have come down to deliver them . . ."

Recall a time when you were called on to take leadership or responsibility—in a job, on a sports team, or in a social situation. Describe your experience: Were you hesitant? How did it turn out? How did it affect your willingness to take on leadership roles in the future?

Form a small group with some of your classmates. Working together, make a collage depicting a modern Exodus by pasting or taping pictures from old magazines and newspapers onto poster board. Here are some images you might include in the collage: all sorts of people who are oppressed or suffering, landscapes symbolizing Egypt or the Promised Land, leaders working for change ("Moses"), barriers to freedom, people living in goodness, and newspaper headlines to serve as captions.

Life in the Promised Land

Before the people enter into the Promised Land, Moses gives them a Law to live by. The requirements of the Law sought to promote goodness and harmony among the people. Moses tells the people that they must live in a way that promotes goodness and peace among them "so that you may live and occupy the land that the LORD your God is giving you" (Deuteronomy 16:20).

Moses was referring to the land of Israel, but, in fact, any place where people live in God's goodness is the Promised Land. Like the Garden of Eden, the harmony and abundant goodness of the Promised Land is a rich symbol of God's life-giving love.

The Law that Moses gave the people included not only the Ten Commandments but also hundreds of very specific rules about the way people were to live. At the heart of all these laws was the **Shema,** which Jews still recite daily. Here is the beginning of that prayer:

> Hear, O Israel: The LORD is our God, the LORD alone. You shall love the LORD your God with all your heart, and with all your soul, and with all your might. (Deuteronomy 6:4–5)

Food drives are one way people today live out the scriptural call to love our neighbors by sharing the first part of our harvest with those in need.

The Israelites lived out the Shema in part by following the many rules about worship and holiness. They saw keeping their worship pure and perfect as a way of loving God with everything they had.

"Love your neighbor as yourself"

The Law also emphasized that true worship is expressed in the way people live with one another. The law commanding the Israelites to "love your neighbor as yourself" (Matthew 19:19) was expressed in many specific regulations that reflected God's compassion for poor and oppressed people. For example, Israel was given the following regulations:

- Leave some of the harvest for gleaning by the poor.
- Do not set dishonest prices.
- Welcome the stranger; treat foreigners as you would your own people.
- Every seven years, cancel all debts.
- Give God thanks for your harvest by giving the first part of it to foreigners, orphans, and widows, "so that they may eat their fill" (Deuteronomy 26:12).

Sprinkled in among these laws are constant reminders of how much God has given the people by bringing them from slavery into the Promised Land. The implication is that these are not just rules to be followed but a way of giving thanks to God by sharing what they have been given. L

The Prophets: Voicing God's Call

Despite the Law, the people of Israel were often unfaithful in their relationship with God. Fortunately for the Israelites, God did not turn

L Make an inventory, or detailed list, of all the things you own, listing how many types of clothes, sports equipment, games, bicycles, or cars you have, and how many tapes and CDs, electronics, shoes, shampoos, jewelry, money, and so on, that you have. Now imagine that you live in ancient Israel. The law asks you to give part of your "harvest" away for the benefit of others. Would you do it? If so, why? What would you give? If not, why not?

away from them but instead chose **prophets** to call the people back to divine friendship. But often the prophets had as little self-confidence about their mission as Moses did; it seems to be a habit of God to choose the lowly or the most unlikely persons for the most important roles.

A common theme of the prophets' call was the important connection between love of God and love of neighbor. Often the people would focus on the laws pertaining to proper worship and sacrifice, but would neglect the laws about loving their neighbors. The prophets made it clear that following all the rules about worship was pointless—even offensive to God—if that worship was not accompanied by compassion for others.

The Book of Isaiah, for instance, describes the practice of fasting, in which people cover themselves in ashes, dress in rough clothes, and bow their heads to show sorrow for their sins and to renew their relationship with God. But these outward signs of repentance are meaningless unless people restore relationships of love with one another, Isaiah says. God says the following to Israel:

> Will you call this a fast,
>   a day acceptable to the LORD?
> Is not this the fast that I choose:
>   to loose the bonds of injustice,
>   to undo the thongs of the yoke,
> to let the oppressed go free,
>   and to break every yoke?
> Is it not to share your bread with the hungry,
>   and bring the homeless poor into your
>   house;
> when you see the naked, to cover them,
>   and not to hide yourself from your own
>   kin?

. . . .

> If you remove the yoke from among you,
>   the pointing of the finger, the speaking
>   of evil,
> if you offer your food to the hungry
>   and satisfy the needs of the afflicted,
> then your light shall rise in the darkness
>   and your gloom be like the noonday.
>   (Isaiah 58:5–10) **M**

In the Book of Micah, God offers a similar response to Israel's question about the best form of sacrificial worship:

> "Will the LORD be pleased with thousands
>   of rams,
>   with ten thousands of rivers of oil?
> Shall I give my firstborn for my
>   transgression,
>   the fruit of my body for the sin of my
>   soul?"
> He has told you, O mortal, what is good;
>   and what does the LORD require of you
> but to do justice, and to love kindness,
>   and to walk humbly with your God?
>   (Micah 6:7–8) **N**

The Call to Justice

In both of the preceding passages, justice is the first thing God names when the people ask what God wants of them. And what happens when justice rules the land? Isaiah says that "your light shall rise in the darkness"—the shadows of suffering are dispelled. Elsewhere, Isaiah describes the rule of justice as a peaceful kingdom in which the wolf lies down with the lamb, and children play in the dens of poisonous snakes: "They will not hurt or destroy on all my holy mountain; for the

M Imagine that the prophet Isaiah was commenting on your school, family, or community. What would he say? Beginning with the phrase, "Is not this the fast that I choose, . . ." write his prophecy in your own words.

N Do you find echoes of the prophets in the music you listen to? Write down the lyrics of songs that you think might be prophetic for people today, and explain why you think they are prophetic.

SOJOURNER TRUTH:
FROM SLAVE
TO PROPHET

God has a habit of choosing the **most unlikely people** to be **prophets.** That was certainly the case with Isabella Hardenbergh, a child born into slavery in rural New York in about 1797.

Slavery, Isabella said, had left her soul crushed and confused. Over time, however, she realized that God loved her just as much as God loved the white men who oppressed her—and that realization gave her a new sense of dignity and strength. When she heard God calling her to preach, she took the name Sojourner Truth. A sojourner is one who is always on the move, which she was as she traveled around the country preaching the truth—the abolition of slavery, the rights of freed slaves, an end to the death penalty, and women's rights—among other things.

Born into slavery, Sojourner Truth eventually became a prophet for her own time.

Sojourner not only preached but took action as well. She escaped from slavery, and later successfully sued in court for the freedom of her son. She protested segregation on public transportation in Washington, D.C., by forcing her way onto whites-only horse cars. During and after the Civil War, she worked to improve living conditions for freed slaves, even urging them to protest unjust treatment. When she was threatened with arrest for this, she retorted that if she were arrested, she would "make this nation rock like a cradle." She attributed all her accomplishments to her unshakable faith in God.

Sojourner Truth is perhaps best known for the impromptu speech that she gave at a women's rights convention in 1851. As feminist Frances Gage tells it, various Christian ministers had come to the gathering to give their own opinion of women's rights—basically, that God had made women inferior to men. No one challenged the ministers, until Sojourner got up to speak. Her words were recalled years later by Gage:

Sojourner walked to the podium and slowly took off her sunbonnet. Her six-foot frame towered over the audience. She began to speak in her deep, resonant voice: "Well, children, where there is so much racket, there must be something out of kilter. I think between the Negroes of the South and the women of the North—all talking about rights—the white men will be in a fix pretty soon. But what's all this talking about?"

Sojourner pointed to one of the ministers. "That man over there says that

women need to be helped into carriages, and lifted over ditches, and to have the best place everywhere. Nobody helps *me* any best place. *And ain't I a woman?*"

Sojourner raised herself up to her full height. "Look at me! Look at my arm." She bared her right arm and flexed her powerful muscles. "I have plowed, I have planted, and I have gathered into barns. And no man could head me. *And ain't I a woman?*"

"I could work as much, and eat as much as a man—when I could get it—and bear the lash as well! *And ain't I a woman?* I have borne children and seen most of them sold into slavery, and when I cried out with a mother's grief, none but Jesus heard me. *And ain't I a woman?*"

The women in the audience began to cheer wildly.

She pointed to another minister. . . . "That little man in black there! He says women can't have as much rights as men. 'Cause Christ wasn't a woman." She stood with outstretched arms and eyes of fire. "Where did your Christ come from?"

"Where did your Christ come from?" she thundered again. "From God and a woman! Man had nothing to do with him!"

The entire church now roared with deafening applause.

Sojourner's "Ain't I a Woman?" speech cleverly showed the contradictions in the logic of oppression. She used her former status as a slave whose dignity and rights had not been respected to prove that women had just as much dignity and as many rights as men. The speech electrified the convention, and only added to her fame. (After Gilbert and Gubar, *The Norton Anthology of Literature by Women,* pages 252–253) ●

She attributed all her accomplishments to her unshakable faith in God.

earth will be full of the knowledge of the LORD, as the waters cover the sea" (11:9). Still elsewhere, justice is described as causing the barren desert to become a fruitful orchard.

It is not a coincidence that these descriptions of the effects of justice contain echoes of the Book of Genesis and the Garden of Eden. God created the world good, but the Fall of our "first parents" disrupted the harmony and goodness of relationships in creation. Justice actively seeks to re-establish the original goodness and order. We might say that **justice** is the establishment of loving relationships among human beings, God, and creation so that life can flourish in the way God intends. **Injustice,** on the contrary, is a condition in which people have put obstacles in the way of loving relationships, thus preventing life from flourishing as God intends.

An impossible dream?

People are called by God to respond compassionately to suffering with justice, so that the world becomes the good place it was always meant to be. That call might seem unrealistic, even impossible—and it would be if people were expected to change the world by themselves. But believers hear the voice of God reply: "Don't be afraid! I am with you."

The longing of God to lead humans out of suffering and into a life of goodness began when God called out, "Where are you?" to Adam and Eve. It continued when God delivered the Israelites from their suffering in Egypt, and when God spoke to the people through the prophets.

God's compassion for humanity is so great that God became human in the person of Jesus. Through Jesus, God dives deep into human suffering and uses that suffering to break open a way through death into goodness and life. When we follow the way opened by Jesus, we too can pass through a world of suffering to a world of hope.

Mother Teresa of Calcutta responded to God's call by compassionately caring for those who were poor, dying, or orphaned.

But believers hear the voice of God reply: **"Don't be afraid!** I am with you."

Is it possible for the world to become the good place envisioned in the Book of Genesis and by the prophets? Explain your answer.

For Review

10. Why does God lead the people out of Egypt and into the Promised Land?
11. Name at least three ways that God asked the Israelites to live out the Law, "Love your neighbor as yourself" (Matthew 19:19).
12. According to the prophets, what kind of worship does God want from humans?
13. Define *justice* and *injustice.*

In Depth

14. Why is worship of God pointless if people do not love one another?

The Compassionate Way of Jesus

Who is Jesus? Christians believe Jesus is the one sent by God to save the world from sin and death. They believe that those who follow Jesus will live a new life, both on Earth and in heaven. This much is familiar to Christians from the time of their childhood.

But what does justice have to do with following Jesus? For Catholics, justice is a central part of Christian faith. In other words, a full response to Jesus involves more than just believing in him, praying to him, and going to church—although those are essential parts of Christian faith. Truly following Jesus means more than just saying yes to God with our lips; it means actually *living* that yes as Jesus did. A closer look at the life and teaching of Jesus reveals the meaning of justice.

God Is with Us

The Gospel of Matthew calls Jesus Emmanuel, a name that means "God is with us." Jesus' followers eventually came to recognize that in Jesus, God was quite literally with them—that Jesus is fully God and fully human.

That must have been a stunning realization: God loved humankind so much and thought humankind was so good that God *became* human. Remember Jean Donovan's decision to stay with the people of El Salvador in order to ease their suffering? The **Incarnation**—God becoming human in Jesus—was God's choice to be with humanity in order to lead us out of suffering and death, just as Moses led the Israelites from Egypt to the Promised Land.

The compassion that moved God to enter humanity is imitated whenever Christians like Jean Donovan have compassion for those who suffer, by being with them.

Jesus' Mission of Justice

In the Gospel of Luke, Jesus begins his public ministry by going to the synagogue in his hometown and reading from the scroll of the prophet Isaiah, whose vision of a just and peaceful world was described earlier. The passage Jesus reads is about one who was sent by God "to bring good news to the poor, . . . to proclaim release to the captives and recovery of sight to the blind, to let the oppressed go free, to proclaim the year of the Lord's favor" (Luke 4:17–21).

In choosing to read that passage, Jesus identified himself with the one who would bring about the just world imagined by Isaiah. In fact, Jesus' ministry was characterized by the same outpouring of God's love that made the world such a good place to begin with. Through his words, actions, and miracles, Jesus worked to restore a world of loving relationships.

But if Jesus' mission was to share God's goodness with people, why would anyone want to kill him?

The official reason for executing Jesus was written on a sign above him on the cross: "This is Jesus, the King of the Jews." Supposedly, Jesus was killed for wanting to be king. Nothing Jesus ever said or did would support that claim, however.

Jesus *did* talk about the coming of a new kingdom, or reign, though—the Kingdom of God.

Through his words, actions, and miracles, Jesus worked to restore a world of loving relationships.

✳ *Student art:* "Brotherly Love." Photograph; Melissa C. Hansen, Ramona Convent Secondary School, Alhambra, California

The Scriptures tell us that God is like a mother comforting her child (Isaiah 66:13). Describe a time when you were suffering from sickness, disappointment, or rejection. How did the presence of a friend or parent make you feel better? Are there times when you would rather be alone when you suffer? Why or why not?

The Kingdom of God

For Jesus, the Kingdom of God was not an earthly kingdom held together by armies and soldiers. Nor was it a specific place at all. Instead, the Kingdom, or Reign, of God is the way things are when God is the "king" who "rules" in people's hearts. Because God's rule is love, we can say the **Kingdom of God** is the way things are when love is more important than anything else in people's lives. We can tell from our experiences that both love and cruel indifference characterize people's actions in the world. We can glimpse God's Kingdom already here when we witness people and communities centered in love. But the Kingdom is not yet completely here, or the world would be a different place. Christians anticipate and work toward the day when God's Kingdom will come completely.

Jesus did not invent the idea of the Kingdom of God. The Israelites had talked about God as king for many centuries. For them, God was their ultimate ruler, and love of God was the greatest commandment in Jewish Law.

But Jesus put his own twist on what it means to love God. In the following passage from the Gospel of Mark, Jesus teaches that love of God (a commandment from the Shema) is impossible without love of neighbor (a commandment from the Book of Deuteronomy):

> One of the scribes . . . asked [Jesus], "Which commandment is the first of all?" Jesus answered, "The first is, 'Hear O Israel: the Lord our God, the Lord is one; you shall love the Lord your God with all your heart, and with all your soul, and with all your mind, and with all your strength.' The second is this, 'You shall love your neighbor as yourself.' There is no other commandment greater than these." Then the scribe said to him, "You are right, Teacher; you have truly said that 'he is one, and besides him there is no other'; and 'to love him with all the heart, and with all the understanding, and with all the strength,' and 'to love one's neighbor as oneself,'—this is much more important than all whole burnt offerings and sacrifices." When Jesus saw that [the scribe] had answered wisely, he said to him, "You are not far from the kingdom of God." (Mark 12:28–34)

Jesus does not answer with just one commandment but with two. The scribe sees that Jesus is teaching that love of neighbor is essential to loving God. Jesus says that those who understand this important lesson "are not far from the kingdom of God." **Q**

Love God by loving one another

Jesus takes his point even further in the well-known story of the final judgment from Matthew, chapter 25. In that story, Jesus says that people will enter the Kingdom of God solely on the basis of whether they loved others:

> "Then the king will say to those at his right hand, 'Come, you that are blessed by my Father, inherit the kingdom prepared for you from the foundation of the world; for I was hungry and you gave me food, I was thirsty and you gave me something to drink, I was a stranger and you welcomed

Q In the Gospel of Luke, Jesus' reply to the scribe is followed by the parable of the good Samaritan. In that story, the priest and the Levite are going to worship at the Jerusalem Temple and do not want to help the beaten man because his blood might make them "unclean" and unable to worship. The Samaritans were despised by the Jews because they did not worship God at the Temple—but, as a result, the good Samaritan is able to help his neighbor. He knows that he honors God by caring for the beaten stranger on the road.

Read the story of the good Samaritan in Luke 10:29–37, then rewrite the parable as if it took place today in your community.

me, I was naked and you gave me clothing, I was sick and you took care of me, I was in prison and you visited me.' Then the righteous will answer him, 'Lord, when was it that we saw you hungry and gave you food, or thirsty and gave you something to drink? And when was it that we saw you a stranger and welcomed you, or naked and gave you clothing? And when was it that we saw you sick or in prison and visited you?' And the king will answer them, 'Truly I tell you, just as you did it to one of the least of these who are members of my family, you did it to me.'" (Matthew 25:34–40)

Jesus and the prophets agree, *True love of God is best shown by loving one another.* Genuine worship comes from a sincere heart, one that recognizes God in the needs of others.

Love Turns the World Upside Down

As strange as it may sound, Jesus' "kingdom of love" frightened the political leaders of the time. If love reigned, they would lose their power. Like Adam and Eve, the leaders had attempted to make themselves into little gods, taking the goodness of God away from others in order to have more power and wealth for themselves. It seems possible that Jesus was killed because his Kingdom would have reversed that situation.

We hear the word *love* so much (especially in religion classes) that it may be difficult to imagine how it could be so threatening. But, in fact, when love, willing the good for each other, is the most important law in a society,

everything changes. By making love the law of the land, Jesus was turning the world of first-century Palestine upside down.

The social world of first-century Palestine

By knowing the social situation of Jewish society at the time of Jesus, we can more fully appreciate the impact of Jesus' mission. As you read about that situation, keep in mind that Jewish society of the first century was in many respects advanced for its time. Jesus did not challenge only Jewish society, but all societies not ruled by love—and his challenge is as valid for Christians in the twenty-first century as it was then.

Imagine Jewish society of Jesus' time as a pyramid, with those at the top of the pyramid closest to God (and therefore "most holy") and those at the bottom farthest from God ("least holy"). At the very top was the high priest, the only man who could go into the holiest part of the Temple.

Next came the other religious authorities. Because they worshiped at the Temple and tried to follow the Law exactly, they thought they were closer to God than everyone else.

All other men who tried to follow the Law were next on the pyramid. Rich and healthy men came first, their prosperity seen as a sign that they had earned God's favor by following the Law.

Women were next down the pyramid. Most of women's worth came from their relationship to their fathers, husbands, or brothers. They were treated like property and had few rights. Men could easily divorce their wives, but women could not divorce their husbands.

R How is the world as you see it today the same as or different from the world of the ancient Jews? Draw a diagram showing how groups of people relate to one another. Your diagram does not have to be a pyramid—it should reflect the shape of society as you see it.

Women generally could not be disciples of rabbis or preachers, nor could they have friendly conversations with men in public.

Next on the pyramid came foreigners. Because the Jewish people were especially chosen by God, people who were not Jewish were considered outside of God's love, although "righteous" non-Jews were often treated with more respect. Samaritans, considered to have a corrupt, inferior version of Judaism, were especially despised.

Next came sinners. Poverty and sickness were seen by many as evidence of sin. People who were poor or sick were thought to have earned their situation by not obeying the Law. People who worked in unclean professions, such as shepherds or tax collectors, were considered to be sinners too.

At the bottom of the heap came people such as prostitutes and murderers.

Those at the top of the pyramid (the ones who followed the Law) did not associate with those at the bottom. If they entered a sinner's house, for instance, or ate with sinners, or touched a leper, they would become unclean and would have to perform elaborate rituals to purify themselves.

Of course, this quick sketch of ancient Jewish society does not reflect its complexities. But the point is clear: Jewish society was one of division, as ours is today. 𝕉

"The last shall be first"

In the Kingdom of God, that pyramid is turned on its head. Jesus taught that far from being unloved by God, people who are poor, suffering, and oppressed are especially loved by God—not because they are better than everyone else, but because they need God's love the most. In the **Beatitudes,** Jesus calls them "blessed." They are blessed not because poverty, suffering, and oppression are good, but because their experience teaches them the importance of love and justice—a lesson that rich and comfortable people may have more difficulty understanding.

On the other hand, anyone who wants to be "first" must not be selfish, but must bring goodness to others—the opposite of what Adam and Eve did. "I am among you as one who serves," Jesus said, urging his followers to do the same: "The greatest among you must become like the youngest, and the leader like one who serves" (Luke 22:26–27).

"Jews do not share things in common with Samaritans," the Gospel of John notes (4:9), and Jewish women were not to speak with strange men in public. It is no wonder that when Jesus asked the Samaritan woman at the well for a drink of water, the disciples "were astonished that he was speaking with a woman" (John 4:27).

Can you imagine what society would look like if instead of trying to get ahead, everyone tried to serve everyone else? Catholic thinker and social activist Peter Maurin put it this way:

Everybody would be rich
if nobody tried to become richer.
And nobody would be poor
if everybody tried to be the poorest.
And everybody would be what he ought to be
if everybody tried to be
what he wants the other fellow to be. §
(*Easy Essays,* page 37)

A new family

In Jesus' kingdom, *all* people are related to one another when they love one another: "Whoever does the will of God is my brother and sister and mother" (Mark 3:35). Throughout the Gospels, Jesus constantly breaks through society's divisions to bring everyone into his family, including the following:

Women. Jesus talked to women in public all the time—his disciples "were astonished that he was speaking with a woman" at the Samaritan well (John 4:27). Jesus touched women to heal them, and was touched by them in return. In one case, a prostitute burst into a room full of male religious leaders and washed Jesus' feet with her tears. Jesus taught women and had them among his disciples. And women, who were not thought to be reliable witnesses, were the first witnesses of the Resurrection.

Sick people. Jesus totally rejected the idea that sickness comes from sin, and he touched the sick to heal them. Over and over, the religious leaders charged Jesus with breaking the command not to work on the Sabbath because Jesus healed people on that day. Jesus said that having compassion for the suffering "keeps the Sabbath holy," but ignoring them in order to honor God does not.

Sinners. Jesus frequently associated with sinners and even ate at their homes, an act that would have made him ritually unclean. Likewise, he forgave sins—an act punishable by death. On the other hand, Jesus said that the ones who think they are holier than everyone else are also sinners because they sin by scorning others.

Rich and powerful people. Jesus must have known that the top of the pyramid can be a lonely place. He challenged rich and powerful people to give up their wealth and power—not just to benefit poor and oppressed people, but because doing so would allow those who are rich and powerful to love. In the Kingdom of God, love is more valuable than gold.

Enemies. Jesus even wanted to bring our *enemies* into the Kingdom of God. He said people should respond to violence not with retaliation but with love: "You have heard that it was said [by some of the teachers of law], 'You shall love your neighbor and hate your enemy.' But I say to you, Love your enemies and pray for those who persecute you" (Matthew 5:43–44). This is a hard saying for people to accept even today because it seems to be the way of weakness. In fact, the power of love is stronger than the power of violence, as we will discuss in a later chapter.

§ Form a small group with some of your classmates. Together, make up a humorous skit about what would happen if people suddenly started living out Peter Maurin's vision. Or write a skit by yourself.

Love's Surprise: The Cross and the Resurrection

As we have seen, the mission of Jesus was to take a world built in large measure on selfishness and turn it upside down to make it a world built on love. But the people in power feared Jesus' new Kingdom based on love. They were afraid of a man who questioned everything about how the world works, everything that made sense to them. In a world based on Jesus' teaching, how would they fare? In fact, love multiplies God's goodness for everyone—but their deep fear kept them from understanding that truth, and so they sought to kill Jesus. ✝

Jesus could have avoided suffering and death by giving up the mission God had given him. After all, he was afraid of pain, suffering, and death just like any other human being. But Jesus was totally committed to following the will of God, which is for people to love one another as God has loved them. Jesus loved God and humanity completely— even though this meant that some people would cause him to suffer and die. On the cross, Jesus gave up everything he had for the sake of love. He did exactly the opposite of what Adam and Eve did when they turned away from God to seek greater power for themselves.

Leaving God's goodness, which had been their source of life, brought the first humans

The cross and the Resurrection are signs that unselfish love, not selfishness, leads to goodness and joy and life.

✝ The political leaders of Jesus' time feared his vision of a world based on love. Have you ever been afraid of love? If so, why? If not, can you imagine reasons that people might fear love?

THE JOY
OF JUSTICE

The dissatisfaction with "the way the world works" that leads people to do justice often results in the surprise of joy. Lou Nanni, now a director of a center for the homeless, discovered this truth during a two-year mission trip to Chile that he undertook after graduating from the University of Notre Dame, and he writes as follows:

> After four enjoyable and affirming years at Notre Dame, I was abruptly displaced, living in a Santiago shantytown under the ruthless dictatorship of a military regime. Distant from family and friends, I struggled with health problems as I adjusted to a new language, culture, political situation and socio-economic reality. Loneliness and self-doubt filled the spaces where pride and confidence had only recently dwelled.
>
> Satisfaction and happiness, which [depend on] external circumstances, were for the first time in my life no longer present. I cried myself to sleep many nights thinking of the profound suf-

fering which surrounded me in our neighborhood. Children not clothed adequately against the cold and rain. . . . Teens and adults tortured, some to death, because they courageously stood for the truth. Masses of people who had lost belief in themselves and hope for the future. What was there to be happy about? In fact, I soon came to feel that I was as powerless as they to change this unjust reality, even for one lost soul. Or so it seemed.

"Nobody ever said the Holy Spirit was going to make us happy, but it is going to make us joyful," [explains theologian Michael Himes]. In fact, [he says,] "the Holy Spirit will make us unsatisfied." I was unsatisfied and disgusted not so much by the military regime and its instruments of destruction as by the majority of individuals who cowardly [gave in] and remained indifferent before it. I was also distressed by the abrupt recognition of my own limitations. I realized to my horror that I was not going to become another Martin Luther King Jr. . . . I was unsatisfied, unhappy . . . and though I did not realize it, the Holy Spirit was at work.

While searching in vain for fulfillment and satisfaction, I discovered joy. I found hope in the common-day prophets all around me. People who had transformed suffering into joy. People who had found resurrection in their own crucifixion, and who shared it with others. A very poor family would invite me into their home and serve hot dogs, and a young child would inadvertently say, "This is the first time we've eaten meat in two years." Or it was a mother who learned that a couple of neighborhoods over, a young man had been tortured to death, and she would protest in the street before the armed forces knowing full well she could be orphaning her own children in the process. She knew it was the right course of action, that it had to be done, and her faith and shared pain with that mother nearby allowed her to rise above her fears and self-interest. . . . This was joy, and I found it emerge through the cracks of broken lives, not from the satisfied and comfortable of this world. (Quoted in Himes, *Doing the Truth in Love,* pages 46–47) ☉ ⋓

This was joy, and **I found it emerge** through the **cracks of broken lives,** not from the satisfied and comfortable of this world.

⋓ Respond to this statement: "Nobody ever said the Holy Spirit was going to make us happy, but it is going to make us joyful. In fact, [it] will make us unsatisfied."

suffering and death. But embracing God's goodness through love brought Jesus the kind of life God always intended for humanity, one filled with goodness that goes on forever. It is through Jesus' death and Resurrection that humanity is freed from sin and a world of justice is restored.

That was not at all what the political leaders expected to happen. They expected that if they took Jesus' life, he would be dead and stay dead. The Resurrection was a complete surprise to them. But to those who believed, it was a sign that God, in Jesus, had succeeded in turning the world upside down; unselfish love, not selfishness, led to goodness and joy and life.

When people follow Jesus by loving God and neighbor even through suffering, they share in his Resurrection. In the process of giving themselves to others, people become more fully who they were meant to be. They become more fully images of God, whose love never runs out even though it is constantly given away. **V**

The Story Continues

Earlier in this chapter, we asked why people such as Jean Donovan would be moved by compassion to ease the suffering of others, even if by doing so they might suffer too.

Christians believe that the source of such compassion is the spirit of God alive and moving within us. God gave God's own self to humanity in Jesus, and Jesus continues to give all of himself—his body and blood—to his followers in the Eucharist. Just as the bread and wine are changed into the body and blood of Jesus, those who receive the Eucharist with an open heart are changed as well. They are called to become like Jesus, giving themselves in love for the goodness of the whole world. Responding to the call of grace unites us more closely with God, who makes it possible for us to transform the world into a place where justice reigns.

Of course, it is easy to talk about the *idea* of justice; responding to God's grace by *doing* justice is a messier matter, one that requires good supplies of imagination, creativity, endurance, courage, and hope. As Jean Donovan and countless others have found, people who seek justice sometimes suffer—and even die—for it. Yet they seek it anyway, because in doing so, they find the true joy that comes only from being united in love with God and one another. **W**

An invitation and a promise

For the remainder of this course, we will focus on how Christians work to cast light on the world's shadows so that it might become a world of justice. Many students find courses in Christian justice to be among the most difficult of their religion courses—not because the material is harder, but because justice challenges people's most basic values today just as much as it did in Jesus' day.

This course is not meant to make you feel guilty about the ways you do not live justly—few Christians are completely just. Nor is it expected that you will agree with everything in this textbook.

So what is this course about? It is an invitation for you to imagine what the world might look like if it were a world of justice. It is an invitation to consider how the Catholic tradition of Christian justice seeks to bring about that world. And it is an invitation to ask yourself how *you* might contribute to a world of justice.

V Describe a time when you were surprised by love. If you cannot think of a personal experience, describe a way you or someone you know might like to be surprised by love.

W Respond to the following statements: (a) God alone can bring justice to the world. (b) Humans can bring justice to the world on their own. Do you agree or disagree with each? Why?

For Review

15. Why did God become human in Jesus?
16. What is the Kingdom of God?
17. According to Jesus and the prophets, how is true love for God best shown?
18. Briefly explain how Jesus invited each of the following groups of people into the Kingdom of God: women, sick people, sinners, rich and powerful people, enemies.

In Depth

19. In two paragraphs, describe the significance of *(a)* the original sin committed by Adam and Eve, and *(b)* Jesus' death on the cross. How are they related?
20. Why do Christians such as Jean Donovan work for justice, even if they might die doing so?

2 CATHOLIC SOCIAL TEACHING

~~injustice~~
dignity
c@mmunity

Envisioning
a world of justice and peace

A
MESSAGE
OF HOPE

1 May 1933: Two hundred thousand **workers** paraded noisily through the streets of New York City, filling the air with a profusion of banners and pennants and signs, most of which were bright red—the color of the Communist Party.

There was a sense of desperation, even anger, in this crowd of people who worked for poverty wages, if they worked at all; the Great Depression was well under way, leaving millions without work, food, or shelter. The previous winter, thousands of farmers and unemployed workers had come together for a hunger march on Washington, D.C., as a dramatic appeal for help from the politicians—only to be rebuffed

Catholic social teaching was a source of hope for these Depression-era New Yorkers, who read about it in the *Catholic Worker* newspaper.

by armed police and soldiers. To many of the hungry and unemployed, the Communist Party seemed to be the only group that cared about their plight.

To dispel that notion, Dorothy Day and three young men ventured into the chaotic crowd of May Day marchers with a new newspaper, *The Catholic Worker.* Some in the crowd probably recognized Dorothy, a journalist and social activist who had frequently run in communist and socialist circles prior to her conversion to Catholicism four years earlier.

"Read *The Catholic Worker!*" they called out, waving copies of their paper. The reaction from the marchers was often hostile—communism claimed that religion was the enemy of the poor, but *The Catholic Worker's* message was the opposite. Those who bothered to read the paper were greeted in this way:

To Our Readers

For those who are sitting on park benches in the warm spring sunlight.

For those who are huddling in shelters trying to escape the rain.

For those who are walking the streets in the all but futile search for work.

For those who think that there is no hope for the future, no recognition of their plight—this little paper is addressed.

It is printed to call their attention to the fact that the Catholic Church has a social program—to let them know that there are men of God who are working not only for their spiritual, but for their material welfare. . . .

In an attempt to popularize and make known the encyclicals of the Popes in regard to social justice and the program put forth by the Church for the "reconstruction of the social order," this news sheet, *The Catholic Worker,* is started. (Based on Roberts, *Dorothy Day and the "Catholic Worker,"* pages 1–3) ☙ 𝐀

"Read *The Catholic Worker!*" they called out, waving copies of their paper.

𝐀 The *Catholic Worker* was started "for those who think that there is no hope for the future." Where have you heard a message that gives you hope for the future? Whether it is from a song, a poem, a book, a movie, or something someone told you, write down that message and why it gives you hope. Be prepared to discuss it in class.

The Church in the World

For many people, church documents about justice are difficult reading. The documents tend to be long, complicated, abstract, and full of fancy words.

But for those who manage to get beyond the difficult reading, those documents—together known as Catholic social teaching—can be a source of excitement and hope. From its humble beginnings, the *Catholic Worker* was soon read by more than one hundred thousand people who wanted to hear about the ideas of Catholic social teaching. Those ideas can change the world—so much so that in some countries, church people who voice them are at risk for their lives.

Even in our own society, Catholic social teaching has been called the church's best kept secret. Why? It calls for society to be transformed in ways that will make it easier for all people to experience the goodness God wants for them—but that transformation requires changes that make some people uncomfortable.

What kind of teaching is this, and where does it come from? That's the question we will explore in this chapter.

What Is Catholic Social Teaching?

At the most basic level, Catholic social teaching is the call of the popes and bishops for people to let the Reign of God's love shape their world. By calling the world to the Reign of God, the church continues the mission of Jesus. In *The Church in the Modern World (Gaudium et Spes),* an important document of the Second Vatican Council, the church describes that mission as one of compassion:

> The joys and the hopes, the griefs and the anxieties of the [people] of this age, especially those who are poor or in any way afflicted, these are the joys and hopes, the

Nobel Peace Prize Laureate Bishop Carlos Felipe Ximenes Belo (front, left) has lived Catholic social teaching by risking his life to take a stand for social justice in Indonesia.

griefs and anxieties of the followers of Christ. Indeed, nothing genuinely human fails to raise an echo in their hearts. (1)

It is this compassion that leads the church to consider seriously the social problems faced by the world's people, and to offer solutions to those problems based on the wisdom revealed by God through the Scriptures and church Tradition. That is why promoting social justice is an essential aspect of the church's mission, as the bishops of the world said in another document:

> Action on behalf of justice and participation in the transformation of the world fully appear to us as a [necessary part] . . . of the Church's mission for the redemption of the human race and its liberation from every oppressive situation. (*Justice in the World,* 6)

Some people might be wondering why the church needs special teaching to guide it in that mission; after all, it already has the Scriptures. Yet the specific social situations of the world today are much different from those of the Mediterranean world some two to three thousand years ago when the Scriptures were written. Catholic social teaching serves as a kind of bridge, applying the timeless truths of the Scriptures—as well as the accumulated wisdom of the church's sacred Tradition—to the new and complex social situations of the modern world.

Catholic social teaching, then, is the teaching of the church that examines human society in light of the Gospel and church Tradition for the purpose of guiding Christians as they carry on the mission of Jesus in the world. It is issued by popes and bishops in letters, statements, and official documents that are addressed to the whole church, and ultimately, the whole world. ℬ

"Signs of the Times"

Of course, it would be impossible for the church's social teaching to be a compassionate response to humankind's "joy and hope, grief and anguish" if it were not based on a deep understanding of the realities faced by people in the world. The church's response to the world flows out of its interpretation of those realities, which it calls the **signs of the times.** Those realities include the religious, political, cultural, and economic factors that shape the overall situation of society.

It was the signs of the times in nineteenth-century Europe, in fact, that first sparked the modern Catholic social teaching tradition. Although the church has always taught about justice in one form or another, the formal social teaching of the bishops and popes began in 1891, when Pope Leo XIII issued the encyclical *On the Condition of Labor.* The encyclical is more frequently called by its Latin title, *Rerum Novarum.* That first document was a response to the social situation brought about by various forces: the Enlightenment,

the Industrial Revolution, capitalism, and Marxism, to name a few.

Although the modern world is considerably different now, the forces that changed the face of nineteenth-century Europe are still major influences on the social situation of the world today. Likewise, the fundamental concerns of *Rerum Novarum*—the suffering of poor people, cooperation between groups, the dignity of work, the role of the state, and so on—have continued to be major themes of Catholic social teaching.

To better understand Catholic social teaching as a whole, it is worthwhile to examine the social context out of which its first modern document was developed.

The new "rulers": Reason, science, individual liberty

Europe in the eighteenth century was full of ferment. New philosophies and approaches to life were springing up that would eventually reshape all Western societies. The **Enlightenment,** the up-and-coming social,

The French Revolution was just one product of the Enlightenment, which said that science and reason—not religion—are the basis for knowing truth.

ℬ The term "Catholic social *teaching*" implies that the church attempts to be a teacher of society through its official documents. In your opinion, who are the most influential "teachers" of society in the world today, and what is their message?

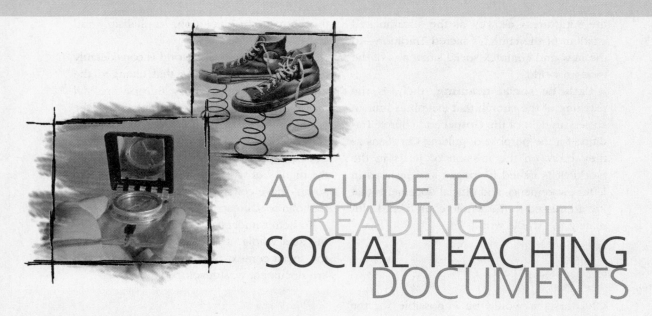

A GUIDE TO READING THE SOCIAL TEACHING DOCUMENTS

Why do many of the **church's documents** have two titles? Catholic church documents published by the Vatican generally have an official Latin title—the opening two or three words of the document—which is printed in Latin, the official language of the whole church. Then there is a title in a modern language, in our case, English. In this text, the English title will be given first, with the Latin title following in parentheses the first time the document is mentioned in a chapter. But *Rerum Novarum* is so well known by its Latin title that we will use that instead of the English title.

What do the numbers in parentheses mean? Church documents are usually numbered by paragraph. When a document is quoted, the quote is usually followed by the paragraph number in parentheses, making it easier to find the quote in the document.

What are *encyclicals, pastoral letters,* and *constitutions*? Church documents are divided into several types, according to author and audience. **Encyclicals** are letters from the pope to all the bishops of the world; sometimes they are also addressed to all Christians and to all people "of good will." **Pastoral letters,** such as the U.S. bishops' *Economic Justice for All,* are typically written by a bishop or group of bishops for all the Catholics in a specific location. And *The Church in the Modern World (Gaudium et Spes)* is a **constitution,** a text from a council of all the world's bishops, including the pope, written for all the world's Catholics and others. ☯

political, and philosophical movement, asserted that reason and science are the basis for knowing truth. The movement dismissed religious teachings, the Bible, and any claims of church or royalty to have authority in matters of truth or in directing human beings. The **liberalist** philosophy of individual rights and autonomy, together with limited government and the ownership of private property, was part of the "program" of the Enlightenment.

The Enlightenment's stance became the basis for at least two political revolutions. In North America, the British colonies revolted against the king of England (see the Declaration of Independence as a classic statement of Enlightenment thinking). And in France, the revolution against the monarchy and the church actually brought about a bloody "reign of terror" by the new rulers, who were hardly people of reason. So the push for individual rights and the rule of reason did not sit well with leaders in the church.

Economic upheaval

By the nineteenth century in Europe, the **Industrial Revolution**—the shift from a farming and craft trade economy to an economy based on factory production—was well under way. As machines in factories enabled goods to be produced faster and cheaper, those who owned the means of producing goods, which is called **capital,** became wealthier. People moved to cities to sell their labor to the factory owners for pitifully small wages, living and working in inhumane, filthy, and dangerous conditions.

Following the Industrial Revolution, the liberalist approach to capitalism resulted in inhumane working conditions for millions of people, including this young girl working in an American cotton mill around 1905.

This new economic system, in which a few owned the means of production for their own profit, and workers sold their labor to the owners for whatever wage they could get, came to be known as **capitalism.** Under the new philosophy of liberalism, capitalism was often left unfettered and unlimited by governments, producing much wealth for a few, but an intolerable life for the masses. The situation was crying out to be challenged. **D**

Marx's challenge

The greatest challenge to unregulated capitalism came through various socialist movements in Europe in the nineteenth century. **Socialism** advocated distributing wealth according to need, not ownership of capital and profits. The German philosopher **Karl Marx,**

C The Catholic church has argued that both faith and reason are necessary to know God and live according to God's wishes. Do you rely primarily on faith or reason in your life, or both? What are the strengths and weaknesses of each approach? Be prepared to discuss your answers in class.

D To demonstrate the impact of the Industrial Revolution, do a scavenger hunt for handmade items (items not made in a factory) in your home. Bring a list of as many items as you can find—or, if possible, the items themselves—to class. As you do this, consider these questions: What might have been some of the benefits and drawbacks of the preindustrial way of making things? What are some of the benefits and drawbacks of industrialization?

Karl Marx advocated revolution as a response to injustice—an approach the church rejects.

with his works *The Communist Manifesto* (1848) and *Capital* (1867), provided a bitter critique of capitalism. His theory of history predicted that the masses would rise up, overthrow the capitalist class, abolish private property, and create a form of socialist state. Eventually, he proposed, socialism would give way to **communism,** an ideal, equitable society in which government and laws would be unnecessary. Marx's atheistic theory, later called **Marxism,** was adopted as a model for social change by many workers' movements around the world, and for the formation of

modern-day socialist and communist states— none of which has been quite the ideal society Marx envisioned. *E*

The Church Responds

All these forces radically changed Western society, as well as the church's role in that society. For the most part, the church strongly resisted those changes, in part because it was losing its political power and authority.

But the church also resisted aspects of the new social, political, and economic systems because it saw these systems as unjust. It was especially concerned with the plight of the new working class. That concern led Pope Leo XIII to issue the encyclical *Rerum Novarum.*

Leo XIII was not the first Catholic to address the injustices faced by the working class. Beginning in the early nineteenth century, a number of bishops around the world were actively supporting the associations and unions that the workers were forming—even though labor unions were widely outlawed in the belief that they disrupted society.

Twenty-year-old Frédéric Ozanam and his friends responded to the social problems of nineteenth-century France by founding the Saint Vincent de Paul Society, which still serves poor people around the world. *Left:* A Marquette University student volunteers her time as a mentor at the Saint Vincent de Paul Family Resource Center in Milwaukee. *Right:* High school and college students distribute school supplies to those who cannot afford them.

Groups of Catholic thinkers and activists also worked on solutions to what was being called the social question. Twenty-year-old **Frédéric Ozanam,** for instance, started the Saint Vincent de Paul Society, a worldwide charitable organization for the poor. In the United States, by 1886 many working Catholics were organizing into a controversial organization known as the Knights of Labor, a union supported by some of the U.S. hierarchy, such as **Cardinal James Gibbons** of Baltimore.

Leo XIII was sympathetic to these early efforts; he himself had taken action by establishing a savings bank for the poor. The foundation was laid for *Rerum Novarum* to appear in 1891.

1. Define *Catholic social teaching.*
2. What are the signs of the times, and what role do they play in Catholic social teaching?
3. Define the following terms: *the Enlightenment, capitalism, socialism, communism.*

4. Choose one of these social influences—the Enlightenment, the Industrial Revolution, capitalism, socialism, Marxism—and in a paragraph or two, explain how it continues to influence society today.

Groups of Catholic thinkers and activists also worked on solutions to what was being called the social question.

E Marxism says that privately owned property is the primary source of conflict between groups of people. Considering the differences between the social groups in your school, do you think Marx was right? Explain why or why not.

The Development of Catholic Social Teaching

Rerum Novarum

Rerum Novarum was hotly debated when it was issued in 1891. Some praised it, and others scorned it—but it certainly was not ignored. Novelist Georges Bernanos would describe the impact of the encyclical in his fictional work *The Diary of a Country Priest* nearly forty years later:

> "When it was published, sonny, it was like an earthquake. The enthusiasm! . . . The simple notion that a man's work is not a commodity, subject to the law of supply and demand, that you have no right to speculate on wages, on the lives of men, as you do on grain, sugar or coffee—why it set people's consciences upside down!" (Page 57)

Pope Leo XIII responded to the plight of nineteenth-century workers by calling for workers' rights and for concern for society's poorest people in *Rerum Novarum,* the first of the modern Catholic social teaching documents.

Why did *Rerum Novarum* cause such a stir in its time, and why is it still so influential? The answers to both questions lie in the encyclical itself.

The themes of *Rerum Novarum*

Like socialism, *Rerum Novarum* criticized the abuses of liberal capitalism that left the majority of workers with lives "little better than slavery itself" (2). But it opposed the socialist solution to that situation, which was for the workers to take over and abolish the private ownership of property so that it would be owned in common by all people.

Rerum Novarum offered an alternative solution, one based on the Gospel and church Tradition. That Tradition includes the notion of **natural law**—the God-given need for creation, including human beings, to follow what God intended it to be. The following are some major elements of the solution offered by Pope Leo XIII:

- *Cooperation between classes.* The social system proposed by *Rerum Novarum* was based on cooperation, not inevitable class warfare, between workers and capitalists, with rights and duties for both.
- *The dignity of work.* Work's primary purpose is to provide a decent life for workers and their families. Workers are owed reasonable work hours, Sundays and religious holidays off, and safe working conditions, with strict limits on child labor.

"A man's work is **not a commodity.**"

- *The just wage and workers' associations.* Workers must receive a **just wage**—an amount sufficient to provide a decent life for a worker's whole family—and must be free to organize associations, now known as **unions,** to negotiate working conditions. These proposals were well ahead of their time.
- *The role of the state.* A balance between the liberalist and socialist philosophies of government is needed. Government should avoid interfering in private matters, but in some situations government has to take action through laws for the good of society.
- *Private ownership of property.* All people have a right to own property, but private property must be fairly distributed and used responsibly for the good of all.
- *Defense of the poor.* Christians and governments should make the protection of the poor a priority.

Like all social teaching documents, *Rerum Novarum* provides general guidance for how society can become more like the Kingdom of God. Although that guidance has changed as the many challenges that face society have changed, Catholic social teaching since then has continued to echo the major themes of its first document. ⫘

Did it work?

In the end, the church's social teaching is only effective to the extent that people actually act on it. In the case of *Rerum Novarum,* the short-term reaction was mixed.

Many Catholics ignored or misunderstood the teaching, but many others took it to heart. Catholic labor unions, mutual-aid societies, cooperatives, and other organizations flourished as a result of the encyclical. It also enabled various Catholic political leaders to more boldly suggest and support legislation to improve the lives of the common people.

Over time, *Rerum Novarum,* along with the influence of socialism, indirectly led to the development of government policies such as minimum-wage laws and the right to strike. As Pope Pius XI would say forty years later, "Great credit must be given [to *Rerum Novarum*] for whatever improvement has been achieved in the workers' condition" (*The Reconstruction of the Social Order [Quadragesimo Anno],* 28).

But perhaps most important, *Rerum Novarum* established a precedent for the church to speak out on social matters. It observed that individual moral choices affect society, and society affects individual morality; the two cannot be separated. Therefore, the church has to be concerned with moral issues not only on the individual level but on the social level as well. ⫸

By making that claim, *Rerum Novarum* helped the church shift its approach to helping poor and vulnerable people. The church had always called for Christians to ease poverty through charitable giving. But now it was also asking Christians to look for the social causes of such problems as poverty, and to change the way society was set up so that the root causes of those problems would be eliminated as much as possible.

In doing that, *Rerum Novarum* opened the doors to more than one hundred years of social teaching and action in the church.

⫘ Consider your own work experience, and talk to your parents and friends about theirs. Based on these experiences, write down some ways that *Rerum Novarum* could be updated for modern workers.

⫸ "Individual moral choices affect society, and society affects individual morality." In several paragraphs, describe some ways your individual moral choices affect society, and then describe several ways society affects your own moral decision making.

MAJOR DOCUMENTS OF CATHOLIC SOCIAL TEACHING

The following list of major documents of Catholic social teaching is provided as a brief introduction to the names and the general themes of the documents. H

Rerum Novarum
(On the Condition of Labor)
Pope Leo XIII, 1891

Prompted by social changes brought about by the Industrial Revolution and the Enlightenment. Addresses the church's right to speak on social issues and the rights and duties of workers and employers. Supports unions and the just wage.

The Reconstruction of the Social Order
(Quadragesimo Anno)
Pope Pius XI, 1931

Written for the fortieth anniversary of *Rerum Novarum,* in the context of the Great Depression and the rise of fascism and dictators in Europe. Reexamines the themes of *Rerum Novarum.* Critical of capitalism and communism. Advocates a just distribution of wealth. Introduces the concept of subsidiarity (see page 61).

Christianity and Social Progress
(Mater et Magistra)
Pope John XXIII, 1961

Says modern society is becoming more complex and interdependent. The gap between rich and poor nations threatens society, as does military spending on nuclear weapons. Although governments should respect individual freedom, when necessary they must act on these problems to protect the common good.

Peace on Earth
(Pacem in Terris)
Pope John XXIII, 1963

Written amid worldwide concern about nuclear war. Says peace can be achieved by respecting rights and duties, and describes these in detail. Says the race among nations for more weapons "must cease." Calls for the strengthening of the United Nations and an end to racism.

The Church in the Modern World
(Gaudium et Spes)
Vatican Council II, 1965

Has the most authority of the social teaching documents because it was written during an ecumenical council of the church. Says the church can and must serve the world, and that it can learn from other cultures in the world. States human beings are the "source, the centre, and the purpose of all economic and social life" (63). Condemns the use of weapons of mass destruction. Maintains peace is not just the absence of war but justice throughout society. Covers many other topics as well.

The Development of Peoples
(Populorum Progressio)
Pope Paul VI, 1967

About human development—in other words, progress toward the economic, social, cultural, and spiritual fulfillment of human potential. Says the gap between rich and poor nations blocks human development. Criticizes capitalism for focusing on profit, competition, and private ownership of property while ignoring social duties. Rich nations must help poor nations. *Peace* means full human development.

A Call to Action
(Octagesima Adveniens)
Pope Paul VI, 1971

An apostolic letter calling individual Christians and parishes to take personal responsibility for promoting justice not only through charity but also through political efforts to change the structures of injustice. Calls for all people to be cared for and allowed to participate in society, regardless of race, age, or gender. Calls for care of the environment.

Justice in the World
World Synod of Bishops, 1971

Written by a gathering of bishops from around the world, many from poor, undeveloped countries. Influenced by liberation theology. Says justice is a necessary and central part of the church's mission. "Christian love of neighbour and justice cannot be separated" (34). Discusses global justice and liberation of the poor and oppressed. Calls for more countries to share power, and for rich nations to consume less.

Evangelization in the Modern World
(Evangelii Nuntiandi)
Pope Paul VI, 1975

Church's central mission is to preach the Gospel to the world. Justice is an essential part of that evangelization. The ways society is organized—its structures—are an obstacle to justice when they are sinful. Christians must liberate people from injustice by transforming the social structures of sin. True liberation is not only political or economic but spiritual as well.

H As you read the summary of the Catholic social teaching documents, consider the following questions: Does any aspect of the church's social teaching surprise you? Do you disagree with aspects of the teaching, and why? In what areas do you think the world best reflects the values of Catholic social teaching? What areas seem to need the most work? Be prepared to discuss your answers in class.

On Human Work
(Laborem Exercens)
Pope John Paul II, 1981

Written for the ninetieth anniversary of *Rerum Novarum,* this encyclical says work is at the center of social issues. The purpose of work is to develop creation and to support family life. All who are able have the right and duty to work, regardless of race, gender, or disability; those who cannot work must be supported by society. Discusses rights of workers. Says people are more important than profits or the things they make.

The Challenge of Peace
U.S. Catholic Bishops, 1983

Written as the United States and the Soviet Union were at the height of the nuclear arms race. Calls the arms race "an act of aggression against the poor" (128) because money that should help the poor is used to build weapons. Calls for an end to the arms race, reduced numbers of weapons, and a ban on nuclear weapons testing. Supports active nonviolence and conscientious objection.

Economic Justice for All
U.S. Catholic Bishops, 1986

Examines economic justice in the United States. Finds both good and bad aspects of the U.S. economic system. Echoes other themes of Catholic social teaching, especially the option for the poor and vulnerable. Says the morality of all economic decisions, policies, and institutions is determined by whether they serve "all people, especially the poor" (24).

On Social Concern
(Sollicitudo Rei Socialis)
Pope John Paul II, 1987

Written for the twentieth anniversary of *Populorum Progressio,* the encyclical addresses the increasing gap between rich and poor countries. Says while poor countries experience underdevelopment, many rich countries experience "superdevelopment"—an overabundance of material goods that leads to consumerism and waste. Calls for rich nations to show solidarity with poor nations through cooperation and sharing.

The Hundredth Year
(Centesimus Annus)
Pope John Paul II, 1991

Written for the centennial of *Rerum Novarum.* Notes that the collapse of communism in Eastern Europe in 1989 came about through nonviolent action, not war; the church played an important role. Says socialism collapsed because it treated people as objects, not spiritual beings. Says capitalism is efficient but flawed when it does not respect human dignity. Calls for a business economy that serves and protects human beings.

The Gospel of Life
(Evangelium Vitae)
Pope John Paul II, 1995

Warns that society is increasingly influenced by a "culture of death," in which people ignore the spiritual side of being human, treating one another as objects and focusing only on their own wants and needs. Abortion, infanticide, capital punishment, and euthanasia are symptoms of the culture of death. Proposes a "culture of life," in which Christian love leads people to actively protect and care for one another. ●

A Dynamic Tradition

The major Catholic social teaching documents that followed *Rerum Novarum* continued to build on it—in fact, four documents have been issued to commemorate its anniversary. The core themes of modern Catholic social teaching have not changed much since its first document was issued.

At the same time, society has undergone considerable change since *Rerum Novarum,* and Catholic social teaching has developed to respond to those changes, as the summary of its major documents on pages 52–54 shows.

For instance, beginning in the 1960s, the documents became more concerned with global issues, rather than just focusing on Western society, because more of the church's bishops were from poor, undeveloped countries. This new global concern allowed the Latin American bishops to call the whole church to a "preferential option for the poor," a theme that has been especially prominent in the church's social teaching since then.

Another example is Catholic social teaching's special attention to international peace and the morality of nuclear weapons during the **cold war.** This was the period between about 1945 and 1990, when the United States and the Soviet Union competed to dominate the world through military might.

Likewise, the church has shifted its attitude toward private property. Leo XIII felt it was important to emphasize the right to own private property because socialism was challenging that right. Since then, however, the church has seen that the Western world, despite its wealth, largely ignores the majority of the world's population that suffers in poverty. So while the church does not dispute the right to private property, it has put more emphasis on the responsibility to use the goods of the earth for the benefit of all.

Despite some changes, however, the social teaching documents have more in common than not. An exploration of their common themes can provide a good overview of what Catholic social teaching is all about.

Beginning in the 1960s, the documents became more concerned with global issues.

The Cuban missile crisis, which brought the world to the brink of nuclear war, prompted Pope John XXIII to issue *Peace on Earth*.

Now that you have been introduced to the Catholic social teaching documents, write your own social teaching document together with some of your classmates. Begin by discussing the various social situations that concern you most, then choose a specific situation to address. Write a letter that expresses your vision for making the situation better. Base your letter on values expressed by the Scriptures and church Tradition.

For Review

5. What are six themes of *Rerum Novarum?*
6. What has been one of the most important results of *Rerum Novarum* for the church?
7. In a short paragraph, describe one way Catholic social teaching has developed to respond to social changes.

8. Review the summary of Catholic social teaching on pages 52–54 and identify what you think might be some of its major themes (for example, human dignity, the gap between rich and poor people). For each theme, describe in a short paragraph how it reflects an aspect of the teaching or mission of Jesus.

Themes of Catholic Social Teaching, 1–3

Although some scholars have listed ten, fourteen, or even twenty basic themes of Catholic social teaching, the U.S. Catholic bishops have limited their list to seven. The following themes are taken from two of their documents, *A Century of Social Teaching* (1991) and *Sharing Catholic Social*

THE SEVEN THEMES OF CATHOLIC SOCIAL TEACHING

As you read through the rest of this book, watch for these icons—they're signals to help you notice the themes of Catholic social teaching in the text.

 1. THE LIFE AND DIGNITY OF THE HUMAN PERSON

 2. PARTICIPATION: THE CALL TO FAMILY AND COMMUNITY

 3. RIGHTS AND RESPONSIBILITIES

 4. THE OPTION FOR THE POOR AND VULNERABLE

 5. THE DIGNITY OF WORK AND THE RIGHTS OF WORKERS

 6. SOLIDARITY

 7. CARE FOR GOD'S CREATION

Teaching (1998). As you learn about the themes of Catholic social teaching, keep in mind that the themes do not stand alone; they cannot be separated from one another. Instead, they are interdependent, woven together to support and complement one another.

The Life and Dignity of the Human Person

Yevgeny Yevtushenko was only a child when he and his mother witnessed twenty thousand German prisoners of war being marched down the streets of Moscow in 1944. Crowds of women lined the streets to show their contempt for the defeated enemy—the enemy who had taken the lives of their brothers, sons, and husbands, and who had caused them to suffer a long winter of near starvation. At first the soldiers and police had to restrain them, so great was their anger. But as the enemy paraded by, the women encountered only bloody, exhausted men and boys who passed with their heads hung low:

> The street became dead silent—the only sound was the shuffling of boots and the thumping of crutches.
>
> Then I saw an elderly woman in broken-down boots push herself forward and touch a policeman's shoulder, saying: "Let me through." . . .
>
> She went up to the column, [and] took from inside her coat . . . a crust of black bread. She pushed it awkwardly into the pocket of a soldier, so exhausted that he was tottering on his feet. And now suddenly from every side women were running towards the soldiers, pushing into their hands bread, cigarettes, whatever they had.
>
> The soldiers were no longer enemies.

German prisoners of war during World War II. Catholic social teaching says that all people, without exception, are given dignity by God.

> They were people. (Yevtushenko, *A Precocious Autobiography,* pages 24–25)

Those Russian women experienced a transformation on that cold day in 1944. The goodness within them overcame their deep pain and anger, allowing them to see their enemies not as monsters but as fellow human beings that suffered just as they did. And by caring for the men as God cared for them, the women became more truly people who reflected the image of God.

All are loved by God

In their compassionate response, the Russian women recognized and acted on the most basic principle of Catholic social teaching: All human beings have dignity because they are loved by God and made in God's image. People, motivated by selfishness, fear, or hate, have always found reasons not to respect the dignity of others: race, gender, nationality, disability, age, and history, just for starters. But Catholic social teaching insists that nothing can take away the fundamental dignity of any person, not even his or her own destructive actions.

The insight that *all* people have equal dignity because they are loved by God has some major implications for Christians. If God loves and wants goodness for every person, and if Christians seek to serve God, then how can Christians do anything less than to love and seek goodness for all people?

For human life

In other words, Christians are called to be for human life. At the most basic level, this means allowing people to live. Respect for human life is the basis for the Catholic church's opposition to abortion, the death penalty, euthanasia, and other forms of violence, including most wars.

But being for human life means a lot more than simply allowing others to live—it also means helping others live to the fullest, experiencing all the goodness that God intended for them in the physical, social, mental, and spiritual aspects of their lives.

Specific examples of the principle of respecting human life and dignity might include the following:

- not using genetic engineering to manipulate human life for the creation of products
- giving poor, rural communities in underdeveloped countries access to clean water and the means to produce their own food
- placing human needs before profits when making business decisions

Promoting the life and dignity of human beings is the most fundamental of the Catholic social teaching principles. It is the one by which Catholicism judges the morality of social institutions and policy decisions, and it is the one on which all the other principles are based. ◡

Nothing can take away the fundamental dignity of any person.

✳ *Student art:* Linocut; Alida Novarese, Saint Agnes Academy, Memphis, Tennessee

◡ Choose one of your favorite songs and write down the lyrics. Then, in a few paragraphs, explain how the lyrics support or oppose human dignity and life.

Participation: The Call to Family and Community

When we arrived at the school, the driver urged me to get out quickly. The white hand of a uniformed officer opened the door and pulled me toward him as his urgent voice ordered me to hurry. The roar from the front of the building made me glance to the right. Only a half-block away, I saw hundreds of white people, their bodies in motion and their mouths wide open as they shouted their anger. "The niggers! Keep the niggers out!" The roar swelled, as if their frenzy had been fired up by something. It took me a moment to digest the fact that it was the sight of us that had upset them.

As I entered a classroom, a hush fell over the students. The guide pointed me to an empty seat, and I walked toward it. Students sitting nearby quickly moved away. I sat down surrounded by empty seats, feeling unbearably self-conscious. One of the boys kept shouting ugly words at me throughout the class. I waited for the teacher to speak up, but she said nothing. My heart was weeping, but I squeezed back the tears. I squared my shoulders and tried to remember what Grandma had said: "God loves you, child. No matter what, He sees you as His precious idea." (Adapted from Beals, in *Stone Soup for the World,* pages 65–70)

During the rest of that first day at the all-white public school in Little Rock, Arkansas, Melba Pattillo Beals was spat upon, hit, and nearly attacked by a mob of angry mothers during gym class. That night, she wrote in her diary: "There seems to be no space for me at Central High. . . . Please, God, make space for me." The next day, President Eisenhower sent in troops to protect Melba and eight other students who were attempting to integrate the school. But the battle over school integration lasted for years after that day in 1954.

In the long run, Melba and other African American students won the right to participate in the mainstream of society. Her experience and the example of those who supported her during those years inspired her to work to make sure *all* people have a "space" in society. She later wrote, "As an NBC television reporter, I would take special care to look into those unexposed corners where otherwise invisible people are forced to hide as their truth is ignored."

Although Melba Beals and eight other students helped to desegregate Little Rock Central High School, barriers such as poverty and discrimination continue to prevent many people from fully participating in the life of society.

Most of the time, the exclusion of people from the mainstream of society is not as obvious as it was in Melba's case. Do you see examples of people being marginalized, perhaps in more subtle ways, in your own school? In your opinion, what are some of the reasons that people are excluded?

Melba's struggle to be fully a part of society reflects the Catholic social teaching theme of **participation**—the right and responsibility of all people to participate in all aspects of human society—educational, political, cultural, religious, economic, and so on. Those who are not able to fully participate in society are often said to be **marginalized**, or forced outside the main group.

In chapter 1, we noted that relationships are an important part of being human. In fact, the human desire to be in relationship is a basic part of what it means to be made in the image of God, who is the relationship of three persons united in one by love. That is why the popes and bishops say human beings "realize," or fulfill, their dignity in relationship with others and in community.

To understand what the popes and bishops mean, just think about all the ways the person you are today has been shaped, in good and bad ways, by the people in your life (not to mention by God and the natural environment around you). The experience of loneliness is a powerful reminder of how much we need to share ourselves with others.

The Christian tradition places special importance on participation in the family. The family is society's most basic building block; it is the place where people are meant to care for and love one another most intimately, and ideally, it is the place where people are able to realize all that God calls them to be. Catholic social teaching emphasizes the need for society to support families so that all people have an opportunity to participate in a family.

At the other end of the spectrum, participation at the international level means that all nations—whether they are rich or poor, weak or powerful—are able to share in making decisions for the global community.

Two aspects of participation—the common good and subsidiarity—are often listed as separate themes of Catholic social teaching. They are important enough to be mentioned briefly here.

. . . Please, God, make space for me.

✳ *Student art:* "Double Space." Pencil and tempera; Dani Maniscalco, Sacred Heart High School, Kingston, Massachusetts

The common good

It is possible, of course, to participate in society in a negative way. But according to Catholic social teaching, people are called to participate in society positively, in ways that will contribute to the common good. The **common good** is the social condition that allows *all* the people in a community to reach their full human potential and fulfill their human dignity. The common good is *not* "the most good for the most people," which would suggest that some people might be left out or might have to live under unjust conditions for the good of the majority. Working for the common good implies paying special attention to groups and individuals that are excluded from the benefits experienced by the rest of society. L

The common good is met only when all people have a place at society's table.

Subsidiarity

The way society is organized affects how well people are able to participate in it. Catholic social teaching says that large organizations or governments should not take over social responsibilities and decisions that can be carried out by individuals and small local organizations. But larger organizations or governments have a responsibility to coordinate and regulate society when individuals and smaller organizations do not or cannot carry out responsibilities necessary for the common good. This concept, known as **subsidiarity,** could also be explained by saying that governments and large organizations exist only to serve the good of human beings, families, and communities, which are the center and purpose of social life.

For example, the concept of subsidiarity would say that it is wrong for the government to take over the responsibilities a family has for its children. But if the family neglects or abuses its children, then the government has a responsibility to intervene for the good of the children. On a larger scale, subsidiarity would suggest that the United Nations should not take over the responsibilities that national governments have for their people. On the other hand, the United Nations has a responsibility to coordinate efforts for global peace and human development that no single nation could accomplish alone.

Rights and Responsibilities

I started living on the streets of Bogotá, Colombia, when I was only seven years old. I left home to live in the gutters because my family couldn't afford to feed me. Over three years, I learned all about poverty and I saw firsthand the cruelty of Bogotá society.

People hated us. At night, a drunk taxi driver would get angry and shoot at us. If a gang didn't like you, they would kill you. The police used to beat me and my friends

L In your local newspaper, find an article about a government, business, or organization doing something that affects society. Write a paragraph or two about whether or not it is promoting the common good, and why. Be prepared to discuss your example in class.

Human dignity is truly respected only when basic human rights—such as the right to safety, food, and shelter—are fulfilled. But even the basic rights of millions of children around the world are often violated.

frequently, just because we were living on the streets and begging for money. . . .

I was ten years old when the Fundación Niños de los Andes took me off the streets and gave me the chance to study and a place to sleep. Now it [has been] six years. I want to finish my studies, go to the university, and get money to help my family. I have three small brothers, and I don't want them ever to live on the streets. Now that I have a future, I want to work with street children who don't yet know they have a future. (*Stand Up for Your Rights,* page 63)

Tens of thousands of street children around the world live as seventeen-year-old Alberto Granada once did: denied basic human rights such as the right to live in safety, the right to adequate food and shelter, the right to education, and the right to equal protection under the law. **Rights** are those conditions or things that any person needs in order to be fully what God created him or her to be.

Survival and thrival

As we discussed earlier, the most basic right is the right to life, because it is impossible to have other rights without it. The rights that are necessary for people to be able to live are known as **survival rights;** these include the right to food, shelter, and basic health care.

But as we saw in the Book of Genesis, God does not want creation to merely survive, but to thrive and flourish, fully realizing the goodness God intended for it. So beyond

survival rights, Catholic social teaching insists that all human beings also have a right to those things necessary for them to become everything God intended them to be. These **thrival rights** include such things as education, employment, a safe environment, and enough material goods to support a family. They also include the right to live by one's conscience and religion, to immigrate, and to live without discrimination.

Human rights that are officially recognized (if not always respected) by most nations in the world are listed in a 1948 United Nations document that the Catholic church has strongly supported as a tool for promoting justice, the **Universal Declaration of Human Rights.**

Responsibilities: Limits on rights

While Catholic social teaching affirms the importance of rights, it also says that rights are not unlimited. An individual's rights are limited by his or her **responsibilities** for the good of others, as well as for the common good of the whole society. It is out of

Rights are balanced by responsibilities, such as the responsibility to care for God's creation.

responsibility for the common good that governments must regulate rights in particular instances.

For example, all people have the right to own property (land, cars, money, clothes, and so on). But Catholic social teaching says that everything in the world is a gift given by God for the good of *all* people, both now and in the future. So people have a responsibility to care for their property, and to use it to promote their own human dignity as well as the dignity of their families and all members of society. When some people have more property than they really need, while others do not have enough to maintain a dignified life, then those with more have a responsibility to fulfill their neighbors' right to the necessities of a good life. **M**

9. Define the following terms: *human dignity, common good, subsidiarity.*
10. Define *participation.* What does participation mean for families and nations?
11. Define *rights.* What general responsibility do people have that limits their rights?

---

12. For each of the following themes, provide your own example (either real or made up) showing the theme or its absence: *life and dignity of the human person, participation, rights and responsibilities.* For example: "A family that decides to serve as a foster family for babies with AIDS is promoting the babies' lives and dignity."

Everything in the world is a gift given by God
for the good of *all* people, both now and in the future.

M Make a list of the rights that you think belong to all people. After each right, list the responsibilities that limit it.

The Option for the Poor and Vulnerable

The number 10 bus lurched to a stop at the County Institutions grounds. The driver yelled at some noisy boys in the back to settle down—other students who, like fourteen-year-old Frank Daily, were coming home from a Catholic high school in Milwaukee.

A very pregnant woman hung onto the handrail and slowly pulled herself onto the bus.

"Where are your shoes, lady?" the bus driver asked her, seeing that she only had stockings on her feet. "It ain't more than 10 degrees out there."

"I can't afford shoes," the woman replied, pulling her frayed coat collar around her neck. "I got eight kids. They all got shoes.

There's not enough left for me. But it's okay, the Lord will take care of me. I got on the bus just to get my feet warm."

Frank looked down at his new Nike basketball shoes, then looked back at the woman with her ripped socks and worn-out clothing. Up until now, Frank had been pondering the fact that he hadn't made the basketball team. Making the team would have been a good way for him as a freshman to fit into his new school. Not being chosen for the team made him feel left out, as if he had become invisible.

But here was another "invisible" person. An invisible person—forgotten by society, but for a different reason, he thought. He would probably always be able to afford shoes. She probably never would. Under the seat, he quietly slipped off one shoe, then the other.

When the bus stopped, Frank waited until his friends had gotten off. Then he picked up his basketball shoes and walked down the aisle.

"Here, lady, you need these more than I do," he said, handing them to the woman. Then he hurried off the bus—managing to step right into an ice-cold puddle.

"Where are your shoes?" one of his friends asked him suddenly. Just then he heard the bus driver calling after him. He turned and saw the woman too.

"Well, Frank, I've never seen anything like that in the twenty years I've been driving this bus."

High school freshman Frank Daily chose the option for the poor and vulnerable on an individual level when he gave his own shoes to someone who needed them more.

"What's your name, kid?" the driver asked. Frank told him. "Well, Frank, I've never seen anything like that in the twenty years I've been driving this bus."

The woman was crying. "They fit me just perfect—thank you," she said. She turned to the driver. "See, I told you the Lord would take care of me." (Adapted from Lewis, *Kids with Courage,* pages 81–85) **N**

Faced with a choice, Frank chose the radical option: he chose the woman's long-term comfort over his own temporary discomfort.

Whose needs go first?

The choice Frank made in this true story is the choice the church advocates when it talks about the option for the poor and vulnerable (also called the *preferential option for the poor*). The **option for the poor and vulnerable** is the choice to put the needs of society's most poor and vulnerable members first among all social concerns. The term *poor and vulnerable* refers not only to those without money but also to those who are deprived of their basic rights or of equal participation in society.

The idea of the option for the poor and vulnerable was developed as part of Latin American liberation theology (see pages 66–67), and has its roots in the Jewish and Christian Scriptures, where God repeatedly expresses special concern for the poor and vulnerable.

Why does God call humanity to place the needs of the poor and vulnerable first? Simply put, their need is greater. Choosing to defend poor and vulnerable people does not imply that they are necessarily better or more valuable than others. Nor does God call people to class warfare; God's love does not exclude anyone. Society is called to place the needs of the poor and vulnerable first in the same way that parents pay special attention to a sick child. The parents do not necessarily love the sick child more than the other children, but they make the sick child their top priority because of that child's greater need.

A call to whole societies

Although the option for the poor and vulnerable can be made by individuals (as in Frank's case), more often it refers to the choice of an organization, a community, or a society. In their historic 1968 conference in Medellín, Colombia, the Latin American bishops described the option for the poor and vulnerable in this way:

> We ought to sharpen the awareness of our duty of solidarity with the poor, to which charity leads us. This solidarity means that we make ours their problems and their struggles, that we know how to speak with them. This has to be concretized in criticism of injustice and oppression, in the struggle against the intolerable situation that the poor person often has to tolerate, in the willingness to dialogue with the groups responsible for that situation in order to make them understand their obligations. (*Document on the Poverty of the Church,* 10)

From the bishops' words, we can see that the option for the poor and vulnerable has two parts. First, it involves freely choosing to become friends or partners with the poor, and taking on their problems as our problems. This is the choice to think of the poor as part of "us"—part of our community of

---

N In your opinion, what are the limits (if any) to helping poor and vulnerable people? For example, if the woman in this story needed a coat, should Frank have given his to her? Should he have given his money to her? If she and her children had been homeless, should he have invited them to his house? Be prepared to discuss your answers in class.

LIBERATION THEOLOGY

During the past few decades, Catholic social teaching has been significantly influenced by what is known as liberation theology. For instance, the social teaching theme of the option for the poor and vulnerable comes from liberation theology.

Liberation theologies began to emerge in the 1960s when poor and oppressed people around the world began questioning their situation in light of their faith. How, they asked, could a just and loving God allow them to suffer?

The answer that came from the faith of the people of Latin America was that it is not God's intention for them to suffer. Rather, they realized, God wants them to experience abundant life—certainly after death, but also now, during their life on Earth. Just as God liberated, or freed, the Israelites from their slavery in Egypt, so too God desired to liberate them from their suffering. As we discussed in chapter 1, God liberates people from suffering by liberating them from sin—including the sin that causes injustice.

Liberation theology calls people to work in solidarity with one another so that all might share in God's goodness.

Liberation theology is a way of talking about God amid the reality of the suffering of innocent people. The term was coined by Peruvian theologian Gustavo Gutiérrez, who wrote the influential book *A Theology of Liberation* in 1971. Ideas from liberation theology worked their way into the documents of the conference of Latin American bishops held in Medellín, Colombia, in 1968, and were later fleshed out by the bishops' conference at Puebla, Mexico, in 1979. The statements issued at those conferences had a significant impact on the Latin American church, as well as the church around the world.

In addition to the option for the poor and vulnerable, liberation theology's main contribution has been to emphasize that *acting* on faith—that is, living it in everyday life in the world—is more important than *talking* about faith. Talking about faith, as we are doing in this textbook, is an important step to living according to faith, but it is not the last step, according to liberation theology.

Liberation theology led many of the poor and oppressed people of Latin America and elsewhere to demand political and economic justice for themselves. It has led to a greater sense of community among people too. Many have been led to form **Christian base communities,** small groups of ten to twenty people who gather to reflect on the meaning of the Gospel for their lives and to support one another. In fact, the realizations brought about by liberation theology have prompted many Catholics, including Archbishop Oscar Romero of El Salvador, to risk their lives and even to die for the sake of justice. ☙

The answer that came from the faith of the people of Latin America was that it is not God's intention for them to suffer.

concern—rather than as "those people." For those who are themselves poor or vulnerable, this choice means standing by other people in the same situation rather than trying to take advantage of them to get ahead. This is what the bishops described as *solidarity,* which will be discussed later in this chapter.

Second, the option involves a commitment to take action to transform the injustice that prevents poor and vulnerable people from becoming everything God wants them to become. In the next chapter, we will discuss how those who seek Christian justice do this.

The Dignity of Work and the Rights of Workers

I was sixteen when I came from my home in central Mexico to Matamoros, on the border. My dream was to get a good job, save money, and return to my hometown to set up a small business.

Instead I worked in a *maquiladora* (a foreign-owned assembly plant) for eighteen years. Every day I rose at 4:30 a.m. and was at my work station by 6:45, where I spent the entire day. I couldn't go to the bathroom without getting permission.

My job was to assemble electronic capacitors with epoxy. Many coworkers developed health problems because of the epoxy. . . .

I was paid $27 for a forty-eight-hour week. [Nearly $6] of that went for transportation. I worked three-and-a-half hours to buy a gallon of milk. . . . Meat, vegetables, and fruit were unaffordable luxuries.

I lived in one room with an outdoor toilet. . . .

I began organizing to improve working conditions in the *maquiladoras* nearly fifteen years ago. As I saw the conditions in which we were forced to work, I got very angry. I said to my coworker, "How is it possible that we continue to put up with this? We have to do something!"

A couple of days later, she told me someone was teaching workers in one of the neighborhoods about the rights of the people.

Fifteen of us went, out of curiosity. We were shocked to realize we *had* any rights. . . . It was tremendous—like someone opening a curtain! We organized within the factory. Slowly, things were added to protect us—like adequate ventilation, air-conditioning, gloves.

It changed my life. I left the *maquiladora* several years ago to work as a full-time organizer with the Border Committee of Working Women. . . . This work fills our spirits. Our spirits are fed because we are doing something for justice. We are doing work that God calls us to do.

As for the companies that come here—I am grateful that there is work. Times are difficult. But tell them that when they come they should bring justice with them. They should bring protection and concern for our health.

We are human beings, not machines. We are persons who feel and cry. We need the work, yes. But let it be a just and good work. Let it be a work that brings us life not death. (Maria Guadalupe Torres, "We Are Not Machines," in *The Other Side*)

 Think about the jobs or work you have had. Have they promoted your human dignity, and how? How do they serve the dignity of others? If they do neither, what would have to happen to change that?

Work is for the benefit of people

When we think about the value of work, we might think immediately of the amount of money paid for it, or the product that is the result of work—a new car, for example. Business executives might think of the value of work in terms of profit.

Catholic social teaching, however, says that, "The basis for determining the value of human work is . . . the fact that the one who is doing it is a person" (*On Human Work [Laborem Exercens]*, 6). Work, and the economy in general, exists for the sake of people, not the other way around. Maria expressed this reality when she said, "We are human beings, not machines." In the context of justice, then, the value of work is measured by whether it promotes the human dignity of the worker.

The dignity of work

Work promotes human dignity by providing families with the things they need to live and flourish. Besides enabling people to live, good work also promotes human dignity simply because it is a reflection of the work God did to bring creation into being.

In the Book of Genesis, God gave humans the privilege of sharing in the work of creation, calling on them to "cultivate and care for" the earth (2:15, NAB). As images of God, humans are made to be creative, to bring order and goodness to the world. When work is done well, whether it is cleaning a floor or creating a database, it contributes to the common good and, ultimately, to the Kingdom of God.

The **dignity of work** is the value that work has because it supports human life and contributes to human dignity. Through good work, as Maria said, "our spirits are fed."

Workers' rights

When Maria Guadalupe Torres realized that the work at the *maquiladoras* did not promote the dignity of the workers, she and others organized to get the minimum necessary for dignified work.

The things that are necessary for dignified work are known as the **rights of workers.** Those rights include the right to employment, to decent and fair pay, to a safe workplace, and to anything else that is necessary for the basic life and health of workers. Workers also have the right to organize and join unions for the purpose of ensuring these basic rights.

Because the dignity of work is about more than just ensuring basic necessities, Catholic social teaching also calls for workers to be given the freedom and responsibility to use their God-given creativity in their work.

Solidarity

In the 1980s, the people of Lebanon divided into factions of Christian, Muslim, and Druse militias, who fought a long, bitter civil war. Although the war turned neighbor against neighbor, the Gospel inspired at least one young Christian soldier to restore a spirit of friendship with his enemy. He tells of how that happened after he was captured by a Druse soldier:

> He led me up the hill towards his camp. But as I was better-trained than he, I was able to set myself free and take his gun, thus reversing the situation.
>
> As I was walking with my prisoner, ready to kill him if he should try to escape, I suddenly saw inside myself the image of Christ on the cross. The passage from the Gospel "Love your enemies and pray for those who persecute you" resounded powerfully in my mind. It was with great urgency that I felt I had to follow the example of Jesus, and I decided to act. I threw down the gun and walked away, ready to be killed by my enemy who could pick it up and shoot at me. And as I walked I heard steps behind me. I did not turn around. Suddenly I felt the arm of the young Druse around my neck and with deep emotion heard him say to me: "You have spared my life. I also shall not kill you. We are brothers!"
>
> We separated, each one walking back to his camp. Later on I found out that he had been executed for not obeying the orders he had received. I left the militia and I refuse ever to return to it. (Goss-Mayr, "Enemies No More," in *Fellowship*)

True friendship is a good thing, bringing out the best in people and making each individual more than what she or he would be

alone. Friends stand by one another in times of trouble, not only sympathizing but also doing what they can to ease the other's suffering. And friends help one another grow and flourish in life by offering mutual support. In other words, friendship helps people become more fully who God intended them to be.

A spirit of friendship with all

Catholic social teaching says that a spirit of friendship—between individuals, groups, and nations—is the basis for a just world. The church calls this **solidarity:** a constant commitment to the common good, based on the belief that "we are all really responsible for all" (*On Social Concern, [Sollicitudo Rei Socialis]*, 38).

Solidarity is based on the understanding that all people are part of the same human family, whatever their national, racial, ethnic, economic, or ideological differences may be. Because we are all children of God, we have the same responsibilities toward one another that any family members have. We are called to work for the good of our brothers and sisters in a spirit of friendship, whether or not they are part of our own social group.

The idea of solidarity may not seem remarkable—after all, we are taught the importance of friendship and cooperation from childhood. But to a great extent, modern societies are still based on the values of competition and conflict, not solidarity. Catholic social teaching rejects the idea of a winners-and-losers society in which people only focus on the good of their nation or group, and proposes solidarity as an alternative. The Christian vision is one of a world in which all people cooperate to bring about goodness for everyone.

Care for God's Creation

Their class hike through the woods started out normally enough for ten students from the Minnesota New Country School. But then they came across frogs hopping around the road, and they started catching them for fun. That's when things started getting very weird.

Catholic Relief Services is an organization whose work promotes solidarity around the world. *Left to right:* Children carry relief supplies to their tents at a refugee camp in Macedonia; an Ethiopian woman sorts beans as part of a women's savings-and-credit program that will help her escape poverty; a man tightens a bolt on one of thirty-seven bridges donated to communities in Honduras and Nicaragua.

 It is true that each of us depends on others every day. To demonstrate this, draw a "map" of all the people you depend on from day to day. Put a circle with your name in it at the center of a page. Draw lines from your name to circles with the names of all the people who help you make it through the day. (For instance: Who makes your breakfast cereal? Who drives you to school? Who provides the gasoline for the bus or car? How do your friends help you?) Then draw lines connecting each of those circles to the people *they* depend on (for example, the people who drill for the gasoline, repair the bus, care for your friends, and so on).

The first frog they caught had a back leg that was so grotesquely twisted, the kids accused each other of accidentally stepping on it. But the next frogs they caught were deformed too. Some had one or three or four back legs, or two feet on one leg; a few had only one eye. More than half the frogs in the area were deformed.

Deformed frogs are one warning sign that the natural environment is suffering as a result of human activity.

The students immediately took out their notebooks and started collecting data, launching a research project that within weeks grabbed the attention of scientists and the national media. Soon, reports of deformed frogs began pouring in from all over the country, and even from around the world. And no one knew what was causing the phenomenon.

The discovery alarmed the scientific community because amphibians are especially good indicators of the health of the environment: whatever was affecting the frogs would likely affect the rest of the environment, even humans.

Thousands of students across the country have continued to assist researchers in finding the cause of the deformities. "It really worries me that more may be going on than we've found," says Betsy Kroon, a ninth grader. "I really hope we find a cause for this problem. . . . I know that this project will have changed something in some way." (Adapted from "The MNCS Frog Project")

Deformed frogs are just one indication of the environmental crisis facing the planet. Catholic social teaching calls all people to **care for God's creation**—to live their faith in relationship with all of God's creation by protecting the health of people and the planet. Care for God's creation, in the words of the U.S. Catholic bishops, "is not just an Earth Day slogan; it is a requirement of our faith" (*Sharing Catholic Social Teaching,* page 6). That requirement is based on God's call in the Book of Genesis for humans to "cultivate and care for" creation (2:15, NAB).

An interdependent world

In the past, many Christians have interpreted the command in Genesis to "subdue" and have "dominion" over creation (1:28) as permission to exploit the resources of the earth without limit. It is true that human beings have more value than any other creature because they alone have been created in the image of God. But, as images of God, people are called to care for creation with love, not to exploit it.

Genesis portrays God's creation as a world of interdependence, a world of peace because all its members—humans, animals, and elements—work together for the good of all. The

God's creation is a world of interdependence.

✳ *Student art:* Acrylic; Adwin Christo, Benilde–Saint Margaret's High School, Saint Louis Park, Minnesota

Christian faith tradition teaches that humans disrupted the original balance of creation, including the natural world, through original sin. Social sin continues to disrupt humankind's relationship with creation.

Christians are called to work for justice for the environment not only because it is necessary for the full development of human beings but also because the environment, as a work of God, has a beauty and value in itself. The beauty of creation can reveal to us something of the beauty of the Creator who made it.

13. Define the following terms: *option for the poor and vulnerable, dignity of work, rights of workers, solidarity, care for God's creation.*
14. Why does God call humanity to place the needs of the poor and vulnerable first?
15. In what two ways does work contribute to human dignity?
16. Why are Christians called to work for environmental justice?

For each of the following themes, provide your own example showing the theme or its absence: option for the poor and vulnerable, dignity and rights of workers, solidarity, care of God's creation.

18. Earlier it was said that the seven themes of Catholic social teaching cannot be separated from each other because they are interdependent. Choose three themes and discuss how each is necessary for the others.

Toward a World Based on Love

This has been a limited introduction to Catholic social teaching. The seven major themes of that teaching form the core of the Catholic vision of a reconstructed social order. Rooted in the Gospels, the aim of this Catholic "program" is to bring about Jesus' vision of a world based on love.

Catholic social teaching may indeed be a powerful tool for transforming the world—but only if Christians take its abstract ideas and live them out in the complexities of their world. Just how Christians have gone about doing justice in the world is the subject of the next chapter.

Go on a nature walk, alone or with some friends, in the area where you live. Bring along a notebook to record your observations. What might God's reasons be for making the things you find? How do they fit into the mutual interdependence of the world?

Choose one of the seven themes of Catholic social teaching and write a prayer or poem that expresses and celebrates that theme. Or if you are musically talented, compose a song around the theme.

3 DOING JUSTICE

barriers
opportunities
direct action

Putting Faith
into action

In This Chapter . . .

A CALL TO PUT FAITH INTO ACTION

As I looked around [the soup kitchen] I saw **so many faces,** faces that were foreign to me and I was foreign to them. I wanted to see their souls, to know their stories, to be able to see what they see and know what they know for just one day. For I'm sure one day is all I could stand. There was a man there, I didn't catch his name, but he had an obvious mental problem, and my classmates and I laughed at his actions. . . . Then I realized that he was going to be

like that forever. There was no one there to help him, and probably no one who cared. It hurt to realize that I was sitting among society's forgotten. The people I read about every day at school and in newspapers. I wanted to cry but I didn't, I couldn't, they didn't need my pity. They needed my actions, and I didn't know what to do. (Youniss and Yates, *Community Service and Social Responsibility in Youth,* page 65)

While volunteering at a local soup kitchen, this Catholic high school student encountered injustice in a way that both moved and overwhelmed her. Many people have had similar experiences—they see the environment being destroyed, or children in Africa orphaned by AIDS, or, as in the case of this student, people struggling to survive on the margins of society—and they are moved with compassion. And like this student, they say, "My actions are needed, but what can I do?"

The Scriptures provide us with a vision for a world ruled by love, and Catholic social teaching guides us in applying that vision to modern-day situations. But neither offers a specific plan for pursuing justice in every situation we might face, because each situation is different. How, then, do we figure out what to do? How can we make justice a reality in the world? This chapter examines one approach that can help to answer those questions. ☉ **A**

"I wanted to cry but I didn't, I couldn't, they didn't need my pity. **They needed my actions.**"

A God calls each of us to act for justice in the world. In what ways do you think God might be calling you to work for justice?

The Circle of Faith-in-Action

In 1971, Pope Paul VI issued *A Call to Action (Octagesimo Adveniens)*, an apostolic letter that called Christians "to bring about the social, political and economic changes seen in many cases to be urgently needed" for justice. The letter offered a three-step process for taking action—a process always guided by "the light of the Gospel" and church teaching. The letter suggested that Christians need not act alone, but could act with the help of the church, other people "of good will," and "the help of the Holy Spirit" (*A Call to Action,* 4).

At about the same time that *A Call to Action* was issued, liberation theology (see the sidebar on pages 66–67) was developing a similar approach to justice that is sometimes called the pastoral circle or the circle of praxis. Basically, **praxis** means living according to one's beliefs, not just in private, but in a way that affects the world. You might say that Christian praxis involves putting faith into action for the world.

The approach to doing justice that we will examine next borrows aspects of both the circle of praxis and *A Call to Action*. To keep things simple, we will call this approach the **circle of faith-in-action**.

Awareness, analysis, action

The circle of faith-in-action involves three basic steps. Because true justice reflects the will of God, each step of the circle is guided by faith—in particular, by the Gospels' and the church's teaching about justice:

- **Awareness.** Before we can work for justice in the world, we must see, hear, and know the world in a spirit of friendship, just as God does. When we perceive the world from God's point of view, we are better able to recognize the ways it can be made a better place to live.

THE CIRCLE OF FAITH-IN-ACTION

Awareness
How does God see the world's people, especially the poor and vulnerable?

Analysis
What is needed for the people of the world, especially the poor and vulnerable, to experience justice?

Action
How are we called to act so that the poor and vulnerable may live in dignity?

New awareness
How has analysis and action deepened or changed our perception of the situation?

- **Analysis.** The next step is to ask: Why is the world the way it is? And how can it be made as good as God intends?
- **Action.** Once we have answered the questions of analysis, we can act for justice in ways that make life better for everyone.

The action people take for justice will often lead them into a deeper relationship with the world, and therefore a deeper awareness of the world—especially if they reflect on and pray about their action. Consequently, the process starts all over again on a deeper level; in that way, it is less like a circle than a spiral.

The circle of faith-in-action is just one approach to bringing justice into the world. In fact, many people did not have any plan when they started working for justice—they had only compassion and courage. However, the circle of faith-in-action represents the wisdom that these leaders have passed on to us as a result of their experiences. That wisdom is a useful guide for those who follow in their footsteps.

Putting the circle into motion at Saint Francis High

When people think of hunger, they usually do not think immediately of Washington, D.C., the capital of one of the wealthiest nations in the world. Yet every day three to four hundred people come to a downtown soup kitchen for a hot lunch. That is where the social-justice students from a nearby Catholic high school, including the student quoted at the beginning of this chapter, volunteered for one semester. The students swept, cooked, served food, and sometimes spent time talking or playing cards with the diners.

From time to time, the students reacted to their experiences at the soup kitchen in short reflection papers and small-group discussions, which were tape recorded. Some of the students' reflections and discussions are presented here to illustrate aspects of the circle of faith-in-action. To protect the students' privacy, we will not use their real names, and we will name their school Saint Francis High.

1. What should guide those seeking justice, according to the apostolic letter *A Call to Action?*
2. Name the three steps of the circle of faith-in-action, and provide a one-sentence description of each.

3. What might be some advantages of working for justice with other people rather than alone?

Awareness: Friendship with the World

Even before the students of Saint Francis High began volunteering at the soup kitchen, they had certain images of and expectations about the sort of people they would be serving. For the most part, the students said they expected the soup kitchen diners to be "dirty," "smelly," "mean-spirited," "unappreciative," "mad at the world," and "disagreeable." With such expectations, naturally some of the students were a bit afraid of going to the kitchen. "I was nervous 'cause I have never personally had a one-on-one conversation with a homeless person," one girl said (Youniss and Yates, *Community Service,* pages 52–53).

After visiting the soup kitchen for the first time, however, the students' perceptions of the diners changed. "I expected them to be all evil and grumpy, but they was nice," one student said. "They chatted, asked you how you was doin', how your day was goin'." "They were funnier than I thought," another student said. "I mean, I didn't know they was going to have such a sense of humor" (Youniss and Yates, pages 52–53).

After reflecting on their first experience at the soup kitchen, these students' perceptions about hungry and homeless people underwent a dramatic change. That raises a question: Why did the students initially have a negative image of homeless and hungry people? In other words, why did their first perceptions not accurately reflect who the soup kitchen diners really were? ℬ

The question is an important one because the way the students approached the problems of hunger and homelessness would have been very different if their visit to the soup kitchen had not caused them to alter their initial perceptions. How we perceive a situation will determine whether, and how, we will pursue justice in it. That's why justice begins with **awareness:** seeing, hearing, and knowing the world in a spirit of friendship, as God does.

Do You See What I See?

At the most basic level, being aware involves interpreting the information provided by our senses in a way that gives us an accurate picture of the world. The differences that arise between people because they interpret the same reality in different ways is a constant reminder that we each have our own awareness of the world—we each perceive it and make sense of it in different ways.

The following story of how photographer Jana Taylor has taught poor and orphaned kids in Los Angeles to see their world in a new way illustrates that point:

ℬ Who in your life, if anyone, perceives you as you really are? If someone wanted to get to know who you really are, what would be the best way for them to do that?

The kids often come from dismal and chaotic surroundings. On the first day of the program, Taylor asks them, "What is beautiful in your home?" The typical response is, "Nothing."

For six weeks, Taylor teaches them photography. "The message of my photography and my teaching is that life is good, even though many of the children got off to a shaky start, and goodness is the foundation of everything," Taylor said. By the end of the program, she gets a completely different response to her question about what is beautiful. "They told me they found beauty in the way 'light hits the kitchen table,' 'dirt reshapes the pattern on the floor,' and 'birds sing in the trees outside the window.' They saw beauty in simple things."

"I can see things I never saw before," said Elisa Sanchez, one of the participants. "I also found ugly can be turned into beautiful." Added Rafael Hous: "The camera can help take you beyond what you see in front of you—see beauty in a piece of wood or even the trash." (Based on Wood, "Poor No More") **C**

Worldviews: Guides for Relating to the World

What enabled the photography students to see their world in a new way? Their eyesight didn't change, but they learned a new way of seeing, one based on Jana's belief in the basic goodness of everything. Their story demonstrates an important point: Our basic beliefs about the world guide the way we relate to the world.

The basic beliefs that guide the way someone relates to the world can be said to be his or her **worldview.** Someone's worldview might include his or her responses to basic questions such as these:

- What is most important in life?
- Do all people have the same rights?
- What responsibilities do individuals have to society, and vice versa?
- Are most people basically good or bad?
- Is there a God, or is life determined by random chance? What is God like? **D**

A particular worldview is made up of the answers someone gives to these and any other important questions about life in the world.

Being able to *see beauty* in their world could *enable them to create beauty* in their life.

✳ Our view of the world affects the path we take in life. *Student art:* "Mirror." Pencil and colored pencil; Bridget Jesionowski, Trinity High School, Garfield Heights, Ohio

C Think of the street on which you live. Before going there, write a detailed description of the place from memory: what can you see, hear, smell, or feel? Then go there and spend ten minutes doing nothing but carefully observing it. After you are finished, write down everything you noticed for the first time. What prevented you from noticing these things before?

D What does your own worldview look like? Write down your perspective on each of the worldview questions listed here. Then list any other important beliefs or values that define who you are and how you act.

At first, the photography students' worldview included the basic belief that nothing in their world was beautiful. Jana Taylor's worldview, on the other hand, included the basic belief that goodness is the foundation of everything. Taylor invited the kids to see through her worldview because she knew that doing so could profoundly change the way they lived. Being able to *see* beauty in their world could enable them to *create* beauty in their life.

Because our worldview has such a profound effect on the way we relate to one another—and therefore on our approach to justice—it makes sense to understand where our worldviews come from.

Experience

One way we develop our own unique worldview is by learning from our experience of the world. For instance, people who grew up in poverty during the Great Depression often value thriftiness and financial security.

Similarly, the kids' experience with Jana Taylor and photography altered their basic perception of the world around them.

It is likely that the Saint Francis students' first perceptions of hungry and homeless people resulted in part from their past experience, or lack of experience, with such people. They may have seen bag ladies on the street or encountered aggressive panhandlers, and assumed that all homeless and hungry people were similar. But their one-on-one experience with the soup kitchen diners provided them with a more realistic picture. *E*

Culture

Personal experience is not the only factor that affects worldviews. Often, our most basic beliefs do not come from our own experience, but from the culture in which we live.

Culture could be described as all of the shared values, beliefs, and ways of relating and living together that characterize a particular group of people. A shared culture enables

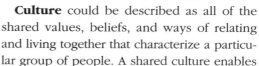

A shared culture enables members of a group to work, play, and live with one another with less conflict and misunderstanding.

✳ *Student art:* "Jus' Chillin'." Black-and-white photograph; Lucia Wharton, Pope John XXIII High School, Sparta, New Jersey

E Describe one of the most significant experiences of your life. How has this experience affected your values and beliefs?

members of a group to work, play, and live with one another with less conflict and misunderstanding.

We each belong to many different groups—defined by race or ethnicity, nationality, religion, school, or sport—and so we are influenced by many different cultures. For example, the dominant culture of the United States includes things like the English language, a certain set of laws, belief in the freedom of individuals, the mass media, and a capitalist economy. Within that dominant culture are many subcultures, such as youth culture, which includes young people's slang, clothing, attitudes, social rules, and music. Youth culture can, in turn, be divided into even more subcultures. **F**

Culture shapes worldviews by teaching its members to adopt the beliefs and behaviors of the group. For instance, *peer pressure* is a term often used to describe the pressure young people might feel to change who they are in order to fit in with the culture of a particular group. But all people, even adults, experience peer pressure. From the time we are children, others in our social group teach us, whether it is intentional or not, what is "normal" for that culture—the ways of thinking and acting that people must follow in order to fit into the group's culture. At first it is our families who teach us what is culturally normal. Later, friends, teachers, and the media all push us to adopt the beliefs, values, and practices of the cultures they represent. As we learn these beliefs, values, and practices, consciously or unconsciously they become part of our worldview. **G**

Blind Spots

Together, experience and culture give us our own unique way of relating to the world. Just as sight helps us get around the physical world, our worldview helps us navigate the social world. But just as our sight has its limitations, so does our worldview. Being aware of the limitations of our worldview can help us avoid being blind to injustice.

Jesus often pointed out such blindness: "How blind you are!" Jesus says to the scribes and Pharisees, ". . . for you . . . have neglected the weightier matters of the law: justice and mercy and faith" (Matthew 23:19–23).

Unfortunately, history is full of examples of people who were blind to injustice. The practice of slavery, for instance, was regarded as normal by most cultures around the world throughout human history. Not all people were blind to the injustice of slavery, but few had the imagination to envision a world in which all would be free. "It is a monstrous thing to do . . . and contradicts . . . our Christianity," wrote one observer of a Savannah, Georgia, slave auction in which families were broken apart. But he went on to ask: "What can be done? The Negroes of the South must be slaves" (PBS, "Judgment Day").

It would be nice to think that had we lived then, we would have known better. But history repeatedly teaches us that otherwise good and intelligent people are capable of being blind to even the gravest injustice. The woman who wrote the following letter was among many educated people who either

F What are the symbols of youth culture? Bring some objects that represent youth culture to class for a "show and tell"—music, clothes, magazines, posters, pictures showing some aspect of the culture, a newspaper report about youth culture, and so on. Be prepared to discuss these questions: What does each symbol say about young people? How does youth culture affect how young people view the world and justice?

G Make a list of the five most important values or beliefs of the culture in which you live. After each item, comment briefly on whether you share the value or belief, explaining why or why not.

ignored or supported apartheid, a system of racial separation and discrimination that existed in the nation of South Africa until it was legally abolished in the early 1990s:

> I am sorry that I did not do more than I did. I also regret not having been aware of the real truth of what was happening in South Africa. I only started to ask questions of myself when my two children started to question the system—they were only twelve and ten at the time. This made me question the system myself, which finally made me aware of the situation. . . . Forgive me! (Parsons, in the Register of Reconciliation, number 93, Truth and Reconciliation Commission home page)

This woman's worldview blinded her to the injustice of apartheid—in part because the culture in which she was raised trained her that apartheid was "normal." But her children, who were still forming worldviews, were able to question what was considered normal by white South African culture. **H**

If seemingly well-intentioned people—whole nations, even—can be blind to glaring injustice, then each of us probably suffers from a certain amount of blindness to injustice too. What can we do about it? We can do what the blind did in the Gospels: turn to Jesus, who can help us to see.

Sharing Jesus' Worldview

Jesus can help us "see" a vision of justice for the world if we look through his worldview, in which love, not selfishness, is the most important value. A love-centered worldview relates to the world in a spirit of friendship—a spirit that Catholic social teaching calls solidarity. Following are the characteristics of that worldview:

Seeing, hearing, and knowing with respect. True friends really want to get to know one another on a deep level, in much the same way that God knew the people of Israel before leading them into the Promised Land: "I have *observed* the misery of my people. . . . I have *heard* their cry. . . . I *know* their sufferings," God told Moses (Exodus 3:7, italics added). People who see through a love-centered worldview enter into solidarity with the world by respectfully seeing, hearing, and knowing it.

A vision of abundant life. True friends want one another to have a good and abundant life. Jesus said, "I came that they may have life, and have it abundantly" (John 10:10). He brought abundant life by healing the sick, reaching out to those on the margins of society, restoring relationships through forgiveness—and ultimately, by giving his own life in order to overcome death. People who see through a love-centered worldview envision the Reign of God: a world in which peace, justice, and goodness bring abundant life to everyone.

Compassion. True friends experience compassion when one of them is suffering, and that compassion moves them to take action—just as God entered the world through Jesus to save us from sin.

Let's see how sharing Jesus' love-centered worldview helped the Saint Francis students envision justice for the soup kitchen diners.

H The next time you watch television, bring a notepad with you. Take notes during one program, including commercials: What messages does the program seem to send about what should be "normal" for the culture? In what ways might the worldview represented by the program be blind to justice? Be prepared to discuss your notes in class.

Seeing, hearing, and knowing with respect

Admittedly, the students of Saint Francis did not go to the soup kitchen with the intention of becoming friends with anyone there—at least not at first. But as the students listened to the diners' stories and opened their eyes to who the diners really were, they found it increasingly difficult to lump "the poor" or "the homeless" into one generic group. Instead, the students recognized them as individual human beings. "I've realized that they are human beings and people's mothers, fathers, sisters, brothers, and someone's child," one student wrote (Youniss and Yates, *Community Service,* page 56).

That realization was possible because the students related to the soup kitchen diners with respect. *Respect* is a word that literally means "to look again." The photography students mentioned earlier "looked again" at the world around them—but instead of looking at it in their usual way, they looked for the goodness in it. To see, hear, and know the world with **respect** is to look beyond outer appearances and first impressions to see the goodness that is the foundation of all God's creation. Respect acknowledges that all the world is good because the world was created from God's own goodness.

Although at first they were nervous about getting to know the diners, the students were willing to see, hear, and know the diners' goodness. The students' attitude of respect al-lowed them to relate to the diners not simply as strangers too poor to feed themselves, but as people with whom they could have a human relationship.

One student's experience demonstrates how mutual respect builds human relationships. He left the kitchen to visit the diners, and was invited to play cards.

I lost, but it wasn't about winning or losing, it was about just showing that you cared, not just that you cared, but you cared enough that you came to them and they didn't [have to] come to you. I mean at that moment we were just people, people that had something in common. (Youniss and Yates, *Community Service,* page 91)

A vision of abundant life

In Jesus' worldview, all people live an abundant life, full of goodness. Many of the Saint Francis students began to develop a similar vision as their relationship with the people at the soup kitchen deepened. As a result, they became more aware of ways the people were prevented from living full, abundant lives.

"Why am I so fortunate and they aren't?" another student asked.

I got up to play with a girl that was sitting eating a saltine cracker. . . . What was her future to be like? I don't think she had a proper home because she was wrapped up in layers and layers of clothes. Her hands

Justice is about more than simply meeting people's physical needs. At its heart, justice is about treating people with respect.

were as cold as ice and wrinkled with dryness. (Youniss and Yates, *Community Service,* page 94)

Jesus' worldview invites us to question what our culture considers to be normal, asking, Is life being lived as abundantly as God intended? The themes of Catholic social teaching are a good guide to the types of questions we can ask to determine whether society fosters a full and good life for all:

- Is all human life being protected and fully supported so that it can thrive? Is everyone's dignity being respected?
- Is everyone able to participate in the life of the community? Are all families being strengthened?
- Are human rights and responsibilities being respected?
- Do all people have good work that respects their dignity and provides them with a good life?

Jesus calls us to provide abundant life for all. *The Lord's Supper,* by Fritz Eichenberg

©Fritz Eichenberg Trust/Licensed by VAGA, New York, NY

- Is the care and protection of poor, vulnerable, and marginalized people a top priority for society?
- Is the integrity of God's creation being respected and protected?

The students found that for many of the soup kitchen diners, the answer to these questions was often no. "Life was not intended to be sustained, it was meant to be lived," one student observed. "The people at the soup kitchen should be out living life to its fullest but they can't" (Youniss and Yates, *Community Service,* page 94).

Compassion

Friendship can be a risky thing because it implies sharing not only the friend's joy but the friend's pain as well. Relating to the world through a love-centered worldview is like that. If you have ever had a friend who was in trouble, then you know that the problem was not just your friend's—to a certain extent, it was your problem too. If you were moved to help your friend, then you experienced compassion.

Compassion isn't always a comfortable emotion—remember the student quoted at the beginning of the chapter who wanted to cry because of the situation faced by the soup kitchen diners? Because she had developed a relationship of solidarity with the diners, compassion led her to be deeply dissatisfied with the situation they faced. But it also prompted her to take action to change the situation.

Compassion led the students to question the underlying causes of the situation faced by poor people, as this student's experience suggests:

What is your vision for a world in which everyone experiences abundant life? In describing your dream world, you might consider some of these questions: How are work and possessions divided among people? How do people relate to creation and use natural resources? How do people relate to one another? How will the government be organized? What do communities look like? What is the education system like? How are conflicts resolved? Brainstorm ideas with other students if you like.

The kitchen was not horrible as my classmates had told me. The only horrible thing was a mother and two-year-old daughter in the line. I didn't think about it for real until the little girl came to the window, stretched out her hand and asked, "Can I have one more sandwich, please?" I felt like giving her one hundred sandwiches, not only one hundred sandwiches but a house and her mother a job. When she walked away with the peanut butter sandwich, I could only ask myself, "Why?" (Youniss and Yates, *Community Service,* page 132)

The question this student asked is critical to justice: Why aren't the poor and vulnerable able to live life fully? The answers we provide to this question can reveal what action needs to be taken for justice.

Friendship can be **a risky thing** because it implies sharing not only the friend's joy but the friend's pain as well.

For Review

4. Define the terms *awareness* and *worldview*.
5. Explain how experience and culture shape a person's worldview.
6. How can we avoid being blind to injustice?
7. Describe the characteristics of a love-centered worldview.

In Depth

8. How can we become more aware of where we are being called to do justice?
9. Describe at least three Gospel passages that illustrate Jesus' desire for people to have abundant life.

Is the kind of sadness and discomfort expressed by this student and the student quoted at the beginning of this chapter something you would prefer to avoid? Why or why not?

Analysis: Asking "Why?"

If we truly care about the world and its people, then eventually we will ask, "Why are so many people unable to live as fully as God intended?"

We already know that injustice doesn't "just happen," nor does it come from God. Rather, original sin introduced injustice into the world, and people continue to promote injustice whenever they choose to seek their own self-interest at the expense of the good of others. Injustice is the result of human choices. That insight allows us to focus the question more narrowly: What human choices cause injustice, and what do people need to do to promote justice?

These are powerful questions, questions with the potential to reveal not only the root causes of injustice but a vision of justice worth working toward. These questions are the beginning of social **analysis,** which is the process of understanding how people's lives are affected by the relationships that shape the society in which they live.

Sharing worldviews in conversation with one another is a good way to begin to analyze injustice.

"I Have a Question . . ."

Their experience at the soup kitchen led the students of Saint Francis High School to question the causes of the poverty they witnessed there. The following excerpt illustrates how they reflected on those questions through group discussion (names have been changed to protect the students' privacy):

Shyla: I have a question. With all the stuff that's going on with homelessness, who is responsible? Do you think it's the persons who got themselves into it or society?

James: [The president] is responsible.

Ben: Society.

Joseph: I think it's more big business.

Ben: Big business?

Joseph: Yeah, check it out.

Marcie: All they gotta do is get a job.

Joseph: I mean, the majority of what I hear of big homeless cases is because a large factory left a certain area and left a whole lot of people out of work. . . . You go find a job. I'll bet you don't find a job in a week.

Russell: I can get a job.

Joseph: You can get a job because you got a house, you got an address.

Ben: If you wanna get a job, where they gonna call . . . to get in touch with you?

Marcie: I know a lot of people on welfare who don't need to be on welfare. They are capable of getting a job and they don't. I think the government should . . . make people work and give them a time limit as to how long they can be on welfare.

Shyla: You can't really give people a time limit to be on welfare. There's no telling how they [got there] and why they're not getting a job.

Marcie: Well, just to say something about that, there's this girl in my neighborhood and she's sixteen and she has a daughter and she's on welfare. . . . She's in school but she could get an afternoon job.

Joseph: But if she's sixteen and has a child and [is] in school, don't you think it's kind of hard to work after school?

Marcie: But she still has that responsibility on herself today. It's nobody else's fault.

Moyra: People, like, who can't work and they need it [should get welfare]—but other people [are able to work] and there [should be] some steps to build them up.

Ben: When you're on welfare, it's like once you in, you trapped, because like, if you get a job, then you're cut off. They need better ways so you can get a job and yet, if [the job] is not fully supporting you—

Shyla: It makes me so mad, when and if you're on welfare and the government's helping you, you're not allowed to save money. I mean, it makes no sense. They want people to get off welfare. But the only way to get off welfare is to have money.

James: Government has to play a major role in it, but seeing how the government's not, somebody's got to solve it. (Youniss and Yates, *Community Service,* pages 57–58, 76–77) 𝍏

The art of asking questions

It was a question—"Who is responsible?"—that began the students' analysis of the problem of homelessness. Questions are perhaps the most important tool of social analysis. When we ask questions, we are acknowledging that we do not know enough about a problem to solve it—and that allows us to consider the problem at a deeper level, where we might find ways to pursue justice that we had not thought of before.

The type of questions we ask about a problem will determine the sort of answers we get. Good questions are based on a love-centered awareness of the world. For instance, several students answered Shyla's question ("Who is responsible for homelessness?") by focusing on the responsibilities of the poor. Personal responsibility is definitely

> The type of **questions we ask** about a problem will **determine** the sort of **answers we get.**

✳ *Student art:* Pen and ink; Brian Szewczyk, Pope John XXIII High School, Sparta, New Jersey

𝍏 Form a small group with some of your classmates and talk about discussions in which people have opposing views on an issue, using the Saint Francis students' discussion as an example. What makes such discussions helpful, and what makes them divisive? Together, draw up a list of tips for discussing differing or opposing views. Be prepared to share them with the class.

an important building block of justice. But because they related to the soup kitchen diners in a spirit of respect, many of the students took a deeper look at the problem. When they did, they realized that the causes of homelessness were more numerous and complex than simply a lack of responsibility on the part of the poor. That awareness led them to ask more questions, such as whether poor people have the resources that would enable them to fulfill their responsibilities.

As the students continued to analyze the problem of homelessness over the course of the semester, one question led to another. Soon they were considering a wide range of issues: unemployment, business ethics, government, the criminal-justice system, discrimination, education, drugs, affordable housing, the minimum wage, and teen pregnancy, to name a few. The fact that all these issues are somehow related to the problem of homelessness might seem surprising, but it reveals an important reality that we first encountered in the Genesis Creation story: our world is one of interdependent relationships.

Finding the way to justice requires identifying the relationships that make it possible—as well as those that prevent it.

A World of Relationships

Independence is a prime value of our North American culture—and one that is necessary for human dignity. But sometimes the emphasis our culture places on independence blinds us to the reality that human beings do not—and cannot—live in complete independence from one another. Rather, all creation is **interdependent:** we depend on one another for our existence. Even a hermit living completely apart from society depends on creation for food and shelter, and at one time depended on his parents and others for those things.

Almost anything we do is possible only because of our life-giving relationships with other people and creation. Just think of all the relationships that make your life what it is: relationships with parents, siblings, friends, and teachers come to mind immediately. But your life is affected by thousands of other people as well, even if your relationship with them is not so personal—think of the hundreds of people involved in bringing you the clothes you wear, for instance, or the water from your faucets or the food you eat.

All creation is interdependent: we depend on one another for our existence.

✳ *Student art:* "Hands of the Future." Tempera; Amanda Irvin, Santa Fe Catholic High School, Lakeland, Florida

Each of us depends on thousands of people, like this strawberry picker, to bring us the food we eat every day.

Moreover, the people who shape your life are themselves affected by their relationships with other people, who are in turn dependent on *other* people, and on and on. Ultimately, our lives are shaped by an intricate web of relationships that connect us, directly or indirectly, to millions of other people.

The relationship map: A blueprint for justice

Justice itself is made possible by many interdependent, life-giving relationships. When those relationships do not exist, or when instead of giving life they actually suppress or harm life, then injustice results.

To build justice we need to ask, What life-giving relationships are necessary to make justice happen? In that way, building justice is like building a house—before we can start construction, we should know what pieces we will need and how they will fit together.

Let's analyze the injustice of hunger as an example. We can begin with the very basic question, What is necessary for people to be well fed every day?

The most basic answer is food. Obviously, the next question is, Where can people get food? Again, the answers are pretty simple: people can get food from their family, from a food shelf or soup kitchen, from a store, or, in a limited way, from a garden. L

If a supportive family or a food shelf is not available, people need money to buy food. How do people get money? The government's food stamp program is one source; family members might be another. But most people prefer to get their income from a good job.

Our analysis continues by asking, What do people need in order to get jobs? Here's where the Saint Francis students found that the seemingly simple issue of hunger suddenly got more complicated. Many things are needed to get a job: transportation to work, a home, job training, child care (if the person is a parent), nearby job openings that pay a living wage, and food—it's hard to work long enough to get paid when you aren't eating.

We could take our analysis even deeper by continuing the questioning process: How do people get transportation, shelter, job training, child care, and food—especially when they don't have money? What happens if an area lacks good job openings? Our questions have begun to reveal that getting enough food every day is not as simple as it might seem—not for those people who lack the basic life-giving relationships that most of us take for granted. These are the questions that the poor struggle with on a daily basis, questions that are shared by those who, in solidarity, try to help them.

This analysis of how people's lives are affected by the various relationships that shape society is an example of a **relationship map**; just as a road map shows the connections between places, a relationship map shows the connections between people that shape our

L Imagine that you are homeless and hungry. You have no money. How would you find food? If possible, check around the community by calling or visiting the places you think would be most likely to provide you with food. Then write a short report of your findings.

society. Of course, our analysis of what people need in order to be well fed is limited—more questions would provide a deeper and more detailed analysis. But even at this basic level, the relationship map can provide us with a vision of what justice for the hungry might look like. We will consider how to put that vision into action later in the chapter.

Social Structures

The shape and quality of a house depend a lot on the parts used for its construction and how those parts are put together. Skip the foundation or a few roof beams and the house might not be such a good place to live. Similarly, society is shaped by the quality of its relationships and the way they fit together.

The patterns of relationships that shape any society are known as **social structures.** The relationship map we just envisioned shows part of the social structure that enables most of us to eat every day. Government, law,

business, labor, education, families—all these are social structures, too, because their existence is sustained and shaped by the relationships within and among them.

We usually take the relationships that structure our world—such as the ones that bring us food—for granted. For example, the analysis above does not consider the basic structures of production and distribution that make food readily available—the natural environment, transportation networks, processing factories, farms, and so on. But these structures are what keep people from going hungry. It is because some of these basic structures are broken that twenty-four thousand people globally, mostly children, die of hunger every day. The structure of our social relationships influences a great deal in our world: who is rich and who is poor, who is included and who is left out—even who lives and who dies. **M**

Building or blocking justice?

People often view social structures as permanent or inevitable. Confronted by images of hungry children, they might be tempted to say, "That's just the way things are." In fact, the structures that shape society are not inevitable. They are the result of the decisions that people make every day.

Each of the relationships that contributes to justice for the hungry, for example, is made possible by individual decisions. The Saint Francis students' soup kitchen was made possible only by the ongoing commitment of

Selfishness is the basic attitude that builds and sustains **structures of sin.**

Injustice is the result of decisions people make every day. The famine that caused these Somali boys to go hungry resulted not from a natural disaster, but from a civil war that destroyed the life-giving structures of their society.

M Describe a relationship map, either in writing or by drawing it, that shows all the relationships that are necessary for you to have a good life. Begin by asking, "What do I need in order to have a life that is good for me?" Write down as many answers as you can. Then, for each of the answers, ask yourself, "What relationships make possible all the things that I need for a good life?" Use the relationship map described in the analysis of hunger on pages 91–92 as a guide.

many different people. The decision of these people to enter a relationship of solidarity with poor people built up justice.

Individual decisions also contribute to the social structures that block justice, which the church calls **structures of sin.** Structures of sin can be identified by asking, What are the barriers to life-giving relationships? In the relationship map about hunger, the barriers that prevent people from having good jobs, good education, shelter, affordable child care, supportive families, and so on, are the structures of sin that cause the poverty that leads to hunger.

The 1987 encyclical *On Social Concern (Sollicitudo Rei Socialis)* made three observations about structures of sin:

1. They can be traced back to the personal sin of individuals (36).
2. They are a result of the interrelated actions of many different people, not just one person (36).
3. The root causes of structures of sin are "on the one hand, the all-consuming desire for profit, and on the other, the thirst for power, with the intention of imposing one's will upon others . . . at any price" (37). In other words, selfishness is the basic attitude that builds and sustains structures of sin.

The underlying message of *On Social Concern* is this: The social structures that lead to injustice are not shaped by chance—they do not "just happen." People have the power to build the structures that shape their world. It is how people choose to use that power that determines whether those structures promote justice or injustice.

Power: Shaping Our World

Human **power** is the God-given ability everyone has to affect their own life, the lives of others, and the world around them—including its social structures—in either positive or negative ways. Power builds relationships.

All people have power because all people have the ability to cause change, at least on some level, although some people have more power than others. To say that power is God-given means that the ultimate source of all power is God. But not all people agree with this perspective. Often, people view human beings as the source of all power. Each of these perspectives has important implications for how people choose to use power.

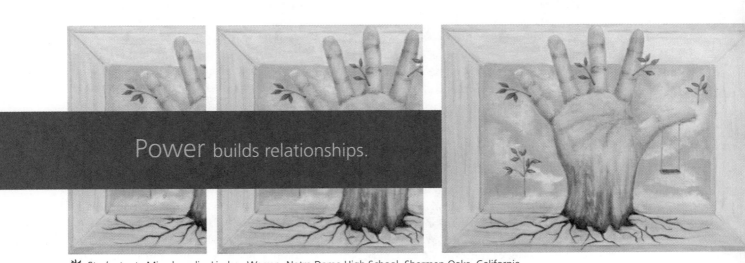

Power builds relationships.

✳ *Student art:* Mixed media; Lindsey Warren, Notre Dame High School, Sherman Oaks, California

Power-over

The belief that human beings are the source of their own power recalls the original sin of the first humans, who believed they could become their own gods. In this view, power might be compared to a limited resource like oil or electricity: it is something that people must work to acquire. Those who acquire power may believe they "own" it and have "earned" the right to use it for any purpose, even at the expense of others. Moreover, if power is something that can be acquired, then it also can be taken away—and that would mean that it needs to be defended from others.

This is known as a **power-over** worldview. Dr. Seuss cleverly depicts this worldview in his book *Yertle the Turtle*. Yertle, king of the turtles, believes that he rules all that he is able to see. In order to see farther—and therefore increase the extent of his rule—he commands the turtles to form a tall stack by standing on each other's backs. Yertle then makes his throne at the top of the stack, from where he can rule over an even greater expanse of land. In the worldview reflected by Yertle's attitude, power is gained at the expense of others; only one person can sit at the top of the stack, while everyone else must remain below.

Such power is often acquired at the expense of the needs of the poor and vulnerable. The result is a structure of sin that fosters injustice. In Seuss's story, the turtles at the bottom of the pile experience pain and hunger as a result of bearing the weight of all the turtles above them.

Ironically, those who abuse their power harm not only those at the bottom of the pile, but themselves as well. The oppressed may live in fear of the powerful, but the powerful also live in fear that the oppressed may take away their power. The division the powerful create between themselves and those they dominate deprives both sides of the solidarity, or friendship, that would otherwise allow them to experience each other's gifts and insights.

When people share power with one another, they can build a more just society. Here, Habitat for Humanity volunteers work together to build affordable housing.

Power-with

In contrast to the power-over perspective, a love-centered worldview understands that God is the source of all power. Therefore, our power—our ability to affect the world around us—is not something that we *own*, but something God has *given* us to use for the good of the world and ourselves. We might say that our power is "loaned" to us by God.

According to this worldview, everyone has God-given power, and because we live in an interdependent world, that power is meant to be shared in relationship with others. This is called the **power-with** worldview, because it sees power as something to be used *with* and for others to bring about the good of everyone.

A power-with worldview does not deny that some people might exercise more power than others. For example, a teacher exercises more power than her or his students, business leaders often have a greater ability to affect society than do low-level employees, and dictators have more power than their subjects. But the extra power these people have is not their own; it comes from others. In Seuss's fable, King Yertle discovers this truth when the turtle at the very bottom of the pile gets fed up and purposely burps, bringing the whole structure tumbling down. Yertle's power was based entirely on the support of the other turtles. Without their cooperation, Yertle was just another turtle in the pond.

Similarly, people who rely on the support of others for their power—such as the dictator or the business owner—would lose much of their power without that support. For instance, the business owner gets her power from her customers and employees. If the customers stopped paying for her company's products, she would lose the economic power she received from them; this is what happens during a **boycott.** And when employees refuse to work for their employer during a **strike,** the employer loses the physical and mental power she gained from their work.

It is not necessarily bad for some people to have more power than others. In democratic countries, people elect leaders who have more political power than ordinary citizens do because it would be impractical for all political decisions to be made by the entire population. However, leaders who have a power-with worldview know that their extra power comes from the people (and ultimately from God), and that they are called to use it with and for the people. $\mathbb{N}$

Power for Justice

Eventually, the Saint Francis students wanted to go beyond asking, Why? Soon they were asking, "What can we do to make life better for hungry and homeless people?" But perhaps even more important, they wondered whether they, as high school students, had enough power to do much of anything:

Tonya: We're sitting here talking about issues, but what are we really doing? That's the question I have for all of you.

Kate: We ourselves, 16-, 17-year-olds, we don't necessarily have to do something right now because we don't have power. . . . If we get enough teenagers together, adults will listen to us, but if it's like five of us, adults are not going to listen.

Tonya: We have the power to change [the world], but we don't do it . . . and if y'all sit here and say it's going to end up bad—

Michael: No one wants to step up!

Celine: I am. . . .

Kate: You're only one person, but the world is real big.

Celine: You got to be committed if you want to change something. You can't just say, "Oh, it's wrong, but there ain't nothing I can do about it."

Tonya: I have power at 16. I'm sorry, I do! (Youniss and Yates, *Community Service,* pages 70–71) $\mathbb{O}$

The students' discussion raises good questions: Just how much power does anyone—especially young people—have to change injustice, anyway? Kate noted that the power of one person acting alone is limited.

But the church believes that God is the source of our power to do justice. When people open themselves to God's grace and share their power in solidarity with one another, their combined power to bring justice into the world is great. Shared power strengthens relationships among people rather than causing divisions among them—and it is the key to transforming structures of sin, according to the encyclical *On Social Concern* (38).

Together we *do* have the power to change the world. But what is the best way to use that power to act for justice? This is the question we will consider next.

$\mathbb{N}$ Research the story of someone who has been a leader in the area of justice. In a three-page report, provide a brief biographical introduction of the person, then describe one significant action the person took for justice. Discuss how power contributed to the injustice the person encountered, and how the person used power to challenge the injustice.

$\mathbb{O}$ Do teenagers have the power to work for justice? Use a specific example to explain your response.

For Review

10. Explain what it means to say that "all creation is interdependent."
11. What does a relationship map show?
12. What is a social structure?
13. In the encyclical *On Social Concern,* what does the church say are the root causes of structures of sin?
14. Define *power.*
15. Explain the difference between the power-over and the power-with worldviews.

In Depth

Choose a justice issue that concerns you and describe how you would analyze it. What kind of questions would you ask? How would issues of power and social structures factor into your analysis?

Action: Bringing Life to the World

Once the process of social analysis reveals the individual choices and social structures that cause injustice in a particular situation, the next step in the circle of faith-in-action is to change the situation in a way that allows all people involved to experience the good life that God intended for them. This is **action.**

As the Saint Francis students recognized, though, taking action for justice is not easy. "You're only one person, but the world is real big," Kate said. She may as well have added that many people—especially those who benefit from unjust social structures—often actively resist any change to those structures. In a big, often hostile world, how does one start taking action for justice?

Opportunities for Action

Let's review how the circle of faith-in-action brings us to the point of taking action for justice. In the first step of the circle, relating to the world in a spirit of solidarity makes us aware of the reality the world faces. In the

Action for justice should address not only the immediate needs of those who suffer but also the social structures that cause injustice.

second step, analysis provides a vision of what justice for the world might look like. Now, in the third step, we can compare the reality to our vision of justice by asking, What relationships need to be built, and what structures of sin need to be transformed in order for the reality of the world to become more like Jesus' vision for justice?

Let's return to the problem of hunger as an example. Our analysis of hunger on pages 91–92 provides us with a basic map for how justice might feed the hungry. Comparing that vision to the reality faced by the soup kitchen diners reveals where action is needed to build life-giving relationships or to transform structures of sin so that people will no longer go hungry. The Saint Francis students found that unemployment, low-wage jobs, homelessness, and a lack of family or community support were among the barriers to justice faced by the soup kitchen diners. Consider some of the following actions that might help the hungry overcome those barriers:

- By volunteering at the soup kitchen, the students created life-giving relationships that overcame the diners' lack of money or family support.
- Supporting job training programs or minimum-wage laws would be two ways to overcome the barriers of unemployment and jobs that don't pay enough to cover both rent and food.
- Recognizing the relationship between hunger and homelessness, some students participated in a demonstration demanding more federal support for affordable housing. "There is . . . a lot of talk about

Look again at the relationship map you developed for activity M. What barriers or structures block the relationships necessary for justice, either for yourself or others?

building more [affordable] houses, but nothing is really being done," one student wrote. "I know that there were not many of us there in protest and that we may not have really changed anything . . . [but] it was the first step of demanding better housing and I was part of it" (Youniss and Yates, *Community Service,* page 70).

These are just a few possibilities; really, the opportunities to create life-giving relationships that build up justice are only limited by our imagination.

Direct Action and Social Action

Given all these choices for action, the Saint Francis students, or any potential hunger fighter, might ask, Which course of action is best? For some people, the best course of action might be that which involves the least work or expense. In a love-centered worldview, however, the best course of action is the one that is the most life-giving for all the people involved in the situation.

We can divide all the opportunities to act for justice into two categories:

- **Direct action** occurs on the level of individual relationships and is usually aimed at meeting an immediate need. The students' volunteer work at the soup kitchen would be an example of direct action.
- **Social action** occurs on the level of social structures. Social action attempts to change the behavior of society and its institutions in a way that promotes justice. The students' attempts to influence federal policy on affordable housing would be an example of social action.

The two feet of justice

Often, the approach that will bring truly abundant life to poor and marginalized people involves *both* direct action *and* social action. Without one or the other, efforts to change injustice may fall short. For example, if the students did not provide food at the soup kitchen (a form of direct action), hundreds of people would have gone hungry. Handing out soup and sandwiches met a real need—satisfying the diners' immediate hunger at the time that they were served.

On the other hand, the students clearly recognized that direct action alone was not sufficient to bring the soup kitchen diners the full and abundant lives they deserved. As the relationship map shows, creating full and lasting justice for all those who go hungry requires action to change the social structures that cause chronic hunger in the first place.

So both direct action and social action are needed to address the injustice of hunger. Direct action is needed to satisfy people's hunger today; social action is needed so that people will not *become* hungry tomorrow and

In a love-centered worldview, the best course of action is the one that is the most life-giving for all the people involved.

beyond. Because direct action and social action work together to move justice forward, they are often called the two feet of justice. Without both, it is difficult for justice to get anywhere.

Action: Always for human life and dignity

The life and dignity of human beings is the foundation of the "house" of justice, so the goal of any action for justice is always to protect and promote human life and dignity. This basic goal has certain implications for the ways we act for justice. On one hand, it implies acting in solidarity with those who experience injustice—but it also means confronting with love, not hostility, those who promote injustice. Let's first look at what it means to act in solidarity.

Acting in Solidarity

Recall that solidarity is like friendship—it is an ongoing commitment to the good of others. Theologian and journalist Margaret Hebblethwaite tells a true story from the base communities of Brazil (see "Base Communities," pages 100–101) that dramatically illustrates the difference between action that respects the dignity of poor people and action that does not:

> Unemployment was taking a hard toll among the metalworkers of São Paulo; in response, the local base communities formed what they called Project Five-Two—named for the Gospel story of the multiplication of five loaves and two fish. Groups of five employed families adopted two unemployed families, and provided them with basic food items—beans, rice, and eggs. It was enough to support the unemployed families while they looked for work. If unemployed families found work, then they too shared their food with others.

But Project Five-Two didn't stop there. It also encouraged the unemployed people to unite together so that they could prayerfully examine the underlying causes of their situation, find solutions, and take action—such as pressuring society to pass work laws with unemployment benefits. "Food distribution is only one aspect of the project; we also want families to become aware of the causes of unemployment," said a project participant, "because the problem is one of social structures that cannot be solved by handouts."

When the host of a popular television show heard of the project, she managed to collect a ton of rice, beans, coffee, and bread from her celebrity friends. She sent the food to the Project Five-Two neighborhood in a truck—along with a television crew to tape the event for her show.

But Project Five-Two stunned the television host by politely refusing the donations. They explained that they did not feel inclined to appear on national television like beggars, with hands outstretched to receive bundles of food: "We don't need assistance, but employment. May [television host] Dona Hebe forgive us if we are judging her wrongly, but it seems she came here looking for self-promotion when she should

Through Project Five-Two, people not only shared food with one another but also worked to change the social structures that trap people in poverty.

BASE COMMUNITIES: WHERE NO ONE WALKS ALONE

The skepticism that some of the Saint Francis students expressed about their ability to affect the world is not uncommon; people often assume that only those with a lot of money or political influence have the power to change the world.

Fortunately, many Latin Americans have shown that even those without economic or political power can affect their world if they combine their power through cooperation. For more than four decades, poor Latin Americans have been doing just that by gathering together in thousands of small Christian groups called basic ecclesial communities.

Basic ecclesial communities (or base communities) are typically composed of fifteen to twenty families, usually from very poor areas. They are called *basic* because, aside from families, they are the smallest unit of the church; *ecclesial* simply means "of the church." Base communities meet several times a week to hear the Scriptures, to discuss the problems they face in society, and to find solutions to those problems through the inspiration of the Gospel.

Base ecclesial communities nourish their life together by celebrating the Eucharist, studying the Scriptures, sharing meals, and working for justice.

The life of a base community is nourished by celebrating the word of God, both in liturgy and in reflection on the Scriptures. But base communities do not keep the new life of the Gospel and the Eucharist to themselves; they cooperate to bring that life to the community. Their action might be as simple as that of the slum dwellers of Cuernavaca, Mexico, who worked to clean and beautify their neighborhood so that it would reflect their human dignity. Or it might mean working to change unjust political structures—even at the risk of death. Whatever they do, base communities act together for the common good, as one organizer from the Philippines describes:

A few weeks ago a man walked in all the way from Na-Salayan, which is about ten kilometers away, carrying his wife on his back. His small children walked alongside him, one of them carrying the baby. His wife was so far gone with tuberculosis that she was only bones. He told me that for a year she had not been able to sleep well. They had no pillow, so at night when they laid down, he would stretch out his arm and she would lie on it the whole night. If Na-Salayan had had a Christian community, that man would not have walked in alone. The men of the community would have carried his wife in a baby's hammock, the women would have looked after the children, and the community health committee would have looked for medicines for the sick woman and told us about her condition months ago. You have a Christian community when you can lie down at night knowing that in your village no one is sick who is not being attended to, no one is persecuted who is not being helped, no one is lonely who is not being visited. (Adapted from Hebblethwaite, *Base Communities,* page 108) ◉

If Na-Salayan had had **a Christian community,** that man would not have walked in alone.

have respected our work. Five-Two is not a social-aid fund but a work of consciousness-raising. Dona Hebe could have helped, but without the TV cameras."

Youth leader Augusto Brito added: "Our plan is to become aware of the reasons for unemployment and at the same time show solidarity for our unemployed companions. No one here is giving alms. If we had accepted those donations we would have been prostituting Project Five-Two."

Dona Hebe would not listen to their explanations. For her, charity meant sending a ton of food to the needy and then broadcasting the scene nationwide as an example for kind hearts to follow. Her idea of charity did not include the type of social action that Project Five-Two advocated.

Assistance might relieve the effects of unjust social structures, but it does not touch the causes. A ton of food from the elite distributed to a handful of families crushed at the bottom does not change the structure of the pyramid. But when that handful at the bottom prays, reflects, acts, and moves together for the common good, the pyramid begins to sway. (Hebblethwaite, *Base Communities,* pages 83–86)

Solidarity: Partnership and commitment

Why would the project leaders reject the television host's help? From their point of view, her actions did not suggest a desire to enter into solidarity with poor people. The television host's actions seemed to say to the unemployed, "You are *so* lucky to have me as a friend; what would you be without me?" But real friendship is a two-way street in which both sides benefit. A true friend doesn't act as if she's doing the other person a favor by offering her friendship.

Solidarity, on the other hand, acknowledges the interdependence of human relationships. Poor people may depend on rich people for assistance—but the economic power of rich people comes in part from poor people. Therefore, the rich are not being extra generous by helping the poor; rather, the rich are only giving the poor what justice says is rightfully theirs. Besides, the interdependent nature of relationships means that when poor and oppressed people are helped, ultimately *all* people benefit, including rich and powerful people. Rather than viewing assistance for poor people as an optional favor, solidarity

Solidarity is the key to overcoming unjust social structures.

✳ *Student art:* ". . . Do What Is Just and Right." Linocut; Jane Richardson, Saint Agnes Academy, Memphis, Tennessee

 Write a letter to either the TV host or the Project Five-Two leaders offering your opinion and advice about the situation. Be prepared to discuss your perspectives in class.

says, "We're in this together: your grief is my grief, your joy is my joy."

In rejecting the host's aid, the project leaders were calling rich people to make a fundamental change in the way they related to poor people: to go beyond a superficial, one-way relationship and enter into a life-giving relationship of mutual respect. They were calling for a basic change in social structures —a change the television host apparently was not willing to make.

Acting in Love

Solidarity is the key to overcoming unjust social structures. But remember that those structures don't just happen; they are the result of human choices, whether or not these choices are intentional. Attempts to change unjust social structures often meet with economic, political, or even violent resistance from those who benefit from them. How should those who work for justice respond to such resistance?

One option would be to take a power-over approach: terrorists, for example, use fear and violence to bring about social change. But the Christian justice tradition takes a power-with approach. That approach is grounded in the belief that, as Jesus announced, "the kingdom of God is among you" (Luke 17:21)—God's love has already overcome injustice through Jesus. God's love, not violence, is the source of all power. Although the human instinct is to fight one's enemies in order to defeat and dominate them, the way of Jesus is to love one's enemies in a way that brings them into God's Reign.

"Love your enemies"

The commandment to love one's enemies has long been considered one of the most challenging aspects of the Gospel. Much of this teaching is collected in the Sermon on the Mount (Matthew 5:1—7:29; a shorter version is Luke 6:20–49). You are probably familiar with the following passage:

> "You have heard that it was said, 'You shall love your neighbor and hate your enemy.' But I say to you, Love your enemies and pray for those who persecute you, so that you may be children of your Father in heaven; for he makes his sun rise on the evil and on the good, and sends rain on the righteous and on the unrighteous. For if you love those who love you, what reward do you have? . . . And if you greet only your brothers and sisters, what more are you doing than others? Do not even the Gentiles do the same? Be perfect, therefore, as your heavenly Father is perfect. (Matthew 5:43–48)

Here is another way of stating Jesus' message: In the world created by humans, it is ordinary to love our friends and family while shunning or hurting our enemies. But the world that Jesus envisions—the Kingdom of God—is different. *Everyone* is invited into the Kingdom, even people we might despise. God gives good things (like sun and rain) to everyone, regardless of whether they are just or unjust. So we should do no less than what God does: we should respond with love even to those who promote injustice. R

R Think about who your "enemy" is—perhaps someone you don't like or have been hurt by. Without naming the person, brainstorm a list of things that you could potentially do that would be good for him or her. Then write a short reflection: Would you be willing to take any of the actions you listed? If so, how might "loving your enemy" change each of you? If not, what would need to change before you could take any of the actions?

Is Jesus suggesting that we must accept and even encourage injustice, or "be nice" to those who harm others? The Gospels provide a clear answer: we need not choose between justice and love; rather, like Jesus, we can be committed to both. Throughout the Gospels, Jesus' commitment to the truth of God's love for all people leads him consistently and boldly to challenge injustice whenever he encounters it.

Challenging injustice is not inconsistent with loving those who are responsible for that injustice. Love is not always the same as "being nice." For example, taking the car keys away from a drunk friend would be a better way of loving her than avoiding a confrontation by letting her drive drunk, because, ultimately, taking away the keys could save her life.

Similarly, challenging the unjust actions of an enemy calls him to respect his own life and dignity. When an enemy is challenged in love, the ultimate goal is not to defeat him or have power over him. Rather, the goal of action based in love is to restore the enemy's relationships—with his own dignity, with other people, and with God. ᔡ

M. K. Gandhi: A model for acting in love

Is Jesus' teaching practical in the real world? Jesus does not promise that his followers won't suffer—he himself was crucified, after all, and thousands of Christians have died in the pursuit of justice since then. Still, those who have followed Jesus' teaching have won freedom and justice for millions of people throughout the world.

Perhaps no one has taken Jesus' instruction to love the enemy more seriously than the Hindu spiritual leader **Mohandas Karamchand Gandhi** (1869–1948). Gandhi developed his own ideas about how to act on Jesus' teaching—and when he put those ideas into action, he and his followers won India's freedom from the British after more than twenty-five years of struggle. His approach to loving the enemy has been imitated by many others since then, including the leaders of the U.S. civil rights movement.

Gandhi believed that all aspects of life should be guided by the principle that nothing is more important than respect for human life and dignity. That principle had two important implications for how people ought to live, Gandhi said. At a minimum, it meant liv-

"Be the change you want,"
Gandhi said.

As part of his long, nonviolent campaign to free India from British rule, Gandhi led a two-hundred-mile march to the seashore in 1930. There, he and his followers defied British law by making salt from seawater.

ᔡ Write a script for a skit, or create one with some of your classmates to present to the class, about loving one's enemy. The skit should show the events that lead up to the conflict and the result afterward.

ing nonviolently: never harming the life or dignity of another person—not even hating an unjust enemy. Fighting an unjust enemy in ways that harm her life and dignity is just another kind of injustice, according to Gandhi.

Gandhi also thought that people should respect human life and dignity by refusing to cooperate with anything that harms it. Recall that injustice doesn't just happen, it arises from the ways people choose to use their power. Gandhi believed that if enough people refuse to cooperate with injustice, then it will not have the power to exist. People should not live as if injustice is inevitable. "Be the change you want," Gandhi said. If people live out their vision for justice as if it were already a reality, then they will soon find it becoming a reality. ✝

Gandhi's approach, which is often called **nonviolent non-cooperation**, led him to organize strikes, boycotts, and acts of **civil disobedience**—intentionally breaking laws that are unjust—during India's long struggle against British rule. Ultimately, India won its freedom, largely without using violence against the British.

Fighting the Nazis with the power of truth and love

If it is difficult to imagine how the principles of Jesus and Gandhi could work in the real world, consider how the people of Norway resisted the Nazis during World War II. Although the Norwegians' armed resistance failed to prevent the Nazis from conquering their country, the principles of Jesus' teaching prevented the Nazis from conquering the Norwegians' dignity. As you read the following story, notice the ways people respected human life and dignity:

The Nazis conquered Norway in June 1940, after two months of armed resistance. They immediately disbanded the parliament, outlawed all but fascist political parties, and installed Vidkun Quisling, a Norwegian fascist, as head of state. Quisling abolished the constitution and all elections. Then he issued a series of decrees demanding that all teachers train their students in the ideology of fascism. Students were ordered to join a fascist youth movement, and teachers were ordered to join a fascist union headed by the military police.

The teachers refused. They agreed on common guidelines: do not obey government orders that conflict with conscience; do not teach Nazi propaganda; do not cooperate with fascist organizations. Within weeks, twelve thousand of Norway's fourteen thousand teachers had refused to join the fascist union, and instead signed a statement declaring that Quisling's orders were against conscience and therefore should not be obeyed. Massive numbers of

The nonviolent non-cooperation of Norwegians foiled Vidkun Quisling and Nazi leaders.

✝ Look again at the vision for a just world that you developed in activity I. What would it mean for you to "be the change you want" in order to bring the world closer to your vision?

students refused to join the youth movement. More than two hundred thousand parents and all of Norway's Lutheran bishops wrote letters of protest to Quisling. When the few fascist teachers attempted to hold classes, students refused to attend.

In exasperation, the government closed the schools. Teachers responded by holding classes in their homes. Thirteen hundred teachers were arrested and sent to concentration camps in northern Norway. Months later, when the schools reopened, the remaining teachers still refused to join the fascist union. They read a letter to their students that said: "The teacher's vocation is not only to give children knowledge; teachers must also teach their pupils to believe in and uphold truth and justice. Therefore, teachers cannot, without betraying their calling, teach anything that violates their conscience. That, I promise you, I shall not do."

The Gestapo spread a rumor that if the teachers did not give in, their arrested colleagues would be killed. After a tremendous struggle of conscience, the teachers decided to continue the resistance. In response, Quisling sent the arrested teachers to a concentration camp above the Arctic Circle. As trainloads of teachers passed through the mountains, students stood at the stations and sang patriotic songs to encourage them.

Although two of them died in the freezing camp, the teachers refused to back down, and their courage inspired the nation. Finally, in November 1942, Quisling released the arrested teachers, who returned home to triumphal processions. "You teachers have destroyed everything for me," an enraged Quisling told them in a speech. (Adapted from Sider and Taylor, *Nuclear Holocaust and Christian Hope*, pages 238–241) ⑾

17. Explain the difference between direct action and social action. Why are both necessary for justice?
18. What does it mean to act for justice in solidarity?
19. How does action based in love confront those who promote injustice?
20. Summarize Gandhi's principle of nonviolent non-cooperation.

 In their confrontation with the Nazis, how did the Norwegians' actions respect human life and dignity through solidarity, love, and non-violent non-cooperation?

⑾ Suppose the Nazis had indeed killed all the teachers because of their nonviolent non-cooperation. Would their nonviolent resistance have been worth dying for? Would it have been better if they had died fighting? Or should they have not resisted at all? Explain your answer.

Justice Is a Journey

The summary of the three basic steps of the circle of faith-in-action at the beginning of this chapter mentioned that the circle does not end with action. That is because action deepens our awareness, leading to a new analysis of the situation and new possibilities for action. Their service at the soup kitchen made some of the Saint Francis students more aware of the causes of poverty, and that deeper awareness led them to another kind of action, demonstrating for more affordable housing. **V**

The call to justice is a call to an ongoing journey. Like Moses and the Israelites, God calls us to journey from a land of oppression and death to a land of justice and new life. God does not promise that it will be easy, however, or that we will not get lost along the way—the Israelites learned that soon enough, as has anyone else who has dared to make the journey since then.

Why make the journey, then? Why respond to the call? Those who have gone before us report that although they may have begun the journey thinking that they were leading others to a better life, in fact the journey brought them to a fuller, richer life as well. One high school student taking a justice course put it this way: Beginning the journey toward justice, she said, "has helped me to see that *God is so real.*" Like so many others, she found that the journey deepened her awareness of the reality of the Reign of God, a reality she was entering through her deepened commitment to the good of others. For wherever people work for one another's good in love, there they will encounter the very real, very awesome presence of God.

The call to justice is a call to an ongoing journey.

A candlelight vigil at Hong Kong University recalls the nonviolent student demonstrators who were killed by the Chinese military at Tiananmen Square in 1989.

V Identify an opportunity for justice from the relationship map you developed for activity M. Outline a plan to work for that justice issue, using the circle of faith-in-action as a guide. Under each step, list specifically what you would do and how you would do it.

4 CHOOSING LIFE

~~death~~
life & healing

children die
No more
women cry

Responding
to abortion and capital punishment

In This Chapter . . .

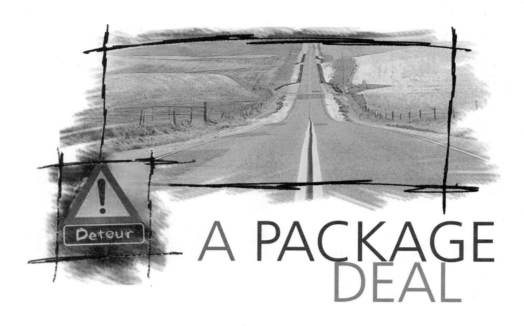

A PACKAGE
DEAL

During my sophomore year of college I started a new relationship. It was a casual relationship, so I was not prepared for the night when it became sexual. I tried not to worry; lots of people had sex without getting pregnant, I told myself. That night I was not one of them.

I went to the campus health center thinking I was sick. After the physician's assistant ran a pregnancy test, he said only two things: "This test is positive," then after a brief pause, "Are you going to terminate the pregnancy?"

Pregnant! I was stunned, not only by the news but also by the abruptness of the decision I was being asked to make. There was no suggestion of talking to my boyfriend or my family, no offer of counseling, no information about prenatal care, no presumption of any outcome but abortion.

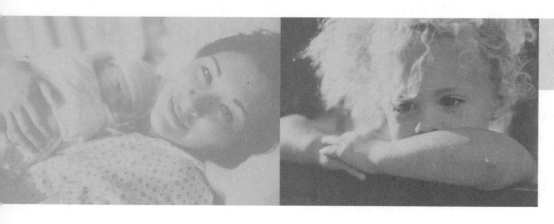

"No," I replied, instinctively. "I guess I'll have to put the baby up for adoption."

I developed my view about life issues in high school. I knew I was solidly against all kinds of killing, abortion included. My parents' involvement in the pro-life movement also left me with some awareness of the alternatives that were available. Yet at that moment, I felt very much alone.

Then the surprises really began. My boyfriend, upon hearing the news, asked if I was going to have an abortion.

"Absolutely not," I said.

"Good," he replied, "because I don't believe in that." He proposed marriage, but I refused; I believe that a baby is the wrong reason to get married. Halfway through the pregnancy he informed me that he could not have anything more to do with me or the baby.

My parents, who I thought would be very angry, were instantly supportive and non-judgmental. "We'll do whatever we can to help you," they assured me. My friends did not quite know what to do. They had never known a pregnant student on campus. And it was clear from the absence of support available to me that the university administration was ill prepared to deal with this situation. I ended up taking a medical leave of absence, shortly after which David was born and I became a single mother at nineteen.

With the help of a supportive counselor, I ultimately decided to keep and raise my child. I set out to be that apparent rarity in American society: a successful single woman raising to work (even though without a degree I would scarcely be able to support us).

Finally, shortly before my son's third birthday and with help from my parents and extended family, I completed my college degree, found a good job, and set up a household. Finding decent child care was a task, but I was lucky to find a wonderful, loving woman who cared for my son for what I could afford to pay her. I even managed a social life, always with the understanding that my child came first for me and that we were a "package deal." As I learned the real story about child support, I researched and used the services of my state's Child Support Enforcement department to win a court order for monetary support and comprehensive health insurance coverage for my son.

It has not always been easy, but my son and I have a pretty good life. I am convinced that my support network is the only difference between me and the young women who, in desperation, resort to an unwanted abortion, or who struggle to escape poverty, with limited education and fading hope for their and their children's future.

Still, my experiences left me angry with a system that on so many levels continues to abandon women and their children. I had a supportive and life-affirming family—but how many women face only harsh judgment and abandonment? How many women must make their pregnancy decision based on what few resources (if any) their college or workplace provides for parents? How many

---

It has not always been easy, but my son and I have a pretty good life.

---

a happy and well-adjusted child. It was a struggle. I applied for and received limited welfare benefits for my son while I finished school, in spite of attempts by the welfare department to force me to leave school and go woman-headed households get caught in a welfare trap that offers them no future and no way out? How many women let their children's fathers off the hook for support, believing they must go it alone?

After college I became involved with an organization called Feminists for Life. I was watching a television talk show about abortion, and a member of the audience was asking the panelist from Feminists for Life, "How can you call yourself a feminist when the basis of feminism is reproductive rights?" To which the woman from Feminists for Life replied, "No, the basis of feminism is that women are people." This is the philosophy of Feminists for Life, that all people, born and unborn, should be treated with the same respect.

Now, one of the things Feminists for Life does is a college outreach program aimed at helping women who face the same difficulties I did. One of the features of the program is a pregnancy forum, which brings together students, the administration, and faculty to examine what pregnancy resources are available and what needs are not being met on campus. Before the forum, the administration may not be aware of the issues that pregnant students face, and the students may not be aware of the support the administration is able to give. With programs like these, we hope to raise awareness on campuses about unexpected pregnancy, so colleges can become sources of support to pregnant students. (Adapted from Jefferson, "Single Motherhood") ⓖ **A**

Groups like Feminists for Life encourage social changes that provide pregnant women with better support.

A Question at the Heart of Justice

When Kelly Jefferson learned that she was pregnant, she faced a fundamental question of justice: How much am I willing to give for the sake of another person's life?

For millions of women like Kelly, it is a particularly difficult and poignant question. But it is not only pregnant women who face this question. It is a question that all people must answer at one time or another. Kelly, for instance, was not the only one confronted with that question as a result of her pregnancy. The physician's assistant, her boyfriend, her family members, the university, her friends, the welfare system, the legal system—all these people and social structures had to decide, How much do we value this new human life?

It is not just an individual question but a social one. Nor is it a question raised by the abortion issue alone; it is central to all justice issues because the heart of justice is all about making it possible for people to live a full and dignified life. The way society answers the question, then, is a good measure of its potential to do justice.

In this chapter, we consider the value of human life by focusing on two issues in which the life of some people is perceived to be in conflict with the well-being of other people: abortion and capital punishment. **B**

A If you knew a young woman who found herself unexpectedly pregnant, what would her primary concerns be? Create a list of at least three concerns and bring it to class for discussion.

B Reflect on this: How much would I be willing to give to save another person's life? Would who the person was or the circumstances of the situation affect your response?

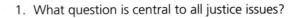

For Review

1. What question is central to all justice issues?

In Depth

2. Name the social structures that affected Kelly's ability to choose a good life for her son and herself. Who had power in Kelly's situation, and how was it used?

Life: A Right for All?

As you probably know, the Catholic church opposes abortion; less well known is that the church strongly opposes capital punishment too. The church bases its opposition to these practices on the principle of respect for the life and dignity of human beings. The right to life is the most basic human right, the church says, because without life it is impossible for someone to have other human rights.

Not everyone agrees that all people have the right to life, however. Abortion and capital punishment have been legal in the United States since the 1970s. People offer many reasons for supporting abortion rights and capital punishment; often these practices are viewed as necessary to overcome injustice. Even if we disagree with the practices themselves, solidarity calls us to seriously consider the injustices they are suggested to overcome. **C**

Choices: Abortion or Birth?

In 1973, the U.S. Supreme Court ruled that women have a right to privacy that includes the right to abortion from conception until birth. Today more than 1.3 million abortions are performed every year in the United States. Before considering the case for protecting new human life, let's briefly look at the reasons some people say abortion should be legal.

C What kinds of ground rules do you think are important for having open, respectful discussions of justice issues in class? Bring your ideas to class.

Few of its supporters deny that abortion ends a human life, because that is a well-established fact. But they do argue that the decision about whether that new human life is a *person,* with all the rights that go along with personhood, is the mother's alone.

Supporters of legalized abortion are often concerned about the life and dignity of women. They suggest that to deny women the right to abortion is to deny them the freedom that is a necessary part of human dignity. Moreover, they say that for some women, an unwanted pregnancy and parenthood are obstacles to living a full and dignified life. Following are some of the situations that they say make abortion necessary. D

Rape

Many people who oppose abortion for other reasons would allow it in cases of rape or incest. Consider the case of Lee Ezell:

Lee's alcoholic father was so abusive that her mother fled to another state with Lee and her siblings. Then, when Lee was eighteen and holding down a job, she was raped by a man who worked for the same

Rape violates the dignity of women.

company. A few weeks after the rape, she learned she was pregnant. A friend offered to take her to Mexico for an abortion, because abortion was illegal in the United States at the time.

Though Lee considered it, the prospect was too daunting. When her mother learned of her pregnancy and her decision not to abort, she told Lee to leave home. (Podell, "You Are My Daughter")

The U.S. Justice Department estimates that 310,000 rapes or attempted rapes occur every year, and that 1 percent of pregnancies that end in abortion were the result of rape. Abortion supporters argue that abortion spares women who have been raped from the further trauma of giving birth to the child.

"I thought there's no way I could have this baby"

✴ *Student art:* "The Boxer." Chalk pastel; Eva Drinka, Boylan Catholic High School, Rockford, Illinois

D Briefly state your position on abortion. Then try to describe the position of someone with whom you disagree on the issue.

E What could schools do to support pregnant students or students who are parents? Think about what the administration, teachers, and other students could do. Bring your suggestions to class.

School and career

Some women experience unintended pregnancy as an obstacle to pursuing their educational or career goals. As Kelly Jefferson found, many educational institutions provide little or no support for students who are pregnant or who are parents. Erin McKasy's case is not unusual:

Erin was a junior honors student at Hill-Murray Catholic High School when she became pregnant after a night of heavy drinking. "I thought there's no way I could have this baby," she says. Having a baby would ruin her dreams of going to college. Her mother agreed, and they scheduled an appointment at a local abortion clinic. (Hrbacek, "I Chose Life")

Erin walked out of the abortion clinic without having the abortion, but many young women do not.

Women might also have abortions because they worry that having a child will interrupt their career plans. Sometimes the problem is employer discrimination against pregnant women. For instance, actress Hunter Tylo was fired from her role in TV's *Melrose Place* for not getting an abortion when she became pregnant. Unfortunately, such cases are not unusual. ⒠

Poverty

Abortion advocates also argue that abortion is necessary to prevent women from becoming trapped in poverty. The following situation faced by nineteen-year-old Melissa

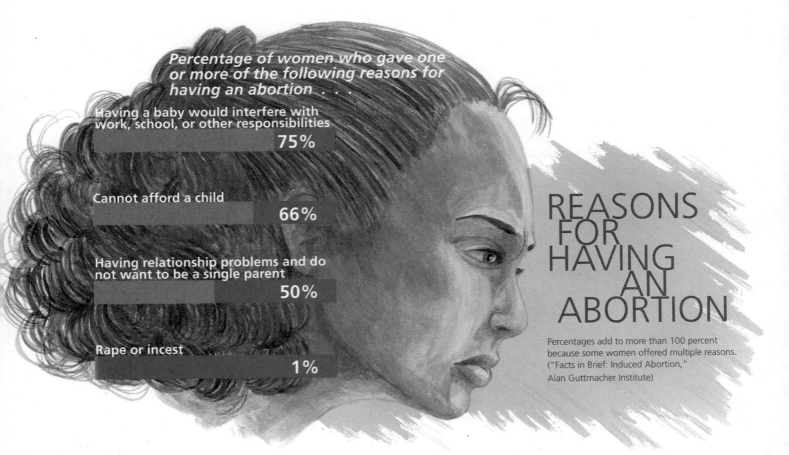

Percentage of women who gave one or more of the following reasons for having an abortion . . .

Having a baby would interfere with work, school, or other responsibilities
75%

Cannot afford a child
66%

Having relationship problems and do not want to be a single parent
50%

Rape or incest
1%

REASONS FOR HAVING AN ABORTION

Percentages add to more than 100 percent because some women offered multiple reasons. ("Facts in Brief: Induced Abortion," Alan Guttmacher Institute)

Rodriguez and her son is a good example of the difficulties that often accompany single parenthood:

> I get free medical for him, and I get $400 a month, and about $130 worth of food stamps. It's the welfare program. And even though it sounds like a lot, it ain't much. You know. I mean there's bills gotta get paid, rent's still gotta get paid . . . $400 disappears in like, a week. I had me a little job. I was a secretary, but it was $6 an hour, so that's like just barely living. You know, it was hard, it was really hard, and I be in school [at a community college] 'til sometimes 5, 6 o'clock and then I would drop him off at the babysitter at like six, and I would go to work from like seven to ten at night. I was barely spending time with him. Barely. (Rodriguez, "Raising Issaiah")

A study of women receiving public assistance in New Jersey found that 71 percent were opposed to abortion. Yet the rate of abortion among these women was more than six times the rate for the whole state. Eighty-five percent of these women who had had abortions said that "not having adequate finances to raise the child" was their primary reason for having an abortion. They felt their financial situation left them no choice. ✒

"I'm just not ready"

These are just a few of the reasons women offer for seeking an abortion. But perhaps the most common reason is simply a feeling of not being prepared to become a mother, or to have another child.

Crime and Punishment

Society debates the question How much is human life worth? not only about its youngest members but about its most violent members as well. In 1976, the U.S. Supreme Court reinstated capital punishment, often called the death penalty. Between 1976 and 2000, more than 630 people were executed. Supporters of capital punishment do not deny that those being executed are human beings—at least not from an objective, biological point of view. But they make two basic arguments to justify their position:

- Certain crimes are so violent that in committing them, the offenders basically forfeit their human rights, including the right to life.
- Certain crimes harm society so much that the only way of restoring justice is to make the offender experience the same level of harm that he or she caused society.

Remember when you were a small child and someone hit you? Probably your first impulse was to hit the person back. That same impulse is played out on a social scale when someone seriously harms human life. This approach to criminal justice, in which the emphasis is on hurting the offender, is known as **retributive justice.** "An eye for an eye and a tooth for a tooth" is the slogan of retributive justice. ✒

Loss and anger

Perhaps the most basic reason for supporting capital punishment is simply a gut-level reaction to horrifyingly violent crimes against the innocent. Reflect on your own gut-level reaction to the following cases:

✒ Where could young people facing an unexpected pregnancy find help in your school and community? What kind of help is available? Work with others to find as much information as possible. Write a brief report, including your evaluation of whether enough help is being provided.

✒ Find an article in a newspaper or magazine about a criminal trial for a serious crime. Identify attitudes of retributive justice in the article—perhaps in quotes or in the author's comments. Write a brief reflection about whether you think those attitudes are justified.

- In the middle of the night, seven-year-old Susie Jaeger is kidnapped from the tent in which she is sleeping with family members during a camping trip. It is later learned that she was held captive for a week by a known sex offender, then strangled to death.
- Two teenagers—a couple who were engaged to be married—are shot to death while they happen to be in a park during a drug deal gone bad. A twenty-seven-year-old man named Anthony Porter is charged with the crime.
- Paul Hines, a twenty-one-year-old college student, agrees to give seventeen-year-old Robert Charles White a ride to his home, where Robert says his mother is deathly ill. But when they arrive at the apartment complex, Robert attempts to steal Paul's car, and shoots and kills Paul in the process.

For the victims' families and friends, a storm of excruciating emotions—fury, despair, grief—follow in the wake of the loss. Often those emotions are channeled into the legal process of convicting the offender. That was the case for Thomas Ann Hines, the mother of the college student who was killed by Robert White:

> When the medical examiner's office called in the middle of the night to inform her that her son had been found shot dead, the words hit hard. A single mother with a scarred and haunting past of abuse, Thomas Ann had focused all the love she could muster on her only child. "All right," she remembers thinking. "I can do this. . . . I can bury my son. But when I'm done, I don't want to live anymore."
>
> First she went to Austin, Texas, where the murder investigation was taking place. "Why would anyone shoot him?" Thomas Ann asked the detective. "Paul was everybody's friend." She soon learned that the killer was Robert White, a seventeen-year-old drug dealer who wanted out of Austin fast—he believed the police were about to arrest him, and he had too many felonies on his record. Near a video arcade, he spotted Paul sitting alone in his car.
>
> Throughout the investigation, Thomas Ann hoped Robert would receive the death penalty. Although he was convicted, he was too young to receive the death penalty. Instead he was sentenced to thirteen years in prison and then probation until he was forty. After Robert was led away in handcuffs and the courtroom emptied, Thomas Ann had never felt so alone in her life.
>
> Thomas Ann prepared to end her own life, buying a one-way ticket to Jamaica, where she planned to walk into the water one calm night and not come back. (Adapted from Wilson, "Crying for Justice") 𝓗

"An eye for an eye and a tooth for a tooth" is the slogan of **retributive justice.**

𝓗 How do you think you would respond if you were involved in one of the situations mentioned in this chapter? What would need to happen for you to be able to forgive the attacker?

3. Why is the right to life the most basic human right?
4. Describe at least three difficulties that cause women to seek abortions.
5. Define *retributive justice*.

Compassion for All

Clearly, some tough situations lie at the root of society's support for capital punishment and abortion. These difficult situations cannot be dismissed or ignored. But Christians are called to have compassion for *all people*—including those who are not yet born and those who are guilty of crimes. Two convictions, human life is sacred and all human beings are equal, lie at the heart of the Catholic approach to issues involving human life.

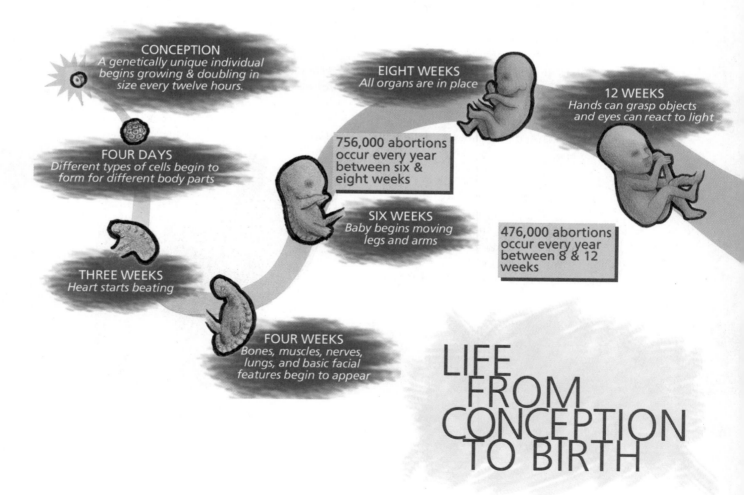

CONCEPTION
A genetically unique individual begins growing & doubling in size every twelve hours.

FOUR DAYS
Different types of cells begin to form for different body parts

THREE WEEKS
Heart starts beating

FOUR WEEKS
Bones, muscles, nerves, lungs, and basic facial features begin to appear

EIGHT WEEKS
All organs are in place

12 WEEKS
Hands can grasp objects and eyes can react to light

756,000 abortions occur every year between six & eight weeks

SIX WEEKS
Baby begins moving legs and arms

476,000 abortions occur every year between 8 & 12 weeks

LIFE FROM CONCEPTION TO BIRTH

Human life is sacred. Each human life is sacred because it comes from God, it is always loved by God, and it is meant to return to God. "God alone is the Lord of life from its beginning until its end" (*Catechism of the Catholic Church,* 2258). Respect for the sacredness of human life and respect for human dignity are closely linked, as this passage from *The Church in the Modern World (Gaudium et Spes)* indicates:

> Whatever is opposed to life itself, such as any type of murder, genocide, abortion, euthanasia, or wilful self-destruction . . . whatever insults human dignity, such as subhuman living conditions, arbitrary imprisonment, deportation, slavery, prostitution, the selling of women and children; as well as disgraceful working conditions, where [people] are treated as mere instruments of gain, rather than as free and responsible persons; all these things and others of their like are infamies indeed. They poison human society, but they do more harm to those who practise them than those who suffer from the injury. (27) |

All human beings are equal. Because all people are created in the image of God, all people have equal dignity and an equal claim to fundamental human rights (adapted from *The Church in the Modern World,* 29).

That all people have equal dignity and an equal right to life is the foundation of Christian justice, as we will see throughout this course. For the moment, let's see how these beliefs apply to the tough issues of abortion and capital punishment. ⟋

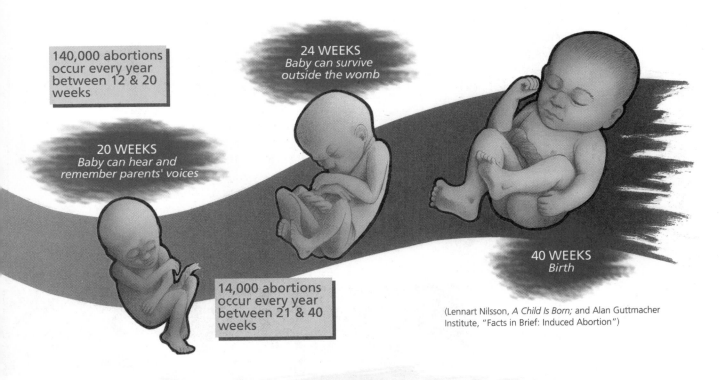

140,000 abortions occur every year between 12 & 20 weeks

20 WEEKS
Baby can hear and remember parents' voices

24 WEEKS
Baby can survive outside the womb

40 WEEKS
Birth

14,000 abortions occur every year between 21 & 40 weeks

(Lennart Nilsson, *A Child Is Born;* and Alan Guttmacher Institute, "Facts in Brief: Induced Abortion")

| What do you think the church means when it says these actions "do more harm to those who practise them than to those who suffer from the injury"?

⟋ Look through the Bible to find a story in which people are understood as sacred and as loved equally in the eyes of God. Bring your story to class for discussion.

Even the Youngest Have the Right to Live

As stated earlier, few people question whether human life begins at **conception**—the moment when the genetic material from a woman's ovum and a man's sperm fuse, creating a genetically unique individual, who immediately begins to grow. From the very start, the new being has all the genetic characteristics—hair color, skin tone, gender, height, and so on—that make her one of a kind.

Supporters of legalized abortion often argue that this new human life is not really a human person because she lacks most of the physical characteristics we associate with personhood. In fact, many of these characteristics develop quickly (see chart, "Life from Conception Until Birth"). Even so, the claim that new human beings are not really persons suggests that personhood—and all the basic human rights that come with it—depends on having certain characteristics. In the case of the person who has not yet been born, those characteristics are said to be age, size, or physical development. Such discrimination is no different from discrimination based on other arbitrary characteristics, such as skin color or gender.

The value of a human being does not depend on his state of development. You were not less human as a baby than you are now. Erin McKasy recognized the humanity of her child when she sneaked a peek at the ultrasound while the abortion technician was out of the room: "I saw the baby and I said, 'There's no way.' After that, I went to the counselor and said, 'I don't think I can go through with this.'" Now, with the help of family and friends, she is raising her son, Cameron, while she attends college.

Neither does the value of human life depend on the circumstances surrounding it. While the evil of rape cannot be overstated, the child who is conceived by rape has the same dignity and rights as any other child. Suppose, for instance, that Lee Ezell had aborted the child who was conceived when she was raped. The abortion would not have erased the rape, but it would have ended the life of her daughter, Julie Makimaa, and all the goodness that would come from that life:

> Lee moved to California and was taken in by a couple she met at church. She decided to place her baby with an adoptive family. After she gave birth to her daughter, she went on to college and was eventually married.

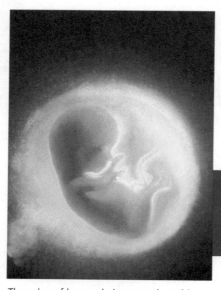

The value of human beings—such as this eight-week-old fetus—does not depend on their physical characteristics or the circumstances surrounding their life.

"God alone is the Lord of life from its beginning until its end."

Years later, Lee's daughter—with the support of her husband and adoptive parents—undertook a search for her birth mother. Twenty-one years to the day after Lee gave birth, she was reunited with her daughter, Julie—and Julie learned about the circumstances of her conception for the first time.

"I asked her, 'Why would you even want to see me, then? How could you want to even be a part of my life?'" recalled Julie. "And she said, 'You know, you don't remind me of the assault at all. You remind me of the good thing that happened out of that tragedy that I went through. And you are my daughter, and I want to have a relationship with you.'

"Most people do not think, 'Well, I could have been aborted,' but I do think of how easily my life could have been ended. . . . Sometimes when my mother and I are together, we just sort of look at each other and know that our story could have been so different, and what a tragedy that would have been. I wasn't planned, but I was loved.

"My mother was a victim of an assault, but she did not choose to victimize me. I was not given the death penalty for the crime of my father. I was given the greatest gift that any of us could give—life." (Podell, "You Are My Daughter")

In opposing abortion, Christians cannot ignore the hardship and suffering that pregnancy causes for many women. But the church calls us to respond to those difficult situations with love, not violence. ✶

All people are created in the image of God.

✶ *Student art:* "Portrait of a Baby." Colored pencil; Sara Berrenson, Notre Dame High School, Sherman Oaks, California

✶ Rape is one of the worst violations any person could endure. Together with some of your classmates, plan a liturgy or prayer service for women who have been raped. What music, prayers, gestures, and symbols could you use? Write down your plan, along with your thoughts about how people in the church could help such women on a practical level.

ABORTION AND MERCY

While the church calls us to **defend the lives** of unborn babies, it also calls us to **respect and care for** the many women who have had abortions. Because our society often does not support families, and especially single mothers, many of these women do not feel they have any other choice. "There is a tremendous sadness and loneliness in the cry, 'A woman's right to choose,'" writes Frederica Mathewes-Green. "No one wants an abortion as she wants an ice cream cone or a Porsche. She wants an abortion as an animal, caught in a trap, wants to gnaw off his own leg" ("Abortion and the Search for Common Ground").

Many women feel tremendous shame, guilt, and grief following abortion—all of which is made worse if they feel the need to hide their emotions. The church has responded to the grief of these women by offering parish-based programs like Project Rachel, through which trained counselors can help women to heal. The process often involves, among other things, writing a letter to the child and reconciling with God.

In *The Gospel of Life,* Pope John Paul II offers this special message to women who have had an abortion:

The Church is aware of the many factors which may have influenced your decision, and she does not doubt that in many cases it was a painful and even shattering decision. The wound in your heart may not yet have healed. Certainly what happened was and remains terribly wrong. But do not give in to discouragement and do not lose hope. Try rather to understand what happened and face it honestly. If you have not already done so, give yourselves over with humility and trust to repentance. The Father of mercies is ready to give you his forgiveness and his peace in the Sacrament of Reconciliation. You will come to understand that nothing is definitively lost and you will also be able to ask forgiveness from your child, who is now living in the Lord. With the friendly and expert help and advice of other people, and as a result of your own painful experience, you can be among the most eloquent defenders of everyone's right to life. Through your commitment to life, whether by accepting the birth of other children or by welcoming and caring for those most in need of someone to be close to them, you will become promoters of a new way of looking at human life. (99) ●

"No one wants an abortion as she wants an ice cream cone or a Porsche. She wants an abortion as an animal, caught in a trap, wants to gnaw off his own leg."

Criminals: Still Loved by God

The claim that the circumstances surrounding human life do not affect its sacredness applies to criminals too. The U.S. Catholic bishops sum up the church's opposition to capital punishment in one sentence: "The antidote to violence is love, not more violence" (*Living the Gospel of Life,* 22). In addition, two other teachings shed light on why the church opposes capital punishment:

- God never stops loving us, even when we reject that love through sin. So although we harm our own dignity when we sin, that dignity—and the right to life that goes with it—is not taken away (based on *The Gospel of Life [Evangelium Vitae],* 9).
- The primary aim of punishment is to heal the harm that was caused through the sin or criminal action. Punishment also serves to protect society from harmful behavior, and to help the guilty person correct his or her behavior (adapted from *Catechism,* 2266). Revenge is not the goal of punishment.

Traditionally, Catholic social teaching has allowed for the execution of violent criminals

Even as criminals are punished, their life and dignity must be respected. Computer and language training will help these prisoners live a better life when they are released.

"if this is the only possible way of effectively defending human lives against the unjust aggressor" (*Catechism,* 2267). However, the church notes that instances where the death penalty is the only way of defending the common good of the community "'are very rare, if not practically non-existent'" (2267). For this reason, the U.S. Catholic bishops have been calling for an end to capital punishment since the early 1970s. And note the following words of Pope John Paul II, speaking at a Mass in Saint Louis in 1999:

> The dignity of human life must never be taken away, even in the case of someone who has done great evil. Modern society has the means of protecting itself without definitively denying criminals the chance to reform. I renew the appeal I made most recently at Christmas for a consensus to end the death penalty, which is both cruel and unnecessary. (Quoted in "A Good Friday Appeal to End the Death Penalty")

Following this statement, the pope made a personal appeal to the governor of Missouri to spare the life of Darrell Mease, who had been convicted of the drug-related murder of three people, and condemned to die. The governor heeded the pope's appeal by commuting the sentence to life in prison without parole.

None of us is completely innocent. Because all people sin, all people bring death into the world. The mercy the church calls for society to show its most violent criminals reflects the generous mercy that God constantly shows each of us. *L*

L Think about a time when you were forgiven for something harmful that you did. What did it feel like to be forgiven?

A flawed punishment

Another reason to oppose capital punishment is because it reflects the flaws of our criminal-justice system. For instance, blacks are about four times as likely as whites to be sentenced to death for similar crimes, and 90 percent of death row inmates could not afford to hire a lawyer when they were tried. Sr. Helen Prejean, whose work with death row inmates was portrayed in the film *Dead Man Walking,* tells of a case that illustrates the flaws of the criminal-justice system:

> For the first time, I believe I befriended a truly innocent man on death row. . . . This man, Dobie Williams, a 38-year-old indigent [totally impoverished] black man, I believe, was railroaded to death for the death of a white victim in a small, racist Southern town. He fit the death row profile perfectly, especially in the South: a poor black man accused of killing a white woman, with an all-white jury as the constitutionally guaranteed "jury of his peers." He had a terrible defense—no defense. The prosecution got everything they asked for—including Dobie's death last night—after 14 years and 12 death dates and stays of execution. But inside the crucible of this terrible ordeal Dobie grew. He grew in faith, in love, in his ability to communicate and feel tenderness, to give of himself to family and friends, to know and love Christ, who became his rock and his protector even as he climbed onto the gurney and was able to forgive those who had wronged him. (Prejean, "Letter from Death Row")

As a result of the structural injustice of the U.S. criminal-justice system, innocent people are sometimes condemned to die. That was the case with Anthony Porter, the man mentioned earlier who was convicted of murdering the engaged couple:

> Porter, who is black and has an IQ of 51, was two days away from being executed by the state of Illinois when the court delayed the execution. Meanwhile, a team of students from a Northwestern University journalism class investigated Porter's conviction by re-enacting the crime and interviewing witnesses. They found that the facts did not add up, and witnesses to the crime said they were pressured by police to lie. With the new evidence, the students tracked down the most likely suspect, who confessed to the crime on videotape. Anthony Porter was released from death row just a few months after his first execution date. (Adapted from McCormick, "Coming Two Days Shy of Martyrdom")

> "For the first time, I believe I befriended a **truly innocent** man on **death row.**"

Anthony Porter celebrates with the Northwestern University students who proved his innocence and won his release from death row.

Convicted murderer Darrell Mease was spared execution at the request of Pope John Paul II.

Nationwide, sixty-seven death row inmates were cleared of the charges against them between 1985 and 2000.

A "Both-And" Approach

Public debate about abortion and capital punishment is often framed in *either-or* terms, as if we must choose either the life of a baby *or* the well-being of a woman; either the life of a criminal *or* dignity for those harmed by her or him.

We do not need to choose between helping only one group or the other, however. In fact, Christians are called to take a *both-and* approach to these issues—to protect both the well-being of women *and* the well-being of their unborn children, to seek both the well-being of those harmed by crime *and* the well-being of the one who causes that harm. We are called, in other words, to build up a whole "culture of life" that looks out for the well-being of all people.

6. What two convictions lie at the heart of the Catholic approach to issues about human life?
7. Summarize the church's argument for why unborn humans should always have the right to life.
8. For what reasons does Pope John Paul II say capital punishment should be ended?
9. What does it mean to take a both-and approach to abortion and capital punishment?

In a paragraph or two, compare and contrast the issues involved in abortion and capital punishment. How are they similar or different?

 Research the case of someone who is about to be executed or has recently been executed. Find at least four stories about the case, preferably from different sources. Write a two-page report about whether the legal process treated the defendant fairly.

The Gospel of Life

In the Book of Deuteronomy, Moses tells the people of Israel:

> I have set before you life and death, the blessing and the curse. Choose life, then, that you and your descendants may live. (30:19, NAB)

For most people, life over death might appear to be the obvious choice—but the widespread practice of all types of killing, legal and illegal, suggests that the choice is not as simple as it might seem.

Cultures in Conflict: Having Versus Being

What does it mean to "choose life"? In his 1995 encyclical *The Gospel of Life,* Pope John Paul II identifies the ways two different cultures answer that question. Each culture bases its answer on a different understanding of what it means to be fully alive.

- One culture says that we are fully alive when we have what we want.
- The other culture says that we are fully alive when we are true to who we are.

Examining these different worldviews can help us better understand the way our society approaches a wide range of justice issues.

Stockbrokers on the trading floor. Justice calls us to make sure that the pursuit of wealth and power does not become more important than respect for the life and dignity of others.

The culture of death: We are what we have

From the perspective of the first worldview, "choosing life" would appear to be the main message of U.S. culture. Advertisements for soft drinks, beer, shoes, and cars urge us to live life to the fullest—a life of excitement, luxury, and convenience. We are told that we should have what we want because we deserve it. The way to live this abundant life is by buying the products being advertised.

According to this worldview, we are what we have: the more we have—in terms of possessions, abilities, good looks, or power—the more fully human we are. So when we start out in life, we are "less human" because all we "have" is our body, and not much of a body at that. A body or mind flawed by physical or mental disabilities is considered less human still. In this worldview, the soul is not part of what it means to be human, because new life is only the result of a biological process, not a gift from God.

If we are what we have, then being fully alive means having what we want—not just in terms of stuff but also in terms of doing what we want. In this view, the basis of human rights is not the sacredness of life and the dignity of the human person, but the ability of people to get what they want.

The Gospel of Life refers to this worldview as the **culture of death** because the culture views human life as separate from God, who is its source. It is a worldview that leads to death for those who are considered to be less valuable.

- It claims that it is the right of people to have more than they need, even as poverty causes death for other people.
- It views people who cause a burden to others as less worthy of life.

- It views the quality of a life as the only measure of whether it is worth living. As a result, **euthanasia**—the intentional killing of someone whose life is deemed to be no longer worth living—is preferred over a natural death that may involve suffering.

The church is *not* saying that it is wrong to have things or to want an enjoyable life. Wanting a better life becomes a problem only when it is viewed as the *only* goal of life. In the Christian view, choosing life is about much more—it is about choosing love.

N Spend an hour watching TV commercials, or scan the ads in a popular national magazine. How do these advertisements emphasize that you are what you have? Do some ads imply that "being who you are" simply is not good enough?

The culture of life: We are images of God

If we are only what we have, then life can only end in death, because cars, careers, and even "the perfect body" will eventually pass away. But in Christian belief, we are more than what we have. According to the following Bible passage, we are images of God:

God did not make death,
and he does not delight in the death of the
living.
For he created all things so that they might
exist.

. . . .

God created us for incorruption,
and made us in the image of his own
eternity.
(Wisdom of Solomon 1:13–14; 2:23)

We are more than just our bodies; we have souls too. United, our body and soul make us fully human, no matter what we have or look like. Being fully alive means reflecting God by loving God and one another. If we do this, then we are complete; we need nothing more. Even death cannot take life away from us because we share in the resurrected life of Christ.

The Gospel of Life calls this worldview the **culture of life** because it recognizes that all human life comes from God and is meant to return to God. Rooted in love, this worldview brings life to the world:

- It calls people to share what they have with others, especially those who do not have enough to live.
- It views all people as gifts of God, even those who require extra care.
- It sees life as worth living even if it involves suffering, because love can transform suffering into something good.

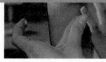

In Christian belief, we are more than what we have.

✴ *Student art:* "Cover Girl." Black-and-white photograph; Lucia Wharton, Pope John XXIII High School, Sparta, New Jersey

Describe someone you know who is true to who she or he is as an image of God. How is she or he more fully alive as a result?

The paschal mystery: A way to life

This last point about suffering is key to a culture of life. Although suffering is not something that God desires for us or that we should seek, it is an inescapable part of life. But how we approach suffering determines whether it deadens us or brings us more fully alive.

If we try to escape suffering in a way that causes suffering or death for others, then part of who we truly are as an image of God dies too. But when we accept suffering in love so that others might live more fully, then, paradoxically, we become more fully alive. This is the paschal mystery of Jesus' cross and Resurrection, a mystery we share when we imitate Jesus' loving self-gift.

The Consistent Life Ethic

All this talk about cultures of life and death might not seem to have much to do with the real-life stories told earlier in this chapter. But, in fact, they do. The social structures that made it difficult for Kelly Jefferson to choose life for herself and her son are rooted in a culture that places little value on those who are poor and powerless. The same culture that placed little value on the life of Kelly's son also placed little value on her ability to live a full and abundant life, because both she and her son were poor and powerless.

Kelly's situation illustrates an important point: Whenever society decides that one person or group is less human than another, or not human at all, it suggests that human dignity is not given by God but depends on the judgment of others. Once society accepts that notion, all people—especially those with less power—become vulnerable. Violating the dignity of women makes it easier to violate the life of their unborn children, and vice versa. Similarly, if we justify executing someone in retaliation for committing murder, then retaliation for other, lesser forms of violence becomes justifiable as well: Why shouldn't a child hit back the person who hit him first?

This is why protecting the life and dignity of any person or group requires that we protect the life and dignity of all people. **Cardinal Joseph Bernardin** of Chicago (1928–1996) called this the **consistent life ethic.** It is also called the **seamless garment,** after Jesus' seamless tunic in John's Gospel account of the Crucifixion. The soldiers could not divide the tunic among themselves by tearing it apart because it was made of a whole cloth, and ripping it would have ruined it. The right to life is the most important human right because all other rights depend on it. That right is most threatened by violence such as abortion, capital punishment, and war. But it is also threatened by *anything* that undermines it. Like the seamless garment that cannot be torn apart, Bernardin argued

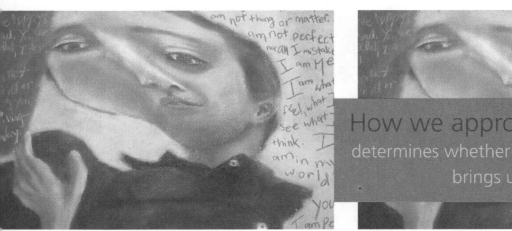

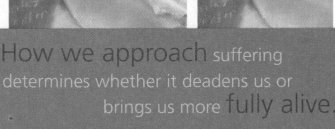

How we approach suffering determines whether it deadens us or brings us more fully alive.

※ *Student art:* Chalk pastel; Michelle Lungin, Notre Dame High School, Sherman Oaks, California

that we cannot "tear apart" the issues of abortion, poverty, capital punishment, racism, war, and other issues that affect human life and dignity:

> If one contends, as we do, that the right of every fetus to be born should be protected . . . , then our moral, political and economic responsibilities do not stop at the moment of birth. Those who defend the right to life of the weakest among us must be equally visible in support of the quality of life of the powerless among us: the old and the young, the hungry and the homeless, the undocumented immigrant and the unemployed worker. . . . Consistency means we cannot have it both ways: We cannot urge a compassionate society and vigorous public policy to protect the lives of the unborn and then argue that compassion and significant public programs on behalf of the needy undermine the moral fiber of the society or are beyond the proper scope of governmental responsibility. ("Cardinal Bernardin's Call for a Consistent Ethic of Life")

The consistent life ethic suggests that far from being in competition with one another, the well-being of each person is really interrelated with the well-being of all other people.

Protecting the life and dignity of **any** person or group **requires** that we protect the life and dignity of **all** people.

Demonstrators promote respect for life by calling for peace in Israel *(left)* and Northern Ireland *(right)*.

For Review

11. How does the culture of death define who we are as human beings? What does it say we must do to be fully alive?
12. How does the culture of life define who we are as human beings? What does it say we must do to be fully alive?
13. Describe the consistent life ethic.

In Depth — Describe how a culture that claims "we are what we have" might affect the way someone views capital punishment or abortion.

Work with some of your classmates to create a montage of music excerpts or images that illustrates the concept of the consistent life ethic.

Building a Culture of Life

Earlier we said that the church approaches issues such as capital punishment and abortion in both-and terms: it seeks the well-being of both women and their children, of both criminals and their victims. Doing so requires that we become a culture that values each person so much that we are willing to make the sacrifices necessary to nurture her and to help her grow.

To see how this is possible, let's return to some of the stories we considered earlier.

From Revenge to Restoration

In a culture of life, the goal of the criminal-justice system is the restoration of life, not revenge. As its name implies, **restorative justice** focuses on restoring the good that has been harmed by criminal activty—for the victims, the community, and the offender too. In contrast to the traditional justice system, restorative justice

- focuses on the harm of wrongdoing more than the rules that have been broken

Restorative justice seeks reconciliation and healing.

- shows equal concern to victims and offenders, involving both in the process of justice
- works toward the restoration of victims, responding to victims' needs as the victims see them
- supports offenders while encouraging them to understand, accept, and carry out their obligations
- recognizes that while obligations may be difficult for offenders, they should not be intended as harms
- provides opportunities for dialogue, direct or indirect, between victims and offenders, as appropriate
- involves the affected community through the justice process

(Quoted in Wilson, "Crying for Justice")

Restorative justice suggests that healing for victims is linked to healing for offenders. The idea of offering healing to someone who has caused incredible pain seems impossible to many. Yet people do offer healing—in fact, the national organization Murder Victims' Families for Reconciliation has four thousand members.

One of its members is Marietta Jaeger, mother of the seven-year-old girl mentioned earlier who was kidnapped and strangled:

> It was when they were dragging the river searching for the body of her daughter that Marietta Jaeger lost her self-control. "That night," she says, "I wanted to kill [the abductor] with my own hands. I wanted him to swing."
>
> But about three weeks after the abduction, Marietta began "a wrestling match with God" about notions of acceptance and forgiveness. In a moment she still remembers, she "gave God permission to change my heart."

Q Restorative justice does not have to apply to the hardest cases alone. Imagine you are a victim or perpetrator of a smaller crime—say, stealing a bike. How could restorative justice resolve such a crime?

"It was hard," she says. "Anyone who says forgiveness is for wimps hasn't tried it." She began trying to picture the kidnapper as a child of God, "someone as precious in God's sight as my little girl. I tried to speak about him with respect. I began to pray for him, and I asked God to let one good thing happen to him each day."

One year to the day after the abduction, the man called Marietta to taunt her. "I'm in charge here," he said, "and you're not." But, in fact, Marietta was in charge because she was able to respond with love. "It's hard to explain," she says, "but I was filled with genuine concern and compassion for him." As the two talked for the next hour, he spoke about his loneliness; at one point, he broke down weeping.

Marietta taped that conversation, then shortly after that, the man was arrested. Although police found the bodies of four missing women and children in his home, he maintained his innocence. Marietta visited him in prison, urging him to free himself from his burdens by telling the truth. Then she approached the state prosecutors and told them she would vigorously oppose the death penalty for the man, whether he confessed or not.

When the man learned of her position, he broke down and confessed in detail to the four murders. Four hours later, he hanged himself.

Marietta has actively campaigned against the death penalty. "In God's eyes, the man who killed our daughter was just as precious as Susie," she says. "To kill someone in her name is to violate her. I honor her life and memorialize her far better by insisting that all life is sacred and worthy of preservation." (Adapted from McClory, "How I Came to Forgive the Unforgivable")

"Anyone who says forgiveness is for wimps hasn't tried it."

Victim offender mediation and dialogue

One way criminal-justice systems can incorporate restorative justice is through **victim offender mediation and dialogue** programs. In these voluntary programs, a mediator helps criminal offenders and their victims carefully work toward the goal of talking to each other. Both the victim and the offender prepare for the meeting by spending lots of time examining their own feelings and attitudes. The goal of the meeting is for the victim to be heard and for the offender to take accountability for her or his actions. When that goal is achieved, healing can happen on both sides.

Thomas Ann Hines found healing through a victim offender mediation and dialogue program:

Following the trial, Thomas Ann flew to Jamaica to drown herself. As she walked to the water's edge, she called out in desperation to her son. "If I just knew where you were," she cried, "and that everything was all right, I would be okay." In response, she had a very powerful sense of Paul saying that he was with God, and that he was all right.

She returned to Texas hoping that it might be possible to find peace. Still, she harbored rage against Robert White, regularly writing the parole board to ask whether he had died yet. She became involved in a program in which victims tell their stories to prisoners.

The turning point came one day when she was waiting to address two hundred

Sr. Helen Prejean, the inspiration for the movie *Dead Man Walking,* provided spiritual guidance to death row inmate Dobie Williams before he was executed.

prisoners. She saw a redheaded man who looked like Paul and thought, "If my son was in this room, I'd want someone to reach out a hand to him."

Slowly, she came to realize her own need to talk to Robert. She arranged the meeting through the state's Victim Offender Mediation/Dialog program.

After extensive preparation in the weeks before the meeting, the two met in the prison chapel. They sat in silence for a few minutes. "This is so hard for me," Thomas Ann said to him at last. "And I know it's hard for you. . . . The hardest thing, though, was to bury Paul. . . . It's really important that I know the last things he said and the last things that happened in his life."

It took Robert a few moments to reply. "I don't know how to start," he whispered, his head lowered. "I don't know how to explain. It was a stupid thing, just stupid. . . . I didn't know I was going to cause so much pain."

The two talked for eight hours straight. Thomas Ann learned that Robert had grown up on the streets. When he was thirteen, his mother told him she could give him a place to sleep, but could no longer feed and clothe him. At the time of his arrest, he was living with a prostitute twice his age and smoking more dope than he was selling.

[Robert] asked [Thomas Ann] why she wanted to help him. "If the only thing good that comes out of burying Paul is that you turn your life around, then Paul will not have died in vain," she said. She told him he was valuable and important, and he began to cry. "I just hate it that I brought all this pain in your life," he said. Before the two parted, Robert spontaneously hugged Thomas Ann, saying, "I'm sorry, I'm sorry."

Since their meeting, the two have cor-responded regularly. Robert no longer got into serious trouble in prison, but started working toward his GED.

"I went in there totally for me," Thomas Ann admits. "But it changed for me as he listened to me, and I listened to him. . . . That sad, troubled boy let me see inside his soul. I began to feel such compassion." (Wilson, "Crying for Justice")

Not everyone agrees with the mediation process. But for many, it is a much more life-giving form of criminal justice than capital punishment. Another participant in the program said that meeting with the death row inmate who murdered her daughter ended twelve years of living with grief and anger: "[It] allowed me to take my *life* back," she said. "I became a person I didn't know I was capable of being."

Making It Easier to Choose Life

When it comes to ending abortion, public attention is often focused on passing laws to restrict it. The harm that abortion causes makes such efforts necessary. But the consistent life ethic suggests that in order to end abortion, we must work to change not only our laws but our whole society:

> It is not enough to remove unjust laws. The underlying causes of attacks on life have to be eliminated, especially by ensuring proper support for families and motherhood. A family policy must be the basis and driving force of all social policies. For this reason there need to be set in place social and political initiatives capable of guaranteeing conditions of true freedom of choice in matters of parenthood. (*The Gospel of Life,* 90)

Brainstorm some specific ways that the social structures of your school, church, or community could be changed to better support single parents and teen parents. If possible, brainstorm with others.

In other words, the church calls us to shape our society in a way that makes it easier for families to choose life for their children. The following are some ways that could happen:

Legislation. Laws permitting abortion need to be changed not only because they are contrary to life but because they reinforce social structures that discriminate against women and children by providing a convenient alternative to dealing with real issues. For example, many states limit the number of children in a given family that can receive welfare. Rather than deal with the issue of poverty, these states encourage poor women to have abortions.

Although abortion is unlikely to be made illegal anytime soon, legislation can curb its harmful effects. **Informed consent** laws require abortion clinics to tell clients about what abortion involves—counseling that many women, like Erin McKasy, never receive.

Changing sexual behavior. Obviously, fewer abortions would occur if fewer women had unintended pregnancies. Nearly one million teens become pregnant every year, contributing to 20 percent of all abortions. Surveys show that the majority of teens are interested in learning how to avoid sexual activity. An increasing trend in the number of teenagers that choose to abstain from sexual activity helped reduce the teen pregnancy rate in the 1990s.

Addressing poverty. Lack of financial resources is a common reason for having an abortion. The issue of poverty will be addressed in more depth later in this course.

The U.S. Catholic church actively lobbies state and federal governments to pass poverty-reducing measures. In addition, many Catholic dioceses around the world have offered direct financial assistance to women who are facing difficult pregnancies. And across the United States, more than three thousand **crisis pregnancy centers** (sometimes called pregnancy care centers) offer material and emotional assistance.

Making workplaces and schools more parent friendly. *The Gospel of Life* calls for changes that will make life easier for working parents. On-site day care, private rooms for breastfeeding, and flexible working schedules can help. Plus, schools can make changes to better accommodate the needs of students who are parents.

Stopping violence against women. Groups like Feminists for Life fight violence against women by lobbying for protective legislation. For instance, the group has worked for legislation that would protect women who become pregnant as a result of rape, and protect children who are conceived in rape from court-ordered visitation with the rapist. Another group, the Life After Assault League, provides support for women impregnated by assault and children conceived as a result of assault. But these groups realize that fighting violence against women also involves changing cultural attitudes toward women by encouraging greater respect and equality.

Encouraging greater involvement by men. Much of this discussion has focused on women, partly because many women who face difficult pregnancies have been abandoned by their boyfriends. Our culture can

"We must also offer simple friendship and support."

Erin McKasy almost had an abortion, but supportive friends, family, and school administrators helped her graduate from a Catholic high school. She went on to attend the College of Saint Catherine, which provided her with on-campus housing and other support necessary for her to care for her son.

ADOPTION:
"BECAUSE
I LOVED HER"

Although nearly **a million teenagers** become pregnant every year, only about **3 percent** consider adoption. The reason is not a shortage of adoptive parents, but the emotional difficulty of carrying a baby for nine months only to give it up to someone else. Still, advocates and opponents of legalized abortion generally agree that adoption is a good alternative to abortion for women who feel unable to raise a child.

One way this option is being encouraged is through the promotion of **open adoption,** which differs from the traditional approach to adoption by allowing ongoing contact between birth mothers and their children. Birth mothers select the family they want to raise their child, and together, they determine the level of contact the birth mother will have with her child. Usually pictures and letters are exchanged throughout the child's life, and visits are sometimes arranged.

The openness of the adoption process is what allowed Misty, who was sixteen when she became pregnant by her twenty-year-old boyfriend, to make the difficult choice of adoption:

When I told him I was pregnant I didn't want money from him. I wanted someone to tell me that I was not going through this alone. He wasn't mature enough to give that to me. . . .

At first I thought I could keep the baby and finish high school. I was determined to do it, so I took a job at Dairy Queen. It didn't take long for me to realize that there was no way I could make it. If I did keep my baby, I wouldn't have been raising it—daycare would. And by the time I got home at night from school and work, the baby would be asleep. Two girls at the high school I'm going to now in Abilene kept their babies and ended up hurting them because of the stress. Even though I hate to say it, I could have been one of them.

My parents said, "You will get an abortion," even though they don't believe in it. And I said, "No I won't. I'm pregnant and you can't kick me out, you'll have to support me and the baby." But they're a lot older and they have dreams, like they want to get one of those R.V.s and travel. So I told them there are other ways like adoption, even though I knew I wouldn't do it. I was just stalling for time. But after thinking about adoption, I knew it was the smartest thing to do.

Two days after Misty gave birth to a healthy baby girl, her mother, the adoptive couple, and others gathered to witness the relinquishment. Everyone cried:

I tried hard to hide my tears. . . . I remember the moment that I felt she's not mine anymore. I thought to myself, I need to get up and do this now and I wrapped her in a baby blanket that I made for her. It was hard to hand her over, but I said to myself, "Let go."

I handed her to Betsy, the adoptive mother, and we prayed. . . . Betsy and Ricky handed me a gift and everybody left because I needed to be alone. Mom just sat there and held me as I cried.

When we were driving home after the relinquishment, I still had to convince myself that I did the right thing. You know, you look down and you don't have a belly and you don't have a baby, and you ask yourself, "Why?" The answer is because I loved her.

Misty sees her daughter frequently. "I know that she's doing well and it helps to see that she's happy. Seeing Payton has helped me to heal. . . . All of the pain was worth it." (Mosher, "Letting Go") ◉ Ⓢ

> "I know that she's doing well and it helps to see that she's happy. Seeing Payton has helped me to heal."

Ⓢ Interview or write a letter to someone involved in the adoption process (a lawyer, a counselor, a birth mother, adoptive parents), asking about the joys and the difficulties. Share your findings in class.

show greater respect and equality toward men by encouraging them and helping them to be responsible parents. ✝

"I needed a friend"

As much as structural changes are needed, at the core of the culture of life is a spirit of solidarity. Frederica Mathewes-Green, a former advocate of legalized abortion who now opposes it, traveled the country talking to women who had had abortions. She wanted to find out why women had abortions:

> To my surprise, what I heard most frequently was that the reason for the abortion was not financial or practical; it had to do with a relationship. It was either the father of the child, or else her own mother, who was pressuring her to have the abortion. The core reason I heard was, "I had the abortion because someone I love told me to."
>
> When I asked, "Is there anything anyone could have done? What would you have needed in order to have had that child?" I heard the same answer over and over: "I needed a friend. I felt so alone. I felt like I didn't have a choice. If only one person had stood by me, even a stranger, I would have had that baby." Over and over I learned

"No woman should feel so alone that abortion seems her only alternative. . . . Come to any Catholic parish in this archdiocese and you will find help." Churches around the world provide direct assistance to people facing difficult pregnancies.

that women had abortions because they felt abandoned, they felt isolated and afraid. As one woman said, "I felt like everyone would support me if I had the abortion, but if I had the baby I'd be alone." In order to support women who have unwanted pregnancies, we have to offer them whatever financial and practical resources we can, but we must also offer simple friendship and support. (Mathewes-Green, "Abortion and the Search for Common Ground")

A Call to Live More Fully

Although we have focused on the issues of abortion and capital punishment in this chapter, the call to choose life is at the heart of all justice issues. The rest of this course, then, really continues the discussion about how to build a culture of life.

It would be wrong to suggest that choosing life does not involve sacrifice, pain, or suffering. And it would be dishonest to suggest that people who choose restoration over revenge, or birth over abortion, live happily ever after without struggles and difficulties. On the other hand, the church believes that choosing to solve difficult situations through the use of violence, while perhaps easier, is not life-giving to anyone involved.

The Christian choice for life is based on the choice Jesus made to suffer and to sacrifice his life in order that all of us might live. It was a choice he struggled with in the Garden of Gethsemane. Even after the Resurrection, Jesus kept the wounds of his suffering, just as Thomas Ann Hines continues to mourn the loss of her son and Erin McKasy struggles to balance motherhood and school. Choosing life does not take away suffering, but it does make us more fully alive. ∪

✝ How do you think society can best help young men be better images of God in terms of relationships and parenthood?

∪ Reflect in writing on the statement, "Choosing life does not take away suffering, but it does make us more fully alive."

15. Define restorative justice and list three of its characteristics.
16. Describe victim offender mediation and dialogue programs.
17. Describe three areas in which social changes might help to reduce abortions.
18. What did Frederica Mathewes-Green find that women facing crisis pregnancies most wanted?

In Depth

From this section, choose one of the stories of a person who chose life under difficult circumstances by rejecting abortion or capital punishment. Describe how the paschal mystery is present in that story.

WHAT YOU CAN DO . . .

- Develop your own culture of life by treating everyone with dignity and respect—even those with whom you disagree on issues such as abortion and capital punishment. Avoid supporting media that promote violence and degrade human sexuality.
- Organize a drive to collect baby supplies for parents who need material assistance. Work with a local crisis pregnancy center or your parish or diocese to find out what is most needed. Use the drive to educate others about the need for social changes that will make abortion less common.
- Volunteer at a local crisis pregnancy center. Young people—male and female—are almost always welcome to help.
- Practice restorative justice in relationships with others by focusing on healing rather than revenge.
- Ask, How does my school (or future college) support pregnant students? Then work with school officials and other students to create support networks.
- Join Amnesty International USA's campaign to abolish the death penalty.
- Contact your Catholic diocese to find out how you can help lobby for legislative change. ☉

5 BUILDING COMMUNITY

✳ *Student art:* Photograph above; Jennifer Safi, Bishop Kearney High School, Brooklyn, New York

exclusion stereotypes

community

Celebrating
unity amid diversity

THE MIRACLE OF THE MENORAH

Early in December, Tammie Schnitzer helped her five-year-old son, Isaac, stencil a menorah on his bedroom window in Billings, Montana. The family was celebrating Hanukkah, the Jewish festival of lights.

The festival recalls a miraculous event in Jewish history. More than two thousand years ago, the Syrian Greeks invaded Judea, ransacking the holy temple and extinguishing the altar's eternal flame. A small band of Jewish fighters waged a guerrilla war against the Syrian army and, against great odds, defeated them. Then the people went about the work of restoring the Temple. Soon all that remained to be done was to light the eternal flame—but there was only enough oil to light the lamp for one day. Still, they lit the lamp; if the flame burned for only one day, so be it. Miraculously, the light didn't die on that day, nor the next. Indeed, it burned for eight days and nights in the presence of the Lord. Ever since, Jewish families have recalled the miracle by lighting the eight candles of the menorah during Hanukkah.

The brick that flew through five-year-old Isaac Schnitzer's bedroom window was supposed to drive his Jewish family out of Billings, Montana. But the Schnitzers' neighbors reacted to the incident in a way that strengthened the community rather than shattering it.

Shortly after Tammie and Isaac had finished stenciling their menorah, a brick flew through the decorated window, shattering it. The image of Isaac's menorah lay in bits and pieces on the bed. The next day, the *Billings Gazette* described the incident. Tammie was reported to be troubled by the advice of the investigating officer. "You'd better remove the symbol from your house," he had told her. But how could a mother explain this to her son? He was so young, too young to be introduced to hatred like that.

Margaret MacDonald, another Billings mother, was deeply touched when she read Tammie's question in the paper the next day. She imagined having to explain to her own children that they couldn't have a Christmas tree in the window because it wasn't safe. She remembered a story she'd heard about the King of Denmark during the Nazi occupation of World War II. Hitler had ordered the Christian king to force all Danish Jews to wear the Star of David on their chests, and he had refused. In an act of courageous defiance, the king placed the yellow star over his own heart, declaring he and all his people were one. His example inspired his countrymen, people of all religions, to wear the stars in solidarity with the Jews. Because of their courage, the Nazis were ultimately unable to find their "enemies."

Margaret wanted to make a similarly powerful statement against hate, for Tammie and Isaac and all the children of Billings. She phoned her pastor, asking him to tell the Danish story during his Sunday sermon and to pass out paper menorahs so that families

churches, businesses, and community groups had followed suit. Soon, hundreds of menorahs appeared in windows of non-Jewish homes. A sporting goods store proclaimed on its large billboard: "Not in Our Town! No hate. No violence. Peace on Earth." A local high school posted a sign reading, "Happy Hanukkah to our Jewish Friends." A vigil was held outside the synagogue during Hanukkah services to protect those who worshiped inside.

But the battle of light against darkness was not easily won. Bullets riddled the high school windows. Two churches that were adorned with menorahs had their windows broken. Six non-Jewish families had car windows smashed; a note left behind simply said, "Jew lover."

The *Billings Gazette* published a full-page drawing of a menorah and invited its readers to cut out the picture and place it in their windows. In this town, with fewer than a hundred Jewish families, the menorah was proudly displayed in thousands of homes. Now the hate groups couldn't find their enemies. In Billings, there were no Jews, no Gentiles: only friends.

As the holidays wore on, incidents of violence slowed. New friendships formed, and greater understanding developed. Ironically, the violence intended to rip the community apart only served to make it stronger. Now, the people of Billings have new reasons to celebrate. If you ask them about their menorahs and what Hanukkah means to them, they'll be proud to tell you. It's about standing together in the face of hatred, overcom-

It's about **standing together** in the face of hatred, overcoming violence with love, and the **miracle** of light shining through the darkness.

could hang them in their windows. That Sunday, members of the congregation could be seen all over town hanging menorahs in their windows. By the following weekend, other

ing violence with love, and the miracle of light shining through the darkness. (Adapted from Hartsig, in *Stone Soup for the World*, pages 81–84)

Two Approaches to Community

In a way, the brick thrown through the window of Tammie Schnitzer's home represented a question lobbed at the whole city of Billings: How will we define our community?

It is a question whose answer has a huge impact on human life and dignity. In the previous chapter, we noted that choosing life means more than protecting people from being harmed—it also means ensuring that people are able to live in a way that reflects their dignity as images of God. Of the many things that allow people to live a full and dignified life, one of the most basic is participation in community. *"Human dignity can be realized and protected only in community,"* the U.S. Catholic bishops say in their 1986 pastoral letter *Economic Justice for All* (14). This is true not only because we depend on our relationships with others to provide us with what we need for a life of dignity, but also simply because human beings are **social:** as images of God, we are made to be in loving relationship with one another.

Our social nature draws us together to form **communities,** groups of people who relate to one another on the basis of common characteristics, circumstances, or interests. The menorah story reflects two ways of thinking about community. **Exclusion** attempts to determine who does and does not belong to the community by focusing on the differences that separate people from one another. Through their actions, the brick thrower and his or her companions were saying that Jews should be excluded from the community because of their religion.

Inclusion, while not ignoring the differences that make each person unique, recognizes that those differences are small compared to the dignity people share in common as images of God. The way we live together should also be a reflection of God, who is the relationship of three different persons united by love in one being. In inclusive communities, love overcomes the differences among people—a reality experienced by the people of Billings who stood in solidarity with their Jewish neighbors.

"Human dignity can be realized and protected only in community."

✳ The family is the most basic building block of society. *Student art:* Photograph; Mary Diaz, Benilde–Saint Margaret's High School, Saint Louis Park, Minnesota

People are excluded from community for many reasons. Poverty is a major cause of exclusion that we will examine later in this course. In this chapter, however, we focus on a type of exclusion that has caused a great deal of harm in the United States: exclusion based on race.

1. Why is participation in community essential to human dignity?
2. What does it mean to say that human beings are social?
3. Describe exclusion and inclusion.

---

4. Whose dignity was affected by the events in the story of the menorah? Explain why and how.

What Makes a Community?

Participation in community is both a right and a responsibility, the U.S. Catholic bishops say in their 1986 pastoral letter *Economic Justice for All:* *"Social justice implies that persons have an obligation to be active and productive participants in the life of society and that society has a duty to en-*

able them to participate in this way" (71). Each person has a right to participate in community in order to become more fully the person God calls him or her to be. Each person has a responsibility to participate because the good of others in the community depends on it.

Just what does it mean to participate in a community? Saint Paul frequently addressed that question in his letters to the early Christian communities.

 What is your vision of a good community? What exactly would make it good? Describe your ideal community in a poem, essay, fictional story, drawing, or some other form.

Varieties of Gifts, Same Spirit

In his First Letter to the Corinthians, Paul says that the Christian community consists of many members who have a variety of gifts:

> Now there are varieties of gifts, but the same Spirit; and there are varieties of services, but the same Lord; and there are varieties of activities, but it is the same God who activates all of them in everyone. To each is given the manifestation of the Spirit for the common good. (12:4–7)

Each person has different gifts to offer the community.

Paul goes on to compare the community, with its variety of gifted members, to the human body. The body has many parts—a hand has a different function than an eye, and the feet cannot take the place of the ears—but the parts work together as one. In the body and the community, "if one member suffers, all suffer together with it; if one member is honored, all rejoice together with it" (1 Corinthians 12:26). **B**

Three key themes are evident in Paul's teaching:

Although we all have different gifts, we are all loved equally by God. No two people are alike; each has different gifts to offer the community. In the excerpt from First Corinthians, Paul celebrates the diversity of the community, but points out three times that differences among people do not mean that one person is less valuable than another. Catholic social teaching echoes Paul:

> Since all [humans] possess a rational soul and are created in God's likeness, since they have the same nature and origin, have been redeemed by Christ and enjoy the same divine calling and destiny, the basic equality of all must receive increasingly greater recognition. (*The Church in the Modern World [Gaudium et Spes]*, 29).

We need one another. All the different members of a community, like the parts of the body, are vital for the common good—that is, the well-being of the entire community—because each brings a unique contribution to the whole. If one person's gifts were ignored or disposed of, the whole community would suffer. But when gifts are offered and received, both the recipient and the giver are enriched. Participating in community is necessary in order for us to give our gifts to others and to benefit fully from the gifts of others.

Solidarity is key. Solidarity is what holds a love-centered community together. You may have experienced the sort of solidarity of which Paul speaks if you have a close-knit family or group of friends: if one is hurt, all hurt; if one is happy, all are happy.

B Read the full description of community found in 1 Corinthians, chapter 12. Write a one-page description of the Christian vision of community, illustrating your points with ideas found in Saint Paul's analogy.

Living Together in Community

In answering the question What makes a community? Catholic social teaching echoes and expands on the teaching of Paul. In *Economic Justice for All,* the U.S. Catholic bishops identify several basic requirements for community life (63–84). When any of these are ignored, the dignity of individuals and groups within the community is violated, and the well-being of the community as a whole suffers.

The right and responsibility to contribute to the common good. Everyone actively working for the good of everyone else is what makes justice happen. Therefore, everyone has a right and a responsibility to use her or his gifts and talents to contribute to the good of the whole community. For its part, the community needs to ensure that all people are able to contribute. When the gifts of members and groups are not recognized because some are considered too young or too old, for instance, everyone loses out.

The right to access the benefits and resources of the community. When people or groups are denied access to the community's benefits and resources, such as adequate education, their ability to live the life that God intended for them is threatened. When members are threatened, the community as a whole is threatened as well. Communities have a duty to organize structures that allow each member to live an abundant life. 𝐂

Human rights. The requirements of participation listed above are fulfilled in basic human rights. Those rights "include the rights to fulfillment of material needs, a guarantee of fundamental freedoms, and the protection of relationships that are essential to participation in the life of society" (79).

When individuals or groups are prevented from participating in community in these ways, they become excluded and marginalized. An inclusive community makes sure everyone is able to live life fully:

> The ultimate injustice is for a person or group to be treated actively or abandoned passively as if they were nonmembers of the human race. To treat people this way is effectively to say that they simply do not count as human beings. . . . The poor, the disabled, and the unemployed too often are simply left behind. (77)

These are only the minimum requirements for a just community. Ultimately, love and solidarity are the glue that holds community together: "Only active love of God and neighbor make . . . community happen" (64).

Justice calls for all members of a community to have fair access to its resources and benefits.

𝐂 Think about a community to which you belong. What gifts do you receive from it? What gifts do you contribute to it?

HUMAN RIGHTS: MINIMUM REQUIREMENTS

In order to **respect human life and dignity,** we must respect **each person's** human rights. These rights make it possible for people to live a dignified life in community.

In the worldview of many North Americans, human rights are regarded as **absolute,** or unlimited. But Catholic social teaching stresses that the human rights of each person are balanced by a responsibility to respect the rights of all other people in the community. The right to freedom, for example, does not entitle someone to endanger the lives of others by driving recklessly.

The right to employment and the right to economic initiative—that is, to start a business—are necessary to ensure full participation in society.

Following are some of the most important human rights identified in *Economic Justice for All* as essential to ensuring human dignity and participation in community.

Basic rights necessary for the protection of human dignity. These include the right to life, food, clothing, shelter, rest, medical care, and basic education.

Rights necessary to ensure basic human rights. To ensure the rights listed above, people also have the right to earn a living, and the right to security in the event of sickness, unemployment, and old age.

Rights that enable participation in community. Full participation in the life of the community requires economic rights, including the right to employment, healthy working conditions, wages and job benefits that allow workers and their families to live a life of dignity, and the possibility of property ownership. Civil and political rights are also necessary for participation; some of these include the right to freedom of speech, the right to freedom of assembly, the right to worship, and the right to political participation (through the vote, for instance).

Catholic social teaching considers these rights to be the minimum necessary for justice and peace. ◦ **ᗡ**

The human rights of each person are balanced by a responsibility to respect the rights of all other people in the community.

ᗡ Imagine you are told that you will be denied three of the human rights listed here—but you are allowed to choose which ones. List the rights you would give up, and explain why. How would you be affected by being denied each of the rights you have chosen to forfeit?

5. Why do people have a right and a responsibility to participate in community?
6. Describe three themes in Paul's teaching about community.
7. In your own words, summarize the requirements for participation in community.

In Depth

8. Choose five different human rights listed in the sidebar on pages 148–149. Briefly explain a responsibility that might balance each right.

The Anatomy of Exclusion

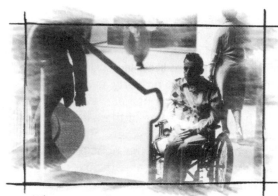

When someone is prevented from fully participating in the life of the community, the whole community is denied the gifts that person has to offer.

Even though justice demands participation for all, the opportunity to participate is often denied. To find out why, let's look at some examples.

Exclusion: Harmful to All

More than likely, each of us has had some experience of being excluded from a community. Listen to the experiences of these students from Humanities High School in New York City:

Nicolette: Because I'm short, everyone calls me Munchkin. . . . My friends always say to each other, "Hi, how are you?" Yet, when they see me, they just squeal, "Oh, cute and cuddly." It gets to the point where I yell, "Get away from me. Can't you just say hello? Must you pinch me on the cheeks every time you see me?" I wouldn't mind if they pinched everyone as a friendly gesture, but they don't. They just do it to me. They would never do that to a tall person. I want people to know there is more to me than cute and cuddly. (Pages 30–32)

Wendy: I don't remember when I started being fat. . . . In elementary school I was teased for lots of things. I was asthmatic. I'd cough a lot and then throw up in class. . . . The kids had a field day. Every class has a kid that the others see and say, "Yyyy-yuuuuuuck." That was me. (Page 22)

Ben: When people meet a stutterer they immediately think that the person is dumb and insecure. . . . In fourth grade if someone didn't like me, the first thing they called me was "stutterer." Kids would tease me. . . . I would immediately go into a defense mode. I wouldn't talk, I would hit, hard. (Page 27)

(Kuklin, *Speaking Out*)

From our own experience, we know that being excluded is painful, but notice how the whole group is hurt too. Nicolette wants her friends to see more than her childlike frame; they may be overlooking the adult-size gifts she has to offer. As for Wendy, it would not be surprising if constantly being teased caused her to withdraw into herself, effectively cutting the group off from what she can bring to it. Ben's story illustrates how exclusion can hurt the group in more obvious ways, leading to resentment and even violence. If we consider exclusion at a societal level, we will see that it causes serious harm to individuals, groups, and whole societies. *E*

Excuses for exclusion

Following are just a few of the reasons—or excuses—offered by those who deny the participation rights of others:

- "If blacks move into our neighborhood, our property values will go down."
- "We have to keep our membership dues high. We have an image to maintain, and some people just don't fit in."
- "We can't have a woman president. She'd let her emotions make decisions for her."

Those who wish to exclude others try to make the case that some people "just don't belong," or that some people, by nature, are "just not fit" to take on certain roles within the community. Even if these excuses are never spoken aloud, they have the potential to influence the way we relate to one another.

When we consider the excuses given for excluding people, we come to the complex issues of stereotypes, prejudice, and discrimination. *F*

Stereotype: A Harmful Assumption

The way we treat others is based on the way we view them; our views are in turn influenced by our culture and personal experience. But as we discussed earlier in this course, the limitations of our experience and culture cause us to view the world in a way that is often inaccurate or incomplete. When our view of a person or group is based on inaccurate or incomplete knowledge, it is a **stereotype.**

Stereotypes give us a distorted view of other people, preventing us from seeing them as they really are.

> The way we treat others is based on the way we **view** them.

E Think of a time you were excluded from a community. How did it affect your sense of dignity? How did you respond to the exclusion?

F Who is excluded from a community to which you belong? Why are they excluded? How does their exclusion hurt them? How does it hurt the whole community?

Stereotypes can be positive (Asian students do well in math) or negative (Asian students belong to gangs). Either way, stereotypes are too broad. It is impossible for stereotypical characteristics to apply to all members of a group. Basing our attitudes toward others on stereotypes demonstrates disrespect for the uniqueness of persons.

Direct experience, faulty logic

Many stereotypes develop from direct experience of others. But the conclusions represented by these stereotypes are the result of faulty logic. In the following examples, the conclusions, which are stereotypes, do not necessarily follow from the observations:

- Three juniors from Westside High were caught cheating on the SATs; therefore, all Westside students are dishonest.
- All the boys I know are into violent video games; therefore, all boys prefer violent games.
- The highest scorers on the team are African American; therefore, blacks are always the best basketball players.

Obviously, all these conclusions represent faulty logic: you may have a dog that's a collie, but it doesn't mean that all dogs are collies. Yet, such logic is the basis for comments such as the following, which also show stereotypical thinking:

- "When kids wearing Westside jackets come into my store, I watch them like a hawk. Otherwise, they'll rob me blind."
- "The only computer games John plays are the ones where you build a city or an amusement park—what's wrong with him?"

- "Their basketball team has mostly black players; there's no way we can win because our team is all white." 🕵

Learned from our culture

Another source of stereotypes is the culture in which we grew up. Many stereotypes are learned from the people around us, such as parents, friends, and teachers. Children can be taught to view certain groups as inferior just as easily as they can be taught that everyone is equal.

News reports tend to present only the bad news, leaving the public with the impression that teenagers, antiabortion activists, police officers (or any other group you can name) are always up to no good. Social institutions such as churches and schools may also promote stereotypes, often because of the way that such institutions are already structured. The fact that in 1999, only nine of the one hundred United States senators were women may lead some people to believe that only men are qualified to assume top leadership roles.

Stereotypes and participation

Stereotyping is an everyday occurrence. Many stereotypes, especially positive ones, seem harmless. So it is easy to lose sight of how much they limit the right of some individuals and groups to participate in community as they choose.

In *Speaking Out,* Wai, who was born in Hong Kong but moved to the United States when he was three years old, talks about the stereotyping he encounters:

🕵 Take notes about how people of different races are portrayed during several TV shows. Write down the race of each character, the role played (doctor, police officer, criminal), and whether she or he was portrayed in a positive, a negative, or a neutral way. Take notes during commercials as well. Then, write a two-page report answering these questions: What racial groups did you see? How often did each group appear? How were people of different groups portrayed? Finally, assess how television might affect perceptions about different racial groups.

H Suppose you overheard someone making prejudicial comments about another person or group. How would you respond? How would your response be different if the comment was directed at your own group?

People think that if you are Chinese you must be a brain. . . . We're supposed to be good at anything that relates to math, physics, or science. . . . My S.A.T. score proved that I'm not that great in math. I'm better in verbal. It's a lot of assumptions. And for us kids, it is a lot of pressure. . . . People also assume that anybody who is Chinese is not athletically inclined. . . . I'm on the soccer team and I take scuba diving. (Kuklin, *Speaking Out,* pages 64–65)

A Chinese American student subjected to these stereotypes might experience a sense of failure, feeling that he *should* be better at math, and he may not receive much encouragement in the areas where he does excel: language and sports, in this case.

Other stereotypes can fuel deep-seated negative attitudes that make efforts to include everyone very difficult. One high school student admits that she stereotypes black males: "When I see a black guy coming down a dark street, or even in the hall, I get the feeling that this is an aggressive person, I don't want to tangle with this person" (Kuklin, *Speaking Out,* page 67). The negative stereotype held by this student, who also happens to be black, creates a barrier between herself and others that harms both sides.

Prejudice and Discrimination

When stereotypes are combined with fear or selfishness, they can develop into **prejudice:** an attitude of hostility that is directed at whole groups of people. Prejudice involves prejudgment, making a judgment about something before all the facts are known—or without considering the facts. The hostility of prejudice blinds one to the dignity shared by all people, creating a kind of poison in relationships. Consider the prejudice witnessed by this homosexual student, for example:

In classrooms, I've heard some teachers use the words homo, faggot, and dyke in casual conversation. They use it to dis somebody, to insult somebody. . . . When a person in authority uses words like that, he's giving kids permission to use them, too. That promotes homophobia and it promotes gay bashing. (Kuklin, *Speaking Out,* page 81)

Prejudicial attitudes harm the human dignity of both those who hold the attitudes and those against whom they are directed. But there is a distinction between prejudice and the power to impose restrictions on other people based on that prejudice. Even if *all* people have

Basing our attitudes toward others on stereotypes demonstrates disrespect for the uniqueness of persons.

✳ *Student art:* Copper tooling; Jessica Newberg, Boylan Central Catholic High School, Rockford, Illinois

some prejudicial attitudes toward people of another race, only *some* people have the power to actively exclude others from resources, activities, and organizations. The greater the level of power combined with prejudice, the greater the potential for damage.

When people who are motivated by prejudice use their power to deny individuals or groups the right to participate in community, **discrimination** results. Discrimination can be seen in actions on an individual level, as when people motivated by prejudice refuse to sell a house or rent an apartment to certain people.

Discrimination can be based on any of the many issues that make people different from one another: gender, age, class, ethnicity, religion, and so on. But one of the most explosive, widespread, and deep-seated examples of discrimination in the United States is racism. Social structures can also promote discrimination, as we will see later.

The Sin of Racism

In their 2000 pastoral statement, *Moving Beyond Racism: Learning to See with the Eyes of Christ,* the Catholic bishops of Chicago define **racism** as

> a personal sin and social disorder rooted in the belief that one race is superior to another. It involves not only prejudice but also the use of religious, social, political, economic or historical power to keep one race privileged.

Although people of any race might be the target of racism and people of any race might be racist, historically in the United States it primarily has been white people who have discriminated against people of other races. The history of white racism against blacks has been particularly influential in shaping thinking and discussion about racial issues.

John Howard Griffin and the man in the mirror

Just as the U.S. civil rights movement was getting under way, **John Howard Griffin** (1920–1980) embarked on a daring experiment to explore the relationship between blacks and whites in the segregated South of 1959. Although much has changed about racism in the United States since then, his experience can still shed light on the issue today.

Griffin, whose heritage was Irish, grew up in Dallas and was educated in Paris. While fighting during World War II, he was blinded by a nearby explosion. Ironically, his blindness led him to a deeper faith, and eventually he converted to Catholicism.

Then, after more than twelve years of blindness, he miraculously regained his sight. With its return, Griffin realized just how much

Civil rights marchers assert their dignity as they pass National Guard troops in Memphis, Tennessee, in 1968.

Prejudicial attitudes harm the **human dignity** of **both** those who hold the attitudes and those against whom they are directed.

the ability to see could be an obstacle to true perception—especially when sight allowed people to discriminate on the basis of skin color. Yet his black friends responded to his thoughts about racism with a challenge: "The only way you can know what it's like is to wake up in my skin" (Ellsberg, *All Saints,* page 261).

Griffin took their words to heart. With the help of drugs, dyes, and radiation, he darkened his skin, shaved his head, and "crossed the line into a country of hate, fear, and hopelessness" (page 261). For two months, he traveled through the Deep South, a white man in black skin, recording his observations for a series of magazine articles that would later become the book *Black Like Me.*

Griffin's disguise was so effective, not a single person of either race ever suspected that he was not black, even though nothing had changed about him but his skin. In fact, he didn't recognize himself when he glanced at his own reflection in a mirror:

> That glance brought a sickening shock that I tried not to admit, not to recognize, but I could not avoid it. It was the shock of seeing my face in the mirror and of feeling an involuntary movement of antipathy [or dis-

like] for that face, because it was pigmented, the face of a Negro. (Bonazzi, *Man in the Mirror,* page 47)

Griffin had begun his experiment to explore racism in the South, but in facing himself in the mirror, he began to face his own unconscious racism as well.

Griffin became the target of racism too. The attitudes he encountered from white people ranged from genuine kindness that was apparently free of racism to open hostility. Mostly, though, he was habitually scorned and rebuffed. He was harassed by teenagers, threatened by others, stared at with open hatred, and routinely denied service that he had received when his skin was light. Once, he took a tense bus ride past the site where a black man had recently been lynched by a white mob. Along the way, the driver refused to let the black passengers off the bus to use the rest rooms.

When Griffin tried to look for employment, he was often hired over the phone but then rejected when he showed up for work. One employer openly admitted the intent behind his discrimination. Griffin offered to work for lower pay and to work harder than the white workers, but the foreman refused to hire him.

"The only way you can know what it's like is to wake up in my skin."

John Howard Griffin dyed his skin to find out what it was like to be a black man in the South in 1959. He is shown here both during his experience *(the man on the left in the first photo)* and one year afterward *(second photo).*

Everyone who saw John Howard Griffin in disguise thought he was black. Did the fact that he appeared to be black actually make him a member of that race? Why or why not?

Suppose you woke up one day and you were a different race than you are now. How would your identity as a person be affected? How would your daily life be affected?

"We don't want you people," he said, adding that his goal was to "weed out" blacks from positions at the industrial plant until the only jobs they held were "the ones no white man would have."

"How can we live?" I asked hopelessly, careful not to give the impression I was arguing.

"That's the whole point," he said. . . . "We're going to . . . drive every one of you out of the state." (Page 95)

The effect of such open discrimination was apparent to Griffin in the deep poverty he encountered among the black people he stayed with during his travels.

Toward the end of his journey, Griffin scrubbed himself raw to make his skin light again; as if by magic, all the friendly smiles, politeness, and opportunities he had known before his experiment magically reappeared. Black people, with whom he had easily conversed while his skin was dark, now were careful and reserved around him. When he dyed his skin again a few days later, he was once again treated "not even as a second-class citizen, but as a tenth-class one" (page 65).

As he reflected on his experiences, Griffin came to realize that at the root of the racism he experienced was fear of **the other**—that is, fear of those we do not know. Although his understanding of the effects of racism was still limited in many ways, his experience helped him more fully appreciate the dignity that all people have in common. By the end of his journey, Griffin no longer reacted with involuntary disdain at the sight of his face in the mirror,

because I was living in the homes of Negro families and I was experiencing emotionally what intellectually I had long known—that the *Other* was not other at all; that within the context of home and family life we faced exactly the same problems as those faced in all homes of all men: the universal problems of loving, of suffering, of bringing children to the light, of fulfilling human aspirations, of dying. (Page 48) *L*

A persistent problem

The point of this story is not so much to recount racism in U.S. history—although that is important because the racism of the past warped relationships in U.S. society in ways that continue to affect people today. But the larger point is to raise questions about how we view one another as people, and why we tend to focus on the differences among us rather than on what we have in common as human beings.

It might be tempting to dismiss Griffin's experience of racism as something that no longer exists. It is true that much has changed since 1959: blatant racism and prejudiced attitudes are less common, and civil rights legislation has enabled greater and broader participation in U.S. society. Surveys conducted during the past thirty years show that a growing number of white Americans believe that African Americans should have the same chance to find employment as those of European descent. Such indications of racial tolerance at the level of personal attitudes are encouraging, but they do not show the whole picture. "In many places, [racism] is powerfully resurgent," writes Bishop Sean O'Malley:

K In what ways does race affect the way you interact with people?

L *The root of racism is fear of those we do not know.* Do you agree or disagree with this statement? Why?

M In what ways does racism or some other form of prejudice continue in your city or town today? Interview five people, preferably of different racial backgrounds, to find their opinions. Summarize in a short report what each person says, then write one page describing your own conclusions. Prepare to discuss your findings in class.

Church burnings and other hate crimes continue, and motorists are still stopped for "driving while black." In the last year, 220 articles on racial violence appeared on the pages of the *New York Times*. ("Solidarity: The Antidote to Resurgent Racism")

Many people who have not experienced race-based exclusion might not realize that even today it creates barriers to full participation. The following account by a young black man is just one example:

I don't know one black person who has never had an encounter with cops.

One day, I'm running to catch the El [elevated train]. This is the third time I got stopped by the cops that year, okay? . . . This time I'm running for an appointment with my barber. I realize I don't have any money. So I stop by my bank on the way. I take out sixty dollars. I take a shortcut through the alley, counting my money. A cop car pulls up. They slam me against the wall, throw me in the car, no *Miranda* rights or anything.

I had a book under my arm. . . . I'm well-dressed. He said, "You stole this woman's purse." I said I didn't steal any purse. They take me to this lady's apartment building a few blocks away. They parade me in front of her window. She's three stories up. I look up. . . . I . . . saw an old woman in her seventies with glasses. The window was dirty. I'm this black kid, three stories down, and she's going to identify me. I can't believe this. They had me walking back and forth.

Fortunately, I was wearing glasses, too. She said it wasn't me because the guy who robbed her wasn't wearing glasses. They gave me my book back and said, "Get out of here." (Quoted in Terkel, *Race*, pages 402–403)

The words of the U.S. Catholic bishops' pastoral letter on racism, *Brothers and Sisters to Us*, are unfortunately as relevant today as when the letter was first written in 1979:

Racism is an evil that endures in our society and in our Church. Despite apparent advances and even significant changes . . . , the reality of racism remains. In large part it is only external appearances which have changed. (Page 10) **M**

Discrimination on a Social Level

When people discriminate against one another on an individual level, patterns of discrimination will build up into social structures. Sometimes such structural discrimination is consciously chosen by an institution or society, as in the case of apartheid in South Africa, in the reservation system that segregated Native Americans in the United States, or in the denial of voting rights to U.S. women before 1920.

Racial discrimination makes it difficult for some people to obtain home mortgages.

Such consciously chosen discrimination is much rarer in the United States today than it once was. But discriminatory social structures persist as the indirect result of many individual acts of discrimination. The following are some examples of structural discrimination.

The wage gap. The **wage gap** is the difference between the amount paid to different groups of people for their work. Women, for instance, earn 74 cents for every dollar that men earn. As much as one-third to one-half of this wage gap cannot be explained by differences in education, experience, or other qualifications, according to a National Academy of Sciences report. The gap applies to men of different races as well: college-educated black and Hispanic men earn $11,258 and $9,495 less per year, respectively, than college-educated white males.

One cause of the gap between wages for women and men is historical. In the past, certain fields were thought of as "women's work." Work that had fallen to women in the home, such as cooking, child care, sewing, and nursing, became the only work open to women seeking employment. Because the assumption was that women didn't need to be breadwinners, these fields paid less than other comparable careers. It is only in recent decades that the salaries of teachers and nurses have risen; child care workers and garment workers are still paid less than other skilled workers.

Educational inequalities. Another example of structural discrimination can be found in the education system. As a group, the academic achievement of nonwhite students tends to lag behind that of white students—not because they have less academic potential, but for a complex variety of reasons, many of which can be traced to patterns of discrimination. Many schools whose students are largely nonwhite do not receive adequate levels of funding, for instance. And stereotypes sometimes cause teachers to have low expectations of nonwhite students. "The black students confront preconceived notions that say that because they are black they aren't academic achievers," says one high school chemistry teacher. "The kids pick up the way they are perceived and they behave in kind. They start to get bad grades" (Dinges, "Blacks, Latinos Flounder at Top 7 High Schools").

Housing segregation. Although laws prohibiting housing discrimination have been in effect for decades, many people still face barriers when they try to buy or rent a home. Studies have shown that in some areas, blacks applying for housing are treated differently about half the time from whites with similar incomes. Discrimination ranges from being shown fewer housing units than white applicants, to being given worse rental terms, to being denied housing that was later offered to whites with the same or worse qualifications.

N In a paragraph, assess how well the social structures of your school provide all students access to the benefits or resources of the school.

C Choose a political body to research (your city council, state legislature, or Congress, for example). Draw a chart showing how many people from different social groups are represented in the body, compared to the population it serves. How well are women and different racial groups represented? Write a reflection about why some groups might be underrepresented and how that might affect their well-being in the community.

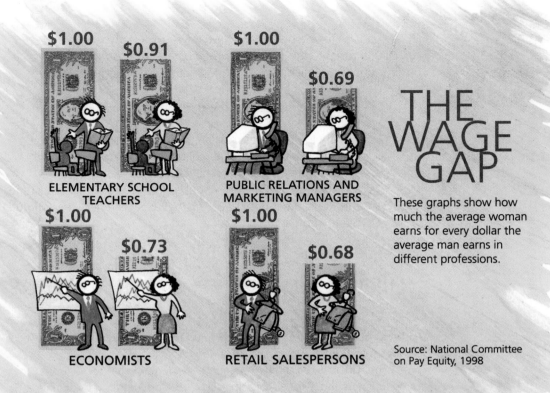

THE WAGE GAP

These graphs show how much the average woman earns for every dollar the average man earns in different professions.

$1.00 $0.91
ELEMENTARY SCHOOL TEACHERS

$1.00 $0.69
PUBLIC RELATIONS AND MARKETING MANAGERS

$1.00 $0.73
ECONOMISTS

$1.00 $0.68
RETAIL SALESPERSONS

Source: National Committee on Pay Equity, 1998

When applying for home mortgages, blacks are denied about 23 percent of the time, Latinos 20 percent of the time, and whites 10 percent of the time—even when they have the same income levels.

Such widespread discrimination helps to explain why many communities remain segregated along racial lines. Housing discrimination contributes to other types of structural discrimination, because the barriers to good housing prevent people from moving to locations where more jobs are available, or where schools are better funded. N

A Cycle of Exclusion

Discriminatory actions, prejudicial attitudes, and stereotyped images all work together to form a cycle of exclusion: a widely held stereotype combines with fear or selfishness to create a prejudicial attitude, which leads to discrimination on an individual level and then becomes incorporated into the structures of society. Structural discrimination leads to conditions that reinforce negative stereotypes. All people are called to work for an end to this cycle:

Racism is not merely one sin among many; it is a radical evil that divides the human family and denies the new creation of a redeemed world. To struggle against it demands an equally radical transformation, in our own minds and hearts as well as in the structure of our society. (*Brothers and Sisters to Us,* page 10)

9. What is a stereotype? How do we develop stereotypes?
10. Define these terms: *prejudice, discrimination, racism, the other.*
11. What is structural discrimination? Briefly describe one example.

In Depth

12. Describe the cycle of exclusion, illustrating your explanation with a specific example (either a real one or one you make up).
13. Review the discussion of having versus being in chapter 4. What aspects of the story about John Howard Griffin reflect the attitude "I am what I have"? What aspects reflect the attitude "I am who I am"?

Building Inclusive Communities

To break the cycle of exclusion, we must reconsider the question, Who belongs to our community and who does not?

Jesus was asked a similar question. Remember that Jesus taught that no commandments were greater than love of God and love of neighbor. In the Gospel of Luke, however, a questioner asked Jesus, "And who is my neighbor?" (Luke 10:29). In other words, the questioner wanted to know, Who deserves my love and who does not?

Who Is My Neighbor?

The term *neighbor* refers to those who are "nigh," or near to us. This can refer to physical nearness, such as the neighbor across the street, or to people we have something in common with. Often, however, we are tempted to think of "something in common" in narrow ways, such as having the same skin color, a similar income level, the same faith, or the same degree of education.

Jesus offers a different definition of *neighbor,* responding to the question by telling the parable of the good Samaritan, in which a Samaritan

P Jesus used a "good Samaritan" to challenge the self-righteousness and stereotypical thinking of his listeners. Who might appear as the "good" person in the story if Jesus were teaching today? Explain why the choice of this person would surprise and challenge modern listeners.

Q Think of someone you have encountered who often is excluded from social activities. Imagine how Jesus might interact with that person. Then write a prayer asking for the ability to be more like Jesus in your daily interactions with others. Be as specific as possible.

helps a wounded traveler after a priest and a Levite have walked by the man (see Luke 10:30–37). At the end of the story, Jesus asks, "Which of these three . . . was a neighbor?" (10:36). Jesus' questioner reluctantly admits that the neighbor was the Samaritan.

That answer probably surprised Jesus' listeners. The priest and the Levite were prominent members of the Jewish community. The people of Samaria, on the other hand, were looked down on as believers in a distorted, even heretical, form of Judaism; as a result, they were usually shunned. Jesus was teaching that love of neighbor means love of all; at the same time, he was challenging his listeners' self-righteousness and deeply held stereotypes.

Jesus embraces humanity

For Jesus, *neighbor* referred to anyone who deserved his love—even those who might be considered enemies (see Luke 6:27). His mission was universal—that is, meant for all people. By example, Jesus taught that the ability of all people to participate in the life of the community is an important dimension of the Kingdom of God:

- The Pharisees and the scribes were reported to have said, "This fellow welcomes sinners and eats with them" (Luke 15:2).
- Those suffering from leprosy were especially singled out as outcasts in Jesus' day, and to even touch a leper would cause "ritual impurity." Yet, when a man covered with leprosy asked Jesus to heal him, "Jesus stretched out his hand, touched him, and said, . . . 'Be made clean'" (Luke 5:13).
- Jesus treated women with respect and included them in the life of his community. For instance, although women were not provided with religious instruction, Jesus taught them (See Luke 10:39–42).

The Christian faith teaches that Jesus' very being represents an acceptance of humanity because he is God incarnate, fully God and also fully human. A still greater demonstration of Jesus' embrace of humanity is his death: he willingly shed his blood for the forgiveness of all. He excluded no one. This is why the U.S. bishops write: "Let all know that [racism] is a terrible sin that mocks the cross of Christ and ridicules the Incarnation. For the brother and sister of our Brother Jesus Christ are brother and sister to us" (*Brothers and Sisters to Us,* page 9).

Love of neighbor **means** love of all.

✳ *Student art:* "Semblance of a Smile in the Ghetto." Photograph; Claire Endo, Ramona Convent Secondary School, Alhambra, California

Searching the Heart

To change exclusive communities into inclusive ones, we must redefine our notions about who belongs and who is excluded—we must change our definition of neighbor. We need to experience conversion—a change of heart—on both the personal and the social levels. Like John Howard Griffin, we can begin to make that change by closely examining our own heart and the heart of society.

Examining our own heart

Attitudes about difference and diversity. When we are around people who are unlike us, how do we feel deep down? Is our behavior different than when we are around people who are more like us, with whom we may feel more comfortable?

Self-acceptance. People who have a hard time accepting themselves often fail to accept others. They make a show out of what they think is wrong with others in order to bolster a false sense of superiority.

The roots of our fear and hatred. Do we fear that others will harm us in some way? Do we believe that their differences somehow hold a threat or a challenge to our own way of doing things? Do our fears have any basis in reality, or are they irrational? Are we taking out our anger toward an individual who has harmed us by hating all those who seem to be like her or him?

Responding to prejudice. How do we respond to prejudice that is directed against us? Do we passively accept it or lash back in anger? Or do we follow the way of Jesus and Gandhi, nonviolently asserting our own dignity in a way that encourages the other person to better reflect his or her own dignity?

Our basic approach to life. Do we put most of our efforts into serving our own needs? Do we have any concern about other people or about contributing to the common good of our communities? To what extent are we guilty of the sins of greed and apathy?

We need to experience conversion —a change of heart.

Student art: "Unveiling." Oil pastel; Elisabeth C. Montana, Boylan Central Catholic High School, Rockford, Illinois

Examining the heart of society

Historical patterns. Because the cycle of exclusion is deeply rooted in history, we need to ask, How have past inequalities affected the ability of people to participate in society today?

Patterns of power. Who holds power in society, and how does that affect the ability of all to participate? Are all types of people represented in government, religious, and business leadership positions? Who lacks the material resources for a life of dignity, and why?

Opportunity for all. Do all people have access to the benefits of society—such as a good education? Do all have the ability to contribute their gifts to society—for instance, by having access to jobs that reflect their talents?

Honesty. Do we as a community honestly acknowledge patterns of exclusion so that they can be addressed, or do we pretend that they do not exist? Do we recognize and celebrate the gifts of diversity? **S**

Part of changing exclusive communities into inclusive communities involves making sure all types of people are fairly represented in government organizations such as the United Nations.

Working to Create Inclusive Communities

Earlier in this chapter, we saw how exclusion is fed by negative stereotypes and how it continues to promote the stereotypes as well. But we also can build a cycle of inclusion: once we include others, it is easier to see them as neighbors; seeing them in this light encourages us to further include them. The story that opened this chapter is a perfect example of how including others in a community can break the cycle of exclusion.

Between individuals

The first step in creating inclusive communities is often simply getting to know "the other," those about whom we might have fears or misconceptions as a result of our lack of knowledge.

Michael Bravly and Forsan Hussein offer a good example of how personal conversion can support efforts to change structures of discrimination at a social level. Both met at Brandeis University in Massachusetts, but they came from worlds apart: Michael is a former officer in the Israeli Defense Forces, while Forsan is a Palestinian. The hostility between Israelis and Palestinians runs deep, the result of more than fifty years of conflict over land Israel now occupies.

The fear and distrust on both sides of the conflict might have been a barrier between the two, but any barrier was soon bridged by the sarcastic sense of humor each had. They quickly developed a friendship. By the end of their first semester at the school, they had formed an informal dialogue group with four other students, two Israelis and two Arabs, for the purpose of bridging the divide between the two cultures.

R Read over the five areas we need to search in our heart. Write a paragraph reflecting on one area that you would want to focus on in changing your own heart.

S Write an essay examining the heart of a community to which you belong, using some or all of the questions listed here as guidance.

The group is called Children of Labaneh—an intentionally silly name that reflects something that unites rather than divides the two cultures: a love of labaneh, a type of thick yogurt enjoyed throughout the Middle East. At the group's weekly meetings, the students eat olives, pita bread, and, of course, labaneh as they learn about each other's culture. Each week, a student delivers a paper explaining some aspect of his or her culture, which the group then discusses. Sometimes discussions turn political and heated; other times, they just hang out and have fun.

The two friends also started a radio show called "Just Like You." The show focuses on Middle Eastern cuisine, personalities, and music, and always concludes with a segment in which the two friends discuss what Palestinians and Israelis have in common—everything from both having a history of British occupation to the cultures' common love of certain foods. Michael and Forsan believe that getting to know one another can help build peace among people—and that, in turn, can contribute to peace among nations.

"Coexistence is a long process," says Forsan. "If you tell a child that one plus one is two, he will believe it. . . . If you tell a child that Palestinians or Israelis are your friends and neighbors, he will also believe it" (Raz, "Partners for Peace"). 🕇

On a community level

The story that opened this chapter is a good example of how cooperation can change local social structures to create more inclusive communities. In South Carolina, many are taking such action by joining clubs aimed at creating more inclusive high school communities.

At Flora High School, for instance, students on the Harmony Committee cleaned up bathrooms containing racist graffiti, painting them in fresh colors and decorating them with posters and plants. Harmony Committee members participate in exercises designed to raise cultural awareness, and they make presentations to middle school students.

Such efforts paid off at another South Carolina high school. Airport High School created its own group, called Living in Peace, after a racially motivated shooting. When posters denouncing Black History Month appeared in the hallways a few years later, the group was prepared to respond. Students disposed of the posters, then held a school assembly. Their call for racial harmony received a standing ovation—twice (based on Roefs, "Better Together").

Once we **include others,** it is easier to see them as **neighbors.**

🌼 National Art Honor Society students at Mount Carmel Academy in New Orleans create more inclusive communities by helping children who are blind to create their own clay sculptures. *Student art:* "Seeing Through Their Eyes and Hands." Photograph; Ilaria Ramzy, Mount Carmel Academy, New Orleans, Louisiana

🕇 What social group in your community do you most need to know better? Either by talking with someone from that group or through research, make a list of the unique gifts people from that group bring to the community—for example, a special kind of food or music or a special way of seeing things.

Reconciliation is an important part of creating inclusive communities. As the Catholic church advocates participation for all people, it attempts to acknowledge its own contributions to the cycle of exclusion. In a letter entitled *Heritage and Hope,* the U.S. Catholic bishops offer an apology to Native Americans for the church's role in perpetuating injustice:

> As Church, we often have been unconscious and insensitive to the mistreatment of our Native American brothers and sisters and have at times reflected the racism of the dominant culture of which we have been a part. . . . We extend our apology to the native peoples and pledge ourselves to work with them to ensure their rights, their religious freedom, and the preservation of their cultural heritage. (Page 2)

On the national level

Governments play a key role in breaking the cycle of exclusion when they enact legislation that promotes participation and justice. For instance, the Americans with Disabilities Act (ADA) addresses the rights of disabled Americans to participate in society by seeking to guarantee their access to schools, workplaces, and so on.

The U.S. Catholic bishops make clear their support for legislation that encourages greater participation by attempting to correct the inequalities that were built into the structures of society as a result of past discrimination:

> Judiciously administered affirmative action programs in education and employment can be important expressions of the drive for solidarity and participation that is at the heart of justice. Social harm calls for social relief. (*Economic Justice for All*, 73)

On the global level

Exclusion on the global level needs to be addressed too. The voices of poorer, smaller nations are often ignored by global organizations determining international agreements: "Whole nations are fully prevented from participating in the international economic order because they lack the power to change their disadvantaged position" (*Economic Justice for All*, 77). Furthermore, the participation of developing countries in the world economy is hampered by their huge debts to rich nations. These debts prevent the poorer countries from providing for the basic needs of their own citizens. Efforts by the church and other organizations in recent years have encouraged some nations to forgive, or write off, a portion of these burdensome debts. But economic inequality must continue to be addressed to ensure the full participation of all nations in the global community. ⊍

Toward a Community of Love

We began this chapter with a question: How do we define community? The example of Jesus reveals that true community is the place where the sharing of gifts and talents among all people makes each person more fully alive. It is a place where differences among people are not a source of division but rather a source of celebration.

The limitations of human sinfulness may make such a community sound like an impossible dream. In fact, the U.S. Catholic bishops acknowledge that

> the fullness of love and community will be achieved only when God's work in Christ comes to completion in the kingdom of God. This kingdom has been inaugurated among us, but God's redeeming and transforming work is not yet complete. (*Economic Justice for All*, 67)

But the more we open ourselves to the Holy Spirit and to one another, the closer we come to experiencing that Kingdom. ⋎

The U.S. Catholic bishops have acknowledged and apologized for the church's racism toward Native Americans. Acknowledging a history of exclusion helps to create more inclusive communities by promoting reconciliation and healing.

⊍ Working with others from your class, brainstorm some specific ways to build more inclusive structures at the local, national, or global level. Summarize your ideas in a one-page plan of action. Be prepared to share it with the class.

⋎ Write a story by yourself or work with a group of friends to create a skit that illustrates something you have learned about participation in community. Be prepared to discuss aspects of your story or skit in class.

14. According to Jesus, who is our neighbor?
15. What do Jesus' Incarnation and Crucifixion imply about how we should treat others?
16. Name three questions that can help us examine our own heart and three questions that can help us examine the heart of society with regard to exclusion.
17. In a short paragraph, explain one strategy for breaking the cycle of exclusion.

---

18. Briefly explain how each of the other themes of Catholic social teaching (listed in chapter 2) affect or are affected by the call to participate in community.

WHAT YOU CAN DO . . .

- Make a conscious effort to get to know and respect people who are different from you. If you feel uncomfortable getting to know someone who is different, search your heart to find out why.
- Challenge stereotypes and prejudicial statements when you hear them.
- Reach out to those who are excluded from your school community and help them to become more involved in a way that they are comfortable with.
- Start a group in which people from different backgrounds can discuss what they have in common as well as how to break down the barriers that divide them.
- If you are part of a group that is excluded by others, help others to know your group better by speaking out about the gifts it has to offer and the ways it is excluded. At the same time, work to change structures of exclusion.
- Organize an event that builds greater understanding of groups that are typically excluded from society—perhaps a celebration of diversity that showcases the gifts of different cultural groups in your community, or a presentation by someone from an excluded group. ☺

6 WORKING WITH DIGNITY

good work

~~unemployment~~

creativity

Participating
in God's creation

In This Chapter . . .

FREE THE CHILDREN

Loud **applause** greeted Iqbal Masih as he rose to the podium. He had traveled to the United States from Pakistan to receive an award in honor of his courage in exposing the horrors of child labor. When the audience quieted down, he began to tell his story, a story not unlike that of many children in South Asia.

Iqbal's parents had borrowed 600 rupees (about $12) from the owner of a carpet factory. In exchange, Iqbal, who was about four years old at the time, was forced to work in the factory until the loan was repaid. For twelve hours a day, six days a week, the children crouched before carpet

Left: "We are free!" Iqbal Masih chanted with the audience when he received the Reebok Youth in Action Award in 1994. *Right:* After being rescued from forced labor in a carpet factory in Varanasi, India, a young boy is reunited with his mother.

looms tying tiny knots to make carpets for the European and North American markets. If the children made mistakes, they were beaten, whipped, or hung upside down in a back room with their legs tied together. Worse, they were fined for every mistake they made. By the time he was ten, Iqbal's family owed 13,000 rupees to the factory owner.

But then, human rights activists bought his freedom. He was able to attend school for the first time—and he began traveling the world speaking out against child servitude.

"We have a slogan at our school," Iqbal told the crowd. "When children get free, we all together say, 'We are free! We are free!'" The audience was rising to its feet.

"We are . . ." Iqbal chanted.

"Free!" replied the crowd of adults and youth.

Iqbal had once told a reporter, "Now I am not scared of the factory owner—he is scared of me!" Indeed, the carpet industry had often threatened to silence him. Four months after his trip to the United States, on Easter Sunday, Iqbal was gunned down while riding a bicycle. The next day his body was placed on a funeral platform next to a large cross symbolizing his Catholic faith, and carried through his village. Among the mourners were many of the child workers he had sought to free.

Three days later, twelve-year-old Craig Kielburger was looking for the comics in the *Toronto Star* when a front-page headline caught his eye: Battled Child Labour, Boy, 12, Murdered. Craig read the story about Iqbal in disbelief.

Craig researched the issue over the next few days, and the following week, he spoke to his seventh-grade class about what he had learned. His presentation motivated twelve of his classmates to join him in forming a group for "children helping children." Free the Children was born.

Soon the small group was speaking to classes of elementary school students, then high school students. As their reputation spread, Craig was invited to speak about child labor to two thousand people at the Ontario Federation of Labor convention in Toronto. After his impassioned speech, the audience gave him a standing ovation, and spontaneously began pledging financial support—$150,000 in all.

It seemed to Craig that the next logical step would be to visit the children his group was trying to help. That winter, he spent seven weeks traveling throughout South Asia with a twenty-four-year-old mentor, meeting and befriending hundreds of child laborers. The children made bricks, fireworks, carpets, metal cups, and candy; they cleaned houses, sold fruit, unloaded ships, and broke rocks. An eight-year-old girl named Muniannal even disassembled used medical syringes so their parts could be resold—often accidentally cutting her bare feet on the dirty needles that covered the floor. In Varanasi, India, Craig met twenty-two boys, ages eight to twelve, who were rescued from forced labor at a carpet factory. He accompanied them home to tearful reunions with their families.

Besides meeting with child laborers, Craig met two other important people during his trip: Mother Teresa, from whom he requested

"When children get free, we all together say,
'We are free! We are free!'"

"Have you read this?" he asked his mother. "What exactly is child labor?"

She was as lost for answers as he was. "Try the library," she suggested.

prayers for laboring children; and Jean Chrétien, the prime minister of Canada. Chrétien was leading a trade mission with Canadian business leaders—but the issue of child labor was not on the agenda. Craig wrangled a fifteen-minute meeting with the prime minister in order to press the point. At first, the prime minister deflected Craig's appeals.

"We are slowly making progress on this issue, Craig," he said. "But things are not always as simple as they seem." He explained that if Canada forbade the purchase of foreign goods made with child labor, other governments might retaliate by refusing to buy products from Canada.

"But if you had a blanket policy that linked all trade to human rights, you couldn't be accused of discriminating against any one country or product," Craig offered.

"It's a very complicated issue," Chrétien said.

"But Mr. Chrétien, will you bring up the issue of child labor with the South Asian governments?"

The prime minister paused for a few seconds; Craig figured he would only offer to consider the issue.

"Yes," he finally said. "Yes, I will bring up the issue. And yes, child labor will be on the agenda."

Today, the youth-led Free the Children is an international organization with thousands of active members in more than twenty countries. Recognizing that education is the key to breaking the cycle of poverty and eliminating child labor, the organization focuses on providing education to poor children around the world. It has raised hundreds of thousands of dollars to build or support hundreds of schools. Moreover, it has bought cows, land, and machinery so poor families can support themselves without sending their children to work. In addition, the youth work for social change by speaking about child labor around the world, urging consumers to boycott products made by children, and lobbying governments to take action—often with impressive results.

When Iqbal Masih was killed, it seemed that death had silenced a voice for freedom. Or did it? A young girl named Shenaz, who, like Iqbal, had been freed from forced labor, held onto hope as she watched his funeral procession. "The day Iqbal died," she declared, "a thousand new Iqbals were born." In Free the Children, perhaps her prediction came true. (Based on Kielburger, *Free the Children*)

What Is the Value of Work?

In Catholic social teaching, work has a value that goes beyond what it produces. As we noted in the previous chapter, work is a basic human right because it is necessary for human life and it enables people to participate

"The day Iqbal died," she declared, "a **thousand** new Iqbals were born."

Moved by Iqbal's story, Craig Kielburger *(back row, center)* started Free the Children. One of the group's first actions was to start a petition to end child labor.

in the life of the community. But in the view of Catholic social teaching, work has value even beyond those basics: it is an expression of the creativity we possess as images of God. For these reasons, the church affirms the dignity of work and the rights of workers.

But the experience of Iqbal Masih and the world's estimated 120 million child laborers—as well as many adult workers—illustrates that not everyone holds that view. When work is valued only for what it produces, workers often lose out. In this case, work might actually harm a workers' life, dignity, and ability to participate in community.

What is the value of work? Is it possible for all people to have good work? These are the questions we will examine in this chapter. **A**

1. List five ways that Free the Children works to end child labor.
2. What does Catholic social teaching say the value of work is? What is an alternate view of work that can harm workers?

3. Write a paragraph discussing how the story of Iqbal and Craig reflects elements of the paschal mystery—the dying and rising of Jesus.

Two Views of Work

Work is any sustained effort expended for a purpose—effort that makes a difference in the world. People often view work as a chore, a necessary but not very enjoyable reality of life. In this view, work is **toil**—it is difficult, challenging, and wearing. This view legitimately reflects part of the reality of work. In the Book of Genesis, the toil of work is portrayed as one of the consequences of humankind's separation from God.

But Christian justice has a different view of work, one that says work still has the potential to be very good. **B**

A Think of one worker who has affected you this week. Write a paragraph reflecting on how this person's work affected your life and dignity, and how it seemed to affect the life and dignity of the worker.

B If you have a part-time job, would you characterize your labor as good work or as toil? Use specific events to back your claim.

Donald Jackson, a scribe for the British queen, is creating a one-thousand-page Bible the way Benedictine monks once did, using handmade inks and quill pens. When we use our creativity for the common good, we participate in God's work of creation.

The Goodness of Work

Listen to how the following people approach their work:

- "Teaching is a job. . . . It gives me the money to eat and pay my bills. . . . Teaching is also a service. . . . My teaching fulfills a need in the community" (quoted in Droel, *The Spirituality of Work,* pages 22–23).
- "The most important part of my job is . . . whether my customers will leave the [grocery] store feeling better or worse because of their brief encounter with me" (Pierce, editor, *Of Human Hands,* page 49).
- "As an engineer, I try not to do anything that will be harmful to the environment; . . . much of what's being engineered today will end up polluting the earth. I try to reduce that" (O'Connell, "Work of Human Hands").

These workers' comments reflect the church's attitude toward work. The U.S. Catholic bishops sum up that attitude in their 1999 pastoral letter *Everyday Christianity.* In it they list four basic aspects of work:

> In the Catholic tradition, work is not a burden, . . . not just how we make a living. Work is a way of *supporting our family, realizing our dignity, promoting the common good,* and *participating in God's creation* (italics added).

A closer look at each of these points reveals a deeper value of work.

Family needs

When we speak of a person's work, we often use the term **livelihood:** work that provides the basic necessities of life. The income from work enables a family to maintain a home and to buy food and clothing. Work also can provide these things directly: workers can build shelters, grow food, and make clothing for themselves and their family. Work is a foundation for family life, meeting the family's survival needs. If a family remains in need even though one or both adults are working, work is not achieving its fundamental purpose.

In addition to providing for the family's material needs, work educates the children in the family. Parents can show their children how to be creative with their life through work, and help their children to grow into full humanness. **C**

Human dignity

Besides providing a livelihood, work allows us to grow as people, learning and putting our natural talents to use:

> Work is a good thing for man—a good thing for his humanity—because through

 Write a script for a scene set in a home in your neighborhood. The scene should illustrate what children might learn at home about the actual work that must be done to maintain a family, and what they might learn about attitudes toward work. Prepare to read your script in class.

work man not only transforms nature, adapting it to his own needs, but he also achieves fulfillment as a human being and indeed in a sense becomes "more a human being." (*On Human Work [Laborem Exercens]*, 9) ◐

Work is the primary means by which each of us becomes all God calls us to be. We do this through our work, in part by contributing to the common good and participating in God's creation.

The common good

Every worker is a member of the larger society, so work enhances the common good. "Work serves to add to the heritage of the whole human family, of all the people living in the world" (*On Human Work*, 10). In a class discussion about the value of work, one student's face lit up with sudden insight:

> Now I understand why my Dad is such a perfectionist about his work! He's a carpenter, and he says that if he's going to put in a door, it will be a door that works perfectly. Now I see that it's not so much the door he cares about; it's the people who will use it. He wants to give them something that's perfect, because that's what they should have.

This student spoke with unmistakable pride; she had not realized before what a valuable contribution her father was making to others' lives. A door that works perfectly—it's a

simple thing that we might not appreciate unless we had to struggle with a balky door. Work is a way for us to provide something good and useful for others. ℰ

Sharing in God's work

The Creation narratives in Genesis tell us that work is central to who we are as persons. Because we are created as images of a God who creates, we are invited to share in God's creative work:

> [Humankind], created to God's image, received a mandate to subject to [themselves] the earth and all it contains, and to govern the world with justice and holiness. . . . While providing the substance of life for themselves and their families, men and women are performing their activities in a way which appropriately benefits society. They can justly consider that by their labour they are unfolding the creator's work. (*The Church in the Modern World [Gaudium et Spes]*, 34).

Although the narrative found in Genesis uses the phrases "subdue the earth" and "have dominion," the role assigned to humans is not really domineering. Remember that at this point in the story, sin has not yet entered

Every worker is a member of the larger society, so work **enhances the common good.**

Work is a way for us to provide something useful for others.

◐ Reflect on some work you have done for the pure pleasure of the activity (a chore, an artistic endeavor, or some volunteer work). What made it enjoyable? What did you gain from doing it?

ℰ Make a list of at least fifteen ways the good work of others has contributed to the quality of your life since you got up this morning.

the picture, so the man and woman would rule in God's place, doing only God's will. Similarly, in the second chapter of Genesis, we read that the man is given the job of naming the animals. His work is to determine how the rest of creation will be used, again in accordance with God's will. Humans are given creation "to cultivate and care for it" (2:15, NAB).

Even though original sin brought toil into the world, good work is still one of the important ways that individuals have of joining in God's work. Whenever our work makes the world a better place, it reflects the work of God. It is for this reason that the church says that work has a natural dignity.

When Good Work Is Denied

Notice that each of the dimensions of the value of work reflects basic relationships necessary for justice: the relationships with one's dignity, family, community, and God. Because work is necessary to maintain these life-giving relationships, all people have a **responsibility to work.** But justice says that whenever people have a responsibility to do something, they also have a corresponding right to do it. The responsibility to work is balanced by the right to work.

What would we expect work to look like if it reflected the values of the Christian worldview? Some of the characteristics associated with good work might include the following:
- a wage sufficient to support a family
- a fair opportunity for advancement, regardless of ethnicity, gender, or personal beliefs

- a workplace where health and safety guidelines for the industry are observed
- medical and retirement benefits
- ongoing training
- the ability to join a union or association to protect worker rights and privileges
- an employer who respects his or her employees, seeking their input and adjusting for the demands of their personal lives
- work that benefits others, or at least does not harm them

All these are characteristics of good work. But many workers around the world are denied even the most basic benefits of work. Many workers don't earn enough to support themselves, have no health or retirement benefits, and work in environments that are unsafe or unhealthy. In developing nations, the situation can be even worse: for many workers there are no rest periods, few days off, and hardly any free time. Some workers are not even free to leave the premises where they work. And, of course, many of these workers are children. **F**

Treating workers like machines

At the root of unjust working conditions is an attitude that regards workers as nothing more than a **means of production**—a way of producing goods and services. Craig Kielburger describes working conditions at a brick kiln in Pakistan:

A landscape of reddish brown clay moulded into a small town, a huge smokestack . . . spewing out thick smoke. Its people worked the clay from dawn to dusk, preparing it to be shipped away in heavy trucks, their only contact with the outside world. The people lived entirely in labour.

F Which of the items in the list from activity E seem most important to your own future work? Which seem least important? Explain your views in two to three paragraphs.

G Reread the description of work in the clay pit. What might you say to the owners to convince them that treating the workers this way is unjust? How might the owners respond?

They started young. Eight years old, and even younger sometimes. . . . They would spend a lifetime at the same endless tasks—chopping clay from the open pit, shovelling it onto wheelbarrows, dumping it into a pile, mixing it with water, slapping it into moulds, turning out bricks, stacking them in wheelbarrows, pushing them to the kiln, lowering them inside, stoking the fires, loading the cooled bricks aboard trucks.

Day after day, for a lifetime.

The debts of people working in the brick kiln can be passed down from generation to generation. In [one] boy's case, his grandmother took out the loan that forced his family into bondage and continues to enslave them. He . . . had never been outside the area of the brick kiln and did not know what a school was. (Kielburger, *Free the Children,* pages 222–223)

This kind of treatment signals a dehumanizing of the workforce. Workers are seen as tools, not as persons, and their treatment is determined solely by economic considerations. In this view, the length of the workday is determined by the number of hours that a worker can stay at her job without collapsing; no consideration is given to the worker, because her worth is measured only in terms of what she can produce. This kind of dehumanization knows no age limits: worldwide 120 million children under age fourteen work at least full-time. Nearly one-quarter of the world's children between six and eleven years old never go to school.

In many countries, labor laws afford little protection to workers. According to Aung San Suu Kyi, human-rights advocate and winner of the 1991 Nobel Peace Prize, her native Burma enacted a law in 1964 guaranteeing minimum wages, setting maximum hours, and requiring disability compensation. However, because unions are not allowed in Burma, she explains, the law has never been enforced. Similar violations of existing laws are widespread, as in sweatshops in the United States, where many workers are illegal immigrants, and as such are unable to bring violations to the attention of the authorities without risking deportation. Others, such as domestic workers, may fall outside the protection of laws because they are hired "off the books."

Speaking through an interpreter to college students, Lorena del Carmen Hernandez described working conditions in a clothing factory in El Salvador:

When we enter into work and all the rest of the day, we suffer a hell inside the factory, they . . . let us go to the bathroom

> He had **never been** outside the area of the brick kiln and did **not** know what a **school** was.

Young people deserve good work too—in school. But as Craig Kielburger saw in this brick factory, too many children are denied an education because their family's poverty forces them to work.

Workers at factories around the world often face conditions that do not respect their human dignity.

. . . once in the morning and once in the afternoon. They scream at us, hit tables where we're working. They don't give us fresh water. The ventilation is no good. It's so hot that many faint. (Levy, "Workers Discuss Labor Conditions")

When National Labor Committee monitors visited the factory, she said, the owners simply reduced demands on the workers until the observers left.

Unemployment

Of course, many people are unable to find any productive work at all. The consequences of unemployment can be devastating. In emerging nations, employment may mean the difference between survival and starvation. Developed nations provide some financial support for the unemployed, but for many workers, the loss of a job can result in poverty.

Another consequence of unemployment is the loss of a sense of personal dignity. "Very few people survive long periods of unemployment without some psychological damage even if they have sufficient funds to meet their needs," the U.S. Catholic bishops note in *Economic Justice for All* (141). Will Reinhard lost his job when the steel mill where he had worked his way up to foreman closed down:

> "It was like losing a friend," Reinhard recalls, "something that you had for over half your life that's not there anymore." In those first weeks at home, unemployed at age fifty-three for the first time in his adult life, Reinhard struggled with the jumble of emotions that accompanied the loss: the bitterness that the company hadn't done more to save the mill, a creeping depression, some fear. (Harris, "Surviving the Age of Insecurity") **H**

Long-term unemployment has the potential to cause great harm to families. In addition to causing financial hardship, it can lead to alcohol abuse, domestic violence, and divorce.

Barriers to work

As we saw in the previous chapter, those who are excluded from full participation in society face special challenges in finding good work. Discrimination based on race and gender form one barrier; poverty is another. Welfare reform legislation passed in 1996 requires aid recipients to find work or lose benefits. But many welfare recipients lack the education and skills to find good work. Take Maria Ortega, for example. Maria is a single mother living in southern California who never finished high school, and has only a tenuous grasp of English. As part of the effort to move welfare recipients into jobs, her county provided her with two years' worth of basic education and computer training. During that time, Maria began volunteering in various neighborhood offices doing clerical work. After the two years were up, she was expected to find a job—or eventually face the loss of

H Write the words "The factory closes" in the middle of a page. Draw a box around these words, then write some of the results of this event in circles, drawing lines to connect them to the box. Fill as much of the page as you can.

her benefits. She looked for work for four months, filling out three applications a day:

> They put so much pressure on me just to get a job. . . . I told them that I haven't worked for such a long time. That I don't have any experience. I went and filled out applications—I went to every store in the entire Whittier Mall! But nobody called me back. . . . I went with my friend to an agency and we applied for anything they had. I told the woman there, "I don't have any experience, but I try. I want to learn." She told me that there isn't anything right now. She said that as soon as something comes up, she will call me. I hope she calls. (Adair, "Climbing the Walls")

Maria eventually did find work with a landscaping company. Jobs often are not located near the highest concentrations of unemployed people, and this was true for Maria—she had to commute over an hour each way. Because she began working, her food stamps were cut, even though the job paid only seven dollars an hour. That left very little for living after she paid for the transportation and child care necessary to maintain the job. Maria's case, unfortunately, is not unique: low wages are a major obstacle to good work for millions of families.

For Review

4. In your own words, restate the four purposes of work identified in church teaching.
5. Why do people have a responsibility to work?
6. What does it mean to treat workers as a means of production?
7. Name at least three ways people are prevented from having good work.

In Depth

8. Create a relationship map (either by drawing or writing) describing the conditions necessary for Maria Ortega to get and maintain good work.

Whenever our work makes the world a better place, it reflects the **work of God.**

As head of the United Farm Workers Union, Cesar Chavez (right, in sunglasses) brought a Catholic perspective to the struggle for workers' rights. In 1983, he led a march from Philadelphia to New Jersey to protest the treatment of workers at a soup company.

Creating Human-Centered Work

Good work is a basic foundation for justice in the world. The lack of good work not only leads to poverty but also prevents people from participating in society and becoming all they are meant to be.

How can we provide good work for all people? According to Catholic social teaching, the key is ensuring that work serves people before products.

A Parable About Work

Jesus himself was a worker, living in a culture that tended to equate a person's means of livelihood with his value as a person. Manual labor was not highly regarded in itself, yet Jesus worked as a carpenter before he began teaching. Jesus clearly directed his message to workers, using all manner of human work to illustrate his teachings: tending sheep, baking bread, making wine, fishing, farming, and housekeeping, for instance.

In Jesus' parable, the just employer pays the field laborers not the lowest possible wage but "whatever is right."

Jesus told a parable about work that says a lot about what work is meant to be in a just world. As you read the parable of the laborers in the vineyard, pay attention to how the workers are treated:

> For the kingdom of heaven is like a landowner who went out early in the morning to hire laborers for his vineyard. After agreeing with the laborers for the usual daily wage, he sent them into his vineyard. When he went out about nine o'clock, he saw others standing idle in the marketplace; and he said to them, "You also go into the vineyard, and I will pay you whatever is right." So they went. When he went out about noon and about three o'clock, he did the same. And about five o'clock he went out and found others standing around; and he said to them, "Why are you standing here idle all day?" They said to him, "Because no one has hired us." He said to them, "You also go into the vineyard." (Matthew 20:1–7)

At the end of the day, each of the laborers is paid. The usual arrangement would be to pay each laborer according to the amount of work he did. But in Jesus' parable, the landowner pays each worker the full daily wage. The laborers who worked all day complain:

> "These last worked only one hour, and you have made them equal to us who have borne the burden of the day and the scorching heat." But [the landowner]

I Is the landowner's payment of the workers fair? Prepare to discuss your views in class.

replied to one of them, "Friend, I am doing you no wrong; did you not agree with me for the usual daily wage? Take what belongs to you and go; I choose to give to this last the same as I give to you. Am I not allowed to do what I choose with what belongs to me? Or are you envious because I am generous?" (Matthew 20:11–15)

Work Is for People

On the deepest level, the parable of the laborers in the vineyard is about God's generosity toward all—even those who, according to the world's standards, do not seem to deserve it.

But the parable also teaches us about the nature of just work. The landowner is concerned with justice, agreeing to pay "whatever is right." He pays all the workers the "usual daily wage"—a wage that is sufficient for living—because, in the landowner's view, the worker is more important than the kind of work being done.

This is a basic insight of Catholic social teaching. John Paul II draws a distinction between the **subjective aspect of work,** which is what the worker experiences; and the **objective aspect of work,** which is what the worker produces. In his 1981 encyclical *On Human Work,* he says that the subjective aspect of work is more important than the objective aspect:

> The basis for determining the value of human work is not primarily the kind of work being done, but the fact that the one who is doing it is a person. . . . This does not mean that from the objective point of view human work cannot and must not be rated and qualified in any way. It only means that . . . in the first place work is "for man" and not man "for work." (6)

The **worker** is more important than the kind of work being done.

✳ *Student art:* Photograph; Mary Diaz, Benilde–Saint Margaret's Catholic High School, Saint Louis Park, Minnesota

Imagine a five-year-old working with poster paints. He shows his mother the masterpiece he has created, looking for approval. Only the most insensitive mother would criticize the artistic merit of the painting. It is the subjective aspect of the work that would be important to the mother; the child's joy in painting and presenting the picture has more value to her than the picture itself. This is not to imply that work has no objective value, but because the mother loves her child, the child is more important; the painting, though the mother may treasure it, is secondary.

In a similar way, because God loves us, *we* are important to God; our work is secondary. Simply put, work should serve the good of the people doing it. When it does not, then it is not just. ✍

The Rights and Responsibilities of Workers

The church's view that work should serve the good of workers leads it to claim that workers have certain rights that should not be violated. These can be divided into rights that protect workers' responsibility to meet family needs and rights that protect the workers' dignity.

Meeting family needs

Obviously, when people cannot work, families will suffer. But to speak of just work means more than earning money. Catholic social teaching on work and the family can be summarized in three ways:

- **The right to work.** Catholic social teaching affirms that everyone has the right to work. Work is the means by which persons fulfill their responsibility to provide for themselves and their families, as well as a way to find fulfillment and to benefit others. It is also the primary way that people take part in God's work of creation. Clearly, if people are denied work, they are missing out on something very important to their humanity.

- **A just wage.** Because church teachings identify work as the basis for family life, the pay for work can only be considered just if it is enough to support the worker's family. What makes a wage fair is not whether the worker has agreed to it: if someone is desperate, he will agree to anything, just or not. In any agreement between employer and worker, only a **living wage**—a wage that enables workers to support a decent life for themselves and their families—can be regarded as a just wage. In addition to actual payment, workers should receive adequate health care and pensions. ✍

Catholic social teaching calls for a living wage, one that pays enough to support both the worker and his or her family.

✍ Open the telephone book yellow pages at random. Using the entries on that page, write down fifteen jobs that would be related to the businesses listed. Rank the jobs from 1 to 15, with 1 for the job generally considered the most prestigious. Does our society tend to equate a person's means of livelihood with his or her value as a person? Write a short reflection that includes factors that determine job prestige.

- **Respect for the worker's family.** As part of the whole person, the worker's home life should be taken into account too. This is particularly true for working women, who are sometimes "punished" for attending to the needs of the family. People should have enough leisure time to develop talents and to take part in the life of their community.

Supporting human dignity

In addition, everything surrounding work should accommodate the worker's dignity:

- **A safe work environment.** For example, in *Rerum Novarum,* Pope Leo XIII explicitly directs the employer not to give workers more work than they can do, not to give them work unsuited to their age, and to avoid harming their savings in any way. Employers have a responsibility for the general safety of their workers, even in dangerous jobs.
- **Permission to join unions.** All workers should be allowed to join unions, which can represent them so they have a voice in corporate decisions. A strike by employees is one of the methods used by unions in the struggle for justice. The strike is a legitimate tool, but one that should be used only as an extraordinary measure. Employees and employers should first strive to work together in solidarity to create justice in the workplace.

- **Equal treatment.** Church teaching urges that all workers should be treated equally. For example, immigrant workers should be housed decently. They should be free to bring their families with them, and they should be helped to become part of their new community. And persons with disabilities should be enabled to participate in work to the extent of their capabilities.
- **The right to private property and economic initiative.** Because all people have the right to work, all people also have the right to **economic initiative**—in other words, to be self-employed, to start a business, and to expand one's business. The structure of society should avoid limiting the right to economic initiative. Associated with the right to economic initiative is the right to own private property. Both of these rights are meant to serve the common good, and are therefore limited by the need to respect human life and dignity as well as to care for God's creation. **L**

Employers and employees have a responsibility to work together in solidarity to create justice in the workplace. But if that fails, workers have the right to strike.

K What would a living wage be where you live? Draw up a hypothetical budget listing expenses a family of four might face over the period of a month (you may want to seek the help of an adult in your family). Find out the approximate cost in your area of five of the items. How much would a worker have to earn in one month, after taxes, to provide those five items? Bring your research to class for discussion.

L In an essay, explain how a work experience has helped you to be more fully what you are meant to be. Your example does not have to be paid work. Describe what you did and how it affected you.

The right to education

To the list above, we can add one more right necessary for good work: the right to a good education. The lack of an adequate education prevents millions of people from developing their talents and finding work that is needed by their communities.

"Most people agree that good primary education is one of the best ways to eliminate exploitative child labour," Craig Kielburger notes in *Free the Children* (page 309). Among developing nations, many governments have directed most of their national budget to the military or to repayment of debts. Little money may be left for education. When the quality of schools is low and the cost of attending them is high, parents send even their youngest children to work. These children are denied the education they deserve; later they cannot find skilled employment as adults. The long-term result is a population unfit for the kind of jobs necessary for their country's development: the people remain poor and their government continues to borrow. We will discuss the role of education in justice at greater length in the next chapter.

Solidarity in Work

Historically, discussions about work, workers, and justice have tended to divide people along ideological lines. As we discussed in chapter 2, the exploitation of workers that occurred during the Industrial Revolution led to a debate between those who favored unrestricted capitalism and those who favored forms of socialism.

The church has responded to this debate by rejecting the extremes of both systems. Catholic social teaching has always advocated that economic systems be based on love of God and neighbor. The key to creating good work for all is solidarity between employers and workers.

The model for this solidarity is Jesus. The church teaches that when we approach our work with love, it can transform the world:

> By enduring the toil of work in union with Christ crucified for us, man in a way collaborates with the son of God for the redemption of humanity. He shows himself a true disciple of Christ by carrying the cross in his turn every day in the activity that he is called upon to perform. (*On Human Work,* 27)

Good primary education is one of the best ways to eliminate exploitative child labour.

✳ *Student art:* Photograph; James Habig, Sacred Heart Preparatory School, Atherton, California

9. What does the parable of the laborers in the vineyard say about human work?
10. Explain the difference between the subjective and the objective aspects of work.
11. Which aspect does Catholic social teaching say is more important, and why?
12. List the rights of workers, including a brief explanation of each.
13. How does inadequate education affect work?

14. Choose one of the stories about work in this chapter. In several paragraphs, explain whether the objective or the subjective aspect of work is emphasized, and why. Support your argument by explaining how the rights of workers are respected or denied.

Restoring Work's Promise

Is the church's vision of just work really practical? Obviously, making just work available to all people would require broad changes in society and workplaces. Those changes are practical only to the extent that we base our work on solidarity with one another.

The primary responsibility for the welfare of workers falls to employers. But the competitive nature of the marketplace makes it difficult for individual employers to make these changes alone. Making changes on a social level lays the foundation for changing the way we work.

Indirect Employers

In his encyclical *On Human Work,* John Paul II discusses the concept of the **indirect employer,** that is, any policy-making institution that helps regulate what employers may or may not do.

An indirect employer could be a labor union, a national government, or a worldwide organization. Although the employer is directly responsible for working conditions, the indirect employer needs to create a climate that encourages just labor practices. For example, both the United Nations and the International Labor Organization have proposed setting regulations on just working conditions worldwide; governments can ratify such standards and enforce them. Doing this would ensure that all economic enterprises have to follow the same rules. Recall that Prime Minister Jean Chrétien objected to Craig's proposal on the grounds that it would be viewed as an unfair trading practice. Creating fair economic structures for everyone would curb such concerns

and help in the fight against dehumanizing working conditions.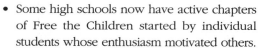

The Power of Cooperation

Acting alone, it may be difficult for us to imagine transforming the experience of workers. But Craig Kielburger demonstrated that the key to changing labor conditions is cooperating with others to influence direct and indirect employers.

Political activism

In a democracy, citizens not only have the right but also the responsibility to influence the decisions made by government. Voting is not the only way to influence public policy: students, even those who are not old enough to vote, can and should let their voices be heard by public policy makers:

- Some high schools now have active chapters of Free the Children started by individual students whose enthusiasm motivated others.
- Students have been involved in demonstrations and letter-writing campaigns to urge

Across the nation, college students—such as these at the University of Michigan—have taken action to end sweatshop labor, beginning with the factories that make their school's clothing.

M Interview a local business leader, asking how economic and government structures—for instance, laws, regulations, international trade rules, competition, and so on—affect her or his ability to create just working conditions. Use the rights of workers as a guide for the questions you ask.

THE COST OF A PAIR OF JEANS

How much of the price goes to the workers

$17.99
$1.50

$17.99
11¢

Average hourly wage of garment workers

$8.31

23¢

Much of the inexpensive clothing sold at discount retailers such as Wal-Mart, JCPenney, and Target is made by workers in developing countries. This chart compares the benefits three groups receive from the sale of a pair of jeans: U.S. garment workers; workers at Chentex, a Taiwanese-owned factory located in Nicaragua; and retail stores.

Source: National Labor Committee

WEEKLY PAY
of the highest paid Nicaraguan garment worker **$17.31**

SOME WEEKLY EXPENSES *of an average Nicaraguan garment worker*

Bus fare to work six days a week	Rent for a two-family one-room dirt-floor hut	Water	Electricity	Wood for cooking on outdoor stove	Powdered Milk	Lunch (beans, rice, cheese, and a little meat)	Total
$2.45	$3.53	$1.41	$1.77	$1.88	$4.08	$6.73	**$21.85**

the establishment of a worldwide labeling system that would let consumers know which manufacturers promote humane working conditions.

- And just as Craig Kielburger has lobbied heads of government for change, other youth have challenged their governments to ratify the International Labor Organization's *Fundamental Conventions,* which provide basic protections for workers.

Purchasing power

Another way that young people can exercise their power for justice is through their purchasing practices. In the 1960s, for instance, seventeen million Americans demonstrated the power of consumers by participating in a successful grape boycott in support of farm workers seeking to establish a union.

Altogether, young people in the United States spend billions of dollars every year. Some have been very influential in boycotts of manufacturers whose labor practices are unfair. For example, colleges and universities receive income from the sale of clothing, such as sweatshirts and caps, that displays their logo. At campuses across the country, college students have asked school administrations to sign agreements only with those clothing manufacturers who can guarantee, through independent inspections, that their clothing is not manufactured under unjust working conditions.

A voice in the workplace

Finally, if you work, you may be able to have some input on policies at your workplace. Every employee can take responsibility to find out about working conditions where he or she works, and about the indirect impact that the business has on other workers.

It can be difficult to picture ourselves questioning accepted practices, especially at work, but justice calls each of us to take a high degree of responsibility and to use whatever influence we do have. We are each called to demonstrate a commitment to solidarity, not just to approve of it abstractly.

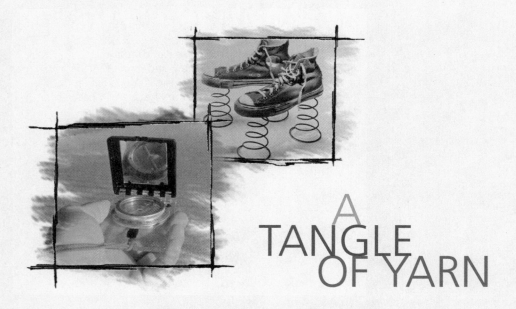

A TANGLE OF YARN

Tracing the causes of the injustice that many workers around the world face begins to reveal the complexity of the problem. Devising solutions is just as complex, as Craig Kielburger discovered soon after Free the Children was founded. During a question-and-answer session following a presentation to a high school class, the students began to ask difficult questions:

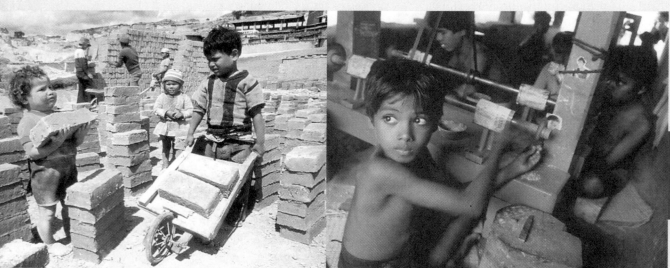

What would happen to these children if they no longer worked? Ending child labor requires overcoming the other injustices that cause it.

- "If you eliminate child labor, won't you send local currencies plummeting, causing unemployment and economic chaos in the countries?"

- "What gives you the right to go to these countries and tell them what to do? Aren't you simply white imperialists coming from a rich country, telling these people in the Third World how to raise their children?"

- "What do you suppose happens to those children after they are taken out of child labor?"

As Craig and his friends discovered, those who are committed to improving the lot of workers around the world may feel as if they have a jumble of yarn to untangle; separating out any one strand may require untangling the whole mass.

In a world of interdependent relationships, solving a problem such as child labor often requires solving other problems simultaneously. That's why Free the Children takes a multipronged approach to the issue. In addition to passing laws curbing child labor, many of the group's initiatives attempt to alleviate the poverty and lack of education that makes poor families dependent on child labor for income. (Based on Kielburger, *Free the Children*, pages 309–311) ☞

In a world of interdependent relationships, solving a problem such as child labor often requires solving other problems simultaneously.

The Special Role of Business Leaders

Business leaders have a good deal of power to shape not only the working conditions of their employees but the structures of society as well. As a result, they have a special responsibility to work for justice in solidarity with workers, the rest of the human community, and God's creation.

What happens when business leaders base their practices on solidarity? Three examples illustrate the good that can result:

Solidarity: "The right thing to do"

Aaron Feuerstein, owner of Malden Mills, in Lawrence, Massachusetts, took the call to solidarity seriously. His mill produces Polarfleece, the light, wool-like synthetic material made from recycled plastic. In 1995, the mill burned down, but Feuerstein continued paying his employees for three years, even though they weren't working, until the mill was rebuilt. "It's the right thing to do," was Feuerstein's answer whenever he was asked about his decision:

I consider our workers an asset, not an expense. If you close a factory because you can get work done for two dollars an hour elsewhere, you break the American Dream. . . . It would have been unconscionable to put three thousand people on the streets and deliver a death blow to the [city] of Lawrence. (Wallace, in *Stone Soup for the World,* page 337)

Solidarity with the marginalized

A special dimension of solidarity is choosing to help the poor and vulnerable. The story of Rachel's Bus Company illustrates how doing so can transform lives:

Rachel Hubka chose to locate her business in a Chicago neighborhood with a 60 percent unemployment rate. She actively recruits welfare recipients and those who are seemingly unemployable to drive her school buses.

"When I opened my business, I wanted to create opportunities for those the system had left behind," Rachel says. "They needed work, and I needed employees. I knew that with the right training, they could become valuable members of society."

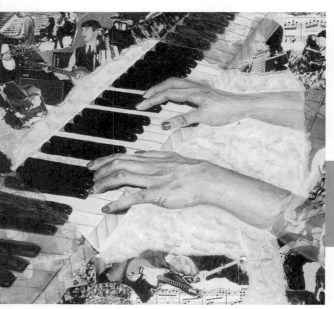

"Her faith in my abilities woke me up to what life was all about."

✳ *Student art:* Acrylic; Lindsey Warren, Notre Dame High School, Sherman Oaks, California

For many employees of Rachel's Bus Company, having a job that offers the opportunity for advancement has been life changing. When Ladell Johnson came to the bus company, for instance, she was a single mother struggling to support three children. Timid and unsure of herself, many employers might have written her off. But Rachel's respect for her employees allowed her to see beyond Ladell's shy exterior. Rachel began giving Ladell increasing responsibility.

As her confidence grew, Ladell discovered a knack for dealing with people that she didn't know she had. Eventually she became head of human resources. Like Rachel, she looks out for the total well-being of employees, an approach that has helped to cut employee turnover. She also became a community leader and a lay minister who helps others; she even received the Sister Thea Bowman Humanitarian Award for her volunteer work.

"Rachel stirred something inside of me," Ladell says. "Her faith in my abilities woke me up to what life was all about. For the first time, I felt I could really live instead of just going through the motions." (Based on Valletta, in *Stone Soup for the World,* pages 341–343)

Rachel's approach to business allowed her company to grow significantly in just seven years. More important, Rachel's Bus Company is an excellent example of how human-centered work allows workers like Ladell to become more fully all they are meant to be. ☯

Solidarity Amid Globalization

In his efforts to eliminate child labor, Craig Kielburger ran headlong into the reality of the **globalization of the economy,** which means that the economies of different nations are increasingly tied together by interdependent relationships. As a result, working conditions in one country are often influenced by business practices in another country. Over the past forty years, Catholic social teaching has emphasized the need for this globalization to be accompanied by solidarity.

Paul Katzeff, the owner of a company that sells expensive gourmet coffee nationwide, illustrates the importance of solidarity in a globalized economy:

It was a spirit of solidarity that led Paul to accept an invitation to visit the fields of Nicaraguan coffee grower Francisco Javier Saenz. Paul wanted to become more aware of his relationship with the people who provided the beans for his coffee.

Paul was shocked by the poverty that he saw among the coffee growers: hungry children, women pounding tortillas hours a day by hand, coffee pickers living in homes with cardboard roofs. He learned that a coffee picker's family might earn only four hundred dollars per year—nowhere close to a living wage.

As a result of what he saw in Nicaragua, Paul developed the Coffee for Peace program: fifty cents of each coffee bag's purchase price would go directly back to the villages where the coffee came from, allowing villagers to buy livestock, plant gardens,

---

𝘕 Make two columns on a sheet of paper, one labeled, "Close the mill" and the other, "Pay workers while rebuilding." In each column, list reasons that mill owner Aaron Feurerstein might have considered in favor of each choice. Summarize your analysis in a brief paragraph.

☯ Talk to your local chamber of commerce (or a similar business organization) to find a business whose practices contribute to the good of its employees as well as the good of the community. Research the company's practices; sources might include media reports, literature from the company, or interviews with company officials. Then write a three- to five-page report relating those practices to Catholic social teaching.

WORK ON THE BORDER IN THE GLOBAL ECONOMY

Rick Ufford-Chase works with an organization called BorderLinks, which helps North Americans become aware of the disparities caused by globalization, and the effect it has on workers. BorderLinks points to the adjacent towns of Nogales, Arizona, and Nogales, Mexico, as an example of the effect globalization has on workers:

> Welcome to Ambos Nogales, two cities balancing precariously on the line between North America and Latin America. . . . Ambos Nogales is the reality behind the world's corporate glitter. It's the scar tissue underlying today's Wall Street "miracles."

Left: Workers in *maquiladoras* (factories) in Mexico are often paid a fraction of what U.S. workers would make, and they lack the same workers' rights. *Right:* A human rights group protests at the border fence in Nogales.

Walk with me, now, through the port of entry from the United States into Mexico. . . . Talk to a few folks, and you'll discover that once you've crossed to this side of the wall, the minimum wage instantly plummets from $4.75 per hour in the United States to less than $3.50 per *day* here. . . .

See those children roaming the streets? . . . By the time they're seven or eight years old, most children are unattended. Their parents are working ten to fifteen hours a day in foreign-owned factories called *maquiladoras*. . . . They sew . . . underwear. They package surgical prep kits. They assemble electronic computer boards or power supplies. . . . In short, their jobs are connected to almost every aspect of your life in the United States.

Cross back now into Nogales, Arizona, and take a look around you. On the surface, the people north of the border may appear to be winners in the global economic adventure. . . . The paved roads, clean sidewalks, shiny fast-food restaurants. . . . But due to air pollution from the *maquiladoras*, Nogales has a higher . . . pollution count than . . . Phoenix, a city 136 times its size. Residents of Nogales have more cases of lupus per capita than in any other place in the world.

. . . Unemployment is also high here [due to jobs going to cheap labor across the border]. . . .

Jesus said that no one can serve both God and money. In an economy that honors only the latter, in a corporate system willing to enslave neighbors, divide cities, and destroy creation for the sake of ever greater profits . . . the time has come to . . . choose to be in community with one another—not just locally but globally. (Ufford-Chase, "Glimpsing the Future")

Ufford-Chase is clearly frustrated with the situation because he cares about working people in both towns. He says that the global economy, increasingly driven by multinational corporations, operates on profits for a few at the expense of huge numbers of workers. People in developing countries need work, and many (although not all) corporations want the cheapest workers and unregulated working conditions to expand their profits. Yet Ufford-Chase is hopeful. The situation is daunting, he says, but ultimately exciting: because we have the chance "to discover what it means to be the people of God," to be in solidarity with one another and live out the implications of God's Reign. ◉ ᴘ

"The time has come to . . . choose to be in community
with one another—**not just locally but globally.**"

ᴘ How does Rick Ufford-Chase's story demonstrate the need for solidarity? Brainstorm with a small group to create concrete examples of what solidarity between these workers on each side of the border would look like.

Entrepreneur Paul Katzeff recognized that he had a responsibility to ensure the good of the Nicaraguan growers who supplied coffee beans for his U.S. business.

for farming according to safe environmental practices: growing coffee in the shade, using natural fertilizers, and so on. But the reward of improved living conditions ensures their future. (Based on Brown, in *Stone Soup for the World,* pages 347–350)

The invitation that Paul Katzeff accepted turned out to be an opportunity to recognize that his business in North America had a direct impact on working families in Nicaragua. Such solidarity is necessary to end inhumane working conditions around the world. **Q**

or even borrow money to start a small business. The workers were pleased, and jumped at the opportunities this provided them.

As Paul learned more, however, he realized that returning cash to the villagers wasn't enough; the environmental impact of the coffee industry was devastating the area, making the land unfit for any other crops. Two decades prior, the coffee brokers forced the growers to plant coffee beans that needed full sunlight, which meant clearing large numbers of trees. Forests, along with the wildlife that lived there, were being lost. Pesticides and coffee pulp were polluting the river. Wages had improved, but the living environment of the workers was going downhill.

Katzeff enlisted the help of experts to develop a system that would encourage coffee-farming practices that protected the environment while earning more for the farmers. The coffee farmers who grow for Katzeff's company are monetarily rewarded

Toward More Human Work

At the beginning of this chapter, we asked, What is the value of work? We have answered that question in many ways. Work has value when it provides good things for both the workers and those who use what the workers produce. But it also has value because through it we continue God's work of creation in the world. Work has value because it makes us "more fully human"— that is, all that God desires us to become.

Ladell Johnson's words sum up the value of work: "For the first time, I felt I could really live." Ultimately, the ability of work to help us really live—by what it provides for each of us and our community, as well as for what it helps us as workers to become—is its true value. **R**

Q Find something in your house that was produced in a foreign country—for instance, food, clothing, electronics. Then contact the manufacturer's customer-service department by phone or via the Internet. Ask for any information the company can provide about the working conditions of the people who produced the product (use the list of the rights of workers as a guide). Write a one-page report describing the company's response and your reaction. If the company does not provide any information, write a one-page essay expressing your opinion about whether consumers have a responsibility to know how products are produced.

R With some classmates, prepare a skit that shows the value of good work. Be prepared to lead a class discussion about how your skit illustrates the dignity of work and the rights of workers.

15. Explain the term *indirect employer.*
16. What are three ways that people can cooperate to change the policies of employers?
17. Define *globalization of the economy,* and explain its implications for work.
18. Briefly explain the role that solidarity should play in good business practices.

In Depth

19. Discuss how just work supports and contributes to these other aspects of justice: human life and dignity, participation in family and community, rights and responsibilities, solidarity, the option for the poor and vulnerable, and care for God's creation.

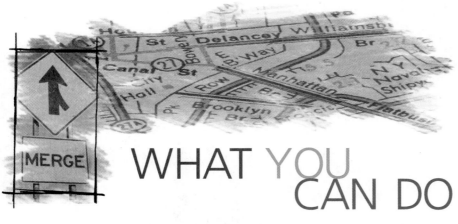

WHAT YOU CAN DO . . .

- When you are making job or career decisions, ask yourself: Will this work help me become who I am called to be? Will it help or harm the common good?
- Make your work a prayer by doing it as well as you can, for the good of yourself and others.
- If your employer's practices or workplace conditions seem to be harming workers, customers, or the environment, tell your supervisor about them. If possible, offer an alternative way of doing things that solves the problem. If the problem is serious and your employer won't do anything to stop it, notify the government agency that regulates your workplace. Confrontation and risk can be uncomfortable—especially if a job is at stake—but justice calls us to take such risks for the sake of the well-being of others.
- Use your purchasing power to practice solidarity with people working under unjust labor conditions. Find out whether the company that produces your school's uniforms, sweatshirts, or athletic wear can guarantee just working conditions at the clothing factories that make its products. If not, work to change the company that provides your school uniforms.
- Working with Free the Children, organize a campaign at your school to raise money to support or build a school in an area of the world that needs one. ☺

7 LIVING THE GOOD LIFE
(PART 1)

living "on the edge"
life-giving care

Breaking
the cycle of poverty

"YOU GAVE ME CLOTHING"

Las Vegas: bright lights, easy money. In the past ten years, the population has grown to almost one million people. Promotional videos seek people to move here, promising thousands of available jobs, affordable housing, an excellent standard of living.

But there is a dark side to Las Vegas, away from the casinos and the hotels. While the population of Las Vegas has boomed, so too has the number of homeless, doubling in the past year alone until most estimates state that there are around eighteen thousand homeless people in the greater Las Vegas area. Homeless shelters and community services deal with a small proportion of these people, but for many, such basic things as food and clothing are a daily struggle.

Students at Bishop Gorman High created Matthew's Closet, "a place where homeless people could come and be treated with respect."

Motivated by retreats and other activities at Bishop Gorman High School, three students wanted to do something about this situation. When Ryan Hall, Andrew Kano, and Caitlyn Barry couldn't think of a way to help, one of their campus ministers, Br. Corey Brost, CSV, suggested creating a "shop" of free clothing for the homeless. The students named the store Matthew's Closet.

"We were going to create a place where the homeless could come and be treated with respect," Andrew says. "We would only put out decent, well-kept clothing and shoes, not stained and tattered clothing. We would only put out new underwear and socks. Our mission was to say to the homeless, 'In spite of your situation, I am going to treat you with as much dignity and love as I can.'"

The trio took over a small, run-down room in the offices of Catholic Charities and they worked to fix it up. "We wanted it to look like any store you would find in the mall, a place where anyone would feel welcome to come in and shop, and that's what it became," Ryan says.

But it was different from the mall stores: "We asked . . . that every volunteer seek to see the face of Christ in every person we serve," says Caitlyn. The students' belief that they serve Christ when they serve those in need is based on Jesus' own words: "I was a stranger and you welcomed me, I was naked and you gave me clothing . . ." (Matthew 25:35–36).

word spread, the students had to create a sign-up system to accommodate all the volunteers. "Once the Closet opened, donations poured in," Andrew recalls. "We had more clothing, socks, underwear, and shoes than our humble little space could handle."

The Closet serves as many as 150 people when it opens each Thursday—some of them regulars who are greeted by name by the volunteers, and many newly homeless coming for help for the first time.

At the end of every Thursday shopping session, the volunteers sit in a circle on the floor and prayerfully reflect on the experience they have just had. They share stories of the memorable people they met, and how stereotypes of the homeless were either challenged or affirmed. The Closet volunteers have seen and heard a lot in their time of service. Customers who suffer from mental illness crouch in the corner, screaming for help. Day workers who have not changed their clothing for a month while working in the Las Vegas sun. Little children who smile. Drunk customers. Stoned customers. Angry customers. The amazing people who stay filled with hope even amid crushing poverty. Customers who return to offer thanks: "I've been homeless in six states," one man said. "This is the first place where I was treated with respect, like a real person."

What keeps the volunteers going is faith. As Ryan says, "Faith gives me hope that this problem of poverty can be overcome. It lets

"We asked . . . that every volunteer **seek to see** the face of Christ in every person we serve."

At first, other students were reluctant to help—some scoffed at the idea of a store for the homeless. But the people who did volunteer found the experience rewarding. As

me see Jesus in every customer who enters the Closet." (Adapted from Pfau, "Matthew's Closet") ⊙ **A**

A What do you think the students meant by trying to "see the face of Christ" in each person who visited the Closet?

Life on the Edge

Food, clothing, shelter, health care, and education are all basic requirements for a good life—things that most of us take for granted. For the first time in the history of the world, humanity has enough resources to provide these things to all people.

Yet, billions of people around the world and millions of people in the United States are prevented from living a good life—a life of dignity that allows them to become fully all that they are meant to be—because they lack one or more of these necessities. It may be impossible for them even to keep themselves and their loved ones alive. The experience of not having the basic things one needs to live a full and dignified life is called **poverty.** Poverty denies people their basic human rights.

"Catholic social teaching does not require absolute equality in the distribution of income and wealth," the U.S. Catholic bishops note in their 1986 pastoral letter *Economic Justice for All* (185). But extreme inequality that causes people to suffer as a result of poverty runs contrary to God's desire for a love-centered world. Catholic social teaching is concerned with poverty because it prevents people from developing their full potential as unique images of God. The way poverty harms people differs from person to person, as we will see in the rest of this chapter. But we can note some common characteristics of poverty that most poor people experience.

The nearness of death. Poor people are always at greater risk of death than people who are not poor. Although the life expectancy of the world's wealthiest people is more than seventy-five years, the average lifespan of the world's poorest people is only forty years. For the poorest people in the United States and the world, survival is an everyday concern. Chronic hunger, health problems, and violence are some of the most common ways people living in poverty experience the nearness of death.

Marginalization. Poverty is both caused by and results in exclusion from the community. In *Economic Justice for All,* the U.S. Catholic bishops describe the marginalization of the poor this way:

> Poverty is not merely the lack of adequate financial resources. It entails a more profound kind of deprivation, a denial of full participation in the economic, social, and political life of society and an inability to influence decisions that affect one's life. (188) 🅱

people who live in poverty live life **"on the edge."**

✳ *Student art:* "Faces of Pain." Charcoal; Sara Berrenson, Notre Dame High School, Sherman Oaks, California

Living on the edge. As a result of marginalization, people who live in poverty live life "on the edge." Because they have so little, it does not take much to make life worse for them. For most families, an illness or an automobile breakdown is an inconvenience. For poor families without medical insurance or money for car repairs, these things can mean the loss of a home or a job.

The cycle of poverty. Poor people often become trapped in a **cycle of poverty,** in which the lack of basic resources creates barriers that prevent people from obtaining those resources. Without a car, for instance, job opportunities are limited; and without a job, it is difficult to get a car. In the cycle of poverty, interrelated problems cause and reinforce one another: homelessness and hunger lead to an inadequate education for homeless children, for instance. Inadequate education leads in turn to reduced job opportunities— and so the cycle continues.

Barriers to full development. Finally, poverty prevents people from developing their full potential—all the unique talents, the self-confidence, and the social skills that allow people to thrive.

Poverty prevents full development in two ways. First, the experience of poverty can lead people, especially children, to develop a worldview in which a better lifestyle seems impossible. People learn how to live a good life through the example of others. When people live on the margins of society, where everyone they know is poor, it is difficult to see a way out.

Second, people who live in poverty are denied the resources necessary for their full development. **Dr. Abraham Maslow** proposed a theory of human motivation based on a hierarchy of human needs. According to him, individuals seek to fill the basic needs first—food, drink, sleep, health. Once these needs are met, people can move on to fill the higher-level needs of safety, love, self-esteem, and self-actualization (becoming who we are meant to be).

If basic needs go unmet, higher needs become more difficult to fill. It is hard for a child who has not eaten for a day to develop her curiosity, and it is difficult for someone who is unable to find a job to maintain self-esteem. People need personal resources like self-esteem and a sense of safety if they are to have the best chance of escaping the cycle of poverty. **C**

An option for the poor

Because poverty prevents people from achieving their full potential as images of God, Catholic social teaching calls society to

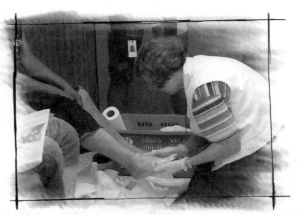

Mary Jo Copeland makes an option for the poor by washing the feet of people who have been homeless and living on the streets. She founded Sharing and Caring Hands, a Minneapolis organization that helps people who are very poor.

B Where would a family of four with an income below the poverty level live in your community? Research rental listings to find housing that costs less than one-third of poverty-level income. Would you be willing to live in the housing you found? Based on your findings, are poor people marginalized in your community? Why or why not?

C Look at Maslow's hierarchy of needs and choose the three that are most important to you. Explain why they are important and how your life would be different if you were unable to fulfill them.

MASLOW'S HIERARCHY OF NEEDS

According to Dr. Abraham Maslow, people focus on **meeting their most basic needs before** moving on to meet higher needs that aid in their full development:

1. Physical needs
- food and drink
- sleep
- health
- exercise and rest

2. Safety needs
- security
- protection
- comfort
- peace
- order

3. Love needs
- acceptance
- belonging
- love and affection
- participation

4. Self-esteem needs
- recognition and prestige
- leadership
- achievement
- competence
- strength and intelligence

5. Self-actualization needs
- fulfillment of potential
- challenge
- curiosity
- creativity
- aesthetic appreciation ⊙

Food is a basic need; without it, it is difficult to meet higher-level needs, like the need for a good education.

make the needs of its poorest and most vulnerable members a top concern. As we discussed in chapter 2, the choice to do so is called the option for the poor and vulnerable (see pages 65–68). Ryan, Andrew, and Caitlyn made an option for the poor by organizing Matthew's Closet. Notice, though, that the purpose of Matthew's Closet went beyond giving away clothes: the students went deeper, trying to create a place where poor people would be treated with a respect that recognized the image of God in each of them. When that happened, the Closet's customers were better able to recognize themselves as "real persons."

Matthew's Closet reflects the true spirit of the option for the poor. It is about more than just giving people the basic resources necessary for living; it is about providing them with whatever they need to fully develop their own unique potential as images of God. The church's call for society to make an option for the poor flows from this conviction: People deserve fair access to the earth's material resources, as well as the resources of the human community, so that they can fully develop their own unique ways of loving God and others (based on *On Social Concern [Sollicitudo Rei Socialis]*, 27–34).

How do we develop a society in which everyone has what they need to live a full and dignified life? We will examine that question in the next chapter. Before we do, though, we need to raise our awareness of the reality of poverty by asking two other questions: How does poverty affect people? And why are so many people so poor? These are the questions we address in this chapter.

1. What is poverty?
2. Briefly describe each of the following characteristics of poverty: the nearness of death, marginalization, living on the edge.
3. Describe the cycle of poverty.
4. What is the basic premise behind Dr. Abraham Maslow's theory of the hierarchy of needs?
5. What is the option for the poor and vulnerable?
6. Why does the church say that people deserve fair access to the resources of the earth and the human community?

---

7. How might the denial of the rights of workers (discussed in chapter 6) affect the cycle of poverty?

Poverty in the World's Wealthiest Nation

The United States is the world's richest country, consuming more than one-fourth of the world's goods and services. Yet, in 1998, about 34.5 million people lived in poverty within its borders.

When people talk about poverty in the United States, they are usually referring to an income level below the poverty threshold set by the U.S. Census Bureau. In 2000, the poverty level for a single adult was $8,350; for a family of four, $17,050. Because each family lives in unique economic circumstances, these numbers are not a perfect measurement of who really is poor. But these measurements give a general picture of the extent of poverty in the United States:

- About 40 percent of the nation's poor people are youth under the age of eighteen. That is one out of every five youth in the nation.

- Although the majority of poor people are white, there is a big difference in the poverty rate within different racial groups: about 1 in 12 white people are poor, compared to about 1 in 4 black and Latino people.

- Contrary to the myth that people are poor because they are lazy, more than 60 percent of poor families have a member who is working at least some of the time.

Writer Pat Schneider helps poor women develop their potential by teaching them to express themselves through creative writing. In doing so, she often has found herself drawn into their struggles with the effects of poverty:

This morning, I left home at 7:45 and returned at 3:00. Remembering where I have been, my heart is heavy. I want to know why, as a nation, we allow mothers and children to suffer.

My day began at a community college where I helped a woman withdraw from a course that I had encouraged her to take and had raised money to send her to. I made a mistake. The course was too hard for her. . . . She needed a course to help her pass the G.E.D. exam, but all the others were offered in the evening. She has no childcare, no money for childcare, and no

About **40 percent** of the nation's poor people are **youth** under the age of eighteen.

Sixteen-year-olds Lloyd Newman and LeAlan Jones educated others about poverty by producing "Ghetto Life 101," an award-winning radio documentary about life in a Chicago public-housing project.

D Why do you think so many people in the United States are poor? Find a book, article, or other resource that provides evidence supporting your ideas. Be prepared to discuss your opinion in class.

way to get to the course site. I've tried to set up tutoring, but she has no telephone, and it has been impossible to make arrangements between her and the tutor.

Later today, I stood in another woman's bedroom where water seepage has corroded and crumbled half a wall and pipes show through two yawning holes in the ceiling. Although she has complained repeatedly, she has been forced to live with water leaking into her bedroom for two and a half years. She threw her mattress away because it got waterlogged. Now her back hurts because she sleeps on a couch with no springs and her skin breaks out in allergic reaction to the moldy air.

I sat today in another woman's kitchen watching her prepare food. She cares for ten children in a very small space. She told me how the noise from the next apartment comes through the walls and how her bathtub needs caulking so badly that she can't wash her hair for fear the water will leak into the next apartment. She doesn't understand why she has a problem with depression.

I looked out of the window of another woman's living room, her child playing on the floor between us. She told me she wants to get a job. She worries about the thousands of dollars she owes for classes she's taken at the college. She is afraid to go on in school. I wonder whether her welfare payments will be cut if she gets part-time work. (Schneider, "The Cost of Love") *E*

Each of these situations is a good illustration of the sort of difficulties people face as a result of poverty. To deepen our understanding of how poverty affects people in the United States, we can look at three of its most harmful consequences: hunger, homelessness, and inadequate education.

Hunger

Nearly everyone experiences ordinary hunger —a growling stomach, maybe some light-headedness—from time to time. But most poor people suffer from **chronic hunger,** meaning that they never have enough food to give the body the nutrients needed to grow and maintain itself properly.

Chronic hunger takes two forms. When the body does not receive enough calories to maintain itself, **starvation** occurs. The metabolism slows down, and the body begins to feed on itself. In other words, lacking food, the body's own fat, muscle, and tissue become the body's fuel. The immune system breaks down, making victims of starvation susceptible to disease. Brain chemistry is also damaged, causing the victim's mental functions to deteriorate. Technically, starvation begins to occur when an individual has lost one-third of his or her normal body weight. Relatively few people actually die of starvation in the United States.

More common, both in the United States and the rest of the world, is malnutrition. A victim of **malnutrition** gets enough calories to prevent his or her body from feeding on itself, but the diet of a malnourished person is extremely limited, often consisting of just three or four foods. As a result, she or he does not receive all the vitamins and minerals needed for proper physical and mental development and maintenance. Nutritional deficiencies can

E How are the characteristics of poverty listed at the beginning of this chapter evident in these women's stories?

cause diabetes, heart ailments, vision problems, obesity, skin diseases, and other problems.

Chronic hunger contributes to the cycle of poverty. It affects the health and development of children, and it seriously harms their ability to learn in school. When people are hungry, they have little energy or motivation to concentrate on other aspects of their life, such as finding work or housing. 🔫

Although the number of hungry people in the world has dramatically decreased since the 1970s, the number of people requesting emergency food assistance from food shelves in the United States has risen every year between 1985 and 2000. Thirty-one million people, approximately one in ten households, experience hunger or the risk of hunger, a figure that includes more than twelve million children.

Homelessness

The typical image of homelessness is one of people sleeping in cars or on the street—and, in fact, this is all too common. According to the National Coalition for the Homeless, more than 700,000 people are homeless in our country on any given night, as many as two million people experience homelessness during a one-year period, and one of every four homeless persons is a child.

Clearly, shelter—someplace to eat, sleep, bathe, and be protected from the elements—is a minimum requirement of human dignity. But to be truly life-giving, homes must provide more than shelter. True homes are safe, stable places where human dignity is respected and each person is free to develop his or her potential. True homes also provide a place for people to participate in a community by building life-giving relationships with others who live nearby. 🄶

Although the housing crisis in our society most visibly affects those who are **literally homeless**—that is, without shelter—millions of people are the **hidden homeless,** people whose poverty prevents them from living in true homes. The hidden homeless include the following:

- **Those whose housing costs consume too much of their income.** According to federal government guidelines, the cost of housing should not exceed more than a third of a family's income. Yet, low-income families typically spend half their income on rent, according to a survey by the mayors of major U.S. cities. Such a situation makes it more likely that people will go hungry or lose their housing entirely.
- **Those who live in inadequate housing.** Often, poor people can afford to live only

But to be truly life-giving, homes must provide more than shelter.

✳ *Student art:* "Laid to Rest." Photograph; Claire Endo, Ramona Convent Secondary School, Alhambra, California

in **inadequate housing**—housing that is unsafe or broken down in a way that degrades the life and dignity of the residents.

- **Those who live in others' housing.** Many people avoid living on the streets by doubling up with other families who live in already crowded apartments.

- **Those who live in unsafe homes.** Violence, crime, and substance abuse are all factors that prevent a home from being a safe, nurturing place.

People who live in poverty often shift between each of these four kinds of homelessness. Consider the true story of this family from New York City—Peter, Megan, and their five children. Peter worked on construction projects as a carpenter, while Megan took care of the children. The family was able to get by on a low income, but one catastrophic event caused a chain reaction. While at the beach one Sunday, the family received word that their apartment was on fire. They rushed home, but the fire had already destroyed all their belongings:

> Peter has not had a real job since. "Not since the fire. I had tools. I can't replace those tools. It took me years of work." He explains he had accumulated tools for different jobs, one tool at a time. Each job would enable him to add another tool to his collection. "Everything I had was in that fire." (Kozol, *Rachel and Her Children,* page 2)

They were forced by these circumstances to apply for welfare, and were placed in a run-down hotel contracted by the city to house homeless families. The conditions at the welfare hotel were quite poor:

> The city pays $3,000 monthly for the two connected rooms in which they live. [Megan] shows me the bathroom. Crumbling walls. Broken tiles. The toilet doesn't work. There is a pan to catch something that's dripping from the plaster. The smell is overpowering.
>
> "I don't see any way out," [Peter] says. "I want to go home. Where can I go?" (Page 2)

The accidental and tragic loss of their belongings, including the tools of Peter's trade, led to a cycle of poverty that the family was unable to break. After two years in the welfare hotel, the children were placed in various foster homes. Their family shattered, Peter and Megan had to live on the streets. *H*

Inadequate Education

A good education is one of the best ways to break the cycle of poverty. This is so not only because a good education opens up good job opportunities but also because education—in and out of the classroom—is one of the ways we develop our full potential as human beings. And successful learning helps to build the self-confidence we need to continue developing our full potential as adults.

Yet, as a group, children who live in poverty lag behind their better-off peers when it comes to academic achievement. This is so even when poor kids come from intact families and safe neighborhoods.

Education leaders debate the reasons why students from poor families tend not to do as well at school as their better-off peers. Race-based stereotypes and discrimination are

---

F With the permission of your parents, try going without food during one day until you feel very hungry—and then wait a few hours before eating. Write a short reflection on how your hunger affected you.

G What does your dream home look like? Draw or describe its physical features, who would live in it, and the kind of neighborhood where it would be located.

H Imagine this scenario: You lost your job two months ago, and with only a high school education, you are having trouble finding another job that pays enough to cover your expenses. Now your landlord is threatening to evict you. Based on the situation in your area, brainstorm a list of strategies for your immediate and long-term survival.

factors, as we saw in chapter 5. Inequalities in school funding play a role too: the tax revenue that funds public school districts (or the tuition revenue that funds Catholic schools) often reflects the economic well-being of the area. Schools in poorer areas receive less funding for materials, facilities, and general maintenance.

But the reasons for the learning difficulties that poor children face go beyond funding issues. Take the Minneapolis school district, for instance:

Many of the city's newest schools are beautifully designed, with up-to-date equipment. Teachers seem fully engaged with their students, even passionate. The district spends $11,000 per student—almost twice as much money as the surrounding suburban school districts. Yet, while suburban school students thrive, more than half the Minneapolis students get poor scores on standardized tests. The Minneapolis chapter of the National Association for the Advancement of Colored People (NAACP) calls the Minneapolis schools "a comprehensive failure" for most students.

Education is key to escaping poverty, and yet children who live in poverty often receive a poor education.

The NAACP says funding is not the issue. It believes the problem is rooted in a range of housing, transportation, and education policies that concentrate poor and minority children in central city schools.

That makes teaching a tough challenge, says Connie Overhue, a teacher and social worker at West Central Academy, a new elementary school. Entire classrooms, she says, are filled with students who show the stress of living in poor, unstable homes.

"One thing is, the kids are falling asleep. Literally falling asleep as we're teaching. Or two is, I had one young boy in my class, for example, today, who just started to cry. It's like, 'Are you okay?' And he's like, 'I'll be okay, I'll be okay.' Or you'll see the violence erupt very quickly. Somebody may say something and it's, like, really blown out of proportion—almost like an explosion. Again, I think some of what's coming from home is coming into the classroom," Overhue says. (Based on Biewen, "Schooling Poor Kids in Minneapolis")

A Tangle of Causes

What causes these problems? To some extent, each problem causes and reinforces the others. Children whose families drift in and out of homelessness move frequently, interrupting their education. A fifth of homeless children do not attend schools due to location and transportation issues. And the sheer stress of poverty poses other barriers to education.

But we can find other reasons for these problems as well, some rooted in the characteristics of poverty listed at the beginning of this chapter, and some rooted in social structures.

What factors enable you to do your best work in school? With another student, write a student's "bill of rights" based on the factors you identified.

Low wages, high costs

In recent years, two trends have made it more difficult for people to afford basic resources like food and housing. On one hand, real incomes—that is, incomes adjusted for inflation—have gone down in recent decades, so that the average worker has less purchasing power. On the other hand, the cost of basic necessities—especially of housing—has increased. The result is more hungry and homeless people.

This is especially evident in the **affordable housing shortage.** As more people work for less money, the need for low-cost housing has increased. But the supply of low-cost housing has decreased significantly because developers are building mostly expensive rental units so they can make a higher profit. In 1998, there were an estimated 4.4 million fewer affordable housing units than there were families in need. One federal survey of people who were homeless found that 44 percent had worked at least part-time during the preceding month. Another report found that nowhere in the United States is the minimum wage sufficient to pay the fair market rent for a two-bedroom apartment.

Limited government aid

The federal government spends about 1 percent of its annual budget on aid to families with children—what is normally called welfare. The aid provides families with a small income (still below the poverty level) that is meant to provide temporary assistance until the head of the family is able to find work.

The majority of families who receive such assistance do so for less than four years in their lifetime. For them, it is a lifeline during a rough period. Others need more help than government aid provides, however. Take Mrs. Harrington, for instance. After much searching, she found a kind landlord who offered to rent her an apartment for $365 a month. But that was more than the government was willing to pay:

> "It's like a dream: This lady likes me and we're going to have a home! My worker denied me for $365. I was denied. $365. My social worker is a nice man but he said: 'I have to tell you, Mrs. Harrington. Your limit is $270.' Then I thought of this: The difference is only $95. I'll make it up out of my food allowance. We can lighten up on certain things. Not for the children, but ourselves. We'll eat less food at first. Then I can get a job. He'll finish his computer course. The house had a backyard. . . . They told me no. I was denied." (Kozol, *Rachel and Her Children*, page 42)

Children whose families drift in and out of **homelessness** move frequently, interrupting their education.

✳ *Student art:* "Pickup Truck." Photograph; Jana Schmid, Benilde–Saint Margaret's High School, Saint Louis Park, Minnesota

Habitat for Humanity is a national organization that brings volunteers together with those who live in substandard housing in order to build new, affordable homes.

In 1996, Congress passed legislation sharply limiting federal welfare benefits. Limiting government assistance to poor families was supposed to motivate more poor people—like Maria Ortega, mentioned in chapter 6—to find work. Many did, although the jobs they found often did not pay enough to lift their families out of poverty. Others were unable to find work because they lacked the necessary training or resources to do so.

Reductions in federal aid have contributed to both hunger and homelessness. For instance, following welfare reform, the number of people who received food stamps (government-issued coupons that can be redeemed for food) declined by one-third—partly as a result of a stronger economy, but mostly due to problems implementing the new welfare rules. Meanwhile, government funding for low-cost public housing has been slashed in recent decades, adding to the housing crunch. Between 1991 and 1997, the number of publicly funded, affordable housing units dropped by almost 400,000.

Physical and mental health issues

Nearly one-third of people living in poverty have no health insurance of any kind, according to the U.S. Census Bureau. Without health insurance, the financial strain of a major illness or injury can lead to the loss of housing. Homelessness, in turn, leads to poor health. Malnutrition, inadequate housing, and stress are among the reasons homeless children experience health problems at twice the rate of other children.

The lack of health care is especially hard on the mentally ill. As much as 25 percent of the single-adult homeless population suffers from some sort of severe and persistent mental illness. While mental illness makes it difficult for people to obtain employment and housing, only a small portion of those who are mentally ill and homeless actually require long-term care in special institutions. Federal programs have demonstrated that the vast majority of mentally ill and homeless people are able to live in the community if they are provided with adequate support, including appropriate housing, counseling, and ongoing contact with social workers. Such services are not widely available, however. ⤻

Hopelessness

People trapped in the cycle of poverty—especially youth who are born into it—frequently lack hope for the future. Hopelessness may not seem like a "real" reason for the poverty that leads to homelessness, hunger, and poor academic performance. Nevertheless, it is a very real reason, and perhaps one of the most powerful. "We haven't even begun to consider how much depression

⤻ Choose one of the aspects of poverty mentioned so far in this chapter and research how it affects your local community. Contact at least three government or nonprofit organizations that work with the poor in your area for information related to your topic. Be prepared to report your findings to the class.

there is among the very poor," says Richard Zorolla, a San Antonio social worker. "We don't seem to think they have a right, or the ability, to feel deeply enough" (Davis, "Who Are the Poor?").

Without hope, people tend to live for the moment, rather than working toward a better future. This may be one reason teen pregnancy rates and high school dropout rates are much higher among poor people.

Hopelessness drives others to look for an easy escape in drugs and alcohol. In the decaying San Antonio public housing projects, for instance, it is common for children to become addicted to mood-altering inhalants—paint, glue, antifreeze—by the age of twelve. Rather than providing an escape, substance abuse only reinforces the cycle of poverty. Often, poor people have little or no access to drug treatment programs.

People trapped in the cycle of poverty—frequently **lack hope for the future.**

Youth Working for Positive Change leaders foster hope for their Des Moines, Iowa, community by working to lessen youth-on-youth violence and by starting a neighborhood-watch patrol so kids can safely walk to school. Their efforts are funded by the Catholic Campaign for Human Development.

8. Compare and contrast how the two forms of chronic hunger affect people.
9. Describe four types of hidden homelessness.
10. Why is education one of the best ways to break the cycle of poverty?
11. In your own words, summarize four factors that contribute to poverty.

12. Review the five characteristics of poverty listed at the beginning of this chapter. Choose three of them, briefly describing how each is evident in one of the poverty-related problems discussed in this section.

With a group of your classmates, brainstorm ways the church can help people who are living in poverty find hope. Then plan a short liturgy around the theme of hope in the face of poverty. Write down the prayers, gestures, symbols, and music you would use.

Poverty in the World's Poorest Nations

All poverty limits the ability of people to develop their full potential. Unlike poverty in the United States, however, poverty in the world's poorest nations is more likely to result in death:

- Half the world's population lives on less than two dollars a day; one in every five people lives on less than a dollar a day.
- About 1.3 billion people do not have access to clean drinking water, and three billion people lack access to basic sanitation, which results in a greater risk of disease.
- In developing countries, one in five children dies before her or his fifth birthday. Every day around the world, an estimated 30,500 children die of preventable diseases.

Life for the World's Poorest Three Billion

The experience of Malekha Khatun, a Bangladeshi woman, illustrates some of the common ways that poverty affects the world's poorest three billion people:

Born in the village of Dhemsha in Bangladesh, she lost her father, the family's wage-earner, when she was very young. Malekha, her younger brother and mother slept outside since they had no house. In this wet climate, they got soaked when it rained unless someone else offered shelter. Her childhood was spent helping her mother work to earn money, attending a few years of school and witnessing the death of her nine-year-old brother from fever.

At 14, Malekha was married off to a man from another village for a small dowry equaling about nine U.S. dollars. She became pregnant right away and lived with her husband's family, while he left to work as a menial laborer so he could send money back to her and the baby. Upon his return, she became pregnant again. When Malekha's husband left a second time, she received no money or word from him. Left on her own with two small children and no means of income, her youngest child died of malnutrition and diarrhea.

Malekha worked at a variety of jobs in order to support herself, becoming skilled at knitting and making nets. She moved out of the home of her husband's family to live with her mother. Hard work and resourcefulness enabled her to run a small grocery store, but competition caused her business to suffer and she sometimes had to fall back on begging.

Malekha's constant hard work and industriousness could not overcome the poverty and hunger that shadow a woman alone at the bottom rung of an already poor nation.

Poverty in the world's poorest nations is more likely to **result in death.**

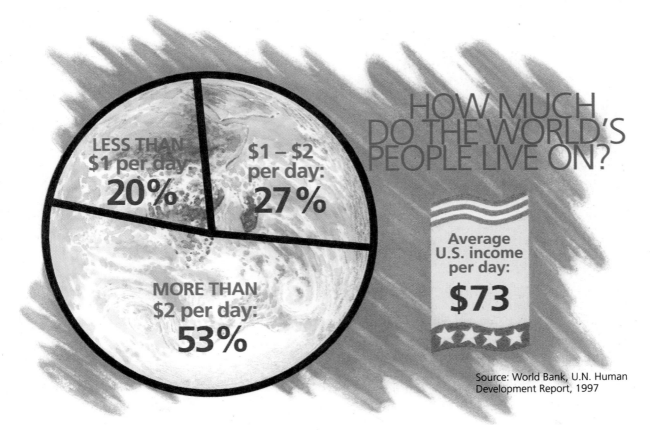

HOW MUCH DO THE WORLD'S PEOPLE LIVE ON?

LESS THAN $1 per day: **20%**

$1 – $2 per day: **27%**

MORE THAN $2 per day: **53%**

Average U.S. income per day: **$73**

Source: World Bank, U.N. Human Development Report, 1997

For all her struggling, Malekha ended up with no food to feed herself, no umbrella to protect her from the rain and only one sari to her name. (Leckman, "Grameen Bank Borrowers") L

To see how poverty affects the world's poorest people, we can look at the same problems that poor people in the United States face: hunger, homelessness, and a lack of access to education.

Hunger

Worldwide, more than one billion people do not have access to the food and water they need. Some are so lacking in daily nourishment that they barely have the energy to do even the most simple activities. Chronic hunger—mostly malnutrition—afflicts more than 841 million people worldwide.

Health issues in impoverished countries are almost completely connected with hunger and poverty. Of the estimated 30,500 children who die of preventable diseases each day, nearly half die of diseases associated with malnutrition, such as diarrhea, acute respiratory infections, and malaria.

Two other symptoms of poverty, unsanitary conditions and unhealthy drinking water, transmit these diseases to people already

---

L Imagine you wake up tomorrow in a place where you have to live on two dollars a day, without access to safe drinking water, toilets, health care, transportation, or education. Write a short essay on how you would try to improve your situation, and bring it to class for discussion.

Girls fetch water in a middle-class neighborhood in Lagos, Nigeria, that had been without running water for months. The city's water and electricity systems deteriorated as a result of government corruption and mismanagement.

weakened by hunger. When human and animal waste is left out in the open or gets into drinking water, the effects are staggering:

- Five million adults every year are afflicted with water-related diseases like cholera, typhoid, and diarrhea.
- Every year five million children younger than five years die from dehydration—the depletion of the body's fluids—caused by diarrhea.
- Malaria, one of the most debilitating diseases linked to bad water sources, affects 800 million people annually, killing one million infants in Africa each year.

The quantity of available water is also important. Keeping the body properly hydrated requires six to eight glasses of water per day. Most of the world's poor people, however, must travel far distances to obtain safe water, or *any* water, and then they must carry it the same long distance back home, usually on foot. **M**

Homelessness

Homelessness for the world's poorest people sometimes resembles the common perception of homelessness in the United States: people sleeping on the streets and in makeshift shelters. This is especially true in nations where changing economic or social conditions displace large numbers of rural people who have traditionally made a living off the land. Often, these people migrate to large cities to look for work; those who are unable to find employment might end up living on the streets. Others build makeshift shelters from scrap wood; whole "cities" of shanties can spring up on the edges of urban areas.

Fr. Pedro Opeka, a priest of the order of Saint Vincent de Paul, witnesses this kind of homelessness and poverty in his adopted home of Antananarivo, Madagascar, every day:

> The city dump teems with men, women, and children who burrow in filth for their daily bread. They have excavated large tunnels through the compressed layers of waste in order to find things they can sell—bones, for example, are used for traditional medicine and animal feed.
>
> In the center of the city, at every junction, barefoot children approach cars and implore the drivers for change. At night, rows of homeless families sleep on the pavement. During the rainy season, competition is fierce to find a place in the road tunnels. As children grow older, begging becomes less lucrative, and so the boys often turn to stealing, while some girls, as young as 14, sell sex for less than the price of a soft drink. (MacFarlane, "Friends in Deed")

Over the past twenty years, Father Opeka has helped to build seventeen new towns to

---

M Look through the Bible for a passage in which Jesus talks about food or water. Write a short reflection about how the plight of the world's hungry and thirsty people affects the way you understand Jesus' words.

house, educate, and employ thousands of Antananarivo's homeless. But millions around the world do not receive such help.

Many of the world's homeless people are **refugees**—people who are displaced from their homes by wars or political persecution. Refugees differ from other migrants in that they cannot return home for fear of persecution. Sometimes refugees are victims of intentional attempts by political factions to displace specific ethnic groups from their homes, a practice known as **ethnic cleansing.**

The church has long urged more stable, wealthy nations to welcome refugees. But despite the fact that there were 35 million refugees worldwide in 1997, the United States accepts fewer than 100,000 annually.

Inadequate education

In his travels throughout Southeast Asia, Free the Children's Craig Kielburger saw the crucial role that education plays in lifting young people out of poverty. A few years of primary education can help those who work the land increase the yield of their crops. Education also opens the door to better employment.

And yet, while 75 percent of children in developing countries attend primary school, access to even the most basic education is still denied to many:

- Nearly one billion adults are illiterate.
- Some 130 million children lack access to primary schooling.
- More than 100 million children a year who do attend school fail to complete even a basic education.

Recognizing the value of education, many children are desperate to attend school, but cannot, either because they are struggling to survive or because they lack access. Craig met one young girl who worked as a prostitute so she could buy schoolbooks and a mandatory uniform in order to attend school.

Global Poverty Is Not Inevitable

Throughout this course, we have suggested that injustice does not just happen. Unfortunately, many people view poverty in the United States and the world as inevitable. This attitude may be partly the result of myths about the causes of poverty.

Take, for instance, the myths about hunger: A common belief is that there is not enough food to feed the world's growing population, but this is false. In fact, enough food is currently grown worldwide to supply every child, woman, and man with 3,600 calories a day, enough to cause weight gain. Almost every hungry country produces enough food for its people. The problem is not the amount of food, but the way it is distributed. Redistributing a small amount of each country's food

Many of the world's homeless people are refugees—people who are displaced from their homes by wars or political persecution.

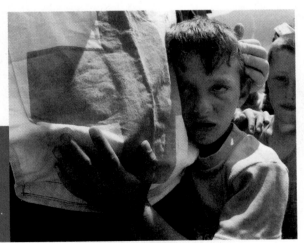

A soldier comforts Samin Hajdoriis, an Albanian refugee left homeless as a result of war.

supply would eliminate hunger. For example, India, the world's second most populous country, has managed to eliminate the threat of famine and starvation. The key to this was investigative journalism and political pressure that forced government officials to respond more quickly and effectively to frequent dips in the food supply and occasional droughts.

Another myth is that most hunger is caused by droughts and natural disasters. But the people of the world have fed themselves for centuries despite drought, floods, and other effects of weather. Strategies for coping with food loss due to natural disasters, such as collectively storing food and distributing it among themselves during periods of major crop failure, have been developed by various traditional cultures. Today, disruptions such as civil wars interfere with traditional life and the coping strategies that have been developed. In addition, many "natural" disasters are actually caused by human action, such as the droughts in Africa that are caused in large part by the elimination of forests.

Others suggest that the world's poor people only need to work harder to obtain the food they need. In fact, the world's poorest people work very hard every day just to survive. They are often unable to support themselves because they are losing access to the resources needed for self-reliance: land, water, tools, animals, credit, and markets for their crops. **N**

The legacy of colonialism

Why, then, are so many of the world's people poor? To a significant extent, the pattern of poverty in the world today is rooted in European and United States history.

As you know, the most powerful European countries conquered native peoples and established colonies as they explored the world between 1500 and 1900. By 1914, Europe, its colonies, and its former colonies (including the United States) controlled 84 percent of the earth's land surface.

The main goal of colonization was to enrich the European powers. Wherever they established colonies, the European nations set up systems designed to extract the human and natural resources of the land for themselves while undermining local economies and peoples. For instance, Britain forbade the manufacture of goods that might compete with British-made goods. In the early nineteenth century, India had a thriving textile industry based in small shops. When India's cheap cloth threatened to compete with the

United Nations peacekeepers distribute humanitarian aid to refugees.

Redistributing a small amount of each country's food supply would **eliminate hunger**.

N Contact an international emergency aid organization such as the Red Cross or Catholic Relief Services to find out about some recent food crises. Choose one crisis to focus on, answering these questions: What were the causes of the crisis? How did the organization respond? What obstacles did it face?

cloth being produced by British mills, steep export taxes were placed on all Indian goods. In Bengal, the British even broke the little fingers of thousands of Indian weavers to prevent them from making cloth. As a result, Indian-owned economic enterprises significantly decreased in number during British rule, causing the country to become under-developed.

In Africa, national borders were drawn by European powers, who divided the continent into zones of control at the Congress of Berlin in 1884. Nations were created with little regard to the reality of the people who lived there: tribes that were traditional enemies were lumped together, while other tribes were split apart, causing ethnic tensions that continue to fuel conflict even today.

In many of the colonies, a handful of people came to control political power and the wealth of land and other natural resources. These powerful elites created plantations producing crops for export—coffee, tea, or sugar, for instance—that replaced the farming of crops meant to feed local populations, such as beans, corn, and rice. Such practices forced native peoples off the land, reducing their ability to feed themselves, and left the economies of the colonies dependent on just a few cash crops for income.

As a result of colonialism, Europe and the United States grew more powerful while the majority of the world's people who lived in their colonies grew weaker. ◉

Barriers to development

Although many former colonies gained their independence in the mid-twentieth century, power-over relationships between the world's richest and poorest countries continue to affect global patterns of poverty today.

Resource extraction. Many poor countries attempt to support their weak economies by exporting the cash crops that were established when they were colonies. As we saw in chapter 6, in the case of coffee grown in Nicaragua, the low prices for these exports impoverish the people who produce them, and at the same time, take away land that could be used to grow food for people locally.

Moreover, multinational corporations based in developed countries extract resources from the poorest nations in the form of cash crops, natural resources, and cheap labor. About $43 billion flows from the poorest nations to the richest nations every year.

War often plunges whole nations into poverty. Children—such as these young soldiers—often suffer the most as a result of armed conflicts.

◉ Choose a nation in Asia, Africa, or Latin America that is a former colony. Prepare a short report about its history, answering these questions: What kind of society did the native population have before colonization? How did colonization change the society? What is the nation like today as a result of colonization?

Government by the elite. Part of the legacy of colonialism is that a tiny number of people continue to control the vast majority of land, resources, and political power in the world's poorest nations. As a result, government policies tend to favor the interests of the wealthy rather than the poor.

Foreign aid problems. Wealthy nations offer small amounts of aid to the world's poorest nations, although not as much as most people may think: U.S. foreign aid comprises less than 1 percent of the federal budget. Such aid is not always put to the best use, however. Donor countries may require that the aid be spent on projects or purchases that end up benefiting the interests of the donor nation and the ruling elite of the recipient nations more than the needs of poor people. Other times, aid is used for unwise development projects. Corruption is still another problem: government officials and the ruling elite of poor nations are capable of stealing billions of dollars meant for development.

Discrimination. Ethnic, religious, and gender discrimination within poor countries also causes poverty. Religious and ethnic minorities are likely to be more impoverished than other groups. Indigenous peoples and women often suffer from prejudice, even if they are not in the minority.

Conflict fueled by arms sales. Military spending by poor countries is encouraged by rich countries that make and sell weapons. As a result, money that could fund programs to end hunger and poverty is spent on weapons. For instance, Pakistan spent 40 percent of its national budget on its military in the late 1990s, compared to about 4 percent on health and education combined. Military spending then fuels the intensity of regional conflicts, which, in turn, are a major cause of famine and a source of refugees.

The debt crisis

Perhaps one of the greatest obstacles blocking the full development of poor nations is the **debt crisis:** poor countries owe billions in loan repayments to banks and wealthy nations, and paying interest on these loans takes money from social programs that could eliminate poverty.

The debt crisis began in the 1970s when poor nations were able to get large loans at low interest rates. Although the money should have been used for social development programs, much of it was either stolen or invested in ways that would not strengthen economies. Some 20 percent of the borrowed money was used for military spending, for instance. Then, when interest rates soared in the 1980s, the interest on the debt soared too. Today, few of the poorest nations have any hope of ever repaying their debts, especially because debt repayments stifle their economic development.

Although poor people received little benefit from the international loans that caused the debt crisis, they bear the greatest burden of their nation's debt. In Uganda, for instance, the government spends $3 per person on health and education every year, but $17 per person on debt repayment. One in five Ugandan children dies of preventable diseases before the age of five.

The Catholic church, along with other groups, has called on international lending institutions and the wealthiest nations to reduce or entirely cancel much of the poorest nations' debt. The call to forgive debts so that people might live more fully goes all the way back to ancient Jewish law, but it is even more urgent for justice today: forty-five of the world's poorest countries owe a combined $235 billion.

Most countries have the resources to feed their people, but violence and injustice make it more difficult for them to do so.

Today, few of the poorest nations have any hope of ever repaying their debts.

Suppose you had so much credit card debt that 25 percent of your current income went to paying the interest. Write a short essay describing how your spending habits would change and how your future plans would be affected. Would it be fair for the credit card company to help you somehow? If so, how?

13. Give two examples of the devastating effects of bad water and poor sanitation.

14. How does the church say that wealthier nations should treat refugees?

15. List three common myths about hunger and give a summary of why they are false.

16. What are three consequences of colonialism?

17. Briefly describe three modern barriers to development for poor nations.

18. Briefly describe how the debt crisis affects the world's poorest people.

19. How would the world's wealthiest countries and poorest countries relate differently if they had a power-with relationship rather than a power-over relationship?

How Do We Respond?

Becoming more aware of how poverty prevents the majority of the world's people from living a good life can be an overwhelming, even discouraging, experience. Faced with such complex and far-reaching problems, the easiest response is to simply ignore the whole issue and go on living our own lives.

Christ calls us to make a different choice—not just because poor people suffer when we ignore their plight, but because, in a very real way, we ourselves become poorer, too.

"Every Gesture Makes a Difference"

Pat Schneider knows the difficulty of responding to poverty with compassion. She is the writer who earlier in this chapter told of her experiences with women in poverty.

By treating these women with respect, Schneider helps them recognize their own dignity. It may seem to be a small thing, but Schneider believes it is vital. When she was growing up in poverty, it was small gestures from a few others that helped her recognize her own dignity:

> When I was a girl, my mother, brother, and I lived in two rooms in a building where eight families used one toilet and nobody cleaned anything. Our apartment was filthy, and there were roaches every-

where. We lived in that place from the time I got out of the orphanage at thirteen until I went away to college at eighteen.

I remember only two people coming there to try to touch my life, each only once. My teacher and my minister. My teacher told me I could write. My minister said he was getting money together to send me to college.

Nobody came into my life and stayed. Nobody made the world over for me. But so help me God, what saved me were the few times that someone reached out, came down, came in, and saw me. Saw me. Believed in me. Wanted to get me out. Helped me see that there was an "out" to get to. . . .

When I was twelve and living in an orphanage, a social worker took me home with her for one overnight. I slept that night in a clean bed in a clean house where the mother and the children ate at a table with clean plates.

I knew, then, that it was possible. I knew, then, that I wanted that life. I knew, then, what to work for, what to dream of. . . .

I know that every gesture makes a difference. It says that somebody cares. It says that there is another way to live; that the struggle is worth the pain. (Schneider, "The Cost of Love")

Recognizing the dignity of those who suffer from poverty—as the students who run Matthew's Closet do—is the first step toward responding to poverty with compassion.

Is compassion enough? It could be. The world contains enough resources to offer everyone a good life. If enough people respond to poverty with genuine compassion, it can be greatly reduced both in the United States and in the world. In the next chapter, we will look at how sharing what we have and living more simply might provide a better life for all the world's people.

"What saved me were the few times that someone reached out, came down, came in, and saw me."

❋ *Student art:* "Trust." Photograph; Lauren Koegler, Mother Guerin High School, River Grove, Illinois

After reading this chapter, how do you think you might be able to make an option for the poor? What specific actions might you be able to take? What would your motivation be?

8 LIVING THE GOOD LIFE
(PART 2)

poverty
joy
eucharistic sharing

Sharing
God's goodness

In This Chapter . . .

THE WEALTH OF JOY

After graduating from Cathedral High School in Saint Cloud, Minnesota, Julie Williams decided to spend a summer living in solidarity *with a poor community in rural Mexico.* She wrote the following letter to her former high school justice teacher:

8 *de Agosto*

Dear Mr. LaNave—

How are things with you? I am doing well, although I am a little hot. It has been four days since the last rain and we are out of water. There are *pilas* about a mile away where we will go for water later when the sun is not

"I love it here," Julie Williams said while spending a summer living in solidarity with poor people in rural Mexico.

too hot. I had gotten used to the late afternoon showers and nightly downpours. This summer I am living in the clouds—perched so high in the mountains that I feel like a bird in its nest. Home is a tin-roof schoolroom that I share with ten other young people aged 18 to 27 from Mexico, Colombia, Spain, Puerto Rico, and Canada (and many fleas, bed bugs, spiders, lice, etc.). We cook over a fire on an earthen stove—tortillas, beans, and rice, tortillas, beans, and rice. Just to live is physically difficult—it's an hour-and-a-half hike up the mountain to cut firewood, we must boil all of our water, wash our clothes with stones, and walk three hours to the nearest market. I love it here. Of course my family thinks I'm masochistic. . . .

I decided to come on this program because of its philosophy—it's different than most other programs I've participated in or heard about. It is a philosophy of respect for differences, and the reality that we are here to support the people and live with them and not [just] to help them. It's an interchange of experiences. Indeed, the people here are helping me more than I am helping them—I don't know which worms are venomous or anything about the land or way of life here.

The people here have nothing of material value—*campesinos* of indigenous origin, they work the land and receive almost nothing in return. The village is almost entirely made up of women and children. The youth and men of their families for the most part are in Mexico City, Monterey, Tampico, or the United States because that's where the money is. It's hard to understand why there is no "work" [for pay] here. It seems like where there are people, there is demand for goods and services, and Mexico is rich with resources, so there should be plenty of jobs and money to go around. There is not.

Slowly, I am learning some of the reasons. On Saturday we had an information session and reflection for the community about 500 *años* [500 years, or the five hundredth anniversary of Columbus encountering the "New World"]. For them 500 *años* of exploitation and destruction of their culture. . . . We also held a discussion about the free trade agreement between Canada, [the] United States, and Mexico. Although this issue is more confusing, it is obvious that the *campesinos* are not the ones who will benefit from this agreement. . . .

Daily we do physical labor in the mornings from 8 a.m. to 1 p.m. We have assisted in building a wall for the school made of rocks we carried from all over (encountering four tarantulas and one viper), leveled a small hill in the schoolyard, planted a garden for the women's union, and now are helping them with a compost pile. . . . In the afternoons we have workshops Monday, Wednesday, and Friday—some we organize, like English class, embroidery, games for kids, . . . math, and sports; others the community and the union organize—like alternative medicine and cooking. Tuesday and Thursday we visit houses in the area. This is my favorite thing to do because you really get to know the people and their life—also because many women do not leave the house because they have too much work to do (lots of kids, cook, wash clothes, etc., etc.,) and also because of *machismo*. The people here in general are very timid and shy, especially before they get to know us. . . .

> Indeed, the people here are **helping me** more than I am helping them.

I love to play with the children and chat with the women. I can experience some of what it feels like to be *campesina*, but I will never completely understand their situation because I know that I will be leaving and have another world to go to. Even here, I don't worry about not having enough food or not being able to feed my children. . . .

Today is a big day for the community—as there is a basketball tournament and dance. What am I doing writing a letter? O.K., I'm out of here—

Sincerely,
Julie Williams ☺

Which Way to True Happiness?

"I love it here." Julie's statement might be surprising, given that she lacked even the most basic comforts—like running water. Somehow, amid poverty and hardship, she managed to find joy. Julie's experience contradicts the message of the commercial culture that dominates life in North America, a message that says happiness is found in having what we want.

God wants all people, rich and poor, to experience the joy that comes from loving one another.

Material things are certainly necessary for human fulfillment, as we saw in the previous chapter. But Jesus announces a different message, one that says true happiness—what we might call joy—is found not in possessing material things but in loving relationships with God and one another.

God wants this joy for all people. This is why we are called to live in solidarity with the world's poorest people, much as Julie did. The choice to do so makes it easier for both those who are poor as well as those who are not poor to develop their full potential as images of God.

Transforming the structures of society so that all people, rich and poor, are able to fulfill their human potential and live dignified lives is a process called **development.** When people talk about development, they usually focus on **economics**—the way societies produce, manage, and distribute material wealth. While the Christian understanding of development focuses on economics too, it also goes beyond economics. True development takes into account all aspects of what it means to be human, including the spiritual dimension.

We do not need to travel to some poor community as Julie did in order to pursue development with those who are poor, but we do need to live in a way that values the sacredness of ourselves, others, and God's creation more than material possessions. This way of living, which we will call **living simply,** is about making choices that deepen our joy because they focus on the essentials of life, not on illusions of what brings happiness.

How does living simply bring about true development for the world's poorest people, as well as for ourselves? We will explore that question in this chapter. ▲

▲ What have been the three happiest, or most joyful, times of your life? For each, write a paragraph describing what qualities of the experience made it joyful. What do these experiences have in common?

1. What did Julie identify as some of the causes of poverty in the village where she was staying?
2. How does the way commercial culture suggests we might find happiness differ from the way Jesus says we can find joy?
3. Define these terms: *development, living simply.*

4. Based on what you have learned in this course so far, what do you think enabled Julie to find joy during her experience?

A Poverty of Riches

In the previous chapter, we saw how material poverty prevents people from developing their full potential; this is the sort of poverty Julie encountered. But material poverty is not the only type of poverty that prevents human development.

The Wealth Gap

Extreme poverty of the type Julie encountered is very rare in the United States. In fact, a huge difference exists between the lifestyle of the world's richest people, which includes most of the people in the United States, and the world's poorest people:

- According to the United Nations, the richest 20 percent of the world's people consume 86 percent of its goods and services. Meanwhile, the poorest 20 percent of the world's people consume less than 1 percent of its goods and services.

Street children warm themselves in a tunnel in Kathmandu, Nepal.

- Although the United States comprises less than 5 percent of the world's population, its people consume more than a quarter of the world's goods and services. If she lived like most North Americans, Julie consumed about sixteen times as much while living in the United States than she did while living in solidarity with Mexico's poorest people.
- A similar gap exists in the United States: the richest 20 percent of the population receives half of the total U.S. income, while the poorest 20 percent receives only 3.6 percent.

The difference between the wealthiest and the poorest people is known as the **wealth gap.**

Stuff:
Necessary, but not sufficient

Our culture tends to view its wealth generally as a good thing. Conventional wisdom says that the more we have, the happier we will be. Most political and business leaders make the decisions that shape our society based on the assumption that the way to improve society is primarily by increasing its ability to produce wealth. As a result, political leaders use economic growth—growth in the ability to produce wealth—as a primary indicator of the health of a society.

Christian justice views material resources as basically good. The Genesis Creation story reveals that God gave humanity the resources of the earth so that each of us can live life to the fullest, developing our full potential. But Christianity rejects the illusion that people can find fulfillment through the possession of material wealth alone. **B**

Living crazily

While it is possible to be both wealthy and happy, material possessions are no guarantee of either a happy life or a happy society. Consider, for instance, the experience of people in the San Francisco area who have become suddenly rich from the growth of computer-related companies. Although some have adjusted well to life with their newfound fortune, others have found that having more has made them *less* happy:

"For many people, part of them would just like to close their eyes and make [the wealth] go away," says Mark Levy, a psychiatrist who treats those suffering from what has been called sudden wealth syndrome. "Life would be simpler and more manageable."

Material possessions are **no guarantee** of either a happy life or a happy society.

✳ *Student art:* Photograph; Nic Marshall, Benilde–Saint Margaret's High School, Saint Louis Park, Minnesota

B What are the three most important things you own? List them, then explain how each contributes to the development of your full human potential.

When Karsten Weide became a multimillionaire, he quit his job—and then did nothing. "The first thing I did was spend two months crashing and burning," recalls Weide. "I found myself in this big black hole where there was nothing to do."

The one thing he did do was worry, a lot. Having a huge pile of cash didn't make his life a breeze. "For me, the opposite happened," he says. "I'm stressing more now than ever. You have to take care of money, invest it somewhere, keep track of it and create something for yourself to do."

Another Internet executive works eighty hours a week. "I see a price paid for not being with my family more," Mark Walsh says. "My family is healthy, happy, and smart, but time is all we have on this planet, and money is meaningless. I'm spending the only asset that matters, my time, a lot of it, on the company and growth. I wish I could clone myself."

Individuals and families are not the only ones who suffer when having money and the things it can buy becomes more important than becoming who we were made to be. Society suffers as well:

The new gold rush in the San Francisco Bay area, where many of the [Internet] rich live, has driven up the median price of a condo to $410,000, a 40 percent hike in just a year. The middle class is fleeing into the suburban netherlands to find a place they can afford, and the homeless population shows no signs of shrinking. Traffic congestion—as well as overcrowded stores and restaurants and buses—only adds to everyone's frustration at the deteriorating quality of life in San Francisco. "In the end, you end up with a much meaner society," says Cornell University economist Robert Frank. "It's ironically a society that the people at the top don't find attractive either."

Poverty of Being

Anyone, rich or poor, is capable of living crazily. In a way, living crazily is another form of poverty. It is clearly not the same as material poverty, but because it prevents us from developing our full potential as images of God, we might say it is a **poverty of being.** This sort of poverty causes us to forget who we really are, to forget that we are called to community, and to forget that we live within the limits of God's creation.

Forgetting our true identity

When we start defining ourselves by what we have rather than who we are, we lose sight of our dignity—our true identity as images of God. The belief that "we are what we have" creates the illusion that we can fill our deepest needs—things like love, self-esteem, and creativity—in the same way that we fill our basic physical needs, such as food and shelter, through material possessions.

The reality is that the things we own are not sufficient to provide us with true happiness. If we do not realize this, though, we can end up buying one thing after another. A new purchase might make us happy for a while, but when that happiness fades, we start feeling the need to buy something better. The attempt to find happiness by buying what we do not really need is called **consumerism.** Pope John Paul II observes that consumerism "easily makes people slaves of 'possession' and of immediate gratification":

> This is the so-called civilization of "consumption" or "consumerism," which involves so much "throwing away" and "waste." An object already owned but now

Living crazily results when having things becomes more important than being true to who we are—images of God.

Karsten Weide agrees. "A lot of people I know are moving away; they can't afford to live here with normal jobs. And the atmosphere has changed a lot, from easygoing, tolerant, laid-back, nonmaterially oriented to a money culture—pushy, aggressive—and they're sad about it."

(Adapted from Fraser, "The Experience of Being Suddenly Rich") **C**

If living simply leads to greater joy in life, we might call the way of life described by the people in the story above **living crazily.** Living crazily results when we value having things more than being true to who we are as images of God. It is a lifestyle that emphasizes *having* over *being,* a concept we first discussed in chapter 4.

C Do you think the dissatisfaction of the people in this story came primarily from being wealthy or from their attitude toward wealth? Be prepared to discuss your answer in class.

D Take a critical inventory of products at a local mall or department store. Make three columns on a sheet of paper, titling the first, "Harms true happiness," the second, "Depends," and the third, "Promotes true happiness." Make a list of twenty products, placing each under the appropriate column. Then choose one from each column and explain why you categorized it as you did.

A throwaway society that seeks fulfillment in consumption neglects the needs of poor people —and of the earth.

superseded by something better is discarded, with no thought of its possible lasting value in itself nor of some other human being who is poorer. . . .

One quickly learns . . . that the more one possesses the more one wants, while deeper aspirations remain unsatisfied and perhaps even stifled. (*On Social Concern [Sollicitudo Rei Socialis]*, 28) ▶

Forgetting our call to community

Living crazily also has consequences for the way we relate to others. As images of God, we find fulfillment in our relationship with God and others. But if we expect to find fulfillment in what we have, we risk losing sight of the social side of who we are: getting more stuff can become a higher priority than the needs of others.

This can lead to individualism, a concept we discussed at the beginning of this course.

In terms of economics, the basic assumption of individualism is this: The world is made up of separate individuals, each seeking his or her own good, indifferent to the success or failure of other individuals seeking their own good. Furthermore, society is simply the sum total of individuals seeking their own good. Looking after the common good is unnecessary because a good society will emerge automatically as more and more individuals achieve their goals. In this individualistic view of economics, moral concerns are kept to a minimum. Genuine fairness and kindness, for example, are not required in economic dealings because social relationships are limited to the impersonal world of contracts, rules, and laws. *E*

Forgetting the limits of creation

Finally, living crazily affects the way we relate to creation because it causes us to view the resources of the earth as something we own rather than as a gift from God that we are called to care for. If the primary way we find happiness is through consumption of the earth's resources, it becomes tempting to overlook the limits of those resources.

As images of God, we find fulfillment in our relationship with God and others.

E In your opinion, when do the needs of others become more important than what an individual wants for himself or herself? Be prepared to discuss your position in class.

While thousands of children die of hunger every day, the world spends $800 billion on its militaries.

Lazarus at the Gate

Catholic social teaching has long seen the wealth gap as a glaring sign of injustice. The injustice lies in the fact that those who have more resources than they need or could ever use are often reluctant to share them with those who lack the basic necessities of life.

The world contains more than enough resources to lift its poorest people out of poverty. For instance, providing the world's neediest people with basic education, basic health care, adequate food, clean water, and sanitation would cost the world $40 billion annually, according to the U.N. 1998 Human Development Report. Although that might seem like a lot of money, consider how much the world spends on other things:

- $800 billion on its militaries
- $400 billion on cigarettes
- $250 billion on advertising
- $160 billion on beer
- $40 billion on golf

At a United Nations meeting some thirty years ago, the world's wealthiest nations promised to give 0.7 percent of their annual gross national product—the value of the goods and services they produce—as foreign aid. With only a few exceptions, they have failed to keep that promise. Among the developed countries, the United States gives the smallest percentage of its wealth as foreign aid—just 0.1 percent of its gross national product. Only a portion of that amount is used for human development.

Pope John Paul II often notes that the wealth gap that divides the world closely resembles the parable that Jesus told about Lazarus and the rich man:

> "There was a rich man who was dressed in purple and fine linen and who feasted sumptuously every day. And at his gate lay a poor man named Lazarus, covered with sores, who longed to satisfy his hunger with what fell from the rich man's table; even the dogs would come and lick his sores. The poor man died and was carried away by the angels to be with Abraham. The rich man also died and was buried. In Hades, where he was being tormented, he looked up and saw Abraham far away with Lazarus by his side. He called out, 'Father Abraham, have mercy on me, and send Lazarus to dip the tip of his finger in water and cool my tongue; for I am in agony in these flames.' But Abraham said, 'Child, remember that during your lifetime you received your good things, and Lazarus in like manner evil things; but now he is comforted here, and you are in agony. Besides all this, between you and us a great chasm has been fixed, so that those who might want to pass from here to you cannot do so, and no one can cross from there to us.'" (Luke 16:19–26)

This parable sounds harsh—but its message is clear. By ignoring the suffering of Lazarus, the rich man hurt not only Lazarus but himself as well. It was not only Lazarus's poverty that separated the two men, but the rich man's failure to love.

The parable of Lazarus and the rich man calls us to reach out across the gap that separates those who "[feast] sumptuously every day" from those who are unable to satisfy their hunger. The way to bridge the gap—and bring true joy for the people on both sides—is through love.

For Review

5. What is the wealth gap? Provide a statistic that illustrates that gap.
6. What is our culture's dominant attitude toward material wealth? How does the Christian attitude toward material wealth differ?
7. Define the term *living crazily*.
8. Name and briefly describe three aspects of poverty of being.
9. Why does Catholic social teaching regard the wealth gap as a sign of injustice?

10. Use your Bible to find three of Jesus' teachings about wealth and poverty, and write them down. In a paragraph, identify common themes in the teachings.

The way to bridge the gap—and bring true joy for the people on both sides—is through love.

★ *Student art:* Ink; Sean Carner, Seton Catholic Central High School, Binghamton, New York

In a brief essay, react to this statement: *Those who have wealth ought to share what they have with those who are poor.* How might individuals, institutions, and countries respond to this statement?

A Eucharistic Response to Poverty

Overcoming poverty is about overcoming the forces of death. Because Christians believe that death can be overcome only in Jesus, they turn to him as they strive to overcome poverty.

The Eucharist: A Source of Life

The central way Catholics turn to Jesus is through the Eucharist. Because the Eucharist is the center of Christian life, all Christian ministries, including ministries of justice, find their source in the sacrament of the Eucharist. The Eucharist is at the heart of a Catholic response to poverty.

What does the Eucharist have to do with poverty? First, the Eucharist is a source of life. When we celebrate it, we participate in Jesus' death and Resurrection; when we receive it, we receive "food that makes us live for ever in Jesus Christ" (*Catechism of the Catholic*

Church, 1405). As bread feeds physical hunger, the Eucharist feeds spiritual hunger.

Second, the Eucharist strengthens the solidarity that is necessary to overcome poverty. Because the Eucharist is the body, blood, and spirit of Jesus, receiving the Eucharist better enables us to become Jesus' presence in the world. Moreover, by deepening our union with Christ, the Eucharist unites Christians with one another and with all for whom Christ died and rose.

Because the Eucharist unites us with all those who yearn for fullness of life, it commits us in a special way to those who are poor and hungry. Saint Paul scolded the Christians of Corinth because at their celebrations of the Lord's Supper, some members were going hungry. By receiving the Eucharist while ignoring those who were hungry, Paul said they "show contempt for the church of God and humiliate those who have nothing" (1 Corinthians 11:22).

Sharing Loaves and Fishes

Breaking the eucharistic bread recalls the story of the miraculous multiplication of the loaves and fishes, a story that is found in slightly different forms in all four Gospels. These accounts have an important lesson to teach about responding to poverty.

> The Eucharist is at the **heart** of a Catholic response to poverty.

Jesus told the disciples to feed the people rather than turn them away hungry: "You give them something to eat" (Mark 6:37). Jesus' multiplication of the loaves and fishes teaches us that when we share, God's abundance provides enough for all.

"Give them something to eat"

Jesus had been teaching a crowd of about five thousand people. Late in the day, his disciples urged him to send the people away so they could buy food for themselves in the surrounding villages.

> But he answered them, "You give them something to eat." They said to him, "Are we to go and buy two hundred denarii [the equivalent of two hundred days' wages] worth of bread, and give it to them to eat?" And he said to them, "How many loaves have you? Go and see." (Mark 6:37–38)

The disciples returned with five loaves and two fish. In a foreshadowing of the Eucharist, Jesus blessed the food, broke the bread, and had the disciples distribute it to the crowds. When the disciples collected the leftovers, they filled twelve baskets. H

"Life is a banquet"

Like the disciples, our first reaction to the crowds of poor and hungry people in the world might be to send them away to fend for themselves. Just as the disciples suggested it would cost too much to feed the crowds, many people today suggest it would cost too much to respond to poverty with compassion.

Yet, Jesus calls us to "give them something to eat." This call comes with the promise that if we respond to one another's needs with love, all people will have enough to live a full and abundant life.

Dorothy Day is one person who took that call and promise seriously enough to act on it. Dorothy is the Catholic convert mentioned at the beginning of chapter 2; together with Peter Maurin, she started the *Catholic Worker* newspaper in 1933 (see pages 236–237). At the same time, the two also founded a movement by the same name. The Catholic Worker Movement, like Dorothy's life, is dedicated to works of mercy such as feeding the hungry, sheltering the homeless, and working to change the social structures that cause poverty and injustice. Catholic Workers choose a lifestyle of voluntary poverty to better serve God and those who have been forced into poverty. They follow the words of Peter Maurin quoted in chapter 1: "Everybody would be rich / if nobody tried to become richer. / And nobody would be poor / if everybody tried to be the poorest."

In her autobiography, Dorothy describes how the Catholic Worker Movement started and grew. The following passage reflects the spirit of the movement, a spirit that reflects a eucharistic response to poverty:

> We were just sitting there talking when lines of people began to form, saying, "We need bread." We could not say, "Go, be thou filled." If there were six small loaves and a few fishes, we had to divide them. There was always bread.
>
> We were just sitting there talking and people moved in on us. Let those who can

Bread is distributed at a refugee camp.

G Listen carefully to the eucharistic prayer during Mass, or find a copy of one of the prayers. Write a one-page reflection on how the words of the prayer might apply to our response to poverty.

H Recall a time when you shared something that you really wanted just for yourself. Write a short reflection on your experience.

LESSONS IN JUSTICE FROM DOROTHY DAY

Although Dorothy Day cofounded a newspaper and a movement dedicated to those serving who live in poverty, perhaps her greatest legacy is the example of her own life. For most of her life, Dorothy lived with poor people in the Catholic Worker's houses of hospitality, while also working to change the "filthy, rotten system" that perpetuated their poverty. Writer Jim Forest came to know Dorothy's spirit through his work as managing editor of the *Catholic Worker*. Here are some of the lessons she taught him about justice.

Justice begins on our knees. I have never known anyone, not even in monasteries, who was more of a praying person than Dorothy Day. When I think of her, I think of her first of all on her knees praying before the Blessed Sacrament [the Eucharist]. I think of those long lists of names she kept of people, living and dead, to pray for. I think

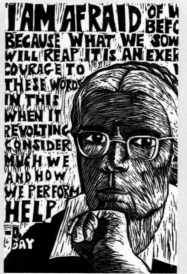

❋ *Student art:* "An Exercise in Courage." Linocut; Jennifer Clark, Saint Agnes Academy, Memphis, Tennessee

of her at Mass, I think of her praying the rosary, I think of her going off for Confession each Saturday evening.

"We feed the hungry, yes," she said. "We try to shelter the homeless and give them clothes, but there is strong faith at work; we pray. If an outsider who comes to visit us doesn't pay attention to our prayings and what that means, then he'll miss the whole point." . . .

The most radical thing we can do is to try to find the face of Christ in others, and not only those we find it easy to be with but those who make us nervous, frighten us, alarm us, or even terrify us. "Those who cannot see the face of Christ in the poor," she used to say, "are atheists indeed."

Dorothy was an orthodox Catholic. This means she believed that Christ has left himself with us both in the Eucharist and in those in need. . . .

Beauty is not just for the affluent. Tom Cornell tells the story of a donor coming into the Catholic Worker and giving Dorothy a diamond ring. Dorothy thanked her for it and put it in her pocket. Later a rather demented lady came in, one of the more irritating regulars at the house. Dorothy took the diamond ring out of her pocket and gave it to the woman.

Someone on the staff said to Dorothy, "Wouldn't it have been better if we took the ring to a diamond exchange, sold it, and paid the woman's rent for a year?"

Dorothy replied that the woman had her dignity and could do what she liked with the ring. She could sell it for rent money or take a trip to the Bahamas. Or she could enjoy wearing a diamond ring on her hand like the woman who gave it away. "Do you suppose," Dorothy asked, "that God created diamonds only for the rich?" . . .

Take the "little way." . . . Change starts not in the future but in the present, not in Washington or on Wall Street but where I stand.

Change begins not in the isolated dramatic gesture or the petition signed but in the ordinary actions of life, how I live minute to minute, what I do with my life, what I notice, what I respond to, the care and attention with which I listen, the way in which I respond. . . .

"What I want to bring out," [she said,] "is how a pebble cast into a pond causes ripples that spread in all directions. Each one of our thoughts, words, and deeds is like that." . . .

[Follow Christ.] . . . Hers was a day-to-day way of the cross, and just as truly the way of the open door.

"It is the living from day to day," she said, "taking no thought for the morrow, seeing Christ in all who come to us, and trying literally to follow the gospel that resulted in this work."

(Forest, "What I Learned About Justice from Dorothy Day") ●

"It is the living from day to day," she said, "taking no thought for the morrow, **seeing Christ in all who come to us,** and trying literally to follow the gospel that resulted in this work."

In your opinion, why did Dorothy view prayer as essential to her response to poverty? If you like, write a prayer that reflects a eucharistic response to poverty.

Compare the story of Dorothy and the diamond ring to the story of the woman who anointed Jesus with costly perfume (John 12:1–8). Then write a short reflection about what these stories teach us about responding to the poor.

take it, take it. Some moved out and that made room for more. And somehow the walls expanded. . . .

I found myself, a barren woman, the joyful mother of children. It is not easy always to be joyful, to keep in mind the duty of delight. . . .

We cannot love God unless we love each other, and to love we must know each other. We know Him in the breaking of bread, and we know each other in the breaking of bread, and we are not alone any more. Heaven is a banquet and life is a banquet, too, even with a crust, where there is companionship. (*The Long Loneliness,* pages 285–286)

At the heart of Dorothy's reflection, and at the heart of a eucharistic response to poverty, is this conviction: *If we share, there will always be enough.* 🕊

Learning to Share

Sharing the world's resources more equitably is key to the economic aspect of human development. Sharing might sound like a simple solution to poverty, but putting it into practice on the scale of whole economies has proven to be more complicated.

Recall that in chapter 2, we discussed the way two major economic systems, capitalism and socialism, approach the distribution of wealth. Catholic social teaching has criticized both these systems, however, for failing to fully respect human dignity. In its communist form, socialism does not respect human freedom and basic human rights. And the church has criticized capitalism for being too individualistic and ignoring the needs of society's poorest members.

Rather than endorse a specific economic system, Catholic social teaching offers principles that should guide economic decision making. The following three principles suggest a way of living together that is the opposite of living crazily.

1. People, especially the poorest, are more important than possessions

Although Catholic social teaching accepts the need for economic growth in order to create living-wage jobs for all people, it rejects the notion that economic growth in itself is the best measure of a society's health. Rather, it says that because people are more important than possessions, concern for human dignity should be the most important guide for all economic decisions. According to *Economic Justice for All:*

The **justice of a society** is tested by how it treats its poorest members.

🕊 If someone came up to you on the street and said, "I'm hungry," how would you respond? Be prepared to discuss your answer in class.

L Make an inventory of everything you own. How much of what you own is surplus—more than you really need? Write a short reflection explaining how you distinguished between what you need and what is surplus. Then discuss how you would feel about giving up your surplus to those who are poor.

Our faith calls us to measure this economy, not only by what it produces, but also by how it touches human life and whether it protects or undermines the dignity of the human person. (1)

Wherever our economic arrangements fail to conform to the demands of human dignity lived in community, they must be questioned and transformed. (28)

Our economic decisions are guided by concern for human dignity in three basic ways: respecting human rights, enabling participation in community, and making an option for the poor.

Human rights and participation. As we have discussed in previous chapters, the extent to which human dignity is being respected can be measured by the extent to which human rights are respected, especially the right to participate in all aspects of the life of the community.

Option for the poor. When promoting human dignity rather than selfishness is the ultimate goal of all economic activity, then the needs of those who are poor become a top concern. The justice of a society is tested by how it treats its poorest members, the church says.

2. The earth is God's gift for all people

The Genesis Creation story teaches us that everything we have comes from God. Therefore, we never really "own" the resources of the earth; God is the earth's only true owner. God calls us to be caretakers of the resources of the earth, to use them to promote our own good, the good of others, and the good of all creation.

The concept that all the resources of the earth are intended for all people is called the **universal destination of goods.** While Catholic social teaching affirms the right of all people to own private property in order to develop their full potential as images of

God, that right is limited by the basic needs of the larger community. We are called to manage our economic resources in a way that benefits the common good of the whole global household:

From the patristic period to the present, the Church has affirmed that misuse of the world's resources or appropriation of them by a minority of the world's population betrays the gift of creation since "whatever belongs to God belongs to all." (*Economic Justice for All,* 34, emphasis deleted)

The concept that "whatever belongs to God belongs to all" guided the economic life of the ancient Jewish community as well as the first Christian communities. Jewish Law called people to ensure that those who were poor would have access to their share of the earth's wealth: "If there is among you anyone in need, . . . do not be hard-hearted or tight-fisted toward your needy neighbor. You should rather open your hand, willingly lending enough to meet the need, whatever it may be" (Deuteronomy 15:7–8).

Catholic social teaching, as expressed by Pope Paul VI, echoes this demand for justice: "No one may appropriate surplus goods solely for his own private use when others lack the bare necessities of life" (*On the Development of Peoples [Populorum Progressio],* 23).

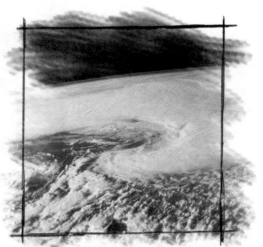

"Whatever belongs to God belongs to all."
Because the earth belongs to God, we are called to care for it and share its resources with all people.

3. We are called to care for God's creation

Recognizing that the earth belongs to God implies that we need to care for the earth's natural resources, not only to preserve them for future generations who have as much a right to use them as we do, but also simply because they are good in and of themselves. We will discuss our responsibility to care for the earth's natural resources at greater length in the next chapter.

Trusting in God, Not Possessions

Fear is a major obstacle to our willingness to share with one another. We fear that we may not be happy if we share our wealth with others, or we hoard resources out of fear that we will not have enough at some future time of crisis.

In the Christian worldview, sharing is made possible because of a deep trust in the providence of God. Jesus taught that loving God before possessions opens our heart to receiving all God's gifts:

"Therefore I tell you, do not worry about your life, what you will eat, or about your body, what you will wear. For life is more than food, and the body more than clothing. . . . Consider the lilies, how they grow: they neither toil nor spin; yet I tell you, even Solomon in all his glory was not clothed like one of these. But if God so clothes the grass of the field, which is alive today and tomorrow is thrown into the oven, how much more will he clothe you—you of little faith! And do not keep striving for what you are to eat and what you are to drink. . . . Instead, strive for his kingdom, and these things will be given to you as well." (Luke 12:22–31)

Jesus is not suggesting that we ignore our own material needs or the needs of others. But his words call us to imagine a new reality for our economic life together. What if trust in God freed us from fear and the accompanying urge to have more than we need? What if our economy was based on love rather than selfishness? What if we shared rather than hoarded? In an economy based on love, there would always be enough—enough resources for everyone's full development, and enough joy to go around. **M**

What if **trust in God** freed us from fear and the accompanying urge to have more than we need?

M Brainstorm with some of your classmates about how living by each of these three economic principles, plus trust in God's providence, would change your community. Then write a three-minute skit based on an advertisement that promotes a community shaped by these principles. Be prepared to present your skit in class.

11. How does the Eucharist call us to commitment to those who are poor?
12. What conviction is at the heart of a eucharistic response to poverty?
13. What does Catholic social teaching say should be the most important guide for making economic decisions?
14. What tests the justice of a society?
15. Define *universal destination of goods,* and briefly explain its major implications for economic life.
16. What does recognizing that the earth belongs to God imply about our relationship with creation?
17. How are Christians called to overcome a fear of sharing what they have with those in need?

In Depth

18. Choose five of the human rights listed on page 149 and explain how each could be used to evaluate whether an economy promotes or undermines human dignity.

Living Simply So Others Can Simply Live

When we apply the spirit of the Eucharist to the way we live our life together, we can begin to live more simply. Because living simply enables us to focus on the essentials of life, it promotes true human development, transforming the structures of society so that all people are able to fulfill their potential and live in dignity. The saying, "Live simply so others can simply live" is what this is all about.

A Different Kind of Wealth

When people hear the suggestion that they should live more simply, they often fear that they are being asked to live a deprived life. But living simply is not the same as poverty. Those who live in poverty lack sufficient resources to take care of their well-being. Simple living, on the other hand, enhances our well-being. It is not a state of destitution, but one of knowing what is enough and sufficient. It is an attitude of being, not having. When we live simply, we allow the spirit of the Eucharist to guide the choices we make in our everyday life:

- **Human dignity.** We value people more than possessions. Our lifestyle decisions are primarily guided by how they affect our own dignity and the dignity of others.

"LIVING SIMPLY" IN A CATHOLIC WORKER HOUSE

The Catholic Worker movement's houses of hospitality are good examples of living simply and eucharistic sharing.

Kitchen scraps and yard waste are composted, saving space in landfills and providing rich soil for gardens.

Volunteers and guests often use bicycles or public transportation to get around inexpensively, saving energy and reducing pollution.

Some houses grow gardens, providing themselves and the community with cheap, fresh, pesticide-free produce.

Most Catholic Worker houses provide hospitality to the homeless, serving between five and fifteen people at a time.

Catholic Workers live in the same house as their guests, receiving no salary for their work.

Usually community members all share one car.

Guests and volunteers share food and conversation at the same table.

Food is donated by people and businesses in the community.

Many houses do not have a television; instead, people talk, read, play games, or participate in neighborhood events.

Washing dishes by hand saves water and energy, and allows for good conversation among guests and volunteers.

Many houses offer used clothes—often as nice as new—to guests.

Catholic Workers raise community awareness of justice issues by distributing their own newspapers or holding public demonstrations.

- **Relationships.** We look for joy in our relationships with others, rather than trying to find happiness only in what we possess. We are aware that we live in a world of interdependent relationships, and so we try to be conscious of how our decisions affect others in the global community. Concern for the common good guides our decisions, not just our own interests.
- **Environment.** We include the well-being of the environment as an important factor in our lifestyle choices.
- **Trust.** We trust that when we live in love, God will provide us with what we need.

Simple living can influence all aspects of our life: the quality and quantity of the goods we buy, the way we earn our money, our attitudes toward learning and recreation, the way we relate to friends and family. Simple living can ease us of the burden of too many possessions and dispel false ideas about who we are. It can eliminate the distractions that prevent us from experiencing deep emotion. In short, simplifying our life can make us more authentic human beings.

A way of living in solidarity with the poor

Living simply is also a way of living in solidarity with the poor. Material poverty and simple living are both economic conditions, but poverty is involuntary, and simple living is a choice. Because both of these economic conditions have to do with how resources are distributed in society, the choice for a simple lifestyle rather than an excessive one can indirectly affect those who live in poverty. Each time we spend a dollar on a certain product, we support the whole system that produced and delivered that product.

So, for example, when the Christmas shopping season comes around, many people who want to live a simple lifestyle decide to buy crafts made by people living in poverty in remote areas of poor nations. In doing so, the purchaser supports economic opportunity for people who have been marginalized in the global economy.

Christina's story

Christina is a young person who grew up in a family that chose to live simply. Her story illustrates how living simply is a good antidote for material poverty as well as poverty of being:

In our family, we never play with war toys. We rarely watch anything on television. We sing lots of songs and we pray together. We have carnivals in our backyard to raise money for our friend who is a Jesuit missionary in Sudan. We very seldom shop for clothes in shopping malls or big department stores. We're not poor. However, we choose to live in solidarity with the poor.

A friend of Christina's who attended the same inner-city Philadelphia parish that she did recalls that "they were the happiest family I've ever met":

I remember noticing that they didn't even watch TV. But they didn't seem to mind. I think by choosing not to watch TV, they were choosing to spend more time with each other, and this helped to make their relationships to each other closer.

They cared a great deal about their community, and they did not want to live a life of excess when there was a lot of poverty around them. They were very active in our

 Most of us have lifestyles that fall in between living simply and living crazily. Using the characteristics of each as a guide, write a reflection on aspects of craziness and simplicity in your life. How does each affect your personal development? How does each affect your relationship with those who are poor?

LIFESTYLES: COMPARING POVERTY, SIMPLICITY, AND EXCESS

Poverty
- is involuntary
- is repressive and debilitating
- fosters a sense of helplessness, passivity, and despair
- degrades the human spirit

Simplicity
- is consciously chosen
- is liberating and enabling
- fosters a sense of personal empowerment, creativity, and opportunity
- nurtures the human spirit by highlighting life's beauty and integrity

Excess
- is voluntary, though many are coerced into excessive lifestyles by advertising and peer pressure
- is addictive and enslaving
- fosters a false sense of self-esteem
- cheapens the human spirit ☻

Living simply builds community.

church, and they worked with others in the neighborhood to provide an after-school program for kids who needed attention and a good meal.

As you might expect, living simply in a consumer culture was often challenging for Christina as she grew up. She recalls the peer pressure she faced:

I remember being in fourth grade and being teased for not having a *real* Cabbage Patch doll. It didn't feel good being so totally "uncool." But as Christians we are called to go against the flow. Thinking about it now, I realize that workers may have been paid unjust wages to produce those dolls. What is "cool" isn't necessarily right.

By living simply, Christina's family promoted true human development, both for themselves and for the community around them.

Sharing to Overcome Poverty

By helping us realize our full potential as images of God, giving us more free time, reducing our dependence on material goods, and deepening our solidarity with others, living simply makes it easier for us to share ourselves and our resources with those who are poor. Ultimately, the principles of living simply must be applied on a social level as well as a personal level if the gap between rich people and poor people is to be bridged.

"I have a job now and a place to live— and I couldn't have done it without you."

How can living simply be applied to society? The following people and communities show the way.

Direct Action: Feeding the Hungry

Although she is not Catholic, seventeen-year-old Amber Lynn Coffman lives the spirit of the Eucharist in her life through an organization she started as an elementary school student. Happy Helpers for the Homeless cares for Baltimore's homeless population:

"I saw a great need," says Amber, who first encountered homelessness while volunteering at a shelter with her mother. "I couldn't live with myself if I didn't do something about it. Mother Teresa inspired me."

So nearly every weekend since 1993, Amber and her friends have gathered at her apartment to make cold meals from perfectly good food that local restaurants and stores would otherwise have thrown away. They make some six hundred meals, which they distribute to homeless people on the streets of Baltimore—many of whom can

Amber Coffman discovered the joy of eucharistic sharing. She and other teen volunteers not only feed and clothe people in need but also celebrate with them.

Brainstorm a list of ways that you could simplify your life today, two years from now, and ten years from now.

not access soup kitchens on the weekends. Over the years, more than five hundred youth volunteers have helped Amber distribute food to some twenty-five thousand people.

Amber's service goes beyond food. She also conducts drives to collect personal-care items like deodorant, soap, and toothpaste. She organizes special events, such as a day of free haircuts or dental care.

And every year on her birthday, Amber throws a huge party for all her volunteers and up to four hundred of the homeless people she serves. The group sings a mile-long, tongue-twisting rendition of "Happy Birthday" that includes the names of everyone present, and they all have pizza and cake. Then Amber hands out gifts. "One year, I handed out watches," she says. "The second year, they had a choice between sleeping bags, tote bags, sweat suits, or sneakers. Sneakers were the favorite."

Amber and her mom are not rich themselves—they have always lived in small apartments. "I wish I had a house," she admits. "And, eventually, I'd like to run my own homeless shelter. It'll be a special family-type shelter where we'll all sit down together to eat dinner and I'll ask everyone how their day was."

In the meantime, Amber's work continues to help people develop their full potential. "I want to thank you," one man told her as she distributed sandwiches in front of City Hall. "This will be my last day coming down. I have a job now and a place to live—and I couldn't have done it without you." (Adapted from Newman, "Love in a Sandwich Bag")

Promoting Self-Sufficiency

Direct aid of the sort provided by Amber Coffman is definitely a necessary response to poverty. Without such action, people die. The ideal, though, is direct assistance that respects human dignity by enabling greater freedom to participate in the economic life of the community.

One such organization that promotes this kind of aid is **Catholic Relief Services** (CRS), an international poverty-fighting organization founded by the U.S. Catholic bishops in 1943.

Besides its emergency relief work in war-torn and famine-stricken countries, CRS helps people to provide for themselves. The organization's work in Cambodia is a typical example. After two decades of civil strife, the

Catholic Relief Services helps women such as these become self-sufficient by creating small community-run "banks" that provide them with loans. *From left to right,* women entrepreneurs assisted by CRS in Gaza, Indonesia, and the Philippines.

Write about some ways that Amber's work reflects the spirit of the Eucharist.

Cambodians' average annual income was just $285, and most had no access to bank loans that they needed to increase their income.

In response, CRS helped to create village banks run by groups of thirty to fifty low-income women. The women are trained in reading, basic math, organizing, and record keeping. They meet once a month to conduct bank business. Ngean Sarem, a single mother of three, used village bank loans to invest in her small grocery stand and her pig-raising business. The profits allowed her to repair her house, expand her business, and save ten dollars. Over five years, 390 village banks provided $3.2 million in loans to nearly twenty-five thousand Cambodians. With continued support and training, CRS sees a time when the banks will become self-sufficient.

Sharing by Changing Social Structures

Of course, grassroots efforts can go only so far to eliminate poverty. Many poor people are prevented from becoming self-sufficient by the larger political, social, and economic structures under which they live. Changes in national and international policies are a critical part of the worldwide efforts to provide economic well-being for all people. Those changes can be guided by the economic principles of Catholic social teaching listed in the "Learning to Share" section in this chapter.

Changing the structures of society is the best way to alleviate poverty in the long run.

But it is often easier said than done; fear and selfishness are powerful forces that cause many people to resist such changes, as one Catholic high school found out. **Q**

Journeying toward a society of love

The students in a Christian justice class at Cathedral High School (the same school Julie Williams attended) in the city of Saint Cloud, Minnesota, decided to work on the issue of homelessness in their community after a speaker from the local housing advocacy group spoke to them about the problem. The students learned that more than one thousand homeless people—mostly families—had been turned away from the local shelter in that year alone.

The housing group hoped to build a larger shelter to accommodate the demand, but it needed the approval of the city council to do so. About fifteen students decided to present their own statement in favor of the larger shelter at a city council hearing. The statement talked about the lessons they had learned as a result of forming relationships with some of the homeless people at the shelter:

> The most important lesson we've learned is that homeless people are just like us. Society's stereotype of homeless people as being unsafe, lazy, and disturbed was quickly changed for us when we came into contact with homeless people and saw the reality of their situation. . . .

Q Write a short research paper on a state, national, or international policy that prevents poor people from living self-sufficiently. (For example, welfare limits that prevent people from going to school, or international trade rules that hurt poor nations.) In your paper, (1) describe the policy and its effects, (2) present the views of people for and against the policy, and (3) analyze it from the perspective of Catholic social teaching. Finally, offer your own reaction to the policy by suggesting ways it could be improved.

Catholic high school students in Saint Cloud, Minnesota, work to raise awareness of the injustice of homelessness in their community.

As a community, we cannot continue to turn homeless people away. . . .

As you make this decision, we ask that you consider how you represent all of the people in Saint Cloud—people who are homeless as well as people who have homes.

Despite the students' plea, the city council denied the housing advocacy group permission to establish the larger shelter.

Two years later, the housing group tried to build support for the expanded shelter by holding a meeting with the residents of the neighborhood where the shelter was to be located. As a result of their ongoing relationship, the housing group invited students from the high school to attend, and about fifteen did. Katie Halupczok, one of the students, recalls how the meeting went:

> During the meeting fellow classmates of mine stood up to talk and take a stand. [Some of] the people of this neighborhood were very prepared; before they even got a chance, the shut-downs began. People there would throw anything [at them].

"Where do you live? You don't pay property taxes! You're just a kid." That was almost terrifying, but still they spoke.

Rather than give up in the wake of this experience, the students deepened their commitment throughout the following year. They focused their efforts on raising the community's understanding of homelessness and raising support for the new shelter. To accomplish this, they lobbied their legislators and city council members about housing issues, made classroom presentations at their own high school and a local university, and organized a two-day and two-night community event that featured informational presentations and displays.

Although the event received considerable support from the community and ample media coverage, the additional shelter was not built; the old shelter was renovated instead. ℝ

Despite the difficulty of the task, each of the students has been enriched by the experience. "I realized we weren't alone in this struggle," said Katie:

> Not only were the fourteen of us students who attended prepared to walk the rest of the way, but so was God—right next to us. . . . With Him all things are possible, and this was only the beginning of a long, long journey. ⓢ

Living Simply in Curitiba

As challenging as it is to transform social structures, we might wonder whether it is at all possible to build a society that lives simply.

While human effort alone can never create the perfect society, the city of Curitiba, Brazil,

---

ℝ Find out if the Catholic Worker, Habitat for Humanity, or another housing advocacy group is active in your community. Interview someone who participates in the organization about local housing issues. How does faith affect that person's work? Write a short report on your interview.

ⓢ Write a short essay identifying principles from the circle of faith-in-action that are present in the students' story.

is a testament to the kind of community we might create if we worked toward living more simply on a social scale. Although this city lacks material wealth, it has managed to apply many of the principles of Catholic social teaching to community life, with a spirit of creativity and joy. As you consider the following examples, watch for how each reflects the principles of eucharistic sharing and living simply.

Transportation. When the city's expanding population began to cause congestion in its small streets, it initially considered knocking down historic buildings in order to build freeway overpasses. Instead, it designed an effective bus system that is fast and easy to use. It preserved the historic buildings by setting aside some streets for buses only, and then it placed extra-long "speedy buses" on those streets.

The result: More than 1.5 million people ride these buses each day—more people than ride the bus daily in New York City. The system is so convenient that the city's residents drive 25 percent less than other Brazilians, which in turn reduces emissions of the gases that cause global warming.

Job creation. Needing jobs for an expanding population in the 1970s, the city of Curitiba sought to lure businesses that would provide good jobs. It might have followed the lead of some other cities by offering large tax breaks to businesses willing to locate there.

But such so-called corporate welfare undermines local tax bases, eroding the ability of governments to provide social services. Instead, officials bought forty square kilometers of land seven miles downwind from the city, put in streets, utility services, housing, and schools. Then the area was linked to the city bus system—including a special workers' bus line directly to the largest poor neighborhood in the city. At the same time, the city enacted strict air and water quality laws in order to prevent industrial pollution. It also provided free child care for the workers' children that included three meals a day.

The result: By 1990, 346 factories employed 50,000 people directly and 150,000 indirectly. Unemployment among the poor decreased, and the children in child care were less likely to go hungry.

Poverty-related health problems. Some of the city's slums experienced an outbreak of a rat-borne disease connected with trash in the streets. One possible solution would have involved hiring garbage collectors, but the streets were too narrow for the trucks. Instead, the city used the money it would have paid the garbage collectors to buy food from local farmers. The food was then given to those in the slums in exchange for bags of garbage.

The result: Greater cleanliness in the slums, better health and less hunger among the city's poorest people, and support for struggling local farmers.

Although it is not as rich as North American cities, the Brazilian city of Curitiba has used its limited resources in ways that respect human dignity, focus on the needs of poor people, and care for the environment.

The city of Curitiba is not perfect; like other cities, it experiences poverty and other problems. What is striking, though, is how the city's leaders use its limited resources in ways that focus on human dignity, participation, an option for the poor, and care for the environment.

"'Integration' is a word one hears constantly from official Curitiba," says writer and environmentalist Bill McKibben. ". . . It means knitting together the entire city, rich, poor, and in-between—knitting it together culturally and economically and physically" (*Hope, Human and Wild,* pages 92–93). ✝

Following the Way to Joy

The call to share God's goodness with all people might tempt us to focus only on what we stand to lose. Yet, the example of Curitiba challenges us to consider whether moving toward simple living might not be more of a gift than a sacrifice.

The citizens of Curitiba enjoy their city. They are not rich—the average annual income in the city is $2,500. Yet, it stands in sharp contrast to the way some of the world's richest people evaluated the changes in San Francisco. McKibben observes the following about Curitiba:

> It is a true place, a place full of serendipity. It is not dangerous or dirty; if it was, people would go to the shopping mall instead. It is as alive as any urban district in the world: poems pasted on telephone poles, babies everywhere. The downtown, though a shopping district, is not a money-making machine. It is a habitat, a place for *living*— the exact and exciting opposite of a mall. (Page 103)

Jaime Lerner, Curitiba's mayor, is responsible for many of the creative ideas in the city. Like Dorothy Day, he suggests that the secret to successful simple living is "the duty of delight":

> You have to have fun. All my work, all my life, we have fun. We're laughing all the time. We're working on things that make us happy. (Page 78) ∪

The secret to successful simple living is "the duty of delight": You have to have fun.

Student art: "Boardwalk." Colored pencil; Lauren Ottaviano, Boylan Catholic High School, Rockford, Illinois

✝ Read the newspaper or talk to your elected representatives to research a specific problem facing your community, as well as the proposed solutions. Drawing on the principles of eucharistic sharing and living simply, brainstorm your own response to the problem. Be prepared to present your work to the class.

∪ Reread "The Joy of Justice" in chapter 1 (pages 36–37). Write a reflection on how the words of theologian Michael Himes apply to the people whose stories were told in this chapter. How could you experience this joy in your life?

19. Name four principles that guide simple living, and briefly explain each.
20. How does living simply better enable us to work to overcome poverty?
21. What is the ideal form of direct action, and why is it preferable?

In Depth

22. Describe the ways the principles of simple living and a eucharistic response to poverty are illustrated in Curitiba.
23. Refer again to the causes of poverty listed in chapter 7. Choose three of those causes and for each, briefly discuss how the principles of eucharistic sharing could help to change or overcome the situation.

WHAT YOU CAN DO . . .

- Start living a simple lifestyle: Avoid prepackaged or processed foods and junk food. Use fewer electric appliances, such as can openers, when hand-operated appliances are available. Buy more locally grown food and locally made products. Use fewer disposable products. Plant home and community gardens. Place more value on family ties and friendship than on making money.
- Practice sharing your possessions with others who might need them more than you do.
- Contact your local school district and volunteer to tutor kids who need help in school.
- Start a food distribution program similar to Amber Coffman's. Ask for help from a respected adult and some of your friends. Start by volunteering with a local program that helps the homeless so you can get to know the people you want to serve. Then ask local restaurants and stores to donate food that is too old to be sold but still good enough to eat.
- Work for more affordable housing in your community by getting involved with local housing advocacy organizations such as Habitat for Humanity.
- Support the political lobbying efforts of your state's conference of Catholic bishops. Contact your diocese to find out what poverty-related issues the church is asking politicians to address, then write or call your representatives.
- Pray for the Holy Spirit to help you and others in your community to bridge the gap between those who are rich and those who are poor. ☉

9 RESPECT FOR THE EARTH

extinction
exploitation
integrity
& stewardship

Caring
for God's creation

In This Chapter . . .

CREAMED
ON BIG GREEN

Eight-year-old Adam Werbach pressed his face up against the airplane window. Down below, the earth was scarred with weird gashes—the result of logging. "Why do they cut trees down?" he asked his parents. Questions like that one prompted Adam to get involved in protecting the earth at a very young age. Fast-forward nine years. Now seventeen, Adam walks into the campaign headquarters of Big Green, a California state ballot initiative pushing for cleaner air, more open spaces, greater fuel economy, and preservation of forests:

As the youngest Sierra Club president ever, Adam Werbach continued to encourage members of the Sierra Student Coalition to work for environmental justice.

"Yeah, what do you want?" a gaunt woman barked at me.

"Well, I, uh, want to help." I figured that I'd lick envelopes until my tongue had a seizure.

"Okay, what can you do?"

"I don't know," I replied. "I'm just a high school student. Who's the person organizing high school students?"

She looked at me with a predatory grin and almost purred, "Well, you are."

"Me? I've never done anything like this before."

"Here's your chance," said the woman, whose name turned out to be Stephanie. She handed me a stack of papers. "Read about the issue and ask me any questions that come up. Coffee's in the kitchen."

I learned everything I could about Big Green and started calling my friends. I didn't ask for much, just that they call the office and offer help. We could write letters, walk precincts, phone, do office work, whatever was useful.

Students all asked me the same questions I had first asked: Why me? What difference can I make? How will I know what to do? Following Stephanie's lead, I told them to get to work. After all, if not them, who? Before long, more than 350 California high school students were canvassing door-to-door and staffing phone banks.

After all that effort, I figured that we had won hands down. Wrong. We got annihilated, whipped, creamed, and had our toast buttered on Big Green, later nicknamed Big Dream. . . . The goal of the grassroots campaign was to change 2 to 3 percent of the overall vote, which we accomplished. But we needed to change 8 to 10 percent to pass Big Green. The oil, mining, and timber industries ran television ads that reached far more people than we could. They outspent us 10-to-1, $30 million to $3 million. I listened and learned.

We had failed. I felt disappointed for leading people down this dead-end path. . . .

I woke up the next morning to the electronic wail of my phone. It was a fifteen-year-old named Tasha. "What's next?" she said anxiously. "I know we lost, but this was fun. It felt good."

"Tasha, I don't know. Let me call you back." I started to hang up. She didn't let me off the hook that easily. "Adam!" she yelled. "Listen. You're going to call me when you know what's next. I'm sorry we lost, but we've got to go on to something else."

What's next turned out to be the birth of the Sierra Student Coalition—now thirty thousand members strong. Victories also followed, which I'll take over defeat anytime. (Adapted from Werbach and Bergman, "Class Acts")

Adam went on to become president of the 600,000-member Sierra Club. At the age of twenty-three, he was the club's youngest president ever. A

I told them to get to work. After all, **if not them, who?**

A What is your relationship like with the natural world? Make a list of all the ways the natural world affects your life, then make a list of all the ways you affect the natural world.

Caring for Creation: A Requirement of Christian Faith

Adam's efforts to pass Big Green highlight the increasing concern many people have for the well-being of the natural environment. At the root of such concern are the many threats facing the natural world—global warming, the extinction of thousands of species, and widespread pollution, among others.

Someone might wonder why Catholic social teaching is concerned about caring for God's creation, because human life and dignity are the foundation of justice. Actually, human dignity and care for God's creation are interrelated issues. For one thing, human dignity calls us to reflect the caring relationship that God has with creation. And on a practical level, human life and dignity are deeply affected by whether the natural world thrives or suffers. In our world of interdependent relationships,

respecting our sisters and brothers—including all future generations—requires respecting the earth.

As a result, the church insists that concern for the well-being of the natural world is an essential part of Christian faith: "Care for the earth is not just an Earth Day slogan; it is a requirement of our faith" (*Sharing Catholic Social Teaching,* page 6). The responsibility that people have to respect and care for all creation is called **stewardship.**

As Adam's story illustrates, stewardship can be challenging when the good of the natural environment seems to conflict with the good of people. When that happens, many people wonder how to find a balance. They might ask, Can we protect the earth without harming human beings? Others may counter with a different question: Can we avoid harming human beings if we fail to respect the earth? **B**

These questions are central to being good stewards of the earth. We'll explore both of them in this chapter.

"Care for the earth is not just an Earth Day slogan; it is **a requirement of our faith**"

✱ *Student art:* Colored pencil; Sarah Jepsen, Boylan Catholic High School, Rockford, Illinois

B Give your opinion in response to each of these questions: *Can we protect the earth without harming human beings? Can we avoid harming human beings if we fail to respect the earth?*

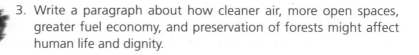

For Review

1. Why is care for the earth a requirement of Christian faith?
2. Define *stewardship.*

In Depth

3. Write a paragraph about how cleaner air, more open spaces, greater fuel economy, and preservation of forests might affect human life and dignity.

The Interdependence of Life

We can begin to find out what the responsibility of stewardship involves by taking a close look at our relationship with creation.

The Integrity of Creation

Think for a minute about all the ways that you relate to the natural world. For most people today, that relationship might seem to be pretty limited— we might think of going hunting or camping, of planting a garden, or of taking a walk in the park.

But the relationship each of us has with creation goes well beyond a hike in the woods. Whether we realize it or not, our daily life is shaped by the natural world because everything that we consume ultimately comes from it: food, air, water, energy, wood, paper. Even synthetic plastics are made from natural resources. Just as our lives are shaped by creation, the way we use natural resources has a huge impact on whether creation thrives or suffers. **C**

In fact, the relationship between the human community and the natural world is just one of the many interdependent relationships that make up the larger community of life. Soils, oceans, grasslands, forests, insects, birds, and animals—each depends on the others in order to thrive:

> God wills the interdependence of creatures. The sun and the moon, the cedar and the little flower, the eagle and the sparrow: the spectacle of their countless diversities and inequalities tells us that no creature is self-sufficient. Creatures exist only in dependence on each other, to complete each other, in the service of each other. (*Catechism of the Catholic Church,* 340)

C What natural resources do you use in your daily life? Keep track of everything you use during one day (including basics like clothing, food, and energy). Make three columns on a piece of paper. List everything you use in the middle column. In the first column, list the natural resources the item was made from. In the last column, list how disposing of the item will affect the environment. Bring the chart to class for discussion.

The way creation's many interdependent relationships fit together as a harmonious whole can be described as the **integrity of creation.**

The integrity of creation is necessary for it to thrive as God intends. Each element within the order of creation—air, soil, water, plants, animals, and even humans—has a specific role that serves the greater good of the whole community of life. If you have taken a biology class, you are aware of the complexity of ecosystems and natural cycles. Plants, for instance, require the proper mix of water, sunshine, soil conditions, nutrients, and atmospheric gases in order to grow; insects and other animals keep away pests, aerate the soil, and aid pollination. Plants, in turn, support all other life on the planet. Disrupt any one of these elements and the disturbance may ripple out to affect the rest of the community of life in unexpected ways. **◗**

The unique role of humanity

Humans live within the integrity of the larger community of life, not apart from it—a reality that is easy for most of us to forget because the conveniences of modern life

God wills the interdependence of all creatures, and calls us to respect the integrity of the larger community of life.

separate us from daily contact with the natural world.

But, in fact, humans have a unique role within the integrity of creation—the role of stewards—because we are made in the image of God. We alone among all creatures have the freedom to choose how we will relate to the rest of creation. Stewardship calls us to relate to creation in a way that respects its God-given integrity:

> Theology, philosophy, and science all speak of a harmonious universe, of a "cosmos" endowed with its own integrity, its own internal, dynamic balance. *This order must be respected.* The human race is called to explore this order, to examine it with due care and to make use of it while safeguarding its integrity. (Pope John Paul II, *The Ecological Crisis: A Common Responsibility,* 8)

Warning signs

The many environmental problems that threaten the well-being of creation are signs that we have failed to relate to it in a way that respects its integrity. Environmental problems are nothing new in the history of humanity. What is new about today's ecological crisis, however, is its extent and severity. Water shortages, the collapse of ocean fisheries, soil erosion, and pollution all threaten the well-being of billions of people. The damage that is being done to the earth today could take hundreds, even millions of years to heal.

To better understand our interdependent relationship with creation, let's examine three related warning signs: the mass extinction of species, rain forest destruction, and global warming. **E**

◗ Find a specific example of something that requires the integrity of all its parts to make it work (for example, a sports team, a song, a machine, a recipe). How would changing some of its parts affect the whole (be specific)? How many parts could be removed before it would fall apart?

E Take an "environmental tour" of your home and neighborhood. Note three examples of how the integrity of creation is possibly being disrupted. Be prepared to discuss your findings in class.

AN ABUNDANCE OF LIFE

A typical four-square-mile patch of rain forest contains:

1,500 flowering plant species
750 tree species
400 bird species
150 butterfly species
125 mammal species
100 reptile species
60 amphibian species

That's not counting all the insects, mosses, bacteria, and nonflowering plants.

Source: "Facts About Rainforests,"
Rainforest Action Network

Vanishing Rain Forests, Vanishing Species

Scientists estimate that the world contains between 3.6 million and 100 million plant and animal species, each of which fits into the integrity of creation in its own way. Nowhere is the diversity of life on Earth more apparent than in tropical rain forests. Although they make up only 6 percent of the planet's land surface (about the area of the contiguous United States), rain forests contain more than half the world's plant and animal species.

As a result of logging and agriculture, the rain forests are being destroyed at an annual rate of fifty million acres—an area half the size of Florida. To understand the impact of this loss, consider the forests of northeastern Ecuador, which once contained some seventeen thousand species found nowhere else on Earth. In a period of ten years, 90 percent of those forests were cleared, mostly for banana plantations, causing the loss of thousands of species. Largely because of the destruction of the rain forest, it is estimated that between eighteen thousand and fifty-five thousand species become extinct every year, threatening the delicate balance that sustains the earth as we know it.

Because most of us never knew so many species existed in the first place, why should we care if they disappear? From a practical point of view, we do not know what natural resources we are losing when species go extinct. Many of our life-saving drugs come from complex chemicals found in rain forest plants and animals, only a fraction of which have been studied. Consider the Australian gastric-brooding frog, discovered in a rain forest in 1974. It swallowed its own fertilized eggs, incubated them in its stomach, and gave birth through its mouth. The frog had the unique ability to turn off its stomach acid, which prevented its eggs from being digested. That ability could have led to drugs for stomach disorders in humans—but the frog went extinct in 1980.

The mass extinction of species diminishes the richness of God's creation. Once species become extinct, they are lost forever—not only to us but also to the future generations whose good we have a responsibility to consider. And it is impossible to predict how the loss of a particular species might affect the rest of the community of life. ☞

A structural problem

Rain forest destruction is primarily caused by commercial logging and subsistence farming.

But as with other issues studied in this course, these immediate causes have deeper roots.

The logging of rain forest timber, for instance, is spurred by demand from developed nations, where it is used in products as diverse as plywood, furniture, and chopsticks. Impoverished, debt-burdened nations are reluctant to restrict logging because it is a source of income, even though the loggers profit more than the people who live in the forests.

The indigenous people themselves often are blamed for rain forest destruction because of their agricultural practices. About 60 percent of rain forest destruction is caused by **subsistence farming**—that is, small-time farming that meets only the basic needs of a family. Subsistence farmers often cut or burn down the forest in order to create space for

The mass extinction of species diminishes the richness of God's creation.

✳ *Student art:* Linocut; Evlyn Wade, Saint Agnes Academy, Memphis, Tennessee

☞ Prepare a one-page report on a plant or animal that has gone extinct within the last one hundred years, or one that is in danger of becoming extinct. Describe the plant or animal, then explain how it fit into the integrity of creation and what caused or is causing it to become extinct.

farming. Because the soil is so poor, however, these fields are usually abandoned after a few years, and the farmers must create new fields by cutting and burning more rain forest. This harmful agricultural practice is the result of the struggle of the poor to survive, as ecologist Norman Myers observes:

> In the tropics, one-third of all parks are already subject to encroachment by landless and impoverished peasants. During the past few decades, 200 million of these people have found themselves squeezed out of traditional farmlands. With no other option if they are to keep getting supper onto the table, they pick up machete and matchbox and head off toward tropical forests. . . . Driven by their desperation and poverty, they are marginal people in marginal environments. Often enough, these marginal environments include parks and other protected areas. ("What We Must Do to Counter the Biotic Holocaust")

In a world of interdependent relationships, the well-being of the natural world cannot be separated from the well-being of our neighbors—especially those who are poor and vulnerable. The U.S. Catholic bishops note this fact in *Renewing the Earth*:

> The whole human race suffers as a result of environmental blight, and generations yet unborn will bear the cost for our failure to act today. But in most countries today, including our own, it is the poor and the powerless who most directly bear the burden of current environmental carelessness.

It is the poor and the powerless who most directly **bear the burden** of current environmental carelessness.

Their lands and neighborhoods are more likely to be polluted or to host toxic waste dumps, their water to be undrinkable, their children to be harmed. . . . Caught in a spiral of poverty and environmental degradation, poor people suffer acutely from the loss of soil fertility, pollution of rivers and urban streets, and the destruction of forest resources. Overcrowding and unequal land distribution often force them to overwork the soil, clear the forests, or migrate to marginal land. Their efforts to eke out a bare existence adds in its own way to environmental degradation. (Page 2)

Rain forest destruction is intertwined with other social structures of injustice, such as the gap between those who consume too much and those who do not have enough to sustain good lives. The story of Francisco "Chico" Mendes and the rubber tappers is a good illustration of the structural causes of rain forest destruction.

Chico Mendes: Saving the forest and its people

Chico was among the people of northwestern Brazil who earned their living by

The destruction of the rain forest is partially rooted in poverty: subsistence farmers often cut or burn down the forest to make space to grow food.

carefully extracting renewable natural resources from the rain forest. Some collected and sold nuts from the forest, while others, like Chico, sold rubber that they tapped from rubber trees.

Such work allowed the people to support their families without destroying the rain forest. But when big landowners and ranchers threatened their livelihood by cutting down the forests to make way for cattle grazing, Chico organized the rubber tappers into a union. The union members lobbied for the government to legally protect the forest, and they formed human chains to block the ranchers from burning and bulldozing the forest that they depended on for their livelihood.

At first, the rubber tappers' main goal was to protect their rights as workers, but soon, Chico's vision led them to see that their own survival and the rain forests' survival were interrelated. The National Council of Rubber Tappers, which grew out of Chico's efforts, puts it this way: "In the Amazon, man and nature are one. . . . There is no real chance to maintain the enormous Amazon forest except with the peoples that are its traditional inhabitants" (de Deus Matos, "The Ideas of Chico Mendes and the National Council of Rubber Tappers"). Although Chico was internationally recognized for his work on behalf of the poor and the rain forests, he was assassinated by ranchers in 1988.

Today, as the nut gatherers and rubber tappers of Brazil struggle to realize Chico Mendes's vision, they continue to face obstacles—in particular, the difficulty of earning enough money to support a family. International competition forces them to sell their rubber to tire companies such as Pirelli, Firestone, Goodyear, and Michelin at the low prices offered by large Asian rubber plantations. As a result, they struggle to live on less than one hundred dollars a month.

The rubber tappers have called on the Brazilian government to subsidize, or help pay for, their rubber so they can make enough money to support their families without harming the forest. But such subsidies are often prohibited by international trade agreements. The rubber tappers have chosen to fit into the integrity of creation, but social structures make it difficult for them to do so.

Rubber tappers such as this one try to support their families while living in harmony with the Amazon rain forest.

In the Amazon, **man and nature are one.**

"There is no real chance to maintain the enormous Amazon forest except with the peoples that are its traditional inhabitants." Write a short reflection about how this statement might apply to your own community and environment.

Global Warming

Deforestation is not only destroying ecosystems—it is disrupting the global climate as well. Rain forests absorb vast amounts of carbon dioxide from the atmosphere, but that gas is released when rain forests are cut down or burned. That makes deforestation a major cause of **global warming,** the rapid increase of the earth's temperature.

In the past thirty years, the earth's temperature has increased at a rate of about 4 degrees Fahrenheit per century—faster than any time in the past ten thousand years. Scientists agree that most of this increase is due to human activity that releases so-called greenhouse gases, such as carbon dioxide, into the atmosphere. **Greenhouse gases** trap heat energy from the sun, thus warming the earth. They have always been present in the atmosphere, but the burning of fossil fuels like gasoline and coal, plus the destruction of rain forests, is expected to double the amount of such gases in the atmosphere. As a result, the average temperature of the earth is expected to rise between 2.7 and 11 degrees Fahrenheit by 2100.

That may not seem like a lot, but even minor temperature changes can have a huge impact on the global environment, especially at higher latitudes. While scientists are unsure what all the consequences of global warming will be, they have enough information to take the problem seriously:

- Ice covering the Arctic has thinned by four feet and receded by 5 percent since 1958.
- Oceans are predicted to rise between one and four feet over the next century, battering coastlines and causing millions of people to be displaced by flooding. Small island nations around the world are already dealing with disappearing beaches, property damage, and saltwater-tainted drinking water.
- Warming of our oceans is destroying coral reefs—upon which millions of marine animals depend—all over the world, according to a study conducted by the U.S. State Department.
- Rainfall patterns and amounts may be dramatically altered, causing more severe floods in some regions and more severe droughts in others.
- Fish, birds, animals, trees, and plants that are unable to adapt to new conditions or to move elsewhere are in danger of going extinct.
- About half of all the Arctic tundra could be lost as forests spread further north, endangering half of the rare bird species that breed there.

To avoid the effects of severe global warming, scientists estimate that the world will need to reduce greenhouse gas emissions by 50 to 70 percent.

Too much of a good thing?

The emissions that cause global warming are driven by the excessive consumption of developed nations. Despite being only 4.6 percent of the world's population, the United States consumes 27 percent of the world's energy, more than any other nation. Not surprisingly, it also emits 24 percent of the world's carbon dioxide, one of the gases that cause global warming—again, more than any other country. So global warming is yet another effect of "living crazily," as the U.S. Catholic bishops noted in their 1991 pastoral statement. *Renewing the Earth:*

The United States emits nearly a quarter of the world's carbon dioxide—a gas that contributes to global warming.

THE POPULATION QUESTION

The earth's environmental problems are often traced to the growing size of the human population. More than six billion people share the earth today; by 2050, that number is expected to reach between 7.3 and 10.7 billion, according to the United Nations. Family planning programs are often promoted as a way of curbing the environmental impact of population growth.

The Catholic church acknowledges the "problems and challenges" that population growth poses to the environment and society (*Renewing the Earth,* page 9). At the same time, it opposes population control programs that promote abortion and pressure the poor to use artificial birth control.

The church has two basic reasons for its position. First, abortion and artificial birth control harm human life and dignity. Often, these practices violate the basic cultural and religious beliefs of the people who are pressured to use them. However, the church does not oppose the use of natural family planning—a birth control method that respects the natural rhythms of the human body.

Second, the church argues that focusing primarily on population control to solve the ecological crisis ignores the basic causes of environmental damage—excessive consumption and poverty:

Regrettably, advantaged groups often seem more intent on curbing Third-World births than on restraining the even more voracious consumerism of the developed world.

We believe this compounds injustice and increases disrespect for the life of the weakest among us. For example, it is not so much population growth, but the desperate efforts of debtor nations to pay their foreign debt by exporting products to affluent industrial countries that drives poor peasants off their land and up eroding hillsides, where in the effort to survive, they also destroy the environment. . . .

Only when an economy distributes resources so as to allow the poor an equitable stake in society and some hope for the future do couples see responsible parenthood as good for their families. In particular, prenatal care; education; good nutrition; and health care for women, children, and families promise to improve family welfare and contribute to stabilizing population. (*Renewing,* page 9)

Besides helping the poor escape poverty, affluent nations can ease the impact of population growth by cutting back on their own consumption of the world's natural resources. ●

The Catholic church acknowledges the **"problems and challenges"** that population growth poses to the environment and society.

Consumption in developed nations remains the single greatest source of global environmental destruction. A child born in the United States, for example, puts a far heavier burden on the earth's resources than one born in a poor developing country. By one estimate, each American uses twenty-eight times the energy of a person living in a developing country. Advanced societies, and our own in particular, have barely begun to make efforts at reducing their consumption of resources and the enormous waste and pollution that result from it. (Page 9) *H*

> By one estimate, each American uses **twenty-eight times** the energy of a person living in a developing country.

Thinning Arctic ice is one sign of global warming.

Reconciling with Creation

Clearly, the way humanity relates to the natural world is causing serious problems, not only for the rest of creation but for the human population as well. Environmental leaders are pursuing solutions to these problems. But any solution to the ecological crisis will only be replaced by new problems if humanity continues to relate to the earth in the same ways that have led to the extinction of thousands of species and the threat of global warming.

If we are to live in harmony with the earth as God intended, then we must reconcile our relationship with creation—and that means returning to our role as its stewards.

4. Define *integrity of creation* and explain why it is necessary.
5. What unique role do humans have within the integrity of creation, and why?
6. Name at least three consequences of rain forest destruction.
7. What do the U.S. Catholic bishops say is the single greatest cause of environmental destruction?

8. In a paragraph, explain how the poverty of indigenous people and the consumption of developed nations contribute to the destruction of rain forests.

H As you reflect on the lifestyle of your own community, why do you think that people in the United States consume so much more than do people in the rest of the world?

Called to Stewardship

The call to stewardship can be found at the very beginning of the Bible, in the Creation stories of the Book of Genesis. Although these stories were written thousands of years ago, they still have a lot to teach us about humanity's place in creation.

Lessons from Genesis

Take a moment to reread both the first and second Creation stories of the Book of Genesis (1:1—2:3 and 2:4–25). As you read, pay special attention to what the stories say about the relationship between God, humans, and creation, both before and after the Fall. |

Here is how God calls humanity to stewardship of creation in the first story:

God blessed [the man and the woman], and God said to them, "Be fruitful and multiply, and fill the earth and subdue it; and have dominion over the fish of the sea and over the birds of the air and over every living thing that moves upon the earth." God said, "See, I have given you every plant yielding seed that is upon the face of all the earth, and every tree with seed in its fruit; you shall have them for food. And to every beast of the earth, and to every bird of the air, and to everything that creeps on the earth, everything that has the breath of life, I have given every green plant for food." And it was so. God saw everything that he had made, and indeed, it was very good. (1:28–31)

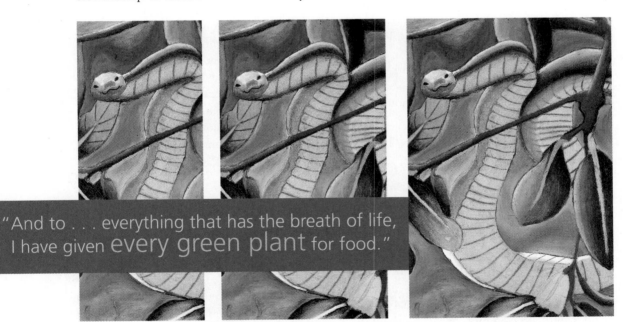

"And to . . . everything that has the breath of life, I have given **every green plant** for food."

✳ *Student art:* "Snake." Pastel; Daniel Pizarro, Notre Dame High School, Sherman Oaks, California

| Design your own modern Garden of Eden—a place where humans live in harmony with nature. Describe in an essay, poem, or some form of visual art what it would be like.

The first Creation story portrays humans living in harmony with the natural world, a harmony that flows from God's loving Reign. The second Creation story paints a similar picture: the garden in which God places the first human is a source of life and goodness. But it also comes with the responsibility of stewardship; humans are to "cultivate and care for it" (Genesis 2:15, NAB). Moreover, humans cannot take whatever they want from the garden—the tree of knowledge of good and evil is off-limits. In Hebrew thought, the "knowledge of good and evil" meant more than just awareness of good and evil. It also signified the power and control over all things that belongs only to God.

Together, the Creation stories make several important points about what it means to be stewards of creation:

- Creation is good because it flows from God's goodness.
- God gives humans dominion over creation—not so they can do whatever they want with it, but so it can be used for the good of humanity.
- God provides for the good of all creation— "everything that has the breath of life." Our right to use creation for the common good is balanced by our responsibility to "cultivate and care for it," which includes respecting its limits.

As you know, Adam and Eve did not respect the limits that God set for using the garden. In taking the fruit from the tree of knowledge, they were essentially saying, "There are no limits for us; we claim the power to do what we want." In so doing, they broke the loving relationship they had with God, the source of creation's life and harmony. The consequences of that broken relationship affected not only humans but also creation.

The ripple effects of sin

The story of the Fall makes an important point: Our relationship with creation is intimately connected to our relationship with God and one another. Because we are part of the integrity of creation, not outside of it, sin within the human community invariably ripples out to harm the wider community of life. When we fail to follow God's way of love, even the earth suffers.

Power Over the Earth

"We are not gods, but stewards of the earth," the U.S. Catholic bishops say (*Renewing,* page 3). Often, though, people have related to the earth in a way that resembles Adam and Eve's desire to exercise the power and control of God (Genesis 3:5). In other words, they take a power-over approach to their relationship with the earth, as *On the Hundredth Anniversary of Rerum Novarum (Centesimus Annus)* points out:

Man thinks that he can make arbitrary use of the earth . . . as though it did not have its own requisites and a prior God-given purpose, which man can indeed develop but must not betray. Instead of carrying out his role as a cooperator with God in the work of creation, man sets himself up in place of God and thus ends up provoking a rebellion on the part of nature, which is more tyrannized than governed by him. (37)

The earth is not a limitless resource. Urban areas that grow unchecked, taking over farmland and wetlands, may be a sign that we have failed to respect the earth's limits.

When people claim sole power over the earth, they claim a power that belongs only to God—much as Adam and Eve did when they took the fruit from the tree of knowledge. A power-over-the-earth worldview is characterized by beliefs that contradict the call to stewardship:

The earth has no value by itself. The earth has value only in terms of what it can produce for us. Therefore, it does not require our respect.

The earth is owned by whoever has the power to take it. This assumption leads to the belief that if we have the power to dam a river, then we can do so without considering the consequences to creation; likewise, if we have the economic power to control natural resources, we can do so without considering the common good.

The earth is a limitless resource. It is like a store whose shelves will refill again overnight, no matter how much we take from it. A power-over worldview does not respect the limits of the earth.

In the power-over-the-earth worldview, humans are above the integrity of creation, not part of it. We can see the power-over worldview at work both in the destruction of the rain forest and in the overconsumption that has led to global warming. ⤴

Short-term thinking

Most of us in the developed nations exercise our power-over relationship with the earth through our habits of excessive consumption. According to some calculations, the equivalent of four Earths would be needed in order for everyone on the planet to live as people do in the United States.

That kind of short-sighted lifestyle cannot be sustained for long, and ignores the obligation we have "to bequeath to future generations an enhanced natural environment and the same ready access to the necessities of life that most of us enjoy today" (*Economic Justice for All,* 250).

In the previous chapter, we saw that excessive consumption is often driven by a culture that regards consumption, rather than relationships of respect, as the way to

Focusing on the short-term benefits of consuming natural resources without considering the long-term consequences harms the earth as well as people.

✳ Student art: Watercolor; Colleen Westman, Cor Jesu Academy, Saint Louis, Missouri

⤴ How do science and technology affect the way humans use power in their relationship with creation?

THE SECRET LIFE OF A T-SHIRT

To appreciate the true impact that excessive consumption has on the environment, just follow the life of one four-ounce, half-polyester, half-cotton T-shirt.

Derrick drills oil off the coast of Venezuela.

Wasted crude oil and drilling muds pollute the oil field.

Crude oil is shipped by tanker to a refinery in the Netherlands Antilles.

During the refining process, 4 percent of the crude oil is burned, causing air pollution.

Refined petrochemicals are shipped to a chemical plant in Delaware.

The petrochemicals are combined to create polyethylene terephthalate (PET), which is then stretched into polyester fibers. Making the polyester fibers releases ten times their final weight in carbon dioxide pollution, which fuels global warming.

Fourteen square feet of cropland in Mississippi was used to produce the two ounces of cotton in the shirt.

To protect the growing cotton, the soil is sprayed with toxic pesticides six times, killing all the organisms in the field. Wind and water runoff carry the pesticides into the environment. Ten percent of the world's pesticides are used on cotton.

Cotton is heavily irrigated.

Water runs off the fields more easily because organisms that aerate the soil have been killed off by the pesticides.

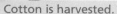

Cotton is harvested.

Before harvest, a crop duster sprays the field with a defoliant so that all the leaves fall off; about half of it drifts outside of the field.

happiness. Focusing on the short-term benefits of consuming natural resources without considering the long-term consequences harms the earth as well as people.

For instance, the fishing industry around the world has focused on catching as many fish as possible from year to year. More fish means more money—at least for that year. But many of the best fishing grounds have been overharvested, causing fish populations to drop dramatically. Consequently, the ocean suffers, but so does the fishing industry. When the North Atlantic cod population collapsed due to overfishing, about thirty thousand people lost their jobs. This same kind of short-term thinking leads to long-term consequences for groundwater, forests, and other natural resources.

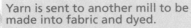

Yarn is sent to another mill to be made into fabric and dyed.

The fabric is bleached, dyed, and finished using industrial chemicals; a third of the hazardous dyes wash off into the wastewater stream.

T-shirt is sewn.

The fabric is shipped to Honduras, where women earning 30 cents an hour cut and sew it into a T-shirt.

Shirt is shipped to Baltimore, sent by train to San Francisco, and trucked to a Seattle department store.

The buyer carries it home in a polyethylene bag from Louisiana. Almost a third of the 64 billion pounds of plastic made in the United States is used for packaging.

Cotton and polyester is sent to a North Carolina textile mill.

The cotton and polyester fibers are combined and spun into yarn, which is then treated with polystyrene.

T-shirt is washed and dried by machine.

Machine washing and drying the T-shirt just once uses one-tenth of the energy that made it. The energy, water, and chemicals used to clean the T-shirt account for its largest environmental impact.

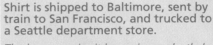

So, stop wearing T-shirts?

Obviously, we still need products like T-shirts, but we can reduce their impact by buying used clothes, buying clothes made from organic cotton, washing clothes in cold water, and drying them on a line.

(Source: John C. Ryan and Alan Thein Durning, *Stuff: The Secret Lives of Everyday Things*)

Strangers to nature

It would be unfair to suggest that most people intend to harm the earth. Many people, especially young people, are very concerned about the plight of the environment and do what they can to avoid harming it. But cultural habits and social structures reinforce our power-over relationship with the earth. For example, the United States leads the world in greenhouse gas emissions partly because U.S. transportation networks favor automobiles over mass transportation, and partly because U.S. culture values the freedom and independence of driving a car.

Moreover, most of us are unaware of the effect our habits have on the planet because modern life has distanced us from the natural world. It has been generations since people in developed nations relied directly on the natural environment for their day-to-day needs. Instead of growing our own food, we buy it in stores. When we are finished consuming something, we no longer have to dispose of it in our immediate environment—instead, the garbage hauler takes it away, allowing us to ignore the impact its disposal might have on the environment. The conveniences of modern life allow us to forget our place within the integrity of creation—at least until creation "rebels," dramatically calling us back to our role as stewards. 𝗞

Keys to Stewardship

Although we are not gods, we are called to be reflections of God; in our relationship with creation, we are called to use our power with love. Earlier, we listed some lessons that the Genesis Creation stories teach about what it means to be stewards of creation. Let's take a deeper look at how those lessons might guide our relationship to the natural world today.

Respect for the sacramental earth

"It was very good" (Genesis 1:31). These words not only signal the dignity of human beings but also the basic goodness of creation, which flows from the goodness of God.

The conveniences of modern life allow us to forget our place within the integrity of creation.

✳ *Student art:* Acrylic; Alexandra Dimakos, Notre Dame High School, Sherman Oaks, California

𝗞 Imagine trying to cut your consumption and waste by half. In what ways do U.S. cultural practices or social structures make it difficult for you to do so?

No wonder many people feel they encounter the presence of God when they stand in awe at the beauty, complexity, power, and mystery of creation.

This is why the church describes the natural world as **sacramental:** it reveals the presence of God in a visible and tangible way (adapted from *Renewing,* page 6). Just as art is a self-expression of the artist, the created world is one way that we understand the love and power of God. Each bird, fish, and blade of grass is God's work of art, and, therefore, has value on its own, apart from its relationship to people.

God's presence in the natural world reminds us of our own place within the integrity of creation: we are creation's caretakers, not its creator. Acknowledging this helps us to avoid acting like "gods" who have absolute power over creation: "Dwelling in the presence of God, we begin to experience ourselves *as part of creation,* as stewards *within it,* not separate from it" (*Renewing,* page 6, emphasis added). Respect for creation, which is the foundation of stewardship, is based on respect for God's presence in it. *L*

The natural world is sacramental because it reveals the presence of God in a visible and tangible way.

A gift for the common good

"See, I have given you every plant yielding seed . . . for food" (Genesis 1:29). God intends for humans to benefit from creation, creating a good life for themselves and others. People need the earth's natural resources, and have a right to use them. That is why God gives us dominion over the earth (1:28).

Unfortunately, these words have often been interpreted to mean that God gives humans ownership of the earth in the sense of having absolute power over it. But the overall message of the Scriptures is that the land ultimately belongs to God, who intends that it be used for the common good: "God has given the fruit of the earth to sustain the entire human family 'without excluding or favouring anyone'" (*Renewing,* page 7).

Human dominion over the earth is meant to be driven by love, not greed or abuse. Part of the responsibility of stewardship, then, involves safeguarding natural resources to ensure that they benefit *all* people, including poor people and future generations—not just those powerful enough to control them.

Caring for creation

We are not gods over creation. But as images of God, we are called to reflect God's care for creation. In the first Creation story, God provides not only for the well-being of the human community but for "everything that has the breath of life" (Genesis 1:30). Therefore, the right to use natural resources for the good of humanity is balanced by the responsibility to ensure the well-being of the natural world. That means actively working to preserve creatures, their habitats, and the earth's natural resources.

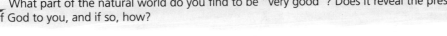

L What part of the natural world do you find to be "very good"? Does it reveal the presence of God to you, and if so, how?

At a minimum, caring for creation involves respecting its limits. In Jewish Law, for instance, every seventh year was to be "a year of complete rest for the land" (Leviticus 25:5), during which it was not to be farmed. Part of the challenge of stewardship today is recognizing the earth's need for "rest" from human consumption. In *Renewing the Earth,* the U.S. Catholic bishops call for **sustainable economic practices,** "that is, practices that reduce current stresses on natural systems and are consistent with sound environmental policy in the long term" (page 2). Sustainable economic practices use natural resources in a way that preserves the earth's ability to nurture itself and the whole human community well into the future. Nonsustainable practices, on the other hand, focus on the short-term benefits of consumption without considering the long-term consequences. **M**

A Spirit of Thanksgiving

At the beginning of this chapter, we raised the question of whether it is possible to protect the earth without harming people. The Scriptures and Catholic social teaching clearly say yes: "Christian love forbids choosing between people and the planet," the U.S. Catholic bishops say. "It urges us to work for an equitable and sustainable future in which all peoples can share in the bounty of the earth and in which the earth itself is protected from predatory use" (*Renewing,* page 11). The integrity of creation depends on justice within the human community, and vice versa; each leads to the other.

It is true that we cannot avoid consuming the earth's natural resources or polluting to some extent. All living things on the planet consume natural resources and create waste, and humans are no exception. The trick of stewardship is to provide for the common good in a way that preserves creation's integrity, the many interdependent relationships that sustain the community of life and make it whole.

To do this, we must begin to respect the natural world. Writer and farmer Wendell Berry offers a metaphor for using the resources of the earth respectfully:

> Part of the challenge of stewardship today is recognizing the **earth's need for "rest"** from human consumption.

M Many products come with an owner's manual or care instructions—a guide for using the product in a way that ensures it will last. Write your own "care instructions" for the earth. Brainstorm with a classmate if possible.

To live, we must daily break the body and shed the blood of Creation. When we do this knowingly, lovingly, skillfully, reverently, it is a sacrament. When we do it ignorantly, greedily, clumsily, destructively, it is a desecration. (*The Gift of Good Land,* page 281)

Like the Eucharist, we must "break" creation in order to have life. But as stewards, we are called to do so in a spirit of respect and thankfulness for God's gift.

9. Name three beliefs that characterize a power-over relationship with the earth.
10. What does it mean to say that the natural world is sacramental?
11. How are humans to exercise dominion over the earth?
12. What are sustainable economic practices?

---

13. Write a short paragraph comparing the ways stewardship of the earth and celebrating the Eucharist are similar and different.

N How would "break[ing] the body and shed[ding] the blood of Creation" with respect change the way you use the gifts of the earth? Provide specific examples.

Sustaining the Earth

The ecological crisis makes it increasingly urgent that we respond to the call to stewardship by living within the integrity of creation, rather than outside it in a power-over role. That means practicing sustainable economics, considering the long-term integrity of creation in the decisions we make as individuals and as a society.

That is often easier said than done, but the good news is that many people are already learning to sustain the earth by tapping into their God-given creativity.

Taking the Earth into Account

Throughout this chapter, we have seen that consumption is one of the leading causes of environmental damage, especially when natural resources are consumed without considering the effect on the environment. One way people are beginning to respect the limits of creation is through **ecological economics,** which seeks to include the value of the environment in economic decision making.

What is the value of clean air or clean water? What is the value of a honeybee or a wetland? In a culture that measures worth primarily in economic terms, these natural resources often have been undervalued. If the natural environment is viewed as having little or no value, then it is likely to be exploited in order to gain something of greater short-term economic value. If a wetland does not make money, then why not fill it in and build a shopping center? If you cannot sell clean air, then why worry about any air pollution a profitable factory might create—especially if the factory owners do not live near it?

Such short-term thinking fails to reflect the real value of the environment on a number of levels:

Hidden economic value. Natural resources that might not appear to have much economic value actually make a huge indirect contribution to the economy. According to researchers, the environment's "free" services —from providing water and creating soil to treating waste and pollinating crops— contribute around $33 trillion annually to the global economy. When the true value of natural resources over their lifetime is considered, exploiting them for short-term gain no longer makes sense. For example, cutting down the mangrove forests of Bintuni Bay in Indonesia for their timber provides a one-time profit of about $3,600 per hectare. But left standing, they contribute resources and services worth $4,800 every year.

Value for life. Sometimes the value of natural resources is difficult to measure in economic terms, even though they are important to human life. How do you measure the value of clean air or drinking water? One way is to ask people either how much they would be willing to pay to have a resource or how much they would want to be paid if it were taken away. How much would you want to be paid if you had to stay indoors one day a month due to high levels of smog? How much would you pay to be able to breathe clean air outdoors every day? Such an assessment can put the true costs of pollution into perspective.

Value as a gift from God. As we have seen, the Scriptures and Catholic social teaching say that natural resources have a God-given value that cannot be measured in terms of money. Good stewardship involves asking whether consuming a natural resource will benefit human life and dignity more than it will harm the environment in the long run.

Taking the real value of the environment into account can guide us as we try to live as stewards within the integrity of creation. The following examples illustrate how.

Living as Stewards Day to Day

With more than six billion people living together on the planet, each of us needs to consider the value of the earth in the decisions we make in our daily life. This may seem overwhelming at first, but a little creative thinking can reveal a wide range of options for living within the integrity of creation.

Exploring options

For example, let's say that Joe is in the enviable position of being given a car by his parents. On one hand, a car can be fun and convenient—even necessary for getting a job. On the other hand, Joe knows that driving contributes to global warming. How does he balance these competing needs? Here are some possible scenarios:

- He chooses a very fuel-efficient car—even though it is not as popular as a light truck or sport utility vehicle.
- He chooses a used car so that he is reusing natural resources rather than consuming them to make a new car.
- Because he has great access to public transportation, he turns down the car and asks to use the money in some other way.
- He accepts the car, but lobbies for legislation that sets higher standards for fuel efficiency and emissions.
- Instead of buying a car, his family moves to a place where they can walk or take public transportation most of the time.
- Instead of using the car just for himself, he starts a car pool with friends in order to cut down on gasoline consumption.

Though Joe's options vary, they do share a common thread: they all take the long-term well-being of the natural world into consideration. The best option is the one that does the least harm to himself, his community, and the integrity of creation.

Each of us needs to consider the value of the earth in the decisions we make in our daily life.

These young people are repairing bikes that will be left around their city for anyone to use; by promoting bicycling, they help to reduce air pollution.

What part of creation do you most value, and why? What would you be willing to sacrifice in order to preserve it?

Of the options Joe considered, which seems best to balance the well-being of the environment with Joe's well-being? Why? Can you think of other earth-friendly options?

How much do you think you can reduce your negative impact on the environment? Brainstorm ten ways you could meet your goal. Be prepared to share them in class.

WHAT YOU CAN DO . . .

- **Reduce your consumption.** U.S. consumption has a huge impact on the environment. Reduce your consumption by bicycling, bussing, or carpooling instead of driving alone. Replace incandescent lights with more energy-efficient and money-saving compact fluorescent bulbs. Before buying, ask yourself, How much will this product benefit me compared to the harm that producing it has on the environment? Buy products that use less packaging. Buy products that you will be able to use for a long time, instead of products that need more frequent replacement.

- **Reuse resources.** Another way of reducing the environmental impact of consumption is to buy used instead of new—and you can save lots of money in the process. Used-clothing stores, for instance, often have like-new clothes. Rather than throwing away an old computer or couch, try selling it or giving it away to someone who could use it.

- **Recycle.** Educate yourself about what can and cannot be recycled. If your community does not have a recycling program, lobby your city or county government for one. Buy recycled products so that companies have an incentive to reuse recycled waste.

- **Share.** Get together with friends, neighbors, or siblings and see what you can share so that each person doesn't have to buy the same thing. Lawn mowers, cars, clothes, and tools are all possibilities.

- **Evaluate the energy use of your home, school, or church.** Most power companies offer to help homes and businesses reduce their energy consumption. Experts audit a building to discover where energy is being wasted. Easy-to-implement advice can cut back on energy use by 6 to 7 percent. Retrofitting a building with energy-saving devices can lower energy bills by 20 to 30 percent, and the cost savings can be used for better things.

- **Lobby businesses.** Research how companies can save money by practicing environmental stewardship. Present your findings to local businesses, and ask them to make earth-friendly changes. ☺

Stewardship on a Social Scale

Individual stewardship can do a lot, but it will not be enough to sustain the earth for future generations. Our brief examination of rain forest destruction illustrated that a web of interconnected social structures—from international trade rules to poverty to blind consumption—contribute to the ecological crisis. To sustain the earth, society needs to change its basic way of doing things to include the responsibility of stewardship.

Businesses: Finding a balance

Businesses have an especially important role in these social changes because their actions can have a huge impact on the environment. Like Joe in the example above, business leaders must weigh the contribution their activities make to the common good against the harm these activities cause the environment.

Although companies may initially resist the costs of environmental stewardship, it often saves money in the long run. An upgrade to more efficient lighting helped Boeing, the Seattle-based airplane manufacturer, reduce the amount of electricity its lights used by 90 percent—which in turn reduced carbon dioxide emissions by 100,000 tons annually. Such energy-saving upgrades can save a company about $1 per square foot of building space every year.

Patagonia, a manufacturer of outdoor recreation equipment and clothing, is a good example of how companies can incorporate stewardship into their business practices. Owner Yvon Chouinard describes his company's philosophy:

 No business can be done on a dead planet. A company that is taking the long view must accept that it has an obligation to minimize its impact on the natural environment.

As we reassessed our operation, we realized that all of Patagonia's facilities should be involved in recycling and composting and have edible landscaping, low-energy-use power, and insulation. We should use recycled paper everywhere, even in our catalogs, encourage ride sharing, eliminate paper cups, and so forth. Could we go further? ("Patagonia—The Next 100 Years")

The employees of Patagonia did go further, evaluating the environmental impact of their products and making appropriate changes. For instance, conventionally grown cotton is typically sprayed with lots of pesticides that kill insects indiscriminately, and toxic defoliants that gradually make fields barren. So Patagonia began using pesticide-free organic cotton in their products.

As the company strove to become a better steward, however, it became clear that it could not entirely avoid harming the earth:

"Sustainable manufacturing" is an oxymoron. It's nearly impossible to manufacture something without using more material and energy than results in the final product. For instance, in modern agriculture it takes three thousand calories of fossil fuel to produce a net of one thousand calories of food. To make and deliver a 100 percent cotton shirt requires as much as five gallons of petroleum. . . .

Other than shutting down the doors and giving up, what Patagonia can do is to constantly assess what we are doing. With education comes choice, and we can continue to work toward reducing the damage we do. . . .

As part of its environmental commitment, Patagonia developed a synthetic fleece made from the plastic in recycled two-liter soda bottles. Making 150 of these fleece jackets uses 3,700 bottles, saving landfill space, 42 gallons of oil, and preventing half a ton of toxic air emissions.

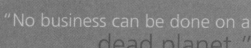

"No business can be done on a dead planet."

Write a letter to the company that makes one of your favorite products (or call the company's customer-service department or visit their Web site). Ask what the company has done to reduce the environmental impact of its manufacturing process. Bring the company's response to class for discussion.

In the final analysis, we have concluded that . . . the most responsible thing we can do is to make each product as well as we know how so it lasts as long as possible. ("Patagonia—The Next 100 Years")

Rather than encourage wasteful consumption by offering more and more products, Patagonia has actually *reduced* the number of products it sells from 375 to 280. Instead of selling more, it focuses on creating quality, multipurpose, long-lasting products "so a customer can consume less but consume better." Moreover, the company practices ecological economics by donating 1 percent of its total sales toward environmental causes, as a way of compensating for the pollution it cannot avoid creating.

What if other companies around the world took the responsibility of stewardship so seriously? Many consumers—who are the source of companies' economic power—are urging business leaders to do so. §

How governments can help

Although stewardship makes sense in the long run, individuals and business organizations often find it difficult to be among the first to get started. If all of Joe's friends are enjoying their cars without worrying about stewardship, why should he be the only one making sacrifices? Governments can help by coordinating the large-scale efforts that are necessary to sustain the environment into the future.

The small Central American country of Costa Rica is a good example. Like many nations, Costa Rica had been depleting its forests, soils, and waters for many years. Recently, the government has cooperated with citizens, businesses, nongovernmental organizations, and labor unions to raise the

country's standard of living while sustaining its natural resources for future generations, a policy known as **sustainable development.** In doing so, it is protecting 5 percent of the world's species that live within its borders.

The government has adopted a wide range of policies to encourage sustainable development:

- Twenty-five percent of the land has been set aside in conservation areas, while the forests that had previously been cleared for cattle grazing are being restored.
- Gasoline and oil is taxed at 15 percent to discourage excessive consumption. A third of the income from the tax is an incentive for small farmers to grow trees that soak up carbon emissions and stop erosion.
- The country is working toward getting 98 percent of its energy from renewable resources such as geothermal power, which is derived from the heat of the earth.
- Electricity is taxed at a rate that reflects its true environmental impact; at the same time, tax credits are given to consumers who buy the most energy-efficient appliances.

Costa Rica has created social structures that encourage the preservation and restoration of its rain forests.

§ Offer your own opinions in response to the idea that companies should make fewer products in order to make better-quality products.

These efforts to protect the environment are made possible by simultaneous efforts made to draw economic benefits from it. **Ecotourism**—tourism driven by natural attractions—is a $700 million industry. The country also hopes to benefit by discovering valuable new medicines and natural chemicals among the many species in its conservation areas. INBio, Costa Rica's National Institute of Biodiversity, has an agreement giving Merck and Company, the giant pharmaceutical manufacturer, the right to research species that INBio discovers and catalogues. In return, Costa Rica will receive a portion of any profits Merck makes from new medicines derived from Costa Rican species.

Only time will tell whether Costa Rica is able to sustain the environment and improve the lives of its citizens. But if it succeeds, it may show the way for the rest of the world.

Tapping into creativity

In each of the previous cases, entering into a new, life-giving relationship with the earth required creativity. Just as creation flowed out of God's creativity, we are called to sustain creation through our own creativity. Today, many young people are leading the way by using their talents, interests, and creativity to sustain the earth:

- At Bellarmine Preparatory School in Tacoma, Washington, students use their research abilities to evaluate more effective ways of restoring natural habitat to roadsides. The Washington State Department of Transportation had been establishing plants along roadsides using an expensive method that involved multiple plantings and lots of herbicides. Students from the school received grant money from the agency to research whether native plants might thrive more easily with the use of fewer pesticides. They established test plots to evaluate how the plants grew with different amounts of fertilizer at different depths. Their project could help to restore natural habitats along roadsides throughout the state. It shows respect for the earth because they are allowing the land to teach them and their community the best way to live within the integrity of creation.
- Young people of the West 181st Street Beautification Project in New York City transformed an empty lot that had once been known for drugs, violence, and vandalism into a garden that houses shrubs, trees, and a playground for toddlers.
- In Covington, Louisiana, high school students worked to restore the local Mile Branch Stream, once a dumping ground for

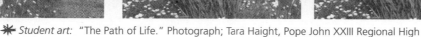

Today, many young people are **leading the way** by using their talents, interests, and creativity to sustain the earth.

✳ *Student art:* "The Path of Life." Photograph; Tara Haight, Pope John XXIII Regional High School, Sparta, New Jersey

✝ Brainstorm five ways that U.S. social structures could be changed to encourage greater environmental stewardship. Bring your list to class for discussion.

furniture and appliances. They tested the water, made an inventory of species, organized a clean-up day, talked to middle school kids about local water pollution, and even built sculptures out of trash to heighten community awareness. Fish and birds are now returning to the clean water.

All these young people used their creativity to enhance the integrity of creation. Their work benefited not only the natural world but the human community as well.

Renewing the Face of the Earth

Ultimately, the relationship we have with creation is a reflection of who we are as people, as the U.S. Catholic bishops observe:

> Our mistreatment of the natural world diminishes our own dignity and sacredness, not only because we are destroying resources that future generations of humans need, but because we are engaging in actions that contradict what it means to be human. (*Renewing,* page 2)

 But if mistreating the natural world diminishes our own dignity and sacredness, the opposite is also true. When we respect creation, when we celebrate it as a sacrament of God's love, when we live within its integrity, we become more fully all God intends us to be.

Renewing the earth means that we ourselves must transform, for the suffering of the earth reflects a breakdown in human relationships. That is why we say, "Send forth thy Spirit, Lord, and renew the face of the earth" (*Renewing,* page 14). With the help of the Holy Spirit, who renews all things, we can build the relationships that restore the integrity of creation. In doing so, we restore our own integrity as well. ⋃

14. How does ecological economics respect the limits of creation?
15. How does short-term thinking fail to reflect the real value of the environment?
16. As stewards of creation, what must business leaders weigh when making decisions?
17. Describe sustainable development. List three policies adopted by the Costa Rican government to encourage sustainable development.

---

 18. In your community, how might human creativity be used to build life-giving relationships between human beings and the earth?

⋃ Write a prayer, poem, or song of thanksgiving for the gifts of the earth.

10 WAGING PEACE

violence ~~division~~
peace solidarity

the Christian
response to violence

In This Chapter . . .

THEIR WEAPONS WERE TRUTH AND LOVE

At fifteen, you don't plan to get involved in a revolution.

But that's what happened to me and my brother during the People's Revolution that swept the Philippines in February 1986. Pardon the history lesson, but I need to explain how two teenage boys ended up in a secret radio station urging the nation to overthrow a dictator. For fourteen years, President Ferdinand Marcos had imposed martial law on the people, denying them their civil rights. Government forces even killed Marcos's arch rival, a senator named Ninoy Aquino, who spoke out for democracy. But Ninoy's widow, Cory Aquino, carried on his cause by running as the pro-democracy candidate in the 7 February 1986 presidential elections.

The church had spent more than a year training about 500,000 volunteers to monitor the elections to keep Marcos from cheating.

Paolo Mercado *(right, first photo)* and his brother, Gabe, volunteered at the Catholic radio station that called Filipinos to peacefully resist the armed troops of Ferdinand Marcos. Tens of thousands responded, meeting the soldiers' guns with love, truth, and prayer.

That's where my brother and I come in. We belonged to a theater group run by a Jesuit priest, Fr. James B. Reuter—who was also head of the church's National Office of Mass Media (NOMM). He asked me and my brother Gabe, who was thirteen, to work at Radio Veritas, the main station in the church's national radio network. When the election monitors called the station, my brother and I wrote down their reports on slips of paper that we handed to Ms. June Keithley, a well-known media personality, to read on the air. For seven days, our national broadcast reported cheating, the harassment and killing of pro-Cory supporters, and also the heroic acts of those protecting the sanctity of the ballot.

Despite our efforts, Marcos declared himself the winner, amid protests of massive electoral fraud. The nation cowered in fear because now the dictator would unleash his wrath on those who had opposed him. In fact, I got thrown out of Radio Veritas that day because the management feared the Marcos backlash and wanted Father Reuter's people out. Because I was the only one at the station, I got all the flack.

Tough as I thought I was, I cried. I cried for being treated so roughly by people who had welcomed us warmly just days before. I cried because I felt so small and insignificant—a scrawny high school kid who supposedly didn't know how much "damage" he was doing. I went home feeling that all we had

key allies—General Fidel Ramos and the minister of defense, Juan Enrile—joined those opposed to Marcos, holing themselves up with a few hundred soldiers in a military base in the middle of Manila. The next day I got a call from Father Reuter asking my brother and me to come to his office immediately.

Father Reuter told us, along with June Keithley, that Marcos's men had destroyed the Radio Veritas transmitter. That was a blow to the church, because Cardinal Jaime Sin (yes, that's his real name!) wanted to call the people to go into the streets to prevent the bloodshed that would result if Marcos's troops ever reached the rebel compound. Father Reuter gave us the assignment of our lives: find another station and broadcast the cardinal's message.

After some searching, we finally found a station, and "Radio Bandido" was born. Father Reuter had volunteers positioned around the city, ready to pass reports to us. I said a prayer, hoping we were doing the right thing.

The broadcast began at midnight with June announcing the cardinal's call for the people to go into the streets to block the tanks. Pretty soon the reports were coming in fast and furious over the two-way radio—my brother and I were too busy writing them down to be scared! As our "field reporters" told us where Marcos's tanks were headed, our broadcast would tell people exactly where to go.

I need to explain how **two teenage boys ended up in a secret radio station** urging the nation to overthrow a dictator.

done in the past week meant absolutely nothing. I tried to forget about the whole thing—but that wasn't the end of the story.

The Catholic Bishops Conference of the Philippines (CBCP) boldly declared the elections fraudulent and immoral, and called on the people to start a civil disobedience movement. About a week later, two of Marcos's

Tens of thousands of people responded to the call, filling the streets of downtown Manila and blocking them with any makeshift barricades they could find . . . trees, trucks, sandbags, lampposts, whatever. When Marcos's soldiers tried to advance, the people would block them by kneeling in front of the tanks and praying. The soldiers were armed with machine guns, tanks, and tear gas. The people were armed only with prayers. They offered the soldiers smiles and flowers and sandwiches—but never budged from the human wall they made. And even when they were attacked, they never became violent.

There were very tense moments. At one point, one of our friends in the field panicked when he saw the tanks rolling forward in their location. He called out to us to tell his mother that he loved her if he didn't make it out of there alive.

June later said that the darkest hour that night was right before dawn, when she could hear the cries of the people being teargassed, and there were reports of helicopter gunships coming. It was about 5:45 a.m., and she began praying over the air: "Lord, you know that there are many people out there. You know what we are going through right now. We ask you to please guide us, Lord. You teach us to always turn the other cheek. We ask you now to show us in many concrete ways that truly nothing good can come from evil. Show us, Lord, that only good will work in this world. Please take care of all who are out there . . . there are children out there, young girls and boys, parents, brothers and sisters, husbands and wives. Who knows what they may have to face this morning? We add our prayers to the prayers of the people in our country. Lord, I am not very good at this, but I ask you please, in Jesus' name, please save our people."

June thought there was a real danger Marcos's men would find us—we even covered the windows with paper so snipers would not get a clear shot at us. Here's a little secret. No one knows this, but I actually had a ninja suit, a pair of nunchakus, and some shurikens (star knives) stashed in my bag in the radio booth. Somehow it was comforting to think that I could "put up a fight" in case the soldiers arrived—as if my nunchakus could deflect M-16 bullets! June had a better plan. She asked Father Reuter's office to send religious sisters and brothers to barricade the building. Before long, the stairwells and hallways were packed with them—which made me feel much safer than if I'd had a bazooka with me for protection!

Throughout the day, the tides were turning against the Marcoses. More soldiers were defecting, more people were packing the streets, and the government-controlled TV stations had fallen. By about 8:00 p.m., it became clear that our role at Radio Bandido was done. There was no one left to call out onto the streets because everyone was already there.

Twenty-four hours later, Marcos and his cronies left the country, and millions of people celebrated in the streets in a huge party. Later, Cory Aquino was inaugurated as president, a position she held for six years.

Now, thirteen years later, I am the father of a one-year-old, and the fight for our freedom continues. Relatives of Ferdinand Marcos are back seeking power, and self-serving politicians want to change our democratic Constitution. The situation is so bad that I was actually thinking of leaving the country for good. But last month, I decided that what we fought for is too important to let slide, and that if my son is going to have a good

Tens of thousands of people responded to the call, filling the streets of downtown Manila.

Priests, nuns, brothers, and thousands of ordinary citizens blocked Marcos's tanks and armored personnel carriers with their own bodies.

life, I had better do something for our society. So I joined a protest rally against those who wish to change the Constitution and return the Marcoses to power. It was my first rally in some time. And it probably will not be my last. (Paolo A. Mercado, with excerpts from Mercado, editor, *People Power*, pages 191–192)

Which Way to Peace?

Like Paolo, millions of young people around the world live under the threat of war, and millions more are threatened by other types of violence.

Most people would agree that the world would be a better place if there were less violence in it. But what is less clear is how to achieve a more peaceful world. How should we respond to the world's violence?

Conventional wisdom tells us that the party with the most strength or weapons will be the one to win a fight. For most people, then, the answer to a violent world is more violence: "Fight fire with fire," they say—violence can only be stopped on its own terms.

But Christianity claims that love, not violence, brings true order and peace to the world. It bases this claim on the belief that although Jesus was crucified and died, the life-giving power of God's love overcame that violence in Jesus' Resurrection. The Filipino people bravely followed Jesus' example by challenging violence with love—and by doing so, they experienced a "resurrection" of their own, defying conventional wisdom. This is the paradox of the cross: love is stronger than violence, even the violence of death.

Of course, it is easier to make that claim in church or religion class than it is to actually rely on it in daily life—especially under the threat of real violence. It's reasonable to ask, How can Jesus' way of love really work in a violent world? That's the question this chapter considers.

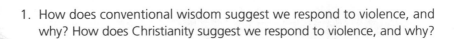

1. How does conventional wisdom suggest we respond to violence, and why? How does Christianity suggest we respond to violence, and why?

2. What types of power are illustrated in Paolo's story? You may find it helpful to review the discussion of power in chapter 3.
3. How does Paolo's story reflect the principles of nonviolent noncooperation discussed in chapter 3? Use specific examples from the story to support your answer.

A What do you think allowed the Filipino people to win against a more powerful opponent who had not hesitated to use violence in the past? Do you think that this sort of peaceful revolution could be successful again?

Violence: Taking a Deeper Look

To understand how love overcomes violence, we need to understand the basic nature of violence itself—specifically, what it is and why it happens.

What Is Violence?

What is violence? The answer might seem obvious: most often, we think of violence as any action that physically injures or kills a person, or damages property. But in the understanding of Catholic social teaching, **violence** is any human action that causes harm to the life or dignity of another person. Because this definition of violence includes harm to human dignity, any action that harms a person's psychological, social, or spiritual well-being can also be considered a type of violence.

When violence is defined to include harm to human dignity, it becomes apparent that we have been examining issues of violence throughout this course: injustice itself is a form of violence.

The sort of violence that occurs as a result of unjust social structures rather than as a direct result of one person's actions is often called **institutional violence.** Racism and poverty are some general forms of institutional violence, as are many of the situations we have examined throughout this course.

The Spiral of Violence

Realizing that injustice is a form of violence offers an important clue for answering our second question, Why does violence happen?

As a strong voice for justice in Brazil, Archbishop **Dom Helder Camara** (1909–1999) had plenty of opportunity to ponder that question. He observed that people usually respond to violence by retaliating with an even greater act of violence. As one act of violence leads to another, it grows in intensity—an effect he called the **spiral of violence.**

At the root of this spiral of violence is **conflict**—disagreements between people or groups that have opposing needs, goals, or beliefs. Conflict is not in itself bad; it is an inevitable result of the fact that each person is different from others. Approached in a spirit of solidarity, conflict does not need to result in violence. But when people attempt to resolve conflict by seeking their own good at the expense of the good of others, injustice results.

Here is one way to describe the spiral of violence:

1. **Basic injustice.** The spiral begins when people resolve conflict by seeking only their own interests at the expense of the good of others, causing injustice and institutional violence.

Anything that causes harm to human life is an act of violence. The church identifies unfair economic practices that cause starvation as a form of murderous violence (*Catechism of the Catholic Church*, 2269).

Violence is any human action that causes harm to the life or dignity of another person.

2. Violent response. If the injustice is severe enough, it prompts a response from those affected by it. People frustrated by injustice often see no other solution than the use of violence against their opponent.

3. Violent counterresponse. Once one side decides to use violence to solve the situation, the other side sees no other choice but to respond with even greater violence.

4. Escalating violence. The level of violence escalates as each side attempts to defeat the other with the use of greater force. Each side may feel its use of violence is justified by the harm caused by the other side.

5. More injustice. When one side manages to use enough force to overwhelm the other, the conflict may appear to end. In reality, although the level of violence may have been greatly reduced, the spiral often returns to the first level when the "winner" imposes its will on the "loser" in an unjust way. In that case, the spiral begins all over again. **B**

To those who ask why we have war and fighting in the world, Helder Camara might suggest looking at how those acts of violence are preceded by other forms of violence. Often, institutional violence lies at the root of more intense forms of violence.

Unfortunately, it doesn't take long to find the spiral of violence at work in our world, both at an individual level and a global level. To see how it works, we can look at two examples: youth violence and militarism.

THE SPIRAL OF VIOLENCE

B Drawing on history books, the news, or your own experience, find an example in which the use of violence led to a more violent response. In a page or two, explain how and why violence escalated in your example, using the spiral of violence as a guide.

Youth Violence

Most young people today are all too familiar with violence, either through their own experience or that of their friends and peers. Consider these true examples:

Seventeen-year-old Robert had a habit of getting into fights. Take the one he got into during a rough pickup game on the basketball court at Islip High School. First there was an argument, then threats, and then fighting. Robert knocked the other boy down by hitting him in the head. Even as the boy lay on the ground, with his eyes rolling back and blood flowing from his head, Robert could only think of hitting him again. Why? The boy had called him names. "I just stood over him and spit at him," Robert recalled later. "I was shaking because I was so furious." (Adapted from Del Valle, "Teenagers, Rage and Tragedy")

Juan never intended to actually fire the gun he began carrying after he started hanging around with his brothers' gang. But then came the night he and some friends were taunted by the leader of a rival gang in a restaurant that Juan's gang considered their territory. Juan went home to get his brothers; they came back with guns. One thing led to another: a member of the rival gang knocked down his brother, causing him to bleed profusely from the mouth. Panicked and scared, Juan and his brother fired wildly, and two people were killed. (Adapted from Wilkinson, "Just Another Face")

"This is a holdup!" screamed the masked figure, pointing a rifle at the head of a petrified cashier. "Give me your money."

Over the next five weeks, a similar scenario unfolded at grocery stores around the affluent community of Kingwood, Texas. The robbers turned out to be four girls who attended the local high school. At school, Malissa, Katie, Michelle, and Krystal were involved in volleyball, drill team, theater, and dance. Their motive? Money for drugs. Their inspiration? "We got it off television," one of them told police. (Adapted from Jerome et al., "Crime: The Lost Girls")

In each of these cases, the young people involved made choices that harmed others— and that ended up harming themselves too. All ended up in court or prison. Why would they make such choices?

People often are quick to offer answers: gangs, drugs, and the general breakdown of morality are commonly blamed. While these answers might be true on the surface, we need to dig deeper to find ways to prevent youth violence. For instance, to say that gangs are responsible for youth violence begs the question, Why do young people form gangs in the first place?

Many factors contribute to youth violence, and it would be a mistake to oversimplify the issue. However, experts who study youth

Young people mourn the shooting death of a friend at Columbine High School in Colorado.

Most young people today are all too familiar with violence.

violence have identified two significant causes worth considering: the breakdown of relationships and the influence of a culture of violence. ☾

Broken relationships

Throughout this course, we have emphasized that a web of life-giving relationships is necessary to provide people with good lives. It should come as no surprise, then, that the breakdown or absence of such relationships might lead young people to respond with violence.

For instance, abused or neglected children are 53 percent more likely to commit crimes when they are teenagers, and 38 percent more likely to commit violent crimes within their lifetime, according to one study. Although Robert was not abused as a child, court-ordered counseling traced some of his feelings of aggression to the bitter divorce his parents went through when he was five years old, and the lack of love he felt from his mother and stepfather afterward. "I grew up feeling like my parents were pushing me away when I needed them most, rather than pulling me closer," he says.

Other young people are a source of abuse and rejection too. Feeling humiliated and dehumanized by such treatment, some young people might see violence as a way to gain respect. That may have been part of what motivated two boys to kill twelve students, a teacher, and themselves at a Colorado high school. "At first, I blamed myself; I could have been a better friend," says seventeen-year-old Devon Adams, a friend of one of the killers. "But then I began to see that all of society was to blame. Eric and Dylan were constantly ridiculed by many kids" ("Mourn for the Killers, Too").

Abused or neglected children are
53 percent more likely
to commit crimes when they are teenagers.

✳ *Student art:* "Aplomb." Watercolor; Jennifer Miley, Sacred Heart High School, Kingston, Massachusetts

☾ Explore the causes of youth violence by surveying at least five of your friends. In your own words, ask them, "What would you say are the main reasons that some young people use violence—like fighting, using guns and knives, or harassing others?" Record their answers, and be prepared to discuss them in class.

Juan's decision to join a gang was motivated not by ridicule but by a simple need to belong somewhere in society. A top student at his largely Latino middle school, Juan floundered when he graduated to a Catholic high school. He struggled with the schoolwork but faced other challenges as well. He sometimes missed school because his family did not have the bus fare; at night, he had to study away from the windows to avoid the bullets shot at his house by gangs targeting his brothers. And as the only Latino kid in his class, he never quite felt like he fit in. The friends from his neighborhood, meanwhile, teased him for studying too much. Lonely and struggling in school, Juan dropped out and got involved with his brothers' gang—where at least he felt like he fit in.

 In reflecting on the events leading to the murders, both Juan and his former school community have concluded that a stronger sense of solidarity within the school could have helped to break the spiral of violence affecting Juan. 🗩

A culture of violence

Although society is quick to condemn young people who use violence, it often sends them a contradictory message by its acceptance of legalized violence such as abortion, capital punishment, and war. Moreover, the media often portray the use of violence in a way that makes it seem acceptable or even heroic.

Lieutenant Colonel Dave Grossman, a retired U.S. Army psychologist who studies the psychological and social effects of learning to kill, argues that the media—movies, television, and video games—have the potential to pass on a culture of violence to young people:

I spent almost a quarter of a century as an Army infantry officer and a psychologist, learning and studying how to enable people to kill. Believe me, we are very good at it. But it does not come naturally; you have to be taught to kill. And just as the Army is conditioning people to kill, we are indiscriminately doing the same thing to our children, but without the safeguards.

After the Jonesboro killings [in which two boys, ages eleven and thirteen, fired on their schoolmates, killing four girls and a teacher], the head of the American Academy of Pediatrics Task Force on Juvenile Violence came to town and said that children don't naturally kill. It is a learned skill, and they learn it from abuse and violence in the home and, most pervasively, from violence as entertainment in television, the movies, and interactive video games. ("It's Time to Stop Training Our Kids to Kill")

Experts suggest that television violence may make the use of violence to solve problems seem socially acceptable—especially to young children.

🗩 Using the definition of violence given in this chapter, keep a record of all the acts of violence you witness in your school and community over three days. Without using the names of the people involved, briefly describe each incident and how it harmed human life or dignity. Then write a short reflection on what you observed. What are the long-term effects of such incidents for the individuals, the school, and the community?

Grossman and others argue that exposure to violence in the media affects children psychologically in ways that make it more likely that they will act violently themselves. In fact, since the 1960s, more than one thousand research studies have shown a link between media violence and real-life violence. Constant exposure to violence in the media may make it seem normal, especially to young children who are unable to distinguish between real and fantasy violence. And action-adventure shows and video games often portray violence as a quick and socially acceptable solution to problems. *E*

Of course, people are influenced by more than just the media. They also learn about the role of violence in society from the behavior of family, friends, and community members. The four girls convicted of armed robbery, for instance, were imitating television violence. But some observers of the case suggested that the local community either ignored or accepted low-level violence such as vandalism, petty crime, and widespread drug abuse among teens and adults alike. Perhaps the local culture contributed to the girls' attitude that their actions were "no big deal."

E Keep a record of all the acts of *physical* violence you witness on television or in the movies in a one-week period, using a phrase or sentence to describe each. Then write a short reflection on what effect, if any, the media have on your attitudes toward violence.

Each of these young people bears a certain amount of responsibility for his or her decision to use violence. But often, young people do not see nonviolent solutions to the problems they face. Families, communities, and the wider culture have the responsibility to teach children these solutions. ⫐

Militarism

While denouncing the use of violence to resolve conflicts on an individual level, society often applies a different standard to the use of violence on an international level. Ultimately, nations resort to violence for the same reason that individuals do: it seems to be the best response to a violent and unjust world. War, many would claim, is necessary to keep the world a just and safe place.

In practice, however, the peace won by war is all too fragile, and often, one war seems to sow the seeds for greater violence in the next. The more than 250 wars fought around the world during the twentieth century claimed the lives of an estimated 110 million people—the great majority of whom were civilians, not soldiers. Far from making the world a safe place, the global habit of war seems only to have made it a more dangerous place.

In their 1983 pastoral letter, *The Challenge of Peace,* the U.S. Catholic bishops warned of the dangers of **militarism,** the reliance on military power to resolve conflict and provide security:

> Reason and experience tell us that a continuing upward spiral, even in conventional arms, coupled with an unbridled increase in armed forces, instead of securing true peace will almost certainly be provocative of war. (219)

In other words, the church argues that building military strength makes the world *less* safe, not more safe, for everyone. Why? Because militarism relies on the threat of violence, rather than solidarity, to ensure peace—and the distrust caused by that threat too often results in real violence.

The arms race

When a nation relies on the threat of violence to ensure its security, that threat must

World War I was to be "the war to end war." Instead, it sowed the seeds of World War II, which in turn led to the cold war, the Vietnam war, and the nuclear arms race.

⫐ What are the best ways to encourage young people to solve their problems without resorting to violence? Brainstorm some ideas with your classmates, listing as many as you can think of. Be prepared to discuss your answers in class.

be credible—that is, the nation must be ready and able to carry out violence in a way that is sure to overwhelm its enemies. According to the theory of **deterrence,** the potential of one country to inflict significant harm on its adversaries will deter, or discourage, those adversaries from attacking it first.

Under the logic of deterrence, the nation with the most potential for violence will be the most secure. This assumption inevitably leads to a "race" between nations and their adversaries to have the greatest capacity for violence. This competition between rivals to have the biggest and best military force is known as the **arms race.** The arms race is fueled by the annual sale of about $50 billion in weapons, mostly to developing countries.

The arms race is a good example of the spiral of violence in action at the international level. Ultimately, the arms race makes the world less safe in at least two ways:

- **More violence.** The arms race tends to be most intense in areas at the most risk for conflict. As each side arms itself more heavily, mutual distrust and aggressiveness grow, making conflict more likely. When conflict does occur, it is more likely to result in greater violence than if the parties had been less heavily armed.

- **Less money for poor and vulnerable people.** The thirty-eight countries that spend the most on their militaries spent $686 billion in 1998 alone. The United States is expected to spend around $300 billion (give or take $15 billion) on military expenses every year through 2004—that's about half of the country's discretionary budget, the part of the federal budget that Congress can decide how to spend (the rest is already committed to things like Social Security payments and interest payments on the national debt).

As Catholic social teaching points out repeatedly, the resources spent preparing for war would better serve the cause of peace if they were used to further human development and justice. Money that is spent preparing for violence is money not spent on preventing violence.

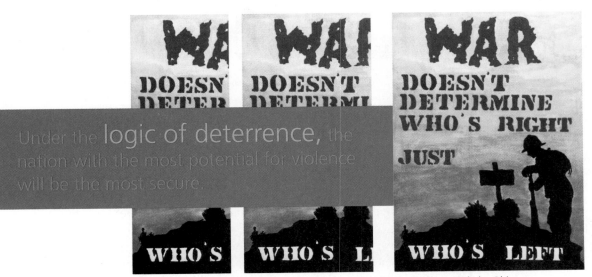

Under the logic of deterrence, the nation with the most potential for violence will be the most secure.

※ *Student art:* "War." Tempera; Jill Napierala, Notre Dame Academy, Toledo, Ohio

 How much would $300 billion buy for human development? Make a shopping list of at least three things that would improve human life and dignity, especially among poor or vulnerable people—for example, a can of food, a medical clinic, or a college education. For each item, research how much one costs and then do the math to find out how many items $300 billion would buy. Record your answers on your list.

PROJECTED U.S. FEDERAL BUDGET SPENDING IN 2003

The U.S. government is projected to spend about $1.89 trillion in fiscal year 2003. The majority of that, $1.3 trillion, is mandatory spending—expenses that the government is already committed to pay, such as interest on the national debt and Social Security. About $636 billion is discretionary spending—money that Congress can decide how to spend. Of that amount, $304 billion, or about 48 percent, is expected to be military spending. This chart shows how military spending stacks up against other spending categories.

In billions of dollars

Military

$304

Social services, education, training, employment

Transportation

Legal justice system

Natural resources and environment

Science, space, and technology

International affairs

Commerce and housing credit

Agriculture

Community development

General government

$15 $10 $19 $9 $18 $24 $10 $28 $69 $52

(Source: Office of Management and Budget, "A Citizen's Guide to the Federal Budget: Budget of the United States Government Fiscal Year 2000")

The nuclear threat

Because the goal of the arms race is to have the greatest possible potential for violence, that goal is reached when nations acquire nuclear weapons.

The deadly force of nuclear weapons was amply demonstrated when the United States dropped atomic bombs on the Japanese cities of Hiroshima and Nagasaki in 1945, killing more than 200,000 residents. Those who survived the immediate effects of the blasts faced a living hell, and radiation poisoning continued to kill tens of thousands of people in the decades that followed.

The atomic bomb ended the war—but it launched a decades-long nuclear arms race between the United States and the Soviet Union. The United States alone has spent more than $4 trillion on nuclear weapons. The result: by 1985, the world nuclear arsenal contained the equivalent of about 1.4 million bombs of the size dropped on Hiroshima.

Under **START II,** the second Strategic Arms Reduction Treaty of 1993, the United States and Russia agreed to reduce their nuclear weapons stockpiles to about ten thousand warheads each by 2007. Still, **nuclear proliferation**—the increase of nations that own nuclear weapons—continues to threaten the world. For instance, the neighboring countries of India and Pakistan, who have long fought a bitter border war, each exploded its first nuclear weapons in 1998 in an attempt to intimidate the other.

Left unchecked, this is where the spiral of violence ends—with the potential destruction of all humanity and great harm to the rest of creation.

Hope for a Violent World?

Given the price of violence, why do people continue to choose it? Faced with a violent situation, many people see only two options:
- do nothing but submit to the violence
- respond with violence

For most people, the first urge is to retaliate if possible. "Fighting fire with fire" is an instinctive and a "commonsense" choice. Responding to violence with violence seems preferable to the humiliating or painful option of submitting to it.

People defend their use of violence in many ways. For instance, they might argue that because the other person was violent first, violent retaliation is justified. Children rely on this argument when they say, "He hit me first!" to explain their fighting. According to the logic of retaliation, the person who commits violence first loses the right not to be harmed. Unfortunately, living by this rule makes it almost inevitable that violence will spiral out of control—as Gandhi once observed, the "eye for an eye" approach to justice soon leaves everyone blind.

Or people might claim that violence is a necessary choice. More often, however, violence seems to be necessary only because people cannot imagine or hope for other options. They may believe that violence is built into the way the world works—just as the Babylonians claimed in their creation myth (see chapter 1, pages 16–17). Whether retaliation is regarded as justified or necessary, the inevitable result is an escalating spiral of violence. *H*

But both of these assumptions overlook a third option for responding to violence—one that offers hope for breaking the spiral.

Those who survived the immediate effects of the blasts faced **a living hell.**

The aftermath of the atomic bomb that was dropped on Hiroshima, Japan

H If you were faced with violence, would you be more likely to fight back, to attempt to escape the situation, or to challenge it without using violence yourself? Explain the reasons for your choice. Is it the choice you would prefer to make? Why or why not?

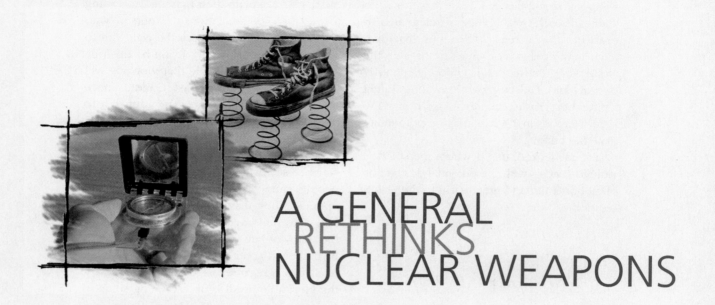

A GENERAL RETHINKS NUCLEAR WEAPONS

Many politicians and military leaders continue to argue in favor of maintaining the United States' large nuclear arsenal to deter any possibility of attack by another nation. But increasingly, some are arguing for the total elimination of nuclear weapons.

Among those taking this position is retired general Lee Butler, who was the top commander of the Strategic Air Command, which managed the nation's nuclear weapons from 1991 to 1994. He eventually concluded that the strategy of nuclear deterrence was not compatible with the values of his faith:

Left photo: This 1952 nuclear test completely destroyed the island on which it took place. *Right photo:* General Lee Butler former commander-in-chief of the U.S. Strategic Air Command, has called for an end to all nuclear weapons.

I was raised to believe in the innate goodness of humanity, developed a deep sense of the dignity of the individual human being, and had a great appreciation for the miracle of life and our existence on this earth. Although that sense of values was deeply embedded in my psyche, what later struck me . . . is how readily for so many years of my life I suspended the tenets of that value system [because I believed] that the threat we perceived during the Cold War was so great it justified a security construct called "mutual assured destruction" that promised the death of hundreds of millions of people. . . .

During [my] last years of active military service, it became clear to me that we had lost all sense of proportion regarding the theory and practice of nuclear deterrence. . . . Finally, I simply answered the voice of my conscience. That's where my religious beliefs intersected most strongly with my sense of professional obligation. (Cortright, "An Unexpected Calling")

As one of those in charge of the nation's nuclear arsenal, Butler answered his conscience by taking action to reduce the nuclear threat. Today, together with other political and military leaders, he continues to work to prevent "mutual assured destruction" from becoming a reality. ●

It became clear to me that we had lost all sense of proportion regarding the theory and practice of nuclear deterrence. . . . Finally, I simply answered the voice of my conscience.

Do some research to find out which elected representatives, military officers, and government officials determine nuclear weapons policy. Write a letter to one of them explaining your position on the issue and requesting information about what he or she is doing about it.

Although civil rights activists were often violently attacked, Martin Luther King Jr. insisted that they should not respond in kind because "hate cannot drive out hate; only love can do that."

Breaking the spiral

The Reverend Martin Luther King Jr. (1929–1968) dramatically demonstrated that people have more than two choices when confronted by violence. He rejected the option of simply submitting to the institutional violence of racial discrimination. But he also insisted that his followers not use violence to achieve their goals—even when attacked. He criticized the logic of violent retaliation in this way:

> The ultimate weakness of violence is that it is a descending spiral, begetting the very thing it seeks to destroy. . . . Returning violence for violence multiplies violence, adding deeper darkness to a night already devoid of stars. Darkness cannot drive out darkness; only light can do that. Hate cannot drive out hate; only love can do that. (Quoted in Pax Christi USA, *Peacemaking*, volume 1, page 126)

King's insight is based on the teaching of Jesus, a teaching echoed by the church: Only love can break the spiral of violence, and only love can bring true peace.

4. Define the following terms: *violence, institutional violence, deterrence, arms race.*
5. Describe the spiral of violence.
6. What are two significant causes of youth violence?
7. Name two consequences of the arms race.
8. What two options do most people see for responding to violence? What is a third option taught by Jesus?

9. Explain the logic of violent retailiation and why the church regards that logic as flawed.

Following Jesus to Peace

Christianity claims that the way of Jesus is the way to true peace for the world. Often, when people refer to "world peace," what they have in mind is the absence of war and physical violence. But the peace to which Jesus calls us goes deeper than that.

Peace: The Fruit of Justice and Love

If we accept the claim that all injustice is a form of violence, then it follows that peace is more than the absence of war or physical violence. Really, true peace cannot be achieved until there is justice for all. This is what Pope Paul VI meant when he said, "If you want peace, work for justice" (quoted in *Peacemaking,* volume 1, page 23).

Here is how the church defines peace in *The Church in the Modern World (Gaudium et Spes):*

> Peace is not merely the absence of war; nor can it be reduced solely to the maintenance of a balance of power between enemies; nor is it brought about by dictatorship. Instead, it is rightly and appropriately called an enterprise of justice. Peace results from that order structured into human society by its divine founder, and actualized [i.e., brought about] by [people] as they thirst after ever greater justice. . . . Since the human will is unsteady and wounded by sin,

the achievement of peace requires the constant mastering of passions and the vigilance of lawful authority.

> But this is not enough. This peace on earth cannot be obtained unless personal well-being is safeguarded and [people] freely and trustingly share with one another the riches of their inner spirits and their talents. A firm determination to respect other [persons] and peoples and their dignity, as well as the studied practice of brotherhood are absolutely necessary for the establishment of peace. Hence peace is likewise the fruit of love, which goes beyond what justice can provide. (78)

If justice leads to peace, then this entire course has been about the pursuit of peace. Working for justice transforms social structures that cause physical forms of violence, such as war, to erupt in the first place.

Peace, then, is the harmony that results when people resolve conflicts by working in love for the good of all.

Paper cranes adorn the Hiroshima Children's Peace Memorial—a symbol of the hope of all children for a world of peace.

But peace is more than even the fulfillment of justice, according to the church: it is also the fullness of love. **Peace,** then, is the harmony that results when people resolve conflicts by working in love for the good of all. ⱱ

The Cross: A Symbol of Peace

Many people view peace as a far-off goal or even an impossible dream—but the church says peace is a real possibility for those who are open to it. Ironically, it is the cross—which many people would view as a symbol of violence—that the church says is the source of all peace. "By the blood of his Cross, 'in his own person [Christ] killed the hostility'" that separates people from one another and God, the church says (*Catechism of the Catholic Church,* 2305).

What does it mean to say that "Christ killed the hostility" by dying on the cross? When people are hurt by violence, they tend to retaliate with violence—such a response "just makes sense." The logic of retaliation fuels the spiral of violence and separates us from one another and God.

But Jesus refused to follow the logic of retaliation. Because he was totally committed to following God's will, he chose to act only in truth and love—even if that meant giving up his life. He responded to those who crucified him not with more violence but with forgiveness (Luke 23:34). By refusing to retaliate, he broke the spiral of violence. And by following God's way of love even in the face of death, he liberated humanity from sin, the root cause of all violence.

Jesus calls us to "take up [your] cross and follow me" (Matthew 16:24). We do that whenever we act in love and proclaim the truth, even though we might suffer as a result. 𝕂

"Blessed are the peacemakers"

As we saw in chapter 1, Jesus challenged injustice throughout his ministry. But he also encouraged peacemaking:

- "Blessed are the peacemakers, for they will be called children of God" (Matthew 5:9).
- Forgive one who sins against you "not seven times, but, I tell you, seventy-seven times" (Matthew 18:22).
- "Love your enemies, do good to those who hate you, bless those who curse you, pray for those who abuse you" (Luke 6:27).
- When one of his disciples attempts to prevent Jesus' arrest by attacking with a sword, Jesus admonishes him, "Put your sword back into its place; for all who take the sword will perish by the sword" (Matthew 26:52).

Clearly, Jesus calls his followers to live in a way that will break the spiral of violence.

Grace: The help we need

"Peace is both a gift of God and a human work," the U.S. Catholic bishops say in *The Challenge of Peace* (68). In other words, peace can be fully achieved only in the Kingdom of God, which we are called to enter by following Jesus' way.

If we stop to consider seriously what Jesus' way requires, we might not be so quick to answer when he asks us to take up our cross and follow him. After all, responding to violence with love is risky, and Jesus does not promise that we will not be "crucified."

ⱱ What does peace look like for you? Choose a photo, painting, song, poem, or story that is an image of peace for you. In two to four paragraphs, explain the image and why it represents peace for you.

𝕂 Few of us will ever be called to sacrifice our life for the sake of peace. But what small, daily sacrifices can people make to contribute to peace? Name some ways you have observed people around you making sacrifices for peace.

The choice for peace can be daunting; to choose that way rather than the way of violent retaliation, we need God's help. But if we are open to the grace provided by the Holy Spirit, we might find that, like the Filipino people who stopped tanks on their knees, we are able to go beyond ourselves to accomplish what we thought was impossible. "No man can stop violence," Gandhi said. "God alone can do so. . . . The deciding factor is God's grace." L

Pacifism: "We No Longer Learn War"

Over the centuries, how Christians have attempted to apply Jesus' teachings on violence to their lives has depended on how they understood those teachings.

For about the first three centuries of the church, most Christians opposed the use of violence under any circumstances. Even though they faced sporadic persecution by the Romans, the early Christians refused to fight back. Nor would they serve in the Roman military, which led to charges that they were disloyal citizens.

The early Christians had various reasons for refusing to serve in the military, but most important was their belief that military service was inconsistent with the teaching and example of Jesus: "For we no longer take up 'sword against nation,' nor do we 'learn war any more,' having become children of peace, for the sake of Jesus," wrote Origen, a second-century Christian leader (Wink, *Engaging the Powers,* page 210). Another second-century Christian apologist, Justin, explained, "We who once killed each other not only do not make war on each other, but . . . gladly die for the confession of Christ" (pages 209–210). Soldiers who converted to Christianity were encouraged to leave the military. "I am a soldier of Christ," declared Martin of Tours, a fourth-century Roman soldier, after his conversion. "It is not lawful for me to fight" (quoted in *The Challenge of Peace,* 114).

Today, such opposition to the use of violence to resolve conflict is called **pacifism.** The church strongly defends pacifism as a legitimate moral choice for individuals, as

> Even though they faced sporadic persecution by the Romans, the early Christians **refused to fight back.**

L Write a prayer, poem, or song for the grace to love enemies, or create a symbolic artistic image of God's grace restoring peace between enemies.

long as it does not harm the rights or duties of others. On the other hand, the church also affirms the right of individuals and the duty of governments to self-defense and the defense of the innocent—even by the use of armed force.

But the church has always taught that violence should be used only as a last resort. Even in the case of self-defense, the church teaches that there are strict moral limits on the use of violence. Beginning in the fourth century, the church began developing criteria for determining when the use of violence could be justified, and how it should be limited in those cases.

The Just-War Theory

The nonviolent practice of the early church changed after Christianity was made the official religion of the Roman Empire in 380. Before, it had been illegal for a Roman soldier to be a Christian; not long after, however, all Roman soldiers were *required* to be Christians. As members of the new majority religion, many Christians felt a responsibility to protect the community.

Augustine of Hippo (354–430), a bishop who became one of the most influential theologians in church history, argued that war could be morally justified in certain cases. Although he viewed war and other forms of violence as tragic and to be avoided, he believed it could be necessary to protect the innocent. Borrowing from Roman ethics, Augustine developed principles for determining the conditions under which war could be justified. Those principles, known as **just-war theory,** were later refined by others, particularly **Thomas Aquinas** (1225–1274).

Just-war theory rests on two assumptions. It begins by presuming that war and violence are always to be avoided and that we should not harm anyone, even our enemy. On the other hand, it also presumes that love calls Christians to restrain an enemy who would harm innocent people. Just-war theory attempts to balance these presumptions by suggesting that when it is necessary, limited violence may be used to protect the innocent—but it can only be justified after other peaceful options have been exhausted, and then only the minimum amount of violence necessary may be used. The purpose of just-war theory is not to encourage war, but first to prevent it and then to limit it as much as possible. In fact, the U.S. bishops have also referred to it as limited-war theory (*The Challenge of Peace,* 80).

War must be the last resort for resolving a conflict.

✳ *Student art:* Technical pen; Robert Green, Boylan Catholic High School, Rockford, Illinois

In *The Challenge of Peace* (85–99), the U.S. bishops restated the criteria for determining why and when going to war is justified. Note that *all* the following criteria must be met for a war to be considered just.

Just-war criteria

Just cause. War is permissible only to confront "a real and certain danger," to protect innocent life, to preserve conditions necessary for decent human existence, and to secure basic human rights. Wars of vengeance are not permissible.

Competent authority. War must be declared by those with responsibility for public order, not by private groups or individuals.

Comparative justice. The party considering war must ask: Are the rights or values at stake consistent with Christian justice, and are they important enough to justify killing? Even if the answer is yes, no one should assume they have "absolute justice" on their side because no one is free from sin. In choosing war, the nation must be aware that its "just cause" for war is limited, and that its actions should therefore also be limited.

Right intention. War can only be waged for the reasons set forth above as a just cause. The intention must also be to use the least amount of force necessary to achieve the goal of justice; for example, soldiers should prefer capturing the enemy over wounding him, or wounding the enemy over killing him. Once war has begun, sincere efforts at peace must continue to be pursued. The enemy should not be forced to accept unreasonable demands, such as unconditional surrender.

Last resort. War must be the last resort for resolving a conflict. All other reasonable possibilities for a peaceful resolution must have been attempted in the time available.

Probability of success. To avoid causing even greater damage than would result otherwise, war should only be attempted if it is likely to succeed in achieving justice. For example, a weak country should not attempt to fight the invasion of a much stronger aggressor if doing so will only result in its greater destruction.

Proportionality. The good to be gained by a war should outweigh the damage and the costs, both material and spiritual, to be caused by it. For example, during the Vietnam war, the U.S. bishops concluded that the damage being done to each side could not justify the continuation of the war.

In addition to these criteria for determining whether it is just to go to war, two criteria apply throughout the war itself. The principle of proportionality just mentioned applies not only to the decision to go to war but also to each decision to use violence during the war. The principle of **discrimination** also applies throughout the war: lethal force may only be directed at those who are threatening to do violence. Noncombatants such as children, prisoners of war, and other civilians may not be targeted. **M**

Is a just war possible today?

As you can see, the criteria for a just war are very difficult to meet. The criteria were originally designed to limit and reduce violence at a time when wars were fought

M Find a short description of a twentieth-century war in an encyclopedia or a history book. In a short written report, tell whether you think the war met just-war criteria. Support your answer by referring to the criteria. (You may not have enough information to address each of the criteria; if so, explain what information is missing.)

with swords and arrows, and some have argued that modern weapons make it virtually impossible to meet all the criteria today. As the U.S. bishops put it, the decision to go to war "requires extraordinarily strong reasons for overriding the presumption *in favor of peace* and *against* war" (*The Challenge of Peace,* 83).

In fact, it is impossible for some forms of warfare to meet just-war criteria under any circumstances. The bishops of the Second Vatican Council condemned what they called total warfare:

> Any act of war aimed indiscriminately at the destruction of entire cities or extensive areas along with their population is a crime against God and [humanity]. It merits unequivocal and unhesitating condemnation. (*The Church in the Modern World,* 80)

The Council's condemnation of indiscriminate destruction can be understood to have

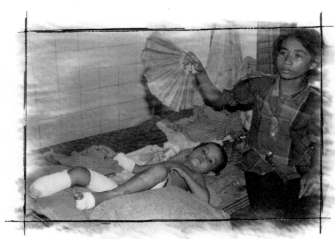

The U.S. Catholic church actively campaigns to ban land mines, which injure or kill twenty-six thousand people— such as this young Cambodian—every year.

condemned all weapons that kill both the aggressors and innocent bystanders—nuclear, chemical, and biological weapons, for example. The church also has condemned land mines, which injure or kill twenty-six thousand people annually—90 percent of whom are civilians.

Still, the church says that for the time being, nations have the duty to defend their citizens in accordance with just-war criteria when no other options are available:

> As long as the danger of war persists and there is no competent and sufficiently powerful authority at the international level, governments cannot be denied the right of legitimate defence, once every means of peaceful settlement has been exhausted. (*The Church in the Modern World,* 79)

Pacifism or Just War?

Although the church accepts both the just-war and the pacifist response to violence, it reminds those who follow each approach of their obligation to meet the concerns of those who take the other way. Those who refuse to fight for the sake of peace are still obliged to seek justice, and those who wage just wars are obligated to always seek peace.

In *The Challenge of Peace,* the U.S. bishops emphasize the right of individuals to refuse to fight—not for reasons of cowardice, but for reasons of conscience. If an individual, in good conscience, sees all wars as immoral, she or he may object to being forced to serve, or drafted, in the military. The legal term for such opposition is

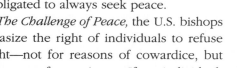

N Do you believe a just war is possible today? Why or why not? Be prepared to discuss your position in class.

called **conscientious objection,** and someone who applies for this status under U.S. law is a **conscientious objector.**

The bishops also teach that individuals may practice **selective conscientious objection,** or "objection to participation in a *particular* war, either because of the ends being pursued or the means being used" (233, emphasis added). Current U.S. law does not allow for selective conscientious objection. Nonetheless, the church insists that Christians, even enlisted soldiers, may refuse to participate in a given war or follow certain orders if he or she views them as immoral. 🕐

For example, when the United States conducted a prolonged low-intensity bombing campaign against Iraq in the late 1990s, the U.S. Catholic bishops seriously questioned whether the action met just-war criteria. So, the U.S. Archdiocese for Military Services reminded enlisted Catholics that they had a responsibility to make conscientious decisions about the morality of their superiors' orders:

> In executing orders that might violate just war requirements, military personnel face a serious moral challenge. . . . Any individual who judges an action on his or her part to be in violation of the moral law is bound to avoid that action.

Any war is a failure of humanity to live up to its **full potential.**

To sum up the church's teaching, we can say that resorting to strictly limited violence, including war, may be better than doing nothing in the face of extreme injustice. On the other hand, the church also insists that resolving conflict through love is always better than resolving it through violence. The history of modern warfare attests that even limited wars cause injury, death, and destruction. As such, any war is a failure of humanity to live up to its full potential.

Although the U.S. Catholic bishops reaffirmed that just-war theory plays an important role in "limiting the resort to force in human affairs," they also emphasized that "it is not a sufficient response to Vatican II's challenge 'to undertake a completely fresh reappraisal of war'" (23). Their insight reflects a growing interest in waging peace, rather than waging war, to achieve justice.

Soldiers in the Gulf war

🕐 Do you think that people who voluntarily enlist in the military should have the right to selectively refuse to fight in conflicts they believe do not meet just-war criteria? Be prepared to discuss your position.

For Review

10. Define *peace*. What are two prerequisites of peace?
11. How is Jesus' cross the source of all peace?
12. What role does grace play in the Christian response to violence?
13. Describe pacifism and just-war theory. How are they the same, and how do they differ?
14. What type of war does the church say is never justified?
15. What rights and obligations does the church say people should consider when deciding whether and how to participate in war?

16. Suppose a nation is considering going to war. What questions does the church say should be asked to determine whether going to war is justified? What questions should be asked during the war itself?

Waging Peace Through Love

While defending the validity of the just-war approach, the U.S. bishops point to nonviolent tactics as the best way to challenge aggression:

> We believe work to develop non-violent means of fending off aggression and resolving conflict best reflects the call of Jesus both to love and to justice. Indeed, each increase in the potential destructiveness of weapons and therefore of war serves to underline the rightness of the way that Jesus mandated to his followers. (*The Challenge of Peace*, 78)

How can the principles of nonviolence be used to promote peace in a violent world?

When the father of Tiffani and Melanie Howell (*far left and far right*) was murdered, students at Loyola College Prep in Shreveport, Louisiana, responded by forming a group that works to overcome the injustice that gives rise to violence.

Peace between individuals can lead to peace between nations.

Waging Peace
One Person at a Time

The spiral of violence teaches us that small-scale violence often leads to large-scale violence. But the opposite is also true: peace between individuals can lead to peace between nations. Here are some specific ways individuals are promoting peace.

Stopping violence *before* it starts

The best time to stop violence is before it starts, and the best way to do that is by promoting justice.

When the father of Tiffani Howell was murdered by two twenty-year-old men, her classmates at Loyola College Prep in Shreveport, Louisiana, got angry enough to take long-term action against the violence in their community.

It began with the freshman class's suggestion to hold a March Against Violence through Shreveport on behalf of Tiffani's father and other local murder victims. They also formed a chapter of the group called Students Against Violence Everywhere (SAVE). The group visits people in nursing homes, educates others about the violence of abortion and hunger, raises money for women facing crisis pregnancies, and holds food drives that provide as many as 750 families with Thanksgiving dinners.

The diversity of the group's activities reflects the students' insight that violence begins with injustice. "We can help reduce violence by examining our hearts and living lives that are consistent with peacemaking," senior Kristi Gallion told her classmates during the March Against Violence. "The path to a more peaceful future is found in a rediscovery of personal responsibility, respect for human life, human dignity, and a recommitment to social justice."

Solidarity

In general, people are less likely to commit violence against people they know and respect. Building relationships with others fosters solidarity, and therefore peace.

Throughout Israel, most Arabs and Jews choose to live apart—the legacy of decades of deadly animosity between them. At The Oasis of Peace, however, Muslims, Jews, and Christians live together in community, choosing to know rather than fear one another. Founded by Fr. Bruno Hussar, the village's School for Peace offers the opportunity for Palestinian and Jewish students to meet and talk with one another in a peaceful environment.

For Ahmad Hijazi, a sixteen-year-old Palestinian student, the facilitated meeting with the Jewish students was life changing. They talked, argued, and, in the end, were able to tell one another with real honesty of the mutual distrust, fear, and anger they bore. Many cried, remembering friends or family who had been killed by one side or the other. "As we envisioned steps to a more peaceful future, we saw each other with new eyes, as human beings," says Ahmad, who later became a leader of the village. "Although governments sign peace treaties, ordinary citizens still have to learn to overcome their fear and prejudices in order to build a peace that endures" (Klippel and Burde, in *Stone Soup for the World,* page 242).

Creating a culture of peace

Cultural pressures may help to cause violence—but they can also be powerful tools for peace. Peacemakers confront and nonviolently oppose those committing violence, and call for the rest of society to do the same. One such peacemaker is Jennifer Flament, a Catholic high school student who has marched, lobbied, and organized for peace.

Jenny first learned about the School of the Americas while preparing to travel to Washington, D.C., to lobby her congressional representatives on justice issues. The "school" is run by the U.S. military to train Latin American military officers in the virtues of democracy and civilian control over the military. "The problem is that they are not only taught the traditional [military] strategies, but declassified teaching manuals have revealed that they are also trained to kill, rape, torture, blackmail, and make people 'disappear,'" Jenny says. Indeed, the United Nations and other human rights organizations have linked the school's graduates to many such atrocities.

After lobbying her congressional representatives to support legislation closing the school, Jenny joined the thousands of protesters who march every year for the school's closing. "Hundreds of crosses [were] being held high [by the crowd], each had a name written across the front, and I knew that each represented a man, woman, or child who had been killed by graduates of the School of the Americas."

Jenny continued her work for peace by starting a student chapter of Amnesty International, an organization that works to fight human rights abuses around the world. "As a Catholic, I feel that it is my duty to fight for those who cannot," she says.

Nonviolent resistance

What would you do if a man kicked in your bedroom door in the middle of the night, the house was empty, and the phone was downstairs? Angie O'Gorman, an advocate of nonviolence, describes her own reaction:

"He was somewhat verbally abusive as he walked over to my bed. As I lay there, feeling a fear and vulnerability that I had never before experienced, several thoughts ran through my head. The first was the uselessness of screaming. The second was the fallacy of thinking safety depends on having a gun hidden under your pillow. Somehow I could not imagine this man standing patiently while I reached under my pillow for my gun. The third thought, I believe, saved my life. I realized with a certain clarity that either he and I made it through this situation safely—together—or we would both be damaged. If he raped me, I would be hurt both physically and emotionally. If he raped me, he would be hurt as well. . . . That thought did not free me from feelings of fear but from fear's control over my ability to respond. I found myself acting out of concern for both our safety. . . ."

She asked him what time it was. When he responded, she commented that his

Every year, thousands of people—including many Catholics—march on the U.S. Army School of the Americas, demanding that it be closed because many of its graduates have violated human rights.

watch might be broken, because it didn't match the time on her clock. She asked how he got in, and commented that it was too bad that he had broken the glass on the back door because she didn't have the money to replace it. He shared his own problems. "We talked until we were no longer strangers and I felt it was safe to ask him to leave," she says. When he refused, she offered to let him sleep downstairs. "He went downstairs, and I sat in bed, wide awake and shaking for the rest of the night. The next morning we ate breakfast together and he left." ("Defense Through Disarmament")

The church teaches that individuals have a right to defend themselves—with limited violence, if necessary. But O'Gorman and other advocates of nonviolence suggest that nonviolent non-cooperation can surprise an attacker who expects his victim to respond either violently or helplessly. In that moment of surprise, he might reconsider his actions—as O'Gorman's experience demonstrates.

Reconciling broken relationships

When we have already been harmed by violence, or have harmed another, we still have an opportunity to break the spiral of violence through **reconciliation,** the mending of broken relationships.

Many veterans of the war in Vietnam have since returned to that country to reconcile with their former enemies, in word and deed. Those efforts have resulted in a number of projects, including a Vietnamese-American Peace Park near Bac Giang, and the creation of Friendship Village. The village provides a caring home for children and adults who were affected by the toxin Agent Orange, which U.S. planes sprayed widely in the Vietnam jungle during the war. "This represents healing and reconstruction," said veteran George Mizo. "Those who have experienced the horrors of war know how precious life is" ("Veteran-Sponsored Village Opens for Kids, Elderly in Vietnam").

Waging Peace on a Global Scale

Although waging peace on a global scale begins with the choices of individuals on a local level, the structures of global injustice and violence are too large for any one person to change alone. Instead, the international community of nations must work together for peace. These four strategies can help: promoting human development, demilitarization, diplomacy, and learning nonviolence.

"As a Catholic, I feel that it is my duty to fight for those who cannot."

 Choose one of the ways of waging peace one person at a time and explain how it could be applied in your school or community.

WHAT YOU CAN DO . . .

- Practice the principles of nonviolence in arguments and disputes by trying to focus on the humanity of your opponent. Say a prayer: "Give me the wisdom and courage to settle this fight in a way that respects the dignity of both of us."
- Avoid media that promote a culture of violence.
- Speak up whenever you see violence—whether it is physical or verbal—being used against someone. If you're afraid to speak up against the violence, get the help of others who might speak up with you, or tell a responsible adult.
- Practice solidarity by reaching out to people outside your social group.
- Join Amnesty International, or form a chapter at your school, and write letters urging foreign governments to release those who have been unjustly imprisoned.
- Start a mediation program for peacefully resolving fights and conflicts at your school. Or offer to start one at a local elementary school.
- Find out what organizations in your community are doing to stop violence, then get involved. Or start your own nonviolent campaign with the help of some supportive adults or community leaders. ☞

"Those who have experienced the horrors of war know how precious life is."

✳ *Student art:* "Peace." Charcoal; Matthew Guerrero, Notre Dame High School, Sherman Oaks, California

Promoting human development

We have already discussed the link between injustice and physical violence. Efforts to combat injustice can eliminate the cause of many wars before they begin:

Injustice, excessive economic or social inequalities, envy, distrust, and pride raging among [people] and nations constantly threaten peace and cause wars. Everything done to overcome these disorders contributes to building up peace and avoiding war. (*Catechism of the Catholic Church,* 2317)

Demilitarization

The Second Vatican Council clearly stated its opposition to a dependence on militarism, calling the arms race "one of the greatest curses on the human race" (*Catechism,* 2329).

If nations were to follow just-war criteria, they would scale back their militaries to only the level needed to defend their own territories, and rely on cooperation with other nations to defend weaker nations against aggression or internal strife. Defense-oriented militaries tend to be smaller, and therefore take fewer resources from other social needs. With a smaller, defense-oriented military, nations tend to be less tempted to wage war for their own economic or political interests.

Demilitarization—reducing the reliance on military force to ensure peace—is not impossible. At least seven nations have given up their nuclear weapons capability after acquiring it. And more than 130 nations have signed a treaty banning the production and use of land mines (although by 2000, the United States had not). Ultimately, though, demilitarization requires a cultural change in attitudes toward violence and war.

Diplomacy

Some of the greatest achievements of global peacemaking have occurred through the use of **diplomacy,** in which nations resolve disputes through talks and negotiations with one another. The goal of diplomacy is to craft a creative solution that addresses the legitimate concerns of each party.

The principle of **reciprocity,** in which each side holds itself to the same standards that it wishes to impose on other nations, provides a useful guide for diplomacy. Reciprocity would suggest, for example, that if the developed nations want underdeveloped nations to limit their pollution, the developed nations must also commit to reducing their own pollution.

Often, the mediation of a third party, one not directly involved in the dispute, can help the adversaries overcome obstacles to a solution. For decades, Catholic social teaching has viewed the United Nations as a potentially powerful instrument of peace, and has called for its increased authority in order to increase its ability to prevent and resolve conflicts peacefully.

South Korean President Kim Dae-jung (left) used diplomacy to reach out to North Koreans after nearly fifty years of hostility between the two nations. He was awarded the Nobel Peace Prize for his efforts, which led to a historic meeting with North Korean leader Kim Jong-il.

Imagine you are an ambassador to the United Nations. Draft a proposal for making the world more peaceful, listing the specific steps the nations of the world would need to take. Keep in mind that according to the principle of reciprocity, your country should do what it asks other nations to do. Be prepared to discuss your proposal in class.

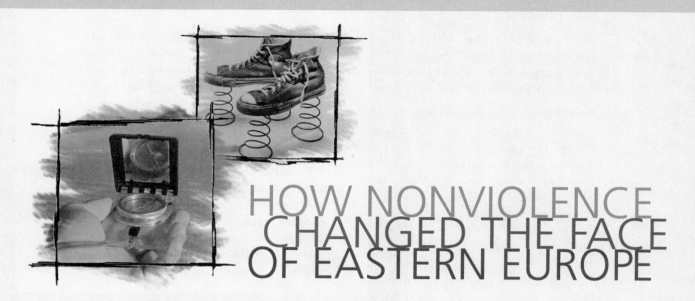

HOW NONVIOLENCE CHANGED THE FACE OF EASTERN EUROPE

For decades during the cold war,

Western powers spent trillions of dollars and lost tens of thousands of lives trying to "contain" communism. But in 1989, it was people with prayers, candles, and songs—not tanks and planes—who liberated Eastern Europe from communism.

Pope John Paul II remarked on that liberation in the 1991 encyclical *On the Hundredth Anniversary of Rerum Novarum (Centesimus Annus):*

> [The fall of communism in Eastern Europe] was accomplished almost everywhere by means of peaceful protest, using only the weapons of truth and justice. . . . It seemed that the European order resulting from World War II . . . could only be overturned by another war. Instead, it has been overcome by the non-violent commitment of people who, while always refusing to yield to the force of power, succeeded time after time in finding effective ways of bearing witness to the truth. . . . I pray that this example will prevail in other places and other circumstances. May people learn to fight for justice without violence. (23)

Left: Czechoslovakians light candles on the spot where nonviolent student demonstrators were attacked by police. The students' demonstration led to the Velvet Revolution and the end of communism in Czechoslovakia. *Right:* A West German hammers away at the Berlin Wall. After forty years, thousands of peaceful Christian protesters brought down the wall.

How could unarmed people win their freedom against one of the greatest military powers in the world? It all began in Poland, where forty years of resistance to communism culminated in the formation of Solidarity, a hugely popular free workers' union. Solidarity initially protested high living costs and food shortages, but quickly became a popular movement to win greater freedom. Being devoutly religious, the Solidarity leadership refused to use violence, even after the union was outlawed in 1981 and many of its leaders were jailed or killed. Its struggle continued until 1989, when it negotiated political reforms that led to the first free elections—which Solidarity won.

The collapse of communism in Poland led to other people's revolutions in Eastern Europe. On 17 November 1989, a crowd of three thousand students holding banners that called for the release of political prisoners, "Justice for all" and "Freedom," attempted to march to Wenceslas Square in Prague, Czechoslovakia. When police in riot gear blocked their way, they sat down and began to sing old Beatles' hits, hymns, and the national anthem. "We have no weapons," they chanted.

The police responded by attacking the crowd with clubs. But outrage over the attack sparked protests by the larger population. Some 200,000 people marched on 20 November, encouraged by Cardinal Frantisek Tomasek, who told them, "With God's help, our

Beginning in the late 1970s, thousands of people met in small base communities in churches to discuss peace, human rights, and concern for the environment.

The revolution that grew out of these church groups in the fall of 1989 was called the Revolution of Light because as people left the Monday-night prayer meetings to gather for small protests in the streets, they held a candle with one hand and shielded it with the other—to show they had no weapons.

At first, the few thousand protesters were met by attacks from the state police. But they continued anyway, week after week through the fall. When the government gave up on the use of force, tens of thousands, then millions flooded the streets of Leipzig and East Berlin. Finally, on the night of 8 November 1989, the government opened the Berlin Wall, which for thirty years had stood as a sign of the regime's oppression: "On the stroke of twelve, both sides of Berlin erupted," said one news report. "Laughing, crying, shouting, and singing, the crowds poured through the crossings, and, where they were packed tight, up and over the wall" (Adapted from Nielsen, *Revolutions in Eastern Europe,* pages 25–48, 85–102).

The revolutions in Eastern Europe and elsewhere show that Jesus' way is a realistic response to violence—although it is not guaranteed to succeed without bloodshed. When

May people learn to fight for justice without violence.

fate now lies in our hands." A general strike by all workers and even larger protests continued until a noncommunist government took power on 10 December. Not one life was lost in what became known as the Velvet Revolution.

It was a similar story in East Germany, where the churches were the only place that people were allowed to freely speak out.

tens of thousands of students in China staged a massive protest for democracy, for instance, it ended with as many as three thousand being massacred by the army.

But a violent response to injustice is just as dangerous as a nonviolent one, if not more so. The question the world must answer is, Which way will ultimately bring true peace? ☙

By acting as if Poland were already a free country, the worker-led Solidarity movement created a free country.

Learning nonviolence

The story of the Filipino people's revolution that opened this chapter is a good example of how nonviolent non-cooperation can prevent armed conflict. Boycotts, strikes, and mass **civil disobedience**—intentionally breaking unjust laws—have all been used successfully as "weapons" in nonviolent struggles. Walter Wink describes how a pervasive spirit of nonviolent non-cooperation helped the Solidarity movement in Poland topple the communist regime without the use of weapons:

> Solidarity in Poland proved that Jesus' nonviolent way could be lived even under the circumstances of a communist regime and martial law. People said to one another, in effect, ". . . Start being what you think society should become. Do you believe in freedom of speech? Then speak freely. Do you love the truth? Then tell it. Do you believe in an open society? Then act in the open." . . . This behavior actually caught on, leading to an "epidemic of freedom in the closed society." By acting "as if" Poland were already a free country, Solidarity *created* a free country. (*Engaging the Powers,* page 265)

To be most successful, nonviolent action requires training—just as any army does. The success of the Filipino revolution, for instance, was due in part to the churches training thousands of people in nonviolence.

Embargoes and economic sanctions are forms of nonviolent action sometimes used by countries to resist a nation committing violence or injustice. **Embargoes** are used to prevent a nation from importing goods, and **economic sanctions** use various methods to "fine" a nation. These tools must be used carefully, however, because they have the potential to cause violence. The United Nations has found that the broad embargo imposed on Iraq was directly responsible for the deaths of hundreds of thousands of Iraqi children. On the other hand, economic sanctions against South Africa—prompted in part by the work of college students—put pressure on that country to end apartheid.

An Option for the Brave

Waging peace requires all the courage, willpower, and perseverance that are needed to wage war—but it also requires imagination, patience, and humility. Peace may be more difficult to wage than war, but in the long run, the benefits for all humanity seem to be worth its added challenges.

If you still are uncertain about how peace can be achieved in such a violent world, then you are not alone—humanity is still learning

Using the quote about Solidarity as an example, make a statement of your personal commitment to peace. List what you believe would make society truly peaceful, then state your commitment to being that peace yourself: "I believe . . . therefore I will . . ."

the ways of peace. Peacemakers are those who are committed to keep learning those ways until true peace is achieved for all.

That is what Paolo and his people have done. Although they still struggle for peace, their nonviolent revolution was a beginning and a cause for hope. At a celebration following that victory, Sr. Sheila Lucey watched twenty white doves fly up into the sky trailing yellow ribbons, "Perhaps they could be a symbol of what we hope will come to our people: peace, accompanied by joy, and always the saving grace of good humor and the spirit of celebration" (Mercado, editor, *People Power,* page 209).

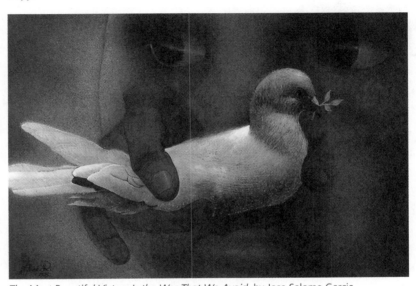

The Most Beautiful Victory Is the War That We Avoid, by Jose Salome Garcia

17. List the five suggested ways of waging peace one person at a time, briefly explaining how each promotes peace.
18. How can demilitarization reduce the likelihood of violent conflict?
19. Explain the principle of reciprocity.
20. What are some of the tools of nonviolent non-cooperation, and what is required for it to be most successful?

21. Based on what you have learned in this chapter, how do you think peace among individual people and peace on a global level are interrelated?

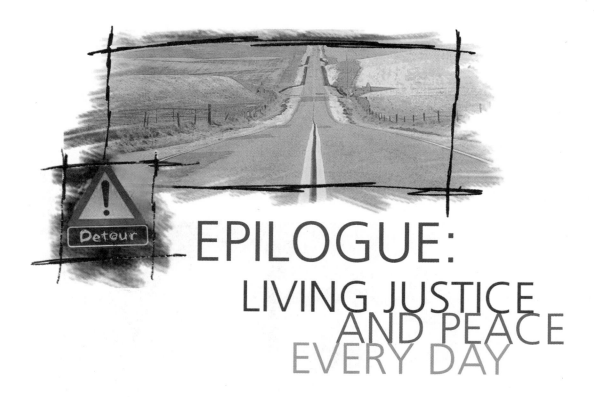

EPILOGUE:
LIVING JUSTICE
AND PEACE
EVERY DAY

As you complete this course, you may be wondering whether Jesus' mission to bring good news to the poor, new sight to the blind, and freedom to the oppressed is realistic in today's complicated world. Sometimes learning about all the world's injustice can leave us feeling overwhelmed and even hopeless about the possibility of changing it.

The church acknowledges that the world cannot become all it is meant to be through human effort alone. And yet it believes that justice and peace will one day reign on earth. The source of its hope is the grace that God has poured out on the world through Jesus. When we seek justice and peace, we allow that grace to work through us to bring the Reign of God closer to fulfillment.

We alone cannot change the world. But by being open to God's grace and by working together, we can build a world of justice and peace.

This is the insight that student Katie Halupczok had in chapter 8: We do not need to work for justice and peace alone, but accompanied by God's grace—and one another. The U.S. Catholic bishops affirm this insight in their 1999 pastoral reflection *Everyday Christianity: To Hunger and Thirst for Justice*. We are called "to be instruments of God's grace and creative power" as members of a larger community:

> This vocation to pursue justice is not simply an individual task—it is a call to work with others to humanize and shape the institutions that touch so many people. The lay vocation for justice cannot be carried forward alone, but only as members of a community called to be the "leaven" of the Gospel.

Although we do not need to feel personally responsible for "saving the world," neither can we leave all the work to church and political leaders, or heroic figures like Mother Teresa, Jean Donovan, or Craig Kielburger. The world is shaped by the actions of each person. Only as each of us chooses to act for justice and peace will the world begin to become all that God and humanity desire for it to be. **A**

Right Here, Right Now

Changing the world around us "does not mean leaving worldly tasks and responsibilities, but transforming them," the U.S. Catholic bishops write in *Everyday Christianity*. In other words, we do not need to wait until we join an organization, have lots of time, or graduate from school before we begin to transform the world. We can begin with our everyday actions, right here and right now. Wherever we are is the best place for each of us to pursue justice.

In families

Because the family is the most basic social group, it is "the starting point and the center of a vocation for justice":

> How we treat our parents, spouses and children is a reflection of our commitment to Christ's love and justice. We demonstrate our commitment to the Gospel by how we spend our time and money, and whether our family life includes an ethic of charity, service and action for justice. *(Everyday Christianity)* **B**

Wherever we are is the best place for each of us to pursue justice.

A As you complete this course, what do you dream a just and peaceful world might look like? Make your description as specific as possible. How has your vision changed since you began this course?

B What can you do in your everyday life, beginning today, to make your dream for a more just and peaceful world a reality? Make a list of the people and places you encounter in your everyday life. For each place, list as many specific ways as you can think of that you might choose justice and peace. Use the seven themes of Catholic social teaching as a guide.

In the workplace

Because we shape the world around us through our work, our workplace offers many opportunities for pursuing justice. We can work with care and creativity, and whether we are employers or employees, we can ensure that concern for people and the environment is a top priority in making workplace decisions. "Catholics have the often difficult responsibility of choosing between competing values in the workplace. This is a measure of holiness" *(Everyday Christianity)*.

In the marketplace

Our purchasing decisions have far-reaching consequences for people and the planet. By one estimate, U.S. teens spend nearly $100 billion annually. This economic power can be used for justice by putting people before products. That means living more simply and educating ourselves about the consequences of our economic decisions. By consuming with care for people and the planet, we can use our economic power to make a better world.

In school

Education promotes justice by helping people realize their talents and become more fully all they are meant to be. It also enables people to participate in the community socially, politically, and economically. We can imitate the example of Kelly Jefferson (chapter 4) and other students by working to ensure that our schools not only teach justice but also reflect justice by treating students with dignity and offering a good education to all.

In the community

As citizens, each of us has a measure of political power—and the responsibility to use it for justice and peace. We can fulfill our responsibility by voting, talking with our

Participating in the political process and voting are ways we can promote justice and peace in our everyday lives.

elected representatives, and, if we are called to do so, becoming community leaders or elected officials ourselves.

Together, We Can Realize the Dream

In short, each of us is called to respond to injustice wherever we happen to encounter it in our life's journey. Throughout this course, we have seen dozens of young people who responded with compassionate action to the suffering they encountered—and so made a difference in their part of the world. Each of us has the power to do the same in our own way. We each have been given unique talents, passions, and life experiences that only we can contribute to the world.

If we do that much, then our dream for a better world will come closer to becoming a reality. Craig Kielburger, (chapter 6) the twelve-year-old boy who accomplished so much by responding compassionately to the story of Iqbal Masih, reflects on the possibilities:

> Some call young people idealists, as if it were a stage they need to outgrow. But I feel the world could do with more idealists, that there are never too many dreamers.
>
> It was the dreamers of the world who thought that one day the Berlin Wall would fall, that apartheid in South Africa would end, and that a human would walk on the moon. Because we are young, full of ideals, and full of dreams, we are not afraid of taking an idea that to some seems impossible and striving to make it a reality. . . .

People have to have faith in themselves and faith that they can change the world. Because it is true—we *can* change the world, one person at a time. Imagine if all the students in a school came together on one issue they believed in. Imagine the power they would have. If people across a community, across a country, across the continents, united to tell the world that no child should have to live in poverty, in abuse and neglect, the power they would have would be incredible. Others would have to stand up and listen, and learn there is a better way for all people to live. (*Free the Children,* pages 291–293) C

C Using the guidelines in this epilogue, write down your own personal pledge of commitment to living justice and peace every day. If you like, include a prayer asking God for the grace to fulfill your commitment.

Italic page numbers are references to photos or illustrations.

conversion, 162–163

Costa Rica, 281–282

Creation story: of Babylonians, 16–17; call to stewardship in, 267–268, 272–273; and the Fall, 19–21; goodness of humans in, 15, 18–19; of interdependent world, 72–73, 256, 257–258; purpose of, 14; work's reflection of, 70, 175–176

criminal-justice system: flaws of, 125–126; retributive justice of, 116–117; victim offender mediation and dialogue programs of, 133–134

criminals: flawed punishment of, 125–126; human dignity of, 124; restorative justice for, 132–133; retributive justice for, 116–117; victim's dialogue with, 133–134

crisis pregnancy centers, 135

cross, the: as sign of love, 35, 38; as source of peace, 304

CRS (Catholic Relief Services), *71,* 246–247

Cuban missile crisis, *55*

culture: defined, 82; questioning the values of, 86; stereotypes from, 151–153; worldview shaped by, 83–84

culture of death, 127–128

culture of life: defined, 129–130; restorative justice of, 132–134; societal aids in, 134–135; solidarity of, 138

Curitiba (Brazil), 248–250

cycle of poverty: defined, 201; and disease, 210, 213–214; and homelessness, 88–90, 206–207, 214–215; and hunger, 205–206, 213; and inadequate education, 207–208, 215; and welfare system, 178–179, 209–210. *See also* poverty

Czechoslovakia, *316,* 317

development: defined, 226; economic principles of, 238–240; global cost of, 232; human aspects of, 241, 243

The Development of Peoples (Populorum Progressio), 53

The Diary of a Country Priest (Bernanos), 50

dignity of work: defined, 69–70, 172–173, 174–175; requirements for, 183; solidarity's role in, 190–191; violation of, 176–178; ways to restore, 186–187. *See also* work

diplomacy, 315

direct action: defined, 98; of feeding the hungry, 245–246; with social action, 98–99

discrimination: defined, 154; in developing countries, 218–219; as principle of just-war theory, 307, 308; racial, 154–157; within social structures, 157–159, 207–208

disease: global statistics on, 213–214; Jesus on, 34; in Jewish society, 33; lack of health care for, 210

Donovan, Jean, 12, 29–30

E

East Germany, 317

ecological economics, 276–277

economic initiative, 183

Economic Justice for All (pastoral letter), 46, 54, 144, 145, 147, 149, 178, 200, 238–239

economics: of consumerism, 227–231; defined, 226; of development process, 238–240; ecological, 276–277; individualistic view of, 231; sustainable practices of, 274, 277–282

economic sanctions, 318

ecotourism, 282

education: of children in poverty, 207–208; global statistics on, 215; right to, 184. *See also* schools

Eichenberg, Fritz, *The First Seven Days,* *14*

embargoes, 318

encyclicals, 46

enemies: command to love, 34, 103–104; Gandhi's respect for, 104–105

enlightened self-interest, 11

Enlightenment, 46–47

Enuma Elish (Babylonian creation story), 16–17

environment. *See* natural resources

ethnic cleansing, 215

Eucharist: response to poverty through, 235, 236–237, 238, 245–246; as source of life, 234

euthanasia, 128

Evangelization in the Modern World (Evangelii Nuntiandi), 53

Everyday Christianity (pastoral letter), 174

exclusion: converting to inclusion from, 163–166; cycle of, 159; excuses for, 151; focused on difference, 144, 156; injustice of, 147; personal experiences of, 150–151; racial, 154–156; structural, 157–159

Exodus, Book of, 23

F

family, the: participation in, 60; pursuit of justice in, 321; subsidiarity's role in, 61; work's support of, 174, 182–183

Feminists for Life (organization), 112, 135

Feuerstein, Aaron, 190

The First Seven Days (Eichenberg), *14*

Free the Children (organization), 171–172, 186, 189

free will, 19–20

French Revolution, 47

friendship. *See* solidarity

Friendship Village (Vietnam), 313

G

Gage, Frances, 27

Gandhi, Mohandas Karamchand, 104–105, 299, 305

Garden of Eden, 19

Genesis, Book of: caring for creation in, 70, 72–73, 267–268; Creation stories in, 14–15, 18–19; the Fall in, 19–21

Gibbons, James (cardinal of Baltimore), 49

globalization of the economy: defined, 191; effects of, on workers, 192–193

global warming, 263, 266

God: Adam and Eve's separation from, 19–21; compassion of, 22–23, 29–30, 38; creative goodness of, 15, 18, 272–273; grace of, 21; humans' intimacy with, 19; is love, 14. *See also* image of God

good Samaritan parable, 160–161

The Gospel of Life (Evangelium Vitae), 54, 123, 127

grace: defined, 21; needed for peace, 304–305, 320–321

Great Depression, 42–43

greenhouse gases, 263, 271

Griffin, John Howard, 154–156

Gulf war, 309

Gutiérrez, Gustavo, 67

H

Hanukkah, 142–143
health care for the poor, 210
Hebblethwaite, Margaret, 99
Heritage and Hope (pastoral letter), 165
hidden homeless, 206–207
hierarchy of needs, Maslow's, 201, 202
Hiroshima (Japan), 298, *299;* Children's
  Peace Memorial in, *303*
homelessness: action to overcome,
  97–98, 198–199, 247–248; analyzing
  causes of, 88–90; awareness of, 80;
  of hidden homeless, 206–207; love-
  centered worldview of, 84–87; of
  refugees, 215; of rural migrants, 214;
  U.S. statistics on, 206. *See also* hunger
hope: compassion with, 12; defined, 10;
  grace's restoration of, 21; during Great
  Depression, 43; for oppressed peoples, 23
hopelessness: defined, 10; of poor and
  vulnerable people, 210–211
housing: discrimination in, 158–159; of
  hidden homeless, 206–207; shortage
  of affordable, 209, 210
Hubka, Rachel, 190–191
human dignity: action to promote, 99,
  102–106; community's protection of,
  144, 145–147, 163–164; creation's ties
  to, 256, 258, 283; of criminals, 124;
  economy's affirmation of, 238–240;
  Gandhi's belief in, 104–105; harmed
  by consumerism, 230–231; harmed
  by original sin, 20–21; harmed by
  prejudice, 153–154; harmed by racial
  discrimination, 154–157; harmed by
  structural discrimination, 93, 157–159,
  207–208; human rights' protection of,
  147, 148–149; of living simply, 241,
  243; through participation, 60–61; of
  the poor, 220–221; poverty's denial of,
  200–201; source of, 15, 18; universal
  principle of, 57–58, 113, 119; violence
  against, 290; of work, 69–70, 172–173,
  174–175, 183. *See also* dignity of work
human life: community's protection of,
  144; from conception to birth,
  118–119, 120–121; creation's
  interdependence with, 72–73, 256,
  257–258, 261, 274–275, 283; in culture
  of death, 127–128; in culture of life,
  129–130; of unborn child, 114, 120;
  universal respect for, 58, 113, 119
human relationships: absence or breakdown of, 292–293; consumerism's
  effect on, 231; fostered by living
  simply, 241, 243, 245–246, 247–248;
  fostered in community, 144, 145–147;
  interdependence of, 90–92, 102–103,

189; of love, 18–19, 34; reconciliation
  of, 313; of respect, 85; use of power
  in, 93–95; work's maintenance of,
  174–176
human rights, 147, 148–149. *See also*
  rights
*The Hundredth Year (Centesimus
  Annus),* 54
hunger: action to overcome, 97–99,
  245–246; analyzing causes of, 91–92;
  myths about, 215–216; in United
  States, 205–206; worldwide, 213. *See
  also* homelessness
Hussar, Fr. Bruno, 311

I

image of God: creativity aspect of, 70,
  175–176; in culture of life, 129–130;
  forgetting our identity as, 230–231;
  free will attribute of, 19; goodness
  attribute of, 15, 18, 57–58; the poor
  as, 201, 203; relationship attribute of,
  18–19, 60, 144
inadequate housing, 206–207
Incarnation, 29–30
inclusion: basic requirements of, 147;
  converting from exclusion to, 163–166;
  defined, 144; in Kingdom of God,
  33–34, 103, 161; Paul's themes of, 146
India, 216–217
indirect employer, 186
individualism, 10–11, 231
Industrial Revolution, 47
informed consent laws, 135
injustice: action to overcome, 97–99,
  321–323; analyzing causes of, 88–90,
  91–92; blindness to, 83–84; of capitalist system, 47–48, 238; defined, 28; of
  exclusive community, 147; Gandhi's
  approach to, 104–105; nonviolent response to, 105–106, 311–313, 316–317,
  318; personal encounters with, 59,
  76–77, 154–157; social structures
  causing, 92–93, 102, 125–126, 157–159,
  207–208; violence tied to, 290–291,
  311, 315; of wealth gap, 227–228,
  232–233; in the workplace, 176–178
institutional violence, 290, 291
integrity of creation, 258. *See also*
  interdependence
interdependence: global level of, 191,
  194; of human relationships, 90–92,
  102–103, 189; of humans with
  creation, 72–73, 256, 257–258, 261,
  274–275, 283
International Labor Organization, 186,
  187
Isaiah, Book of, 25, 28, 30

Israelites. *See* Jews

J

Jesus: delivery from suffering through,
  28, 29–30, 35, 38; inclusiveness of,
  33–34, 103, 161; love-centered
  worldview of, 31–32, 84, 85–86,
  103–104; nonviolence of, 304; parable
  of workers by, 180–181
Jews: Exodus of, from Egypt, 23;
  Kingdom of God for, 31; prophets of,
  24–25; Shema prayer of, 24; social
  world of, 32–34
John Paul II, Pope, 54, 127, 232; on
  abortion, 123; on capital punishment,
  124; on consumerism, 230–231; on fall
  of communism, 316; on work, 181,
  186
John XXIII, Pope, 52, 53
Jonesboro killings, 294
justice: action to create, 97–99, 102–103;
  Catholic social teaching on, 44–45;
  circle of faith-in-action for, 78–79; as
  criteria for war, 306, 307–308; defined,
  28; Dorothy Day's lessons on,
  236–237; for the environment, 72–73,
  256, 257–258, 273–275; everyday
  pursuit of, 107, 321–323; fundamental
  question of, 112; Gandhi's approach
  to, 104–105; God's call to, 25, 28;
  grace needed for, 304–305, 320–321;
  of inclusive community, 146–147; from
  interdependence, 91–92, 102–103;
  Jesus' mission of, 29–30, 33–35,
  44–45, 84, 85–86; joy of, 36–37;
  leading to peace, 303–304, 311;
  restorative, 132; retributive, 116–117;
  social structures blocking, 92–93, 102,
  125–126, 157–159, 207–208; of
  universal destination of goods, 239;
  workers' rights to, 69–70, 176–178,
  180–181
Justice in the World (pastoral letter), 53
Justin (Christian apologist), 305
just wage, 51. *See also* living wage
just-war theory, 306–308

K

Katzeff, Paul, 191, 194
Kielburger, Craig, 171–172, 176–177, 186,
  322–323
Kim Dae-jung, *315*
Kim Jong-il, *315*
King, Martin Luther, Jr., 302

START II (1993), 299
starvation, 205
stereotypes, 151–153
stewardship: by businesses, 279–281; Creation stories of, 267–268, 272–273; defined, 256; by governments, 281–282; humanity's role of, 258; by individuals, 277–278, 282–283; power-over approach versus, 268–270; sustainable economic practices of, 274, 276–277
strikes, labor, 95
structures of sin: how to identify, 93; how to transform, 97–98, 103
Students Against Violence Everywhere (SAVE), 311
subjective aspect of work, 181–182
subsidiarity, 61
subsistence farming, 260–261
suffering: causes of, 14, 20–21, 22; delivery from, through Jesus, 28, 29–30, 35, 38; love-centered world-view of, 130, 138; ways of responding to, 10–13
survival rights, 62
sustainable development (government policy), 281–282
sustainable economic practices: defined, 274; by governments, 281–282; by individuals, 277–278; by industry, 279–281; using ecological economics, 276–277
Suu Kyi, Aung San, 177

T

Teresa, Mother, *28,* 171
A Theology of Liberation (Gutiérrez), 67
thrival rights, 62
Tiananmen Square (1989), *107*
toil, 173
Truth, Sojourner, 26–27

U

Ufford-Chase, Rick, 192–193
unemployment, 99, 102, 178–179
unions, 48, 49, 51, 183, 262
United Nations, 62, 315
United States: affordable housing shortage in, 209; annual refugees to, 215; chronic hunger in, 205–206; education in, 207–208; energy use in, 263, 266; foreign aid budget of, 218, 232; homelessness in, 206–207; income statistics in, *213,* 228; military budget of, 297, *298;* poverty statistics in, 204, 228; spending in, by category,

298; welfare benefits in, 178–179, 209–210
Universal Declaration of Human Rights (United Nations document), 62
universal destination of goods, 239
U.S. **Army School of the Americas,** 312
U.S. **Supreme Court,** 113, 116

V

Velvet Revolution (Czechoslovakia), 317
victim offender mediation and dialogue, 133–134
violence: Babylonian creation story of, 16–17; the church on, 305–306, 308, 309, 310; defined, 290; early Christians on, 305; Gandhi on, 104–105, 299, 305; injustice tied to, 290–291, 311, 315; just-war theory of, 306–307; Martin Luther King Jr. on, 302; love's response to, 289, 304; in the media, 294–295; military use of, 296–297, 298–299; pacifist opposition to, 305–306; in the Philippines, 286–289; youth's experience of, 292–296. *See also* militarism; spiral of violence; war

W

wage gap, 158, *159*
war: conscientious objection to, 308–309; deaths from, 296; just-war criteria for, 306–308; pacifist opposition to, 305–306. *See also* militarism; violence
wealth gap: in parable of Lazarus, 232–233; statistics on, 227–228
welfare: annual U.S. budget for, 209; reform legislation on, 178–179, 210
Werbach, Adam, 254–255
women: Jesus' relations with, 34, 161; protective legislation for, 135; rights of, 27; status of, in Jewish society, 32–33; wage gap of, 158, *159*
work: education requirements for, 184; four purposes of, 174–176; human dignity of, 69–70, 172–173, 174–175, 183; Jesus' parable of, 180–181; objective aspect of, 181–182; pursuit of justice at, 322; responsibility to, 176; right to, 176; solidarity model of, 184, 190–191; subjective aspect of, 181–182; in support of family, 174, 182–183; as toil, 173; unemployment from, 99, 102, 178–179; for welfare recipients, 178–179, 209–210. *See also* dignity of work; rights of workers

worldview: of colonialists, 216–217; cultural origins of, 82–84; of culture of death, 127–128; of culture of life, 129–130; defined, 81; of Gandhi, 104–105; as love-centered, 84–87, 129; personal conversion of, 162–163; of the poor, 201; power-over, 94, 268–270; power-with, 94–95, 103

Acknowledgments (continued)

The quote by M. K. Gandhi on the back cover was found at the M. K. Gandhi Institute for Nonviolence Web site at *www.gandhiinstitute.org,* accessed 24 January 2000.

The scriptural quotations in this book are from the New Revised Standard Version of the Bible. Copyright © 1989 by the Division of Christian Education of the National Council of the Churches of Christ in the United States of America. All rights reserved.

The scriptural quotations in this book marked NAB are from the New American Bible with revised New Testament and revised Psalms. Copyright © 1991, 1986, and 1970 by the Confraternity of Christian Doctrine, Washington, DC 20017-1194. Used with permission. All rights reserved.

The excerpts in this book marked *Catechism of the Catholic Church* or *Catechism* are from the *Catechism of the Catholic Church,* second edition, by the Libreria Editrice Vaticana, translated by the United States Catholic Conference (USCC) (Washington, DC: USCC, 1997). English translation copyright © 1994 by the USCC—Libreria Editrice Vaticana.

The excerpts in this book marked *The Gospel of Life* are from the encyclical letter *The Gospel of Life* (Evangelium Vitae): *On the Value and Inviolability of Human Life,* by Pope John Paul II (Washington, DC: USCC, 1995).

The excerpts in this book marked *Economic Justice for All* are from *Economic Justice for All: Pastoral Letter on Catholic Social Teaching and the U.S. Economy,* by the National Council of Catholic Bishops (NCCB) (Washington, DC: USCC, 1986). Copyright © 1986 by the USCC, Washington, DC. All rights reserved. Used with permission.

The excerpt from Jean Donovan on page 12 is from *Salvador Witness: The Life and Calling of Jean Donovan,* by Ana Carrigan (New York: Simon and Schuster, 1984), page 218. Copyright © 1984 by Ana Carrigan.

The excerpts on pages 17, 305, 305, and 318 are from *Engaging the Powers: Discernment and Resistance in a World of Domination,* by Walter Wink (Minneapolis: Augsburg Fortress, 1992), pages 14–15, 210, 209–210, and 265, respectively. Copyright © 1992 by Augsburg Fortress. Permission applied for.

The excerpt from Saint Augustine on page 19 is from *The Confessions,* Book I, 1.

The excerpt about Sojourner Truth on pages 26–27 is after *The Norton Anthology of Literature by Women: The Tradition in English,* by Sandra M. Gilbert and Susan Gubar (New York: W. W. Norton and Company, 1985), pages 252–253. Copyright © 1985 by Sandra M. Gilbert and Susan Gubar. Used with permission. All rights reserved.

The poem on page 34 is from *Easy Essays,* by Peter Maurin (New York: Sheed and Ward, 1936), page 37. Copyright © 1936 by Sheed and Ward. Reprinted by permission of Sheed and Ward, an Apostolate of the Priests of the Sacred Heart, 7373 South Lover's Lane Road, Franklin, WI 53132.

The excerpt from Lou Nanni on pages 36–37 is quoted in *Doing the Truth in Love: Conversations About God, Relationships, and Service,* by Michael J. Himes (Mahwah, NJ: Paulist Press, 1995), pages 46–47. Copyright © 1995 by Michael J. Himes. Used with permission of Paulist Press, *www.paulistpress.com.*

The excerpt on pages 42–43 is based on *Dorothy Day and the "Catholic Worker,"* by Nancy L. Roberts (Albany, NY: State University of New York Press, 1984), pages 1–3. Copyright © 1984 by State University of New York.

The excerpts from the Catholic social teaching documents that are described in chapter 2 and noted throughout the text are taken from *Proclaiming Justice and Peace: Papal Documents from "Rerum Novarum" through "Centesimus Annus,"* edited by Michael Walsh and Brian Davies (Mystic, CT: Twenty-Third Publications, 1991). Compilation copyright © 1991 by CAFOD. All rights reserved. Used with permission.

The excerpt on page 50 is from *The Diary of a Country Priest,* by Georges Bernanos, translated by Pamela Morris (New York: Macmillan Company, 1937), page 57. Copyright © 1937 by the Macmillan Company.

The summary of the seven themes of Catholic social teaching in chapter 2, and the excerpts on pages 72 and 256 are from *Sharing Catholic Social Teaching, Challenges and Directions: Reflections of the U.S. Catholic Bishops,* by the National Council of Catholic Bishops (NCCB) (Washington, DC: USCC, 1998), entire document, page 6, and page 6, respectively. Copyright © 1998 by the USCC. All rights reserved. Used with permission.

The excerpt on page 57 is from *A Precocious Autobiography,* by Yevgeny Yevtushenko, translated by Andrew R. MacAndrew (New York: Dutton Signet, a division of Penguin Books USA), pages 24–25. Translation copyright © 1963 by E. P. Dutton, renewed 1991 by Penguin USA.

The excerpts on pages 59, 142–143, 190, 190–191, 191 and continued on 194, and 311 by Melba Pattillo Beals, Jo Claire Hartsig, Jeanne Wallace, Diane Valletta, Laura Brown, and Nina Mermey Klippel and Sharon Burde are adapted or based on *Stone Soup for the World: Life-Changing Stories of Kindness and Courageous Acts of Service,* compiled by Marianne Larned (Berkeley, CA: Conari Press, 1998), pages 65–70, 81–84, 337, 341–343, 347–350, and 242, respectively. Copyright © 1998 by Marianne Larned. Permission applied for.

The excerpt on pages 61–62 is from *Stand Up for Your Rights,* by Peace Child International (Chicago: World Book, 1998), page 63. Copyright © 1998 by World Book.

The excerpt on pages 64–65 is adapted from *Kids with Courage: True Stories About Young People Making a Difference,* by Barbara A. Lewis, edited by Pamela Espeland (Minneapolis: Free Spirit Publishing, 1992), pages 81–85. Copyright © 1992 by Barbara A. Lewis. Permission applied for.

The excerpt on page 65 from the *Document on the Poverty of the Church,* is from *The New Dictionary of Catholic Social Thought,* edited by Judith A. Dwyer (Collegeville, MN: Liturgical Press, Michael Glazier Book, 1994), page 593, number 10. Copyright © 1994 by The Order of Saint Benedict, Collegeville, MN.

The excerpt on page 68 from "We Are Not Machines," by Maria Guadalupe Torres is from *The Other Side,* January–February 1997. Used with permission.

The excerpt on page 70 is from "Enemies No More," by Hildegard Goss-Mayr, in *Fellowship,* July–August 1995. Used with permission.

The excerpt from the MNCS Frog Project on pages 71–72 is adapted from "The MNCS Frog Project," 8 September 1999, at *www.mncs.k12.mn.us,* accessed 20 March 2000. Used with permission.

The excerpts on pages 76–77, 80, 85, 85, 85–86, 86, 87, 88–89, 95, and 97–98 are from *Community Service and Social Responsibility in Youth,* by James Youniss and Miranda Yates (Chicago: University of Chicago Press, 1997), pages 65, 52–53, 56, 91, 94, 94, 132, 57–58 and 76–77, 70–71, and 70, respectively. Copyright © 1997 by the University of Chicago. Permission applied for.

The excerpt on page 81 is based on "Poor No More: New Beauty in Child's Pictures," by Daniel B. Wood, in *Christian Science Monitor,* 5 January 1988. Copyright © 1988 by the Christian Science Publishing Society. All rights reserved.

The excerpt on page 83 is from "Judgment Day: Part 4," by PBS, at *www.pbs.org,* accessed 29 February 2000.

The excerpt on page 84 is from Cathy Parsons, in the Register of Reconciliation, number 93, Truth and Reconciliation Commission home page, *www.truth.org,* accessed 21 December 1997.

The statistic about hunger on page 92 is from "The Hunger Project," 6 December 1999, found at *www.igc.org.*

The summary of the story of Yertle the Turtle on page 94 is from *Yertle the Turtle and Other Stories,* by Theodor Seuss Geisel (Dr. Seuss) (New York: Random House, 1958). Copyright © 1958 by Theodor S. Geisel and Audrey S. Geisel, renewed 1986.

The excerpts on pages 99 and continued on 102 and 101 (adapted) are from *Base Communities: An Introduction,* by Margaret Hebblethwaite (Mahwah, NJ: Paulist Press, 1994), pages 83–86 and 108. Copyright © 1994 by Margaret Hebblethwaite. Used with permission of Paulist Press, *www.paulistpress.com.*

The excerpt on pages 105–106 is adapted from *Nuclear Holocaust and Christian Hope,* by Ronald J. Sider and Richard K. Taylor (Downers Grove, IL: InterVarsity Press, 1982), pages 238–241. Copyright © 1982 by Ronald J. Sider and Richard K. Taylor. Used with permission of the authors.

The excerpt on pages 110–112 is adapted from "Single Motherhood," by Kelly Jefferson, in *The American Feminist,* Spring 1999. Used with permission.

The statistics about abortions performed in the United States on pages 113 and 118–120 are from the Alan Guttmacher Institute, "Facts in Brief: Induced Abortion," February 2000.

The excerpts on pages 114 and 120–121 are from "You Are My Daughter: An Interview with Julie Makimaa," by Janet Podell, in *The American Feminist,* Fall 1998. Used with permission.

The excerpts on pages 115 and 120 are from "I Chose Life," by Dave Hrbacek, in *The Catholic Spirit,* 11 May 2000.

The excerpt on page 116 is from "Raising Issaiah," by Melissa Rodriguez, on National Public Radio (NPR), 10 November 1997.

The statistics about abortion and women receiving public assistance on page 116 are from "Common Ground for Pro-Life and Pro-Choice," by James R. Kelly, in *America,* 16 January 1999.

The statistics about the number of people executed on page 116 are from "A Life or Death Gamble," by Jonathan Alter and Mark Miller, in *Newsweek,* 29 May 2000.

The excerpts on pages 117, 132, and 133–134 are adapted from "Crying for Justice," by Jon Wilson, in *Hope,* Winter 2000. Permission applied for.

The chart on pages 118–119 and the information on page 120 are based on information from *A Child Is Born,* by Lennart Nilsson, translated by Clare James (New York: Dell Publishing, A DTP/Seymour Lawrence Book, 1990). English translation copyright © 1990 by Bantam Doubleday Dell Publishing Group.

The excerpts on pages 122 and 138 are from "Abortion and the Search for Common Ground," by Frederica Mathewes-Green, in *The New Religious Humanists,* edited by Gregory Wolfe (New York: Free Press, 1997), pages 218 and 283. Copyright © 1997 by Gregory Wolfe. Permission applied for.

The excerpt from *Living the Gospel of Life,* number 22, on page 124 is based on a 1998 statement by the U.S. Catholic bishops (Washington, DC: USCC, 1998) at *www.nccbuscc.org/prolife/gospel.*

The statistic about death sentences for blacks versus whites on page 125 is from "The Death Penalty in Black and White: Who Lives, Who Dies, Who Decides," by Richard C. Dieter (Death Penalty Information Center, 1998).

The statistic about death row inmates being unable to afford a lawyer on page 125 is from an American Civil Liberties Union quote in "Stat House: Capital Punishment," found in *Salt of the Earth* online.

The excerpt from Sr. Helen Prejean on page 125 is from "Letter from Death Row," in *America,* 13 February 1999.

The excerpt from John McCormick on page 125 is adapted from "Coming Two Days Shy of Martyrdom," in *Newsweek,* 15 February 1999.

The statistic about death row inmates cleared of charges on page 126 is from "A Life or Death Gamble," by Jonathan Alter and Mark Miller, in *Newsweek,* 29 May 2000.

The excerpt on page 131 is from "Cardinal Bernardin's Call for a Consistent Ethic of Life," by Cardinal Joseph Bernardin, in *Origins,* 29 December 1983.

The excerpt on pages 132–133 is an adaptation of "How I Came to Forgive the Unforgivable," by Robert McClory, in *U.S. Catholic,* August 1998. Used with permission of the author.

The statistics about teens and abortion on page 135 are from the Alan Guttmacher Institute, "Facts in Brief: Teen Sex and Pregnancy," September 1999.

The information about Feminists for Life and the Life After Assault League on page 135 is from "Violence Against Women Act: Round II," by Jamie Hanson Smith, and "Choosing Life," by Juli Schwartz, in *The American Feminist,* Fall 1998.

The excerpt on page 137 is from "Letting Go," by Jenn Mosher, in *Hope,* September–October 1997. Permission applied for.

The excerpts on pages 150 and 153 are from *Speaking Out: Teenagers Take on Sex, Race, and Identity,* by Susan Kuklin (New York: G. P. Putnam's, 1993), pages 30–32, 22, 27 and 64–65, 67, 81. Copyright © 1993 by Susan Kuklin. Permission applied for.

The excerpt on page 154 is from the pastoral statement *Moving Beyond Racism: Learning to See with the Eyes of Christ,* at *www.archdiocese-chgo.org,* accessed 3 April 2000.

The excerpt on page 155 is from *All Saints: Daily Reflections on Saints, Prophets, and Witnesses for Our Time,* by Robert Ellsberg (New York: Crossroad Publishing, 1997), page 261. Copyright © 1997 by Robert Ellsberg.

The excerpts on pages 155 and 156 are from *Man in the Mirror: John Howard Griffin and the Story of "Black Like Me,"* by Robert Bonazzi (Maryknoll, NY: Orbis Books, 1997), pages 47 and 95, 65, 48. Copyright © 1997 by Robert Bonazzi.

The excerpt on page 157 by Bishop Sean O'Malley is from "Solidarity: The Antidote to Resurgent Racism," in *Origins,* 3 February 2000.

The account by a young black man on page 157 is quoted in *Race: How Blacks and Whites Think and Feel About the American Obsession,* by Studs Terkel (New York: New Press, 1992), pages 402–403. Copyright © 1992 by Studs Terkel. Permission applied for.

The excerpts from the U.S. Catholic bishops on pages 157, 159, and 161 are from *Brothers and Sisters to Us: U.S. Bishops' Pastoral Letter on Racism in Our Day,* by the NCCB (Washington, DC: USCC, 1979), pages 10, 10, and 9, respectively. Copyright © 1979 by the USCC, Washington, DC 20017. All rights reserved.

The statistics about the wage gap on page 158 and the statistics in the chart on page 159 are from the National Committee on Pay Equity, "Face the Facts About Wage Discrimination and Equal Pay," 1 September 1998.

The excerpt on page 158 is from "Blacks, Latinos Flounder at Top 7 High Schools," by Barnaby Dinges, in *The Chicago Reporter,* September 1990.

The statistics about home mortgages on page 159 are from "Doors to Home Ownership Remain Locked in Discriminatory Practices for Minorities," by Paul Barton, Gannett News Service, 6 September 1998.

The quotation from Forsan Hussein on page 164 is from "Partners for Peace," by Guy Raz, in *Hope,* Fall 1999.

The story of the Flora High School students on page 164 is from "Better Together," by Wim Roefs, in *Teaching Tolerance,* Fall 1998.

The excerpt on page 165 is from *Heritage and Hope: Evangelization in the United States,* by the NCCB (Washington, DC: USCC, 1991), page 2. Copyright © 1991 by the USCC, Washington, DC 20017. All rights reserved.

The excerpts about the Free the Children organization on pages 170–172, 177, 184, 188–189, and 323 are from *Free the Children: A Young Man's Personal Crusade Against Child Labor,* by Craig Kielburger, with Kevin Major (New York: HarperCollins Publishers, 1998), based on the entire book, quoted from pages 222–223, quoted from page 309, based on pages 309–311, quoted from pages 291–293, respectively. Copyright © 1998 by Craig Kielburger. Permission applied for.

The quotation about teaching on page 174 is quoted in *The Spirituality of Work: Teachers,* by William Droel (Chicago: National Center for the Laity, 1989), page 22–23. Copyright © 1989 by National Center for the Laity.

The quotation about the grocer on page 174 is from *Of Human Hands: A Reader in the Spirituality of Work,* edited by Gregory F. Augustine Pierce (Minneapolis: Augsburg, 1991), page 49. Copyright © 1991 by Maxine F. Dennis.

The quotation about the engineer on page 174 is from "Work of Human Hands: Fifteen People Talk About Faith on the Job," by Mary O'Connell, in *U.S. Catholic,* September 1992.

The excerpts from the U.S. Catholic bishops on pages 174, 321, and 322 are from the pastoral letter *Everyday Christianity: To Hunger and Thirst for Justice,* by the NCCB (Washington, DC: USCC, 1999). Copyright © 1999 by the USCC, Washington DC 20017. All rights reserved.

The statistics about children who work on page 177 are from the ILO Washington Branch Office, "Child Labor 101," at *www.us.ilo.org.*

The information about Aung San Suu Kyi on page 177 is from *Witness,* "Exclusive Interview with Aung San Suu Kyi for the Hearing of European Commission on the European Generalized System of Preference," at *www.witness.org.*

The quote from Lorena del Carmen Hernandez on pages 177–178 is from "Workers Discuss Labor Conditions," by Jaime Levy, in *The Chronicle Online* (Duke University), 24 September 1999.

The quote from Will Reinhard on page 178 is from "Surviving the Age of Insecurity," by Mark Harris, in *Hope,* May–June 1998.

The excerpt on page 179 is from "Climbing the Walls," by Benjamin Adair, in *Hope,* July–August 1997.

The excerpt on pages 192–193 is from "Glimpsing the Future," by Rick Ufford-Chase, in *The Other Side,* January–February 1997. Permission applied for.

The story on pages 198–199 is adapted from "Matthew's Closet: Students Impacting the Lives of the Homeless," by Tim Pfau. Used with permission.

The information about life expectancy on page 200 is from *World Military and Social Expenditures 1996,* by Ruth Leger Sivard (Washington, DC: World Priorities, 1996), page 32. Copyright © 1996 by World Priorities.

The excerpts on pages 204–205 and 220–221 are from "The Cost of Love: A Journal Entry," by Pat Schneider, in *The Other Side,* March–April 1999. Permission applied for.

The statistics on hunger in the world on pages 205–206 are from the USDA, and can be found on the Bread for the World Web site, *www.bread.org.*

The statistics about homeless people on page 206 are from the National Coalition for the Homeless, "Homeless Families with Children," at *www.nch.ari.net.*

The excerpts on pages 207 and 209 are from *Rachel and Her Children: Homeless Families in America,* by Jonathan Kozol (New York: Crown Publishers, a division of Random House, 1988), pages 2 and 42. Copyright © 1988 by Jonathan Kozol. Used with permission of Crown Publishers, a division of Random House, Inc.

The excerpt on page 208 is based on "Schooling Poor Kids in Minneapolis," by John Biewen, from *The Forgotten Fourteen Million,* by American Radio Works, *www.mpr.org.* Copyright © 1999 by Minnesota Public Radio.

The statistics about the affordable housing shortage on page 209 are from the National Coalition for the Homeless Web site, *www.nch.ari.net;* and "Homeless and Hungry" and "Scarcer Housing for the Poor," editorials in *America,* 29 January–5 February 2000 and 11 December 1999, respectively.

The excerpts on pages 210–211 are from "Who Are the Poor?" by Peter Davis, in *Hope,* September–October 1996.

The statistics on poverty in the world's poorest nations on page 212 and the information in the chart on page 213 are from "A Dialogue in Hope," by Leo O. Donovan, SJ, in *America,* 11 September 1999.

The excerpt on pages 212–213 is from "Grameen Bank Borrowers," by Scott A. Leckman, in *Pearls of Bangladesh* (RESULTS Educational Fund, 1993). Accessed at the Bread for the World Web site, *www.bread.org.* Permission applied for.

The statistics about malnutrition and disease on pages 213–214 are from the Bread for the World Web site, *www.bread.org.*

The excerpt on page 214 is from "Friends in Deed," by Magnus MacFarlane, in *U.S. Catholic,* October 1999.

The information about the legacy of colonialism on pages 216–217 (adapted) and statistics about military spending on pages 297–298 are from *Justice and Peace: A Christian Primer,* by J. Milburn Thompson (Maryknoll, NY: Orbis Books, 1997). Copyright © 1997 by J. Milburn Thompson.

The excerpt on pages 224–226 is from a letter written by Julie Williams to her former high school teacher Kevin LaNave.

The statistics about the wealth gap on pages 227–228 are from "It's a Poor World After All," by Kevin Clarke, in *U.S. Catholic,* October 1999; *State of the World Atlas,* by Dan Smith (New York: Penguin Reference, 1999). Copyright © 1999; and "Press Briefing on 1998 Income and Poverty Estimates, U.S. Census Bureau," by Daniel H. Weinberg, accessed 30 September 1999, at *www. census.gov.*

The excerpt on pages 228–230 is adapted from "The Experience of Being Suddenly Rich," by Laura Fraser, in *The Standard.com,* posted 29 Nov. 1999 at *www. thestandard.com,* and accessed 17 July 2000. Permission applied for.

The excerpt on pages 235 and contined on 238 by Dorothy Day is from *The Long Loneliness: The Autobiography of Dorothy Day* (New York: Harper and Row, 1952), pages 285–286. Copyright © 1952 by Harper and Row.

The excerpt on pages 236–237 is from "What I Learned About Justice from Dorothy Day," by Jim Forest, in *Salt of the Earth,* July–August 1995. Reprinted with permission from *U.S. Catholic* magazine, Claretian Publications, *www.uscatholic.org,* 800-328-6515.

The story about Christina on pages 243 and continued on 245 is by Christina Puntel.

The excerpt on pages 245–246 is adapted from "Love in a Sandwich Bag," by Aline A. Newman, in an insert in *Guideposts for Teens,* October–November 1998. Permission applied for.

The story on pages 247–248 about homeless people in Saint Cloud, Minnesota, is by Katie Halupczok.

The excerpts on page 250 are from *Hope, Human and Wild,* by Bill McKibben (New York: Little, Brown and Company, 1995), pages 92–93, 103, and 78. Copyright © 1995 by Bill McKibben.

The story on pages 254–255 is adapted from "Class Acts," by Adam Werbach and B. J. Bergman, in *The Next Generation,* volume 82, 21 November 1997. Copyright © 1997 by the Sierra Club. Permission applied for.

The excerpt on page 258 is from *The Ecological Crisis: A Common Responsibility,* number 8, a message from Pope John Paul II for the celebration of the World Day of Peace, 1 January 1990, at *www.library.catholic. org,* accessed 21 February 2000.

The facts about rain forests on pages 259–260 are from "Vanishing Before Our Eyes," by Edward O. Wilson, in *Time,* April–May 2000; the Rainforest Action Network fact sheet, "Facts about Rainforests," at *www.ran.org;* and the Rainforest Information Centre, "The Causes of Rainforest Destruction," at *www.forest. org.*

The information about the Australian gastric-brooding frog on pages 259–260 is from "Nature's Gifts: The Hidden Medicine Chest," by Mark Plotkin, in *Time,* April–May 2000.

The excerpt by Norman Myers on page 261 is from "What We Must Do to Counter the Biotic Holocaust," in *International Wildlife,* volume 29, 1 March 1999. Copyright © 1999 by National Wildlife Foundation. All rights reserved.

The excerpts from the U.S. Catholic bishops on pages 261, 265–266, 268, 273, 273, 274, 274, 283, and 283 are from *Renewing the Earth: An Invitation to Reflection and Action on Environment in Light of Catholic Social Teaching,* by the NCCB (Washington, DC: USCC, 14 November 1991), pages 2, 9, 3, 6, 7, 2, 11, 2, and 14, respectively. Copyright © 1992 by the USCC, Washington, DC 20017. All rights reserved. Used with permission.

The excerpt on page 262 is from "The Ideas of Chico Mendes and the National Council of Rubber Tappers," by Atanagildo de Deus Matos, at the Environmental Defense Fund Web site, *www.edf.org.* Copyright © 1998 by the Environmental Defense Fund.

The statistics about global warming on page 263 are from the Environmental News Network (ENN), "Salmon Headed for Hot Water," 10 June 1999; the *Minneapolis Star Tribune,* "Study Suggests Earth's Climate Is Warming at an Unprecedented Rate," 23 February 2000; ENN, "Arctic Warming Signals Dire Straits for Birds," 5 April 2000; *The Regional Impacts of Climate Change: An Assessment of Vulnerability,* edited by R. T. Watson et al. (Cambridge, MA: Cambridge University Press, 1998). Copyright © 1998 by the Intergovernmental Panel on Climate Change; ENN, "Arctic Changes," by John Roach, 27 July 1999, at *www.enn.com;* "Surf's Up—Way Up," by Colin Woodard, in Special to the *Christian Science Monitor,* 15 July 1998; and "Valuable Lessons," by Brian Staszenski, in *Time,* April–May 2000.

The statistics about emissions that cause global warming on page 263 are from *State of the World Atlas,* by Dan Smith.

The excerpt on page 275 is from *The Gift of Good Land: Further Essays Cultural and Agricultural,* by Wendell Berry (San Francisco: North Point Press, 1981), page 281. Copyright © 1981 by Wendell Berry.

The statistics about the hidden economic value of natural resources on page 276 are from "Earth's Worth As Much As $54 Trillion Annually," Associated Press, in the *Denver Rocky Mountain News,* 15 May 1997; and "Learning to Value Nature's Free Services," by Janet N. Abramovitz, in *The Futurist,* 1 July 1997.

The information about Boeing's energy-saving upgrades on page 279 is from "The Battle for Planet Earth," by Sharon Begley, in *Newsweek,* 24 April 2000.

The excerpt on pages 280–281 is from "Selected Essays: Patagonia—The Next 100 Years," by Yvon Chouinard at *www.patagonia.com,* accessed 15 February 2000.

The information about Costa Rica on pages 281–282 is from "The Greening of Costa Rica," by David Tenenbaum, in *Technology Review,* 1 October 1995.

The story on pages 286–289 and the excerpt on page 319 are from an essay by Paolo A. Mercado, with excerpts from *People Power, An Eyewitness History: The Philippine Revolution of 1986,* edited by Monina Allarey Mercado (New York: Writers and Readers Publishing, 1986), pages 191–192 and 209. Copyright © 1986 by Monina Allarey Mercado.

The excerpt about Robert on page 292 is adapted from "Teenagers, Rage and Tragedy," by Christina Del Valle, in *Newsday,* 20 July 1998.

The excerpt about Juan on page 292 is adapted from "Just Another Face," by Jim Wilkinson, in *Teaching Tolerance,* Fall 1998.

The excerpt about the holdups on page 292 is adapted from "Crime: The Lost Girls," by Richard Jerome et al., in *People,* 13 September 1999.

The crime statistics on page 293 are from "Stop Crime Where It Starts," by John J. Dululio Jr., in the *New York Times,* 31 July 1996.

The quotation on page 293 is from "Mourn for the Killers, Too," by Devon Adams, in *Newsweek,* 23 August 1999.

The excerpt on page 294 is from "It's Time to Stop Training Our Kids to Kill," by Lieutenant Colonel Dave Grossman, in *U.S. Catholic,* June 1999.

The excerpts from the U.S. Catholic bishops on pages 296, 304, 305, 306, 307, 308–309, 309, and 310 are from the pastoral letter *The Challenge of Peace: God's Promise and Our Response* (Washington, DC: USCC, 1983), numbers 219, 68, 114, 80, 92–99, 83, 233, 23, and 78, respectively. Copyright © 1984 by the USCC, Washington, DC 20017. All rights reserved. Used with permission.

Many of the statistics about military spending on pages 297–298 are from the International Institute for Strategic Studies, Department of Defense, in *The Defense Monitor,* volume 28, number 1, 1999; "Loosing the Nuclear Genie," Reuters, 23 June 1999; and "Suffering from the Bomb More Than 50 Years Later," by Akiko Kusaoi, in the *International Herald Tribune,* 1 July 1998.

The information about India and Pakistan's nuclear weapons on page 299 is from "Tracking Nuclear Weapons," in *Time,* 25 May 1998.

The excerpt on page 301 is from "An Unexpected Calling: An Interview with General George Lee Butler," by David Cortright, in *Sojourners Online,* January–February 1999 at *www.sojourners.com,* accessed 4 January 1999.

The words of Martin Luther King Jr. and Pope Paul VI on pages 302 and 303 are from *Peacemaking,* volume 1, by Pax Christi USA (Erie, PA: Pax Christi USA, 1983), pages 126 and 23. Copyright © 1985 by Pax Christi USA.

The statistics about land mines on page 308 are from the Vietnam Veterans of America Foundation, "VVAF Factsheet: The Global Landmine Tragedy."

The quotation from the U.S. Archdiocese for Military Services on page 309 is from "Military Archbishop Questions Bombing of Iraq," in *America,* 16 January 1999.

The quotations about the group SAVE on page 311 are from a speech by Kristi Gallion during the March Against Violence, held in Shreveport, Louisiana.

The story about the School of the Americas on pages 311–312 is by Jennifer Flament.

The excerpt on pages 312–313 is from "Defense Through Disarmament" in *The Universe Bends: A Reader on Christian Nonviolence in the U.S.,* edited by Angie O'Gorman (Philadelphia: New Society Publishers, 1990). Copyright © 1990 by New Society Publishers. Permission applied for.

The quotations from George Mizo on page 313 are from "Veteran-Sponsored Village Opens for Kids, Elderly in Vietnam," by Paul Alexander, at *AP Online,* 29 October 1998.

The excerpt on page 317 is adapted from *Revolutions in Eastern Europe: The Religious Roots,* by Niels C. Nielsen (Maryknoll, NY: Orbis Books, 1991), pages 25–48 and 85–102. Copyright © 1991 by Orbis Books. Permission applied for.

Photo and Art Credits

Sara Berrenson: pages 121, 200

Annie Bursiek: page 21

Sean Carner: page 233, bottom

Adwin Christo: page 72 (bottom)

Jennifer Clark: page 236 (bottom)

Mary Diaz: pages 144, 181

Alexandra Dimakos: page 272

Eva Drinka: page 114 (bottom)

Claire Endo: page 161, 206

Robert Green: page 306

Matthew Guerrero: page 314 (bottom)

James Habig: page 184

Tara Haight: page 282

Melissa C. Hansen: page 30

Amanda Irvin: page 90

Sarah Jepsen: page 256

Bridget Jesionowski: page 81

Lauren Koegler: page 221

Michelle Lungin: page 130

Dani Maniscalco: page 60

Nic Marshall: page 228

Jennifer Miley: page 293

Elisabeth C. Montana: page 162

Jill Napierala: page 297

Jessica Newberg: page 153

Alida Novarese: page 58

Jason Oglio: page 20

Lauren Ottaviano: page 250

Daniel Pizarro: page 267

Ilaria Ramzy: page 164

Jane Richardson: page 102

Jennifer Safi: page 140

Jana Schmid: page 209

Brian Szewczyk: page 89

Evlyn Wade: page 260

Lindsey Warren: pages 11, 93, 190

Colleen Westman: page 269

Lucia Wharton: pages 82, 129

The following images were used as icons throughout the book: "For Review" (sign), photo by Laurie Geisler; "In Depth" (magnifying glass), image by Artville Stock Images; "Journeys in Justice" sidebar (compass), image by Philip and Karen Smith/Stone; "Journeys in Justice" sidebar (shoes with springs), image by Nick Vedros and Associates/Stone; "Detour" (sign), image © Charles O'Rear/Corbis; "Detour" (road), image by SuperStock; "What You Can Do . . ." (map and merge sign), images by Artville Stock Images.

© AFP/Corbis: pages 75, 107

AP/Wide World Photos: pages 40, 62 (top), 72 (top), 124, 126 (top), 131 (middle left and right), 155 (bottom right), 163, 202 (bottom), 204, 208, 212, 214, 215, 290, 300 (bottom right), 315, 322

Artville Stock Images: cover wrap, cover inset, pages 4 (left and right), 5 (left and right), 8 (bottom left, middle, and right)

Bruce Ayres/Stone: page 182

Scott Barrow, International Stock: page 231 (top)

Johan Berglund, Impact Visuals: page 188 (bottom right)

Elie Bernager/Stone: page 294

© Bettmann/Corbis: pages 12, 59 (left and right), 97, 141, 154, 179 (bottom), 302 (top)

Ken Biggs/Stone: pages 253, 264 (bottom)

Photo courtesy of the *Billings Gazette,* Billings, MT: page 142 (bottom right)

Donna Binder, Impact Visuals: page 196

Wade Britzius: pages 80, 194

Photo by Karen Callaway for Catholic Campaign for Human Development: page 211 (middle)

Demetrio Carrasco/Stone: pages 36 (bottom middle), 100 (bottom middle)

Catholic Relief Services–USCC, 209 West Fayette Street, Baltimore, MD 21201: pages 71 (bottom left, middle, and right), 246 (left, middle, and right)

Ann Cecil/Photo 20–20/PictureQuest: page 18 (top)

Paul Chesley/Stone: page 166 (left)

Photo courtesy of Amber Coffman, Happy Helpers for the Homeless: pages 222, 245

Stewart Cohen/Stone: page 70

Photograph courtesy of Colby Memorial Library, Sierra Club: page 254 (bottom)

Photo courtesy of Community Cycling Center, Portland, OR: page 277 (left and right)

© Corbis: pages 47, 105, 239, 296 (left), 300 (bottom left)

Tony Demin, International Stock: page 273

Mary Kate Denny/Stone: page 87 (middle right)

Mary Farrell: page 244

Photo courtesy of Feminists for Life of America, Washington, DC: pages 109, 112

Ken Fisher/Stone: page 226

Tim Flach/Stone: page 127

© Owen Franken/Corbis: page 232

Photo courtesy of Free the Children International, www.freethechildren.com: pages 170 (bottom right), 172, 177

Ricardo Funari, Imagens Da Terra, Impact Visuals: page 261

Laurie Geisler, back cover (top left)

© Bill Gentile/Corbis: pages 22 (bottom middle), 217

Mark Gervase/Stone: page 110 (bottom left)

Hulton Getty/Stone: pages 26 (bottom), 28, 48 (top), 55 (left and right), 299

Giraudon/Art Resource, NY: page 45

Pam Hasegawa, Impact Visuals: page 303

David Hiser/Stone: pages 36 (bottom left), 100 (bottom left)

© Historical Picture Archive/Corbis: page 16 (bottom)

Manuela Hoefer/Stone: page 10

Cliff Hollenbeck, International Stock: page 266 (top)

Ansell Horn, Impact Visuals: page 114 (top)

Jeremy Horner/Stone: page 151

Dave Hrbacek/The Catholic Spirit: page 135

© Hulton-Deutsch Collection/Corbis: pages 57, 104, 296 (right)

Andre Jenny, International Stock: page 275 (top)

© 2000 Journal Sentinel, photo by Jack Orton, reproduced with permission: page 64

Photo courtesy of Julianne Williams Foundation for Social Justice: page 224 (bottom)

Zigy Kaluzny/Stone: pages 88, 158

© Layne Kennedy/Corbis: page 252

Marilyn Kielbasa: page 258

© Christophe Loviny/Corbis: page 308

Sandy Malone, Saint Vincent de Paul: page 48 (bottom left)

Marquette University Archives: pages 41, 42 (bottom)

Marsolek, Maryknoll: page 66 (bottom left)

David Maung, Impact Visuals: page 192 (bottom left)

Buddy Mays, International Stock: page 281

© Stephanie Maze/Corbis: pages 99, 262

© Kevin R. Morris/Corbis: page 274

Adrian Murrell/Stone: page 223

© Amos Nachoum/Corbis: page 263

Nicaraguan Cultural Alliance, P.O. Box 5051, Hyattsville, MD 20782: page 319 (middle)

Linda Panetta, SOA Watch NE: page 312 (left and right)

Photo courtesy of Patagonia, Ventura, CA: page 280

Photo by Nicholas Patrinos: page 48 (bottom right)

Peace Corps, Washington DC: page 238 (left and right)

Chuck Pefley/Stone: page 166 (right)

Jeff Perkell, Impact Visuals: page 22 (bottom left)

Photo courtesy of Tim Pfau, Bishop Gorman High School, Las Vegas, NV: page 198 (bottom left and right)

Digital imagery © copyright 2001 PhotoDisc: pages 18 (middle), 136 (bottom), 148 (bottom right), 323

Jim Pickerell/Stone: page 230

Greg Probst/Stone: page 276

Photo courtesy of Sr. Sharon Rambin and Mary Ann Whited, Loyola College Prep, Shreveport, LA: page 310 (bottom)

The Reebok Human Rights Foundation: page 170 (bottom left)

Photo by Don Rutledge: page 155 (bottom left)

The St. Cloud Visitor: page 248

Photo courtesy of Saint John's University, Collegeville, MN: page 174

© Pablo San Juan/Corbis: page 192 (bottom right)

Scala/Art Resource, NY: page 305

James L. Shaffer: pages 85 (bottom left and right), 94, 142 (bottom left), 145 (bottom), 146, 147, 231 (bottom)

Photo courtesy of Sharing and Caring Hands, Minneapolis, MN: page 201

Skjold Photographs: pages 15, 61, 76 (bottom left and right), 132

Sovfoto/Eastfoto/PictureQuest: page 18 (bottom right)

Sean Sprague, Impact Visuals: page 44

Vince Streano/Stone: page 168

SuperStock: pages 18 (bottom left), 50, 110 (bottom right), 175 (left)

Thor Swift, Impact Visuals: page 268

© Sygma/Corbis: pages 6, 7, 24, 91, 98, 100 (bottom right), 108, 125, 133, 157 (left and right), 169, 178, 183, 186, 188 (bottom left), 197, 216, 235, 249 (left and right), 284, 292, 309

C. Takagi, Impact Visuals: page 210

Mario Tapia, Impact Visuals: page 22 (bottom right)

Chris Thomaidis/Stone: page 180

Thomas, Maryknoll: page 66 (bottom middle and right)

Patrisha Thomson/Stone: page 71 (top)

© Peter Turnley/Corbis: pages 92, 285, 316 (bottom left and right), 318

© Robert van der Hilst/Corbis: page 219

Gandee Vason/Stone: page 120

All rights reserved Vie de Jésus MAFA, 24 rue du Maréchal Jaffre, F-78000 Versailles: page 234

Carlos Villalon, Impact Visuals: page 36 (bottom right)

© Karl Weatherly/Corbis: page 240

Jim West, Impact Visuals: page 62 (bottom)

Jerry Windley-Daoust: page 138

W. P. Wittman Limited: pages 122 (bottom), 148 (bottom left), 150 (middle)

© Alison Wright/Corbis: page 227 (bottom)

© Tim Wright/Corbis: page 117

Reprinted with permission from People Power: An Eyewitness History, Writers and Readers Publishing, 1986: pages 74, 286 (bottom left and right), 288

David Ximeno Tejada/Stone: page 175 (right)

Endnotes for Documents of the U.S. Catholic Bishops

Page 147
Endnote for *Economic Justice for All* 79: Pope John Paul II, Address at the General Assembly of the United Nations (2 October 1979), 13, 14.

Page 178
Endnote for *Economic Justice for All* 178: Richard M. Cohn, The Consequences of Unemployment on Evaluation of Self, Doctoral dissertation, Department of Psychology (University of Michigan, 1977); John A. Garraty, Unemployment in History: Economic Thought and Public Policy (New York: Harper and Row, 1978); Harry Mauer, Not Working: An Oral History of the Unemployed (New York: Holt, Rinehart, and Winston, 1979).

Page 239
Endnote for *Economic Justice for All* 34: St. Cyprian, "On Works and Almsgiving," 25, trans. R. J. Deferrari, "St. Cyprian: Treatises," 36 (New York: Fathers of the Church, 1958), 251. Original text in Migne, "Patrologia Latina," volume 4, 620. On the Patristic teaching, see C. Avila, "Ownership: Early Christian Teaching" (Maryknoll, NY: Orbis Books, 1983). Collection of original texts and translations.

Page 305
Endnote for *The Challenge of Peace* 114: Sulpicius Severus, The Life of Martin, 4.3.

Page 309
Endnote for *The Challenge of Peace* 23: Vatican II, *The Pastoral Constitution on the Church in the Modern World,* 50.